Critical Essays on Gertrude Stein

Critical Essays on Gertrude Stein

Michael J. Hoffman

G. K. Hall & Co. • Boston, Massachusetts

Library of Congress Cataloging-in-Publication Data
Main entry under title:

Critical essays on Gertrude Stein.

(Critical essays on American literature)
Includes index.
1. Stein, Gertrude, 1874–1946 – Criticism and interpretation –
Addresses, essays, lectures. I. Hoffman, Michael J., 1939–   . II.
Series. PS3537.T323Z585   1986   818'.5209   85-14004
ISBN 0-8161-8696-0

This publication is printed on permanent/durable acid-free paper
MANUFACTURED IN THE UNITED STATES OF AMERICA

CRITICAL ESSAYS ON AMERICAN LITERATURE

This series seeks to anthologize the most important criticism on a wide variety of topics and writers in American literature. Our readers will find in various volumes not only a generous selection of reprinted articles and reviews but original essays, bibliographies, manuscript sections, and other materials brought to public attention for the first time. This volume by Michael J. Hoffman is the most substantial collection of criticism available on Gertrude Stein. It contains forty reviews and essays on Stein's works including reprinted selections by Sherwood Anderson, Kenneth Burke, Edith Sitwell, Marianne Moore, Katherine Anne Porter, Thornton Wilder, and Edmund Wilson. In addition to a lengthy introduction by Hoffman, there are original essays by Elyse Blankley, Jane Bowers, Lisa Ruddick, and Laura Riding Jackson. We are confident that this volume will make a permanent and significant contribution to American literary study.

James Nagel, GENERAL EDITOR

Northeastern University

For my parents
Nathan and Sara Hoffman

CONTENTS

INTRODUCTION

Criticism of Gertrude Stein has always been complicated by her extraordinary personality. Magnetic and imperious, contentious and serenely arrogant, Stein affected everyone strongly, particularly those with whom she had personal contact. A lifelong admirer, Carl Van Vechten, gave some hint of the already mythic Stein when he described her in the *Trend* (7 August 1914) as being "massive in physique, a Rabelaisian woman with a splendid thoughtful face," and went on to talk about "her velvet robes, mostly brown, and her carpet slippers," her "walking staff, and a trim unmodish turban." By 1922 Sherwood Anderson, another friend and admirer, could be so affected by the Stein myth as to write in "The Works of Gertrude Stein" that before he met her he had "heard stories of a long dark room with a languid woman lying on a couch, smoking cigarettes, sipping absinthes perhaps and looking out upon the world with tired, disdainful eyes. Now and then she rolled her head slowly to one side and uttered a few words, taken down by a secretary who approached the couch with trembling eagerness to catch the falling pearls."[1]

With such imagery surrounding the name of Stein, it is no wonder that her work attracted such extreme responses from admirers and detractors alike. In 1913, for instance, Mabel Dodge in *Arts and Decorations* (March 1913) described Stein as working "in a large studio in Paris, hung with paintings by Renoir, Matisse and Picasso . . . doing with words what Picasso is doing with paint . . . impelling language to induce new states of consciousness, and in doing so language becomes with her a creative art rather than a mirror of history." Stein was to receive such encomia throughout her career, but equally hyperbolic comments emerged from her detractors. Her brother Leo asserted that she was "not an intelligent thinker."[2] Contributors to *Testimony against Gertrude Stein*, a supplement published by *transition* (July 1935) — which included such writers as Henri Matisse, Georges Braque, and Tristan Tzara — testified to the shallowness, lack of understanding, and self-serving inaccuracies in *The Autobiography of Alice B. Toklas.* The Marxist critic Michael Gold called her a "literary idiot" in 1936; as late as 1958 Benjamin Reid, in *Art*

1

by Subtraction, wrote an entire book designed to define Stein out of literature; and Hilary Corke's long article in the *Kenyon Review* (Summer 1961) contained more than twenty pages of intemperant invective.

In addition, throughout her life many parodies of her style appeared: from one in 1912 in the old humor magazine *Life*,[3] to scornful passages in a number of Hemingway works,[4] to a review by W. H. Auden in the *Saturday Review* (22 February 1941) of Stein's late novel, *Ida.* Some of the parodies are quite skillful; most are not. Perhaps it is true that, as Stein claimed, she did it better herself.[5] Her style is both too easy and too difficult to parody successfully in the way that the best parodies — such as Max Beerbohm's of the late style of Henry James[6] — illuminate their subjects.

Sorting through the small mountain of prose produced by admirers, detractors, biographers, journalists, and critics poses many problems for an editor. How many cries of delight or anguish does one include? What is the best way to reflect the changing points of view about Stein's work as a whole? How much does one represent the increasing tendency in Stein criticism to do lengthy analyses of individual works? Since it is also the case that many of the best-known writers of our age have written about Stein, how many of their responses does one represent as part of the history of twentieth-century letters?

This book attempts to balance all these concerns. The first section consists of reviews and essays, most of which appeared during and immediately after Stein's long lifetime in letters. The beginnings of more formal Stein criticism can be dated from Donald Sutherland's *Gertrude Stein: A Biography of Her Work* (1951), which remains one of the most interesting books written about her. The common belief that little of worth was written about Stein before that time has no basis in the record. In spite of the negative, often scornful remarks made about her work, Stein received many thoughtful, appreciative reviews and essays, even in the earlier years. In addition to the writers already mentioned, such poets and critics as Edith Sitwell, Richard Aldington, Edmund Wilson, Kenneth Burke, Laura Riding, Robert Graves, Wyndham Lewis, Katherine Anne Porter, and William Carlos Williams had written serious estimates of her work by 1930. Wilson published perhaps ten pieces about Stein, mostly in book reviews; but in *Axel's Castle* (1931) he gave her a full chapter along with such prominent contemporaries as Proust, Valery, Joyce, Eliot, and Yeats.

Throughout the 1930s and 1940s, and particularly after *The Autobiography of Alice B. Toklas*, Stein received much attention in both the popular and "literary" press from such writers as Thornton Wilder, B. F. Skinner, Clifton Fadiman, Henry Seidel Canby, Malcolm Cowley, and Perry Miller. I have included a number of these essays and reviews, some because they are quite instructive and others because they demonstrate the history of Stein's critical reception.

The second part of the book contains pieces that assume Stein to be an important writer worthy of serious assessment. Twenty years ago I was able to claim that nothing in Stein scholarship was comparable to the burgeoning "Joyce industry."[7] That claim can no longer be made. More than thirty books have been written on Stein in the past three decades, and an equal number of Ph.D. theses. The scholarly articles now number in the hundreds, and the listing in the annual *MLA International Bibliography* now exceeds a column every year. I have included a generous selection from such sources, including both overviews of Stein and close readings of particular works. In addition, I have attempted to represent as many Stein titles as possible (more than forty of her books have been published), and in the process to represent diverse styles of literary criticism: descriptive essays, attempts at literary history, analyses in what used to be called the New Criticism, structuralist analyses, recent essays in the "deconstructive" mode, and feminist criticism—a point of view that was unusually late in being applied to Stein. I have tried, where possible, to publish essays from journals that have not previously appeared as chapters in books. Recently published books on Stein are readily available. I have also tried to publish excerpts from full-length books only when the books were either out of print or otherwise hard to obtain.

In the remainder of this Introduction I shall describe the history of Stein criticism, giving particular emphasis to works that are reprinted in this volume.

For most of her life Stein could not publish her work until long after she had written it. *The Making of Americans*, for instance, whose final passages were written in 1911, was not published between hard covers until 1925. *Three Lives*, allegedly written while Stein posed for Picasso's famous portrait of her, was completed around the end of 1905, but was not published until more than four years later. In early 1906, she sent the manuscript to the journalist Hutchins Hapgood, whom she had met in Italy. His thoughtful letter in response (22 April 1906) is published here as the first review of a work by Stein, although it did not appear in print for almost fifty years. Despite his excessive tact, Hapgood strikes themes that were repeated by publishers who rejected the book and by the most perceptive of her early reviewers: themes that reflect a concern with psychological accuracy in character portrayal and realism in setting, dialogue, and narrative.

The public history of Stein criticism begins on 18 December 1909 with an anonymous review of *Three Lives* in the *Kansas City Star*, a short piece as positive and perceptive as a new author might want. It characterizes Stein's first book as "fiction which no one who reads it can ever forget, but a book for a strictly limited audience." The narrative originality is "notable," and the book has "a sweet enlightened sympathy, an unsleeping sense of humor and an exquisite carefulness in detail." *Three Lives* is "a very masterpiece of realism." The next anonymous review, which appeared in the *Nation* the following month (20 January 1910), also focuses on *Three Lives* within the context of realism. Although the stories lack "construction and focus" and are repetitious and circular, they are nonetheless about "real people" and display a "sense of urgent life." Stein is compared to Browning and to the Russian realists. Both reviewers attempt to deal seriously with the book, but they are limited in their ability to cope with Stein's experimentation by the dominant contemporary paradigm of realism.

The time was soon to come, however, for a new set of norms to be established, more by the arts of painting, sculpture, and music than by modernist writers, most of whom followed rather than preceded Stein. The exhibitions of "Post-Impressionists" organized in London by Roger Fry in 1910 and 1912, followed by the famed Armory Show in New York City (1913), developed for the first time in English-speaking countries, and particularly in the United States, a receptive climate for those artists who were creating the modernist consciousness. In August 1912 Alfred Stieglitz published Stein's portraits of "Matisse" and "Picasso" in a special number of *Camera Work*, these being the first magazine publications of Stein since two articles that appeared in the *Psychological Review* in the late 1890s.[8] This issue of *Camera Work* also reproduced a few works of each artist, thus linking Stein with the painters. This linkage of her name with the growing fame of modernist art was continued in the article that Mabel Dodge wrote to coincide with the Armory Show. In "Speculations, or Post-Impressionism in Prose," as we have seen, Dodge's vivid, urgent style insists on Stein's importance amid references to great names of the School of Paris and a reproduction of Brancusi's bust of Mlle Pogany (misspelled in the caption as Pognay). It was clear that to respond properly to the fauves and cubists, one would also have to admit the importance of the writer most closely associated with them.

Dodge was returning a favor to Stein who had recently composed "A Portrait of Mabel Dodge at the Villa Curonia," thereby making her subject famous. The "Portrait" had only a limited circulation, but one copy of it did get into the hands of the *Atlantic Monthly* (September 1914) where it received a notice in "The Contributor's Club." The anonymous writer describes Dodge as the "victim" rather than the subject of the portrait. "After a hundred lines of this I wish to scream, I wish to burn the book, I am in agony . . . Some one has applied an egg-beater to my brain." The addled reviewer goes on to describe Stein as being "merely a red flag waved by the *Zeitgeist*." But the *Zeitgeist* was about to wave an even redder flag.

In 1914 Stein published *Tender Buttons*, a collection of still lifes she wrote while traveling in Spain a few years earlier. Although this "outrageous" book was to become the Stein work most subject to parody, it was little noticed when it came out, there being only two reviews that have been discovered, a somewhat scornful one by Alfred Kreymborg in the *Morning Telegraph*[9] and the other by Robert Emons Rogers in the *Boston Evening Transcript* (11 July 1914), the latter influenced by Mabel Dodge's earlier piece. Entitled "New Outbreaks of Futurism," it reviews not only Stein's book but the *Patagonian Sonnets* by her publisher Donald Evans. In attempting to understand *Tender Buttons* Rogers follows Dodge's lead in using Picasso to explain Stein's method.

Although not a review of *Tender Buttons*, Carl Van Vechten's "How to Read Gertrude Stein," in the *Trend* (August 1914), was occasioned by publication of that book. It is a survey of Stein's work until that time, including reference to such unpublished writings as "a very long autobiographical work," supposedly even "longer than 'Clarissa Harlowe,' " an obvious reference to *The Making of Americans*. While Van Vechten's remarks are primarily appreciative noises made between lengthy quotations, this essay continued the introduction of Stein's work to avant-garde circles and indicates that she received appreciative critical notice early in her career.

The intervention of the Great War during the summer of that year curtailed Stein's literary productivity for quite a while. As residents of Paris, Stein and Toklas became involved in the War three years earlier than most Americans, driving with the American Fund for the French Wounded a model-T they named Auntie. Stein received little critical notice throughout the rest of the decade, but her reputation was by then secure, and after the war her literary career was rejuvenated when many writers of the new generation either took notice of her work or came to meet her. If Stein's literary reputation developed initially from relationships with the great modernist painters, its next evolution came from relationships with writers of the Twenties, particularly with Sherwood Anderson, Edith Sitwell, Ernest Hemingway, and F. Scott Fitzgerald, many of whom recognized her as both mentor and precursor.

The extent of Stein's reputation was indicated in "The Disciples of Gertrude Stein," an essay by Richard Aldington in *Poetry*.[10] The topic is the American influence on French poetry, but Aldington scarcely mentions Stein at all, assuming that his readers simply understand Stein's relationship to the avant-garde in poetry. Probably the largest boost to her reputation arose from the interest expressed by Sherwood Anderson who wrote about her first in the *New Republic*[11] and then in "The Work of Gertrude Stein," an introduction to *Geography and Plays*, a collection of many items Stein had been writing both before and since the advent of the War. Anderson's essay is, once again, the enthusiastic prose of a booster, telling more about Stein's influence on him than about the nature of her achievement. Still, such praise from the author of *Winesburg, Ohio* was instrumental in connecting Stein to what was new and important in American letters. Soon after that Anderson sent a letter introducing the young Ernest Hemingway, and soon after Hemingway came F. Scott Fitzgerald, among the first in a long line of young writers who continued to seek out Stein the rest of her life. It should also be noted that Hemingway was an important agent in bringing *The Making of Americans* to print. He convinced Ford Madox Ford, then editing the *Transatlantic Review*, to publish excerpts from Stein's unpublished manuscript. Shortly thereafter, Stein contracted with Robert McAlmon to publish the full work as one of his Contact Editions.

Geography and Plays brought forth a number of reactions in prominent places, including one by Edmund Wilson in *Vanity Fair*,[12] the first in his long series of writings on Stein; one by Kenneth Burke in the *Dial* (published herein); another by Edith Sitwell in *The Nation & The Athenæum* (also reprinted here); and a puzzled, derogatory one by Stuart Pratt Sherman in the *Literary Review*.[13] In many ways the essay by Burke, "Engineering with Words," is the first piece of serious literary criticism on Stein, and it still has something to teach us today. Reading Stein in the context of Milton, Burke seeks the nature of her "significant form," using that phrase in the sense developed by Clive Bell but without evaluative connotations. Burke systematically identifies Stein's peculiar dichotomy between form and content, finding her form "significant" but without the reinforcement of significant content. Contemporary critics deal with this phenomenon by distinguishing between signifier and signified. Burke talks about Stein's excision of content as an "art by subtraction."

Sitwell's review reveals the honest struggle of a contemporary poet to come to terms with Stein's radical originality. Complimenting Stein on doing "valuable pioneer work," Sitwell also finds that *Geography and Plays* contains "an almost insuperable amount of silliness, an irritating ceaseless rattle. . . . great bravery, a certain real originality, and a few flashes of exquisite beauty." It was Sitwell who soon arranged for Stein to give the lectures at Oxford and Cambridge that became "Composition as Explanation," one of Stein's most well-known pieces of "theory."

Stein's good fortune continued in 1925 with publication of *The Making of Americans*, "History of a Family's Progress." Reviews of that book continued to attract other important writers into taking account of the Stein phenomenon. One of the best reviews was written by the poet Marianne Moore, who, in the *Dial* (February 1926), called the book one of the "extraordinary interpretations of American life" and "a truly psychological exposition of American living." She found the story to be "engrossing" and asserted that "there is great firmness in the method of this book." It is fascinating to follow the tortuous, anxious logic by which a poet who worked in polished cameos discovers the very different formal method of a fellow poet in the garden.

A year later Katherine Anne Porter reviewed the same novel for the

New York Herald Tribune Books (16 January 1927), calling it "a very necessary book." Her impressionistic reading vividly recreates Stein's methods and their effects on the reader. Porter, who was to end her own career with an attempt at the Great American Novel in *Ship of Fools*, is, like Moore, known primarily as an artist who worked on a small narrative scale. While her ability to empathize with Stein's formal repetitions is remarkable, in later essays such as "The Wooden Umbrella,"[14] she was to be much less sympathetic.

The most furious of Stein's early critics was Wyndham Lewis, who devoted four chapters to Stein in *Time and Western Man* (two of them published herein), a general attack on what Lewis defined as the decadent time consciousness of modernist literature. With great urgency Lewis describes Stein's prose as "a cold, black suet pudding," calling her a celebrator of the "child-cult," and accusing her of being deliberately naive and primitive, the very qualities that Laura Riding praised in an article in *transition* (June 1927) entitled "The New Barbarism and Gertrude Stein." Writing in the most prominent expatriate journal, Riding places Stein among such theorists as T. E. Hulme, T. S. Eliot, and Allan Tate, finding in "Composition as Explanation" a justification for Stein's experimental program. "No one but she," says Riding, "has been willing to be as ordinary, as simple, as primitive, as stupid, as barbaric as successful barbarism demands."[15] It is Riding more than any other critic to this point who understands the consistent revolutionary stance embodied in Stein's willingness to reduce the associative resonance of language so much that the subject of her language becomes the language itself. Shortly after, in "A Note on the Writing of Gertrude Stein," Ralph Church states that in "Miss Stein's writing . . . there is nothing not given in the presented character of her words." In this way, "her writing is often in every word final,"[16] and by implication it is not subject to conventional interpretation.

By the end of the Twenties, Stein's name had been spread by the single most important stimulus to her reputation, an epigraph to *The Sun Also Rises* which attributes to Stein the statement, "You are all a lost generation." When the novel became a best-seller Stein's name and the sybilline utterance she claimed not to have originated[17] became part of the lore of American literature.

In 1928 Payson & Clarke published the enigmatic *Useful Knowledge*, a collection of shorter pieces. In addition, Stein and Toklas began to publish some of Stein's manuscripts in the Plain Edition of the Writings of Gertrude Stein. The first volume, *Lucy Church Amiably*, was published in 1930, to be followed by *Before the Flowers of Friendship Faded Friendship Faded* (1931), *How to Write* (1931), *Operas and Plays* (1932), and *Matisse, Picasso and Gertrude Stein* (1933).

The most pivotal events of that decade began to occur in 1933, with the publication — serially, in the *Atlantic Monthly*, and then as a book with Harcourt Brace — of *The Autobiography of Alice B. Toklas*, Stein's memoirs of her life to that time, ostensibly written by her companion and lover, Alice Toklas. Eccentric but comprehensible, witty, irreverent, and full of delicious, malicious gossip and many names, *The Autobiography* was both a best-seller and a selection of the Literary Guild. Stein's name became a household word, and thousands who had only heard her name could now enjoy one of her books. Her fame was such that she returned the next year to the United States for the first time since 1903 to give a series of lectures and travel the country as a celebrity, interviewed incessantly by the press and radio. Stein's public addresses were published as *Lectures in America.*

While Stein was in the States, the opera on which she and Virgil Thomson had collaborated, *Four Saints in Three Acts*, was elaborately produced on Broadway and was, according to some critics, the theatrical event of the season. Through Bennett Cerf, Random House became Stein's publisher, taking on that role in 1934 with an abridged version of *The Making of Americans* and continuing with *Four Saints* (1934), *Portraits and Prayers* (1934), *Lectures in America* (1935), *The Geographical History of America* (1936), and *Everybody's Autobiography* (1937), the latter containing an account of her American tour. Most of these works were written in her "comprehensible" style, a fact that not only enlarged her audience, but also gave Stein much exposure in the popular press. Many pieces about her now appeared in such outlets as *Time,* the *New Yorker,* and the *New York Times Book Review.*

The essay on Stein that opened the Thirties was published by William Carlos Williams in *Pagany* (Winter 1930). Entitled "The Work of Gertrude Stein," and published herein, it takes the position that because science has subverted writing, authors must "ascend to a plane of almost abstract design." By becoming "abstract" enough to shed "scientific and philosophic lumber" Stein "has placed writing on a plane where it may deal unhampered with its own affairs." But the great leap forward in Stein criticism was taken by Edmund Wilson who placed Stein amid the chief modernist figures in his classic work, *Axel's Castle.* The benefit to Stein emerged largely from her association with the great modernists, because the chapter on her is the weakest in a book marked by excellent close readings of such figures as Proust and Joyce. Wilson's greatest gift was always an ability to reconstruct a narrative subtly from within either a novel or a poem. Without the subject matter to free that gift, Wilson was often reduced to assertion from within a theoretical context that considered all his writers — including Stein — as inheritors of the French symbolist tradition, a point of view on Stein that is no longer widely held. Still, the association of Stein with the classic modernists gave legitimacy and method to critics who might choose to write about her.

With Stein's fame securely established, *The Autobiography of Alice B. Toklas* and *Four Saints in Three Acts* received close to twenty reviews apiece. *The Autobiography* was the subject of a cover story in *Time,* written by James Agee,[18] which contains a balanced appraisal of Stein's life and her latest book. Such prominence must have been a shock even to her monumental self-esteem. There was a thoughtful piece in the *New Republic* by Edmund Wilson,[19] and one in the *Nation* (6 September 1933) from an underrated critic, William Troy, who wrote that "there have always been only two questions about Gertrude Stein: What, precisely, has she been trying to do these many years? What, if any, is the value of what she has done?" Troy places Stein in an American tradition that includes Poe, Hawthorne, Melville, and Henry James, and is characterized by "an orientation from experience toward the abstract, an orientation that has been so continuous as to constitute a tradition, if not actually *the* American tradition."

The Autobiography inspired another article that has played a prominent role in Stein criticism ever since, "Has Gertrude Stein a Secret?," an essay in the *Atlantic Monthly* (January 1934) by the young Harvard psychologist B. F. Skinner. Inspired by Stein's account of her work in the Harvard Psychology Laboratory as a precocious undergraduate, when she worked on habits of attention under Hugo Münsterberg and did experiments on automatic writing, Skinner examined Stein's early articles in the *Psychological Review*, concluding that Stein's characteristic method derives from these experiments. Skinner reconstructs the experiments and quotes from the elicited passages of "automatic" writing. By juxtaposing those passages with some others written "in the *Tender Buttons* manner," Skinner concludes that the latter were "written automatically and unconsciously in some such way as that described in this early paper." Skinner further concludes that Stein's automatic writing is performed by a "second personality successfully split off from Miss Stein's conscious self . . . intellectually unopinionated . . . emotionally cold . . . [with] no past." These assessments are close to those expressed a few years earlier by Laura Riding, and then again by Williams, although they were positively construed in both cases. Skinner's construction is negative, however, for he does "not believe in the importance of the part of Miss Stein's writing that does not make sense."

Skinner's article has received a number of responses, the earliest of which appeared in Conrad Aiken's "We Ask for Bread," an unsympathetic review in the *New Republic* that calls the abridged *Making of Americans* "a complete esthetic miscalculation."[20] Since that time many other writers, including this one, have sought to defend Stein against Skinner's accusations. This kind of argument ultimately comes down to assertion and counter-assertion. It is probably safe to say that while Stein's writing retains some superficial characteristics of the automatic writing done in the Harvard experiments, the prime value of those experiments was to expose her to the buried consciousness that lies beneath the formal linguistic conventions we all obey in speech and writing. It is this buried linguistic consciousness which Stein tries to elicit in her "experimental" writing and which provides her with a structure through which she can consistently concentrate her own attention in a way impossible in pure automaticity.

Four Saints in Three Acts received a number of thoughtful reviews in the popular press and journals of opinion, most of them understandably concerned with production values in the "musical event of the season." Many prominent critics wrote assessments, including Paul Rosenfeld[21] and Joseph Wood Krutch,[22] but perhaps the most striking essays were two that Stark Young wrote for the *New Republic* (7 March 1934: 11 April 1934). In his opinion the production of *Four Saints* was "the most important event of the theatre season: it is the first free, pure theatre that I have seen so far." A month later Young attempted to make a further case for this work of pure theater. Later critical discussion has tried to determine how much of the play's success is due to Stein's libretto. Many others were involved in the first production of *Four Saints:* Maurice Grosser produced the scenario, John Houseman directed, Florine Stettheimer did the costumes and sets, Frederick Ashton was the choreographer, and Virgil Thomson wrote the charming score. Richard Bridgman, for instance, asserts that *Four Saints* "occupies a more important position in Gertrude Stein's canon than its intrinsic worth can justify."[23] But if one listens to a recording,[24] one can see how complementary the words and music are; and since the words were written first, one is tempted to praise Stein heavily.

While a number of interesting reviews were written about *Lectures in America, Narration, Portraits and Prayers, Everybody's Autobiography,* and *The Geographical History of America,* the two remaining pieces I wish to highlight from the 1930s are an essay by Michael Gold, "Gertrude Stein: A Literary Idiot," and Thornton Wilder's introduction to *The Geographical History of America.* Michael Gold, though largely forgotten today, was one of the leading American Marxist writers, a man for whom Stein represented the ultimate in bourgeois decadence. It is instructive to compare Stark Young's delight in the free play of drama in *Four Saints* with the furious condemnation contained in Michael Gold's suggestion that Stein's words "resemble the monotonous gibberings of paranoiacs in the *private* wards of asylums" [my italics], for it is easy to forget that the American public was then contending with the Great Depression, and that even writers like Edmund Wilson and John Dos Passos shared Gold's concerns on other topics, though in a lower key.

Of more lasting value to Stein criticism is Thornton Wilder's "Introduction" to *The Geographical History of America* (1936), the first of a number of his pieces that remain among the best things written on Stein. *The Geographical History* is one of Stein's more problematic works, although it does construct a somewhat consistent argument about Stein's distinction between Human Nature and the Human Mind, between the part of us that clings to identity and personality, and the other more basic, essential part of the self that is much closer to pure being and pure perceiving. The former is concerned with audience and reception, the latter with the purity of expression that exists without concern for an audience. Wilder's lucid expository prose is written out of a sympathy for an author he had recently come to know when she lectured at the University of Chicago. One of the first writers to take Stein seriously as a thinker as well as artist, Wilder makes clear how we are to respond to Stein's humorous playfulness and her sense of "gaiety."

Through the end of the thirties, Stein published a series of "accessible" books including *Paris France, The World Is Round*, and *Picasso* (the only one of her works originally written in French). But at the height of her international celebrity, Stein once again found herself caught in the straitened circumstances of a world war that involved her adopted country a few years before her native one. When Paris became threatened by the German army in 1939, Stein and Toklas decided to spend the war years at their country home in the Midi, rejecting a safe exile in another country for the dangerous existence of being elderly Jewish women in a part of rural France occupied by the Nazis. They moved to Bilignin in 1939 and then to Culoz, a small town nearby, in 1943, not returning to Paris until December 1944, after the liberation of France.

Stein's publishing was curtailed by her situation during these difficult years. A few books, such as *Ida*, were reviewed early in the forties, and at the end of her life she published *Wars I Have Seen*, a chronicle of the life she and Alice led during the war, and *Brewsie and Willie*, a short tale about the G.I. Joes who gathered round her during the months after the liberation. Stein's death in 1946, from cancer, preceded the publication of her *Selected Writings* (1946), *The Mother of Us All* (1947), *Four in America* (1947), *Blood on the Dining Room Floor* (1948), *The First Reader and Three Plays* (1948), and *Last Operas and Plays* (1949).

W. H. Auden begins our survey of Stein criticism in the 1940s with a review of *Ida* in the *Saturday Review* (22 February 1941) that is one of the better parodies of Stein. A gentle parody, unlike those of Hemingway and some others, it is written out of a sympathy for Stein's work and an understanding of its humor. Jean Wahl's review of *Wars I Have Seen* reflects the point of view of an exiled Frenchman on the subject of Stein's evaluations of the German occupiers, of those who collaborated in the Vichy government, and of the *maquis*, or members of the resistance movement. This was a sticky subject, and Wahl's criticisms of Stein's political naïveté are pointed but polite. Although Stein considered herself one of the innovators of the twentieth century, for Wahl she is "like many of the intelligentsia of the dying nineteenth century . . . too intelligent and not intelligent enough."[25]

Shortly after her death Perry Miller reviewed the *Selected Writings of Gertrude Stein*. With his usual sense of historical perspective, Miller places Stein within both the twentieth century and the Western philosophical tradition, mentioning Descartes a number of times as one of her precursors in clearing the air of impediments to the clarity of thought. Miller uses the occasion to call for a "comprehensive estimate of Stein's place in modern literature and for defining her real influence on her contemporaries." As for himself, Miller makes the judgment that "she did largely succeed," even though the measure of her success might well be limited by the fact that her "intention [was] not widely enough conceived."[26]

An overall estimate of which Miller might have approved was Thornton Wilder's introduction to *Four in America*,[27] a problematic work completed just after Stein wrote *The Autobiography of Alice B. Toklas*. The early part of the essay is concerned with the general import of what Stein was trying to do, and it contains a description of Stein's compositional methods. The latter part remains the best discussion of *Four in America* we have, with the possible exception of Richard Bridgman's in *Gertrude Stein in Pieces*. Wilder also captures Stein's extraordinary persuasiveness in conversation, a hint of which is available to anyone who listens to a recording of Stein reading her own work.[28]

In 1949 Rosalind Miller brought out one of the first books wholly devoted to Stein, *Gertrude Stein: Form and Intelligibility* (Exposition Press). The first part contains a straightforward discussion of Stein's career, life, genres, and styles. While Miller's criticism makes little lasting contribution to Stein scholarship, the second part of the book, "The Radcliffe Manuscripts," reproduces with some commentary by her teachers[29] the themes Stein wrote when a student at Radcliffe (then called the Harvard Annex). Aside from revealing certain matters of biographical interest, these compositions strike a number of emotional and thematic issues that are relevant to Stein's later writing. They also exhibit Stein's grammatical and punctuational weaknesses, which she later developed into stylistic idiosyncracies justified *post facto* in such essays as "Poetry and Grammar" in *Lectures in America*. Serious students of Stein will want to examine these early writings.

The final work in this section is Edmund Wilson's *New Yorker* review (15 September 1951) of Stein's early novella, *Q.E.D.*, published in 1951 in a limited edition as *Things as They Are*. Aside from containing a perceptive reading, this is the first essay to deal directly with lesbianism in Stein's work. Wilson believes that the linguistic ambiguities in Stein's experimental writing stem from the elaborate measures she developed to mask what she could not at that time express directly. The theory that Stein's difficulty stems from her desire to obscure a psychic wound antedates later critics such as Richard Bridgman and Elizabeth Fifer for whom Stein's experimental language becomes a form of code. Wilson's essay-review brings to an end the early period of Stein criticism.

Academic interest in Stein began to develop in the early 1950s when the Yale University Press published Donald Sutherland's *Gertrude Stein: A Biography of Her Work* concurrently with the first volume of the Yale Edition of the *Unpublished Writings of Gertrude Stein*. The Edition ran to eight volumes and was completed in 1958, bringing into print the great bulk of Stein's work, even though a few other volumes continued to appear thereafter. Sutherland was a friend of Stein, and while his tone is often too partisan, his knowledge of the materials and his sympathetic understanding of what Stein was trying to do makes this still one of the better books on the subject. Sutherland quotes at too great length and he often does not analyze as closely as he should, but he has insights that other critics continue to use and he has a fine understanding of the milieu that produced the literary experimentation of modernism. The selection reproduced from this book outlines Stein's intellectual background, discussing her work in the Harvard Psychology Laboratory with William James and Hugo Münsterberg, and placing her literary experiments in the context of Freud, Proust, and Joyce.

Many publications on Stein during the 1950s were biographical. In 1954 *The Alice B. Toklas Cookbook* appeared, with its famous recipe for brownies. The book actually contains a delightful series of anecdotes about Toklas's life with Stein, with a number of interesting recipes thrown in. Three years later Elizabeth Sprigge published the first full-length biography.[30] Although interesting at the time, it is not a highly analytical book, often accepting at face value the facts as Stein had Alice present them in *The Autobiography of Alice B. Toklas*, and not tying the significance of Stein's writing to the facts of her life. A much more persuasive picture of Stein as a creative artist capable of producing the things she wrote is John Malcolm Brinnin's *The Third Rose: Gertrude Stein and Her World* (1959). This lively account of her career and life is based to some extent on original materials and interviews, but it is distinguished less for its scholarship than for insights into Stein's works and their relationship to the Parisian milieu and the painters who constituted so much of her artistic companionship. Although now superseded as a story of her life by James Mellow's *Charmed Circle: Gertrude Stein & Company*, it remains one of the best accounts of the modernist School of Paris during Stein's early years there.

Toward the end of the 1950s, a number of serious critical assessments began to appear. Allegra Stewart's essay in *American Literature* (January 1957), "The Quality of Gertrude Stein's Creativity," developed a theory based heavily on the work of Jung which described Stein as engaged in a form of religious meditation. The essay, which enhances our understanding of Stein's intellectual milieu, is reproduced here, a microcosm of Stewart's full-length work *Gertrude Stein and the Present* (1967), which was published ten years later. John Ashbery's review in *Poetry* (July 1957) of *Stanzas in Meditation*, "The Impossible," transcends its genre by dramatizing the early confrontation of an important contemporary poet with one of his precursors. Ashbery talks about the monotony in Stein, but he says "it is the fertile kind, which generates excitement as water monotonously flowing over a dam generates electrical power." Comparing Stein's poetry to the late novels of James, Ashbery commends her for attempting "the impossible"; but even though "we feel that it is still impossible to accomplish the impossible, we are also left with the conviction that it is the only thing worth trying to do."

Not all critics were as enthusiastic about Stein's "monotony." Another *bête noire* of Stein criticism, B. F. Reid's *Art by Subtraction: A Dissenting Opinion of Gertrude Stein*, was written to erase Stein from the literary canon. The following statement expresses a frustration typical of many academic readers:

> It seems to me that Miss Stein is a vulgar genius talking to herself, and if she is talking to herself, she is not an artist. It is because she does talk to herself that she offers insuperable difficulties to both reader and critic. I suggest, therefore, that she be defined out of existence as an artist. To be an artist, she must talk to us, not to the dullest or the most tradition bound or the most unsympathetic of us, but to those of us who are flexible, those willing to be fruitfully led. There is not world enough or time enough for Gertrude Stein's kind of writing; too much in literature is both excellent and knowable.

Reid's easy, dismissive assertiveness was challenged a few months later in a long essay (published herein) by William Gass, soon to become known as a distinguished novelist and philosopher. Gass accuses Reid's book of being "a muddled and angry piece of journalese whose only value lies in how well it expresses the normal academic reaction," and his anger generates an excellent overview of Stein's work. Gass's collection of essays, *The World within the Word* (1978), includes "Gertrude Stein and the Geography of the Sentence," which contains one of the best accounts yet of *Tender Buttons*.

Critical interest continued to develop during the 1960s at about the same rate of speed. An early (1961) Minnesota Pamphlet on American Writers, written by Frederick J. Hoffman, contains a brisk overview of Stein's work and career, with a number of good insights as well as a number of factual errors. Difficult to get hold of, this work is now of interest only to beginners. Also published in 1961 was the first of Richard Bridgman's pieces on Stein, this one an essay on "Melanctha" in *American Literature* (November 1961), much of which appeared in the distinguished chapter on Stein's style in *The Colloquial Style in American Literature* (1966).

Although no full-length biographies were published in the 1960s, a few contributions to Stein biography appeared during that time. In 1963 Alice B. Toklas published her own memoir of life with Stein, *What Is Remembered*. By then, however, Toklas was quite old, her legendary wit had lost most of its bite, and what is remembered is too little to be satisfying. Nonetheless, a few critics have noticed resemblances between the style of *What Is Remembered* and that of *The Autobiography of Alice B. Toklas,* an observation that leads to one of two conclusions: either Stein was a wonderful mimic, or Toklas played a greater hand in writing *The Autobiography* than is commonly believed. Richard Bridgman has discussed the matter at some length,[31] but since no conclusive evidence has ultimately been found, readers may draw their own conclusions.

A year later Ernest Hemingway's memoirs of Paris, *A Moveable Feast,* were published posthumously. The book contains cattily malicious chapters on Stein and Toklas, where innuendoes about lesbianism fly and an incident is described in which Stein and Toklas argue off stage. Hemingway also describes how Stein entertained all the authors (presumably male) while Toklas spoke separately with the wives. Hemingway managed to have the last word in an indecorous battle of words that had been going on for more than thirty years and had certainly been fueled by the accusation in *The Autobiography* that Hemingway was "yellow."[32] Another of Stein's artistic compatriots, Virgil Thomson, published his own autobiography, *Virgil Thomson,* in 1966, filling it with many references to Stein and their collaboration on such "operas" as *Four Saints in Three Acts, Capital Capitals,* and *The Mother of Us All.* This book is especially of interest for its account of the composition and production of *Four Saints.*

Three full-length critical works appeared during the 1960s. The first was Leon Katz's Ph.D. thesis, a detailed study of the composition of *The Making of Americans.*[33] Of use to all Stein scholars, this study should have been published long ago. Bits and pieces of it have appeared as articles, introductions to books, and chapters in books,[34] and Katz's edition of Stein's unpublished notebooks has been announced as imminent for many years. The notebooks have still not been published, and the only lengthy manifestation of them is a typescript to which only a few scholars have had access. Reprinted in this volume is Katz's essay "Weininger and *The Making of Americans,*" which outlines the extraordinary influence on Stein of Otto Weininger's *Sex and Character,* a strange mélange of antifeminism and anti-Semitism written by a Viennese Jew who committed suicide at age 25. The book influenced a number of other authors, including James Joyce.

My own book, *The Development of Abstractionism in the Writings of Gertrude Stein,* appeared in 1965, the first full-length attempt at a methodical, nonpartisan analysis of a discrete body of Stein's writing. Limited to the first ten years of her career, the book examines Stein's work from *Q.E.D.* (1903, first published in 1950 as *Things as They Are*) through *Tender Buttons* (1914). Starting from a definition of abstractionism as "the act or process of leaving out of consideration one or more qualities of a complex object so as to attend to others," the book examines the development of Stein's abstractionism as being constituted by the progressive leaving out of elements of the "complex object" of realistic verisimilitude. Each of Stein's writings became a new stage in this progression, culminating in the "cubist" poetry of *Tender Buttons* which did not attempt to portray the external world in the usual way of fiction, but treated words that normally referred to that world as plastic counters that could be manipulated in the manner of a cubist collage.

Less detached was Allegra Stewart's *Gertrude Stein and the Present* (1967), a book that brought the apparatus of Jungian psychology to bear on a number of Stein's works. Proposing Stein as a writer of religious contemplation, Stewart's ingenious readings of *Dr. Faustus Lights the Lights* and of *Tender Buttons* as a mandala give a sense of richness to what most analysts had found to be a writing style designed to minimize significance. It was a valuable counterbalance to the somewhat detached "new critical" stance of my own book, even though subsequent critics have often found Stewart to be a bit too ingenious.

If the 1960s showed only a modest increase of interest in the work of Stein, the 1970s saw the development of a burgeoning critical industry. By the time of her centennial in 1974, Stein criticism had come of age.

Norman Weinstein's modest book, *Gertrude Stein and the Literature of the Modern Consciousness* (1970), brought to bear on Stein's work some of the discoveries of modern linguistics. While certainly a worthwhile endeavor, Weinstein's own command of linguistics remained largely at the theoretical level, and his readings of Stein were not consistently illuminating. A book marked more by its stimulating insights than its systematic reading of texts, it has provided ideas for others to explore with more authority.

The next book is not burdened by such limitations. Richard Bridgman's *Gertrude Stein in Pieces* is the one book on Stein that deserves to be called indispensable. Bridgman set himself the task of writing about the entire Stein canon in the order it was written. In the process of ascertaining the order of Stein's compositions, he examined the papers in the Yale Collection of American Literature and corrected the standard bibliographies of Stein's work. He modestly describes his book as "a preliminary inventory of Gertrude Stein's literary estate" (p. xiii).

Bridgman does not apply a systematic methodology to analyzing all of Stein's difficult works. He accepts the fact that "the greater part of Gertrude Stein's writing was improvisational (p. xv)," that she experimented relentlessly, recording her many doubts and insecurities, as well as the quotidian details of her life. As a result, any critic must accept the fact that dull spaces exist throughout Stein's writing, but that fact should not be used as a weapon to attack Stein and avoid understanding what she was about. Bridgman further believes that the progressive obscurity of Stein's writing arises from her own difficulty in channeling a somewhat chaotic emotional life, a theory adumbrated in Edmund Wilson's review of *Things as They Are.*

Bridgman's readings are thorough, nonideological, and full of common sense. While not afraid to make judgments about individual works, he is more interested in establishing what Stein was about than in judging definitively the value of her career. A book like this makes it possible for others to build on its insights and comprehensiveness in order to do the more specialized studies needed to understand a difficult, complex author. Much of the remarkable development of Stein criticism throughout the 1970s is indebted to Bridgman.

The same year (1970) New York's Museum of Modern Art organized "Four Americans in Paris," an exhibition also shown at museums in Baltimore and San Francisco, two cities associated with Stein. Thousands of individuals became familiar with Gertrude, Leo, Michael, and Sarah Stein as this century's great art collecting family. The catalog, *Four Americans in Paris*, includes interesting essays by Leon Katz and Douglas Cooper, art critic and historian of Cubism. Published concurrently was a handsome art volume, *Gertrude Stein on Picasso*, edited by Edward Burns, containing the Stein portraits, "Picasso" (1909) and "If I Told Him" (1923), as well as Stein's short book, *Picasso* (1938). The volume also contains selections from Stein's notebooks concerned with Picasso and many reproductions of the Stein collection and photographs of Stein and Toklas among their paintings at 27 rue de fleurus. The graphics are spread throughout the book as a running commentary on the various texts.

The approach of Stein's hundredth anniversary brought about more and more publishing activity. Robert Bartlett Haas edited three books during the early 1970s. The first, *A Primer for the Gradual Understanding of Gertrude Stein* (1971), is an anthology of Stein's writings intended to introduce the new reader to her work. It also contains Donald Sutherland's essay, "Gertrude Stein and the Twentieth Century." The other two volumes publish previously uncollected writings: *Reflection on the Atomic Bomb* (1973) and *How Writing Is Written* (1974). In 1972 the University of North Carolina Press brought out a volume that contains the correspondence of Stein and Sherwood Anderson and the essays they wrote about one another.[35] All these volumes continued to flesh out our knowledge of Stein. In addition, Leon Katz published *The Making of Americans: An Opera and a Play* (1973), a dramatization of Stein's long novel, including passages from her unpublished notebooks, which was produced at Judson Poets' Theater during the Fall of 1972, with a musical score by Al Carmines.

In honor of the centennial three journals devoted entire issues to Gertrude Stein: *The Widening Circle* (Fall 1973), *White Pelican: A Quarterly Review of the Arts* (Autumn 1974), and the *Lost Generation Journal* (Winter 1974). A number of works for a popular audience were also published, including a number of biographical volumes. The more ephemeral ones include Avis Burnett, *Gertrude Stein* (1972); Howard Greenfield, *Gertrude Stein: A Biography* (1973); Janet Hobhouse, *Every-*

body Who Was Anybody: A Biography of Gertrude Stein (1975); Lois Rather, *Gertrude Stein and California* (1974); W. G. Rogers, *Gertrude Stein Is Gertrude Stein Is Gertrude Stein: Her Life and Work* (1973); Linda Simon, ed., *Gertrude Stein: A Composite Portrait* (1974); and Ellen Wilson, *They Named Me Gertrude Stein* (1973). That a number of these are written for juveniles suggests how widely accepted Stein had become. None of these works are based on primary scholarship and none do more than transmit some form of received opinion about Stein.

Books of more lasting value were also published at that time. One was a full-length descriptive bibliography of all Stein's published works, prepared by Robert A. Wilson and published by the Phoenix Bookshop (1974). This supersedes previous bibliographies but should now be brought up to date. Of serious biographical interest are two works. James R. Mellow's *Charmed Circle: Gertrude Stein & Company*, based on solid research among the Stein materials as well as a deep understanding of modern artistic movements, takes its place as the best life yet of Stein. The picture of Stein and her "company" is vivid and solidly documented, but the book is limited by Mellow's inability to deal well with Stein as a writer. One looks in vain for a complex understanding of the relationship between Stein's life and her work, but her life is so interesting that Mellow's book remains an important contribution. Also valuable is *Staying on Alone: Letters of Alice B. Toklas* (1973), edited by Edward Burns. Although these letters were written after Stein's death in 1946, the subject of many of the letters is, in fact, Stein, and so our understanding of the relationship of Stein and Toklas is much enhanced by the latter's astringent, vital prose.

The middle 1970s saw no slackening of interest in Stein. Carolyn Faunce Copeland's *Language & Time & Gertrude Stein* (1975) is a study of Stein's narrators. Based on an interesting idea, it is largely unrealized, because of Copeland's shaky scholarship and her lack of sophistication about contemporary theories of narratology. The following year (1976) this writer's *Gertrude Stein* was published in the Twayne United States Authors Series. My intention was to write a clear, concise, and comprehensive overview of Stein's career that would serve as a useful reference work and a critical introduction to Stein. In 1977 Samuel M. Steward published *Dear Sammy: Letters from Gertrude Stein & Alice B. Toklas*, containing letters and a lengthy memoir of how the young Steward had met and spent time with Stein and Toklas in France in the 1930s. The same author has just published a novel called *Parisian Lives* (1984), a fictionalized account of life in the gay community of Paris with portrayals of Stein and Toklas *in propriae personae*. Stewart is always amusing, but he tells us little we can't find out elsewhere. Nor does Linda Simon, who, in *The Biography of Alice B. Toklas* (1977), a slick piece of journalism, goes over most of the ground of Mellow and Brinnin and adds an account of the years Toklas survived after Stein's death. One can learn more about Toklas, however, from the letters in *Staying on Alone*.

More important than any of these titles, however, were two new trends in Stein scholarship, manifested in the late 1970s in articles and a few books. The first was the application of structuralist and poststructuralist critical theory to the analysis of Stein's work. The second was the reading of Stein from a feminist perspective, an ironically belated occurrence given the nature of Stein's writing. As a concomitant of this maturity scholars began writing about a number of works that had not yet received serious critical scrutiny. Some of the pieces in this volume reflect the greater variety in recent Stein criticism. A few appeared in the special Stein issue published by *Twentieth-Century Literature* in Spring, 1978, which contains a number of articles written from both the feminist and poststructuralist points of view.

Wendy Steiner's *Exact Resemblance to Exact Resemblance: The Literary Portraiture of Gertrude Stein* (1978) is a structuralist study of Stein's literary portraits, stemming more from the Russian than the French school. It relates Stein's portraits to the historical genre of the literary portrait; explores the developmental stages in Stein's own use of the genre; places the portrait within the context of Stein's other genres; and explores the relation of Stein's portraiture to that of the cubists. While Steiner's own assertion of structures sometimes seems a bit schematic, her book embodies a great advance in Stein criticism. In particular, she is excellent on one of the cruxes of Stein scholarship, the relationship of Stein to cubism, because her structuralist methodology adds precision to her practice of periodization. Steiner is represented in this volume by an article entitled "The Steinian Portrait," which concisely prefigures the overall theory of her book.

Also useful is a short monograph by S. C. Neuman, *Gertrude Stein: Autobiography and the Problem of Narration*[36], which applies contemporary concepts of narratology to the "comprehensible" works Stein wrote from *The Autobiography of Alice B. Toklas* through *Wars I Have Seen.* Neuman studies the problem of time and the use of different types of narrators and narrative voices; her readings of Stein's late works are among the best we have.

In 1979 a valuable scholarly tool was also published: Maureen R. Liston's *Gertrude Stein: An Annotated Critical Bibliography.* Liston covers (through 1977) bibliographies, biographies, critical books, articles, book chapters, dissertations, introductions to Stein's works, reviews of Stein's works, and reviews of the secondary literature. Her work was certainly an indispensable aid to me in preparing the present volume. The years since 1977 can be adequately covered by the current MLA bibliographies.

Serious feminist readings began to appear around the middle of the 1970s. In the recent past it had become possible to discuss Stein's lesbianism openly, particularly after Bridgman's frank treatment of it and the openness of discussion in Mellow's biography. To relate Stein's sexual preference to the buried life it led in her writings has become a task of feminist critics. One of the first valuable attempts is the chapter on Stein in Dolores Klaich's *Woman + Woman: Attitudes toward Lesbianism* (1974) in which the author analyzes the submerged lesbian linguistic code Stein uses in her writing. Development of this kind of discussion is continued at a less sophisticated level in Jane Rule's chapter on Stein in *Lesbian Images* (1976). More sophisticated efforts are by Catharine R. Stimpson in "The Mind, the Body, and Gertrude Stein,"[37] a study of sexuality in Stein's very early writings and "The Somagrams of Gertrude Stein," published herein; by Cynthia Secor's more militant reading of "Ida, a Great American Novel";[38] and especially by Elizabeth Fifer in a series of articles on Stein's use of language and buried forms, one of which is reprinted here.[39]

Stimpson, Secor, and Fifer all seem to be working on full-length studies of Stein, and Stein scholars and enthusiasts can only look forward to their appearance. Two full-length works in 1983 combined a feminist reading with the application of poststructuralist theories of language. Marianne DeKoven's *A Different Language: Gertrude Stein's Experimental Writing* explicitly applies the terminology of "current French feminist, poststructuralist, and psychoanalytic criticism" to the experimental works of Stein. DeKoven believes that all experimental writing is antipatriarchal because it opposes modes that are "linear, orderly, closed, hierarchical, sensible, coherent, referential, and heavily focused on the signified." Stein's modes are "incoherent, open-ended, anarchic, irreducibly multiple," and are "focused on what Roland Barthes calls the 'magic of the signifier.' "[40] DeKoven's chronological analysis of the various categories of Stein's writing is quite fresh and demonstrates not only continuities in Stein's writing but also gives the critic a new way of writing about the *dis*continuities that define her various stylistic stages.

Neil Schmitz's witty book, *Of Huck and Alice: Humorous Writing in American Literature* contains two lengthy chapters on Stein. Schmitz's method is deconstructive, locating the irresolvable cruxes (the *aporias*) of Stein's style in a way that points out their humor and the relevance of a hidden lesbian linguistic code to that humor. One of the chapters contains readings of Stein's autobiographical works. The other, "The Gaiety of Gertrude Stein," with its obvious pun, is concerned with the difficult, experimental works *Tender Buttons, Lifting Belly,* and *A Long Gay Book,* all of them rich in the lesbian coding to which Schmitz deconstructs the text. Included in the present volume is an earlier version of Schmitz's remarks on *Tender Buttons,* not as full of his brittle wit but more straightforward and pointed in presenting the same content.

Two books published just at the time I was writing this introduction are concerned with Stein's modernism and her relationship to modern painting. Randa Dubnick's *The Structure of Obscurity: Gertrude Stein, Language, and Cubism* (1984) is based on some of the linguistic distinctions that "have been made by structuralists and semiologists, such as Saussure, Barthes, and Jakobson." Dubnick uses Stein's own differentiations to distinguish between two basic Stein styles, "poetry" and "prose." She applies Jakobson's distinction between the vertical and horizontal ordering of language, between "*selection* (choice of signifying elements; vocabulary) and *combination* (ordering of elements: spatial or syntactic)."[41] Her readings of works such as *Tender Buttons* and *The Geographical History of America* are good examples of the value of semiological theory for practical criticism.

Jayne Walker uses contemporary linguistics and semiotics in *The Making of a Modernist: Gertrude Stein from "Three Lives" to "Tender Buttons"* (1984). She also makes extensive use of the unpublished notebooks. Her readings of Stein's early work, through *Tender Buttons*, are amplified by both her basic scholarship and her theoretical sophistication. In addition, Walker, like Dubnick, has written a convincing account of the relationship of Stein's early work to that of the cubists.

The final four essays are being published for the first time in this volume. Lisa Ruddick, who is writing a book on Stein, contributes a Lacanian analysis of Stein's concepts of female character as they are manifested in her early works. She focuses heavily on Stein's word play, deconstructing her metaphoric and metonymic structures to reveal their sexual origins. Elyse Blankley also focuses on the early Stein, from *Q.E.D.* through *Tender Buttons*, to show the connection between Stein's expatriation and her developmental experience "as an American college girl and New Woman in the 1890s." Stein's experience as an expatriate has been much more interesting to her biographers than to her critics who have not until now found a way to make it a critical tool. Blankley is writing a book on twentieth-century expatriate women writers in Paris. Jane Bowers's reading of *Four Saints in Three Acts* is part of a full-length work she is preparing on Stein's "operas" and plays. Building on Richard Bridgman's approach to the opera, Bowers treats *Four Saints* as a "landscape" and explores Stein's attempts to create a new theatrical genre. The final essay is by Laura Riding Jackson, who has contributed her views on Stein in "The Word-Play of Gertrude Stein." As Laura Riding, Mrs. Jackson first wrote on Stein in *transition* (see note 15). An important modernist poet in her own right, she reemerged into print in recent decades after a long silence. Her piece places Stein within the modernist linguistic revolution and measures her against such contemporaries as T. S. Eliot. It is a serious summary statement by a major twentieth-century poet-critic.

When Stein's unpublished notebooks as well her voluminous correspondence are finally published, many more insights will be available into the character of this remarkable woman, and much of the critical literature will have to be rethought. We shall certainly need a new biography that makes full use of this information. In addition, much of Stein's important work has still not received enough serious commentary.

Except for Bridgman's book, many of Stein's plays have not yet had their first serious critical reading—even such an important one as *The Mother of Us All*. The same is true for *Mrs. Reynolds* and *A Novel of Thank You* as well as numerous shorter pieces of prose such as those collected in *As Fine as Melanctha*. Stein's poetry is beginning to be read now that both feminist and deconstructive theory has caught up with what she was doing, but much of that writing has only begun to find receptive readers. Stein may well be one of those writers whose work lends itself best to what is going on in contemporary criticism. At least the recent spate of writing about her work and the prospect of much more to come would tend to suggest that she is finally receiving the kind of critical attention appropriate to so well known a writer.

Books are usually collaborative efforts, and this one is no exception. I am grateful to the following individuals for their aid and advice: Anne Cabello and Diana Dulaney, for speedy and accurate typing of the text; Barbara Vargas for constant last-minute help and for making sure I kept up with my deadlines; James Woodress, editor of *Critical Essays on Walt Whitman*, also in this series, for his careful reading of my introduction; Diane R. Hoffman, my wife, for her continued love, support, and advice, for helping me make time for my work, and for taking time from her own busy schedule to give a critical reading to my introduction. The University of California supported me with generous research funding and a sabbatical leave.

Most of all, I wish to thank my student and research assistant, Patrick Murphy, for being a true collaborator. He helped me during every stage of the project, not only in routine research activities too numerous to mention, but in many matters of judgment. He aided me in choosing the texts for this volume, advised on which ones to omit, which to include, which to reduce and how to reduce them; and he read my introduction with an editor's eye. This volume could not have been completed nearly so well without his very able assistance.

Notes

1. Both these works are reprinted in this volume. Bibliographical data relating to all works reprinted in this volume will be found in notes accompanying those essays. In an attempt to keep notes to a minimum I have included as much bibliographical reference as possible within the text of the Introduction, particularly in the case of books easily available in a university library.

2. Leo Stein, *Journey into the Self: Being the Letters, Papers and Journals of Leo Stein*, ed. Edmund Fuller (New York: Crown Publishers, 1950), 230.

3. John Malcolm Brinnin, *The Third Rose: Gertrude Stein and Her World* (Boston: Little, Brown, 1959), 220.

4. See, for instance, *For Whom the Bell Tolls* (New York: Scribner's, 1940), 289.

5. Brinnin, *Third Rose*, 220.

6. "The Mote in the Middle Distance," in *A Christmas Garland* (London: William Heinemann, 1912).

7. *The Development of Abstractionism in the Writings of Gertrude Stein* (Philadelphia: University of Pennsylvania Press, 1965), 18.

8. Leon Solomons and Gertrude Stein, "Normal Motor Automatism," *Psychological Review* 3 (September 1896): 492–512; Gertrude Stein, "Cultivated Motor Automatism," *Psychological Review* 5 (May 1898): 295–306.

9. "Gertrude Stein — Hoax and Hoaxtress: A Study of the Woman Whose 'Tender Buttons' Has Furnished New York with a New Kind of Amusement," *Morning Telegraph* 7 (March 1915): 6.

10. Richard Aldington, "The Disciples of Gertrude Stein," *Poetry* 17 (October 1920): 35–40.

11. "Four American Impressions," *New Republic* 32 (11 October 1922): 171.

12. "A Guide to Gertrude Stein," *Vanity Fair* (September 1923): 60, 80. This article is only in part about *Geography and Plays*.

13. "Really Quite Extraordinary," *Literary Review* (11 August 1923, 891). Reprinted in *Points of View* (New York: Scribner's, 1924).

14. See Porter's *Collected Essays and Occasional Writings* (New York: Delta, 1970), 256–70.

15. Laura Riding, "Composition as Explanation," *transition* 13 (June 1927): 157. I shall refer later in this text to her original essay, "The Word-Play of Gertrude Stein," which appears for the first time anywhere in this collection.

16. Ralph Church, "A Note on the Writing of Gertrude Stein," *transition* 14 (Fall 1928): 167.

17. See the discussion in James Mellow, *Charmed Circle: Gertrude Stein & Company* (New York: Praeger, 1974), 273–74.

18. James Agee, "Stein's Way," *Time* 22 (11 September 1933): 57–60.

19. Edmund Wilson, "27 rue de fleurus," *New Republic* 76 (11 October 1933): 246–47. Reprinted in *The Shores of Light: A Literary Chronicle of the Twenties and Thirties* (New York: Farrar, Straus & Young, 1952), 575–80.

20. Conrad Aiken, "We Ask for Bread," *New Republic* 78 (4 April 1934): 219.

21. Paul Rosenfeld, "Prepare for Saints!" *New Republic* 78 (21 February 1934): 48.

22. Joseph Wood Krutch, "A Prepare for Saints," *Nation* 138 (4 April 1934): 396, 398.

23. Richard Bridgman, *Gertrude Stein in Pieces* (New York: Oxford University Press, 1970), 176.

24. RCA Victor Red Seal #LM 2756.

25. Jean Wahl, "Miss Stein's Battle," *New Republic* 112 (19 March 1945): 398.

26. Perry Miller, "Steinese," *New York Times Book Review* (3 November 1946): 30.

27. Thornton Wilder, introduction to *Four in America* (New Haven: Yale University Press, 1947), v–xxvii.

28. Caedmon Records #TC 1050.

29. Including the poet William Vaughn Moody, who was a Harvard instructor before moving to the University of Chicago.

30. Elizabeth Sprigge, *Gertrude Stein: Her Life and Work* (London: Hamish Hamilton, 1957). W. G. Rogers, *When This You See Remember Me: Gertrude Stein in Person* (New York: Rinehart, 1948) is more a memoir than a biography.

31. See *Gertrude Stein in Pieces*, 209–17.

32. Gertrude Stein, *The Autobiography of Alice B. Toklas* (New York: Random House, 1933), 216.

33. Leon Katz, "The First Making of *The Making of Americans:* A Study Based on Gertrude Stein's Notebooks and Early Versions of Her Novel (1902–1908)," Ph.D. diss., Columbia University, 1963.

34. See, for instance, "Matisse, Picasso and Gertrude Stein," in *Four Americans in Paris: The Collections of Gertrude Stein and Her Family,* ed. Irene Gordon (New York: The Museum of Modern Art, 1970), 51–63; and Introduction to *Fernhurst, Q.E.D., and Other Early Writings,* by Gertrude Stein (New York: Liveright, 1971), ix–xiii.

35. Ray Lewis White, ed., *Sherwood Anderson/Gertrude Stein: Correspondence and Personal Essays* (Chapel Hill: University of North Carolina Press, 1972). Also edited by White, see *Gertrude Stein and Alice B. Toklas: A Reference Guide* (Boston: G. K. Hall, 1984).

36. S. C. Neuman, *Gertrude Stein: Autobiography and the Problem of Narration,* English Literary Studies, Monograph 18 (Victoria, B.C.: University of Victoria, 1979).

37. Catharine R. Stimpson, "The Mind, the Body, and Gertrude Stein," *Critical Inquiry* 3 (Spring 1977): 489–506.

38. Cynthia Secor, "Ida, a Great American Novel," *Twentieth-Century Literature* 24 (Spring 1978): 96–107.

39. See the following: "Is Flesh Advisable? The Interior Theater of Gertrude Stein," *Signs* 4 (Spring 1979): 472–83; "Guardians and Witnesses: Narrative Technique in Gertrude Stein's *Useful Knowledge,*" *Journal of Narrative Technique* 10 (Spring 1980): 115–27; "Rescued Readings: Characteristic Deformations in the Language of Gertrude Stein's Plays," *Texas Studies in Language and Literature* 24 (Winter 1982): 394–428.

40. Marianne DeKoven, *A Different Language: Gertrude Stein's Experimental Writing* (Madison: University of Wisconsin Press, 1983), xiii–xiv.

41. Randa Dubnick, *The Structure of Obscurity: Gertrude Stein, Language, and Cubism* (Urbana: University of Illinois, 1984), xiv.

[Letter to Gertrude Stein]　　　　　Hutchins Hapgood*

Villa Linda, Via Poggio di Gherardi 2, Settignano,
Apr 22 [1906]

Dear Gertrude—

I have been reading your stories with a very great deal of interest. In the essentials they seem to me extremely good—full of reality, truth, unconventionality. I am struck with their deep humanity, and with the really remarkable way you have of getting deep into human psychology. In this respect, the Negro story ["Melanctha"] seemed to me wonderfully strong and true, a powerful picture of the relations between a man and a woman and the inevitable causes of their separation. The characters in all the stories are real and clearly drawn, and the atmosphere and setting is all in tone. I really feel like complimenting you highly on what is most fundamental in your work. You have grasped some big things and have been able to make a picture of them. They show, too, a remarkable sympathy in you. Without that, you could not have done any work of that kind. The Negro story especially is extraordinary in this way. It is the very best thing on the subject of the Negro that I have ever read.

Saying all this, means of course, that in some way you have done an artistic thing. And yet somehow you have attained your end without any of the ordinary devices of plot, piquancy, conversation, variety, drama, etc. Your stories are not easy reading, for that reason. They lack all of the minor qualities of art,—construction, etc., etc. They often irritate me by the innumerable and often as it seems to me unnecessary repetitions; by your painstaking but often clumsy phraseology, by what seems sometimes almost an affectation of style. You may say you couldn't have attained your effects otherwise—but I think you could improve them much by cutting and by manipulations in other ways. But that sort of thing must be left to the author. He knows best what *moyens* he can avail himself of. The gist of my criticism is: *au fond*, they are excellent—superficially irritating and difficult and I fear to most people unattractive.

*Reprinted from *The Flowers of Friendship: Letters Written to Gertrude Stein*, ed. Donald Gallup (New York: Alfred A. Knopf, 1953), 31–32.

I fear you will have difficulties with the publishers; partly for the very idiotic but real reason that they are not the right length, and partly (and this the most important) because to get their real quality, patience and culture are demanded of the reader. . . . I think that . . . you will surely find an ultimate publisher, but it may take you a long time. [Pitts] Duffield is the most likely man to get into the quality of your work, that I know; and, if he likes it, he is less likely to allow strictly commercial reasons to interfere with his publishing it, than many others. I will gladly write him, if you like, and call his attention to what I think the great excellence of your work. . . .

Your stories really have a remarkable amount of quality and they would certainly be successful if published and public were what they ought to be. Perhaps they will be anyway.

Auf Wiedersehen
Hutchins Hapgood

Fiction, but Not Novels   Anonymous*

Three Lives by Gertrude Stein, is fiction which no one who reads it can ever forget, but a book for a strictly limited audience. The three lives are "The Good Anna," "The Gentle Lena," and "Melanctha." The good Anna was Miss Mathilda's housekeeper. The gentle Lena, when she had been in this country long enough to know the English, married the good son of German parents. Melanctha is a colored girl, her lover the very best type evolved in the race, a young physician. In this remarkable book one watches humanity groping in the mists of existence. As character study one can speak of it only in superlatives. The originality of its narrative form is as notable. As these humble human lives are groping in bewilderment so does the story telling itself. Not written in the vernacular, it yet gives that impression. At first one fancies the author using repetition as a refrain is used in poetry. But it is something more subtle still; something involved, something turning back, for a new beginning, for a lost strand in the spinning. It makes of the book a very masterpiece of realism, for the reader never escapes from the atmosphere of those lives, so subtly is the incantation wrought into these seeming simple pages. Here is a literary artist of such originality that it is not easy to conjecture what special influences have gone into the making of her. But the indwelling spirit of it all is a sweet enlightened sympathy, an unsleeping sense of humor, and an exquisite carefulness in detail. But it is tautology to praise Miss Stein's work for this quality or that. Enough has surely been said to call the

*Reprinted from the *Kansas City Star*, 18 December 1909, 5.

attention of those who will value her work to this new and original artist come into the field of fiction.

[*Three Lives*] Anonymous*

These stories of the Good Anna, Melanctha, and the Gentle Lena have a quite extraordinary vitality conveyed in a most eccentric and difficult form. The half-articulated phrases follow unrelentingly the blind mental and temperamental gropings of three humble souls wittingly or unwittingly at odds with life. Whoever can adjust himself to the repetitions, false starts, and general circularity of the manner will find himself very near real people. Too near, possibly. The present writer had an uncomfortable sense of being immured with a girl wife, a spinster, and a woman who is neither, between imprisoning walls which echoed exactly all thoughts and feelings. These stories utterly lack construction and focus, but give that sense of urgent life which one gets more commonly in Russian literature than elsewhere. How the Good Anna spent herself barrenly for everybody in reach, the Gentle Lena for the notion of motherhood, while the mulattress Melanctha perished partly of her own excess of temperament, but more from contact with a life-diminishing prig and emotionally inert surroundings, readers who are willing to pay a stiff entrance fee in patient attention may learn for themselves. From Miss Stein, if she can consent to clarify her method, much may be expected. As it is, she writes quite as a Browning escaped from the bonds of verse might wallow in fiction, only without his antiseptic whimsicality.

Speculations, Or
Post-Impressionism in Prose Mabel Dodge*

Many roads are being broken today, and along these roads consciousness is pursuing truth to eternity. This is an age of communication, and the human being who is not a "communicant" is in the sad plight which the dogmatist defines as being a condition of spiritual non-receptivity.

Some of these newly opened roads lie parallel and almost touch.

In a large studio in Paris, hung with paintings by Renoir, Matisse and Picasso, Gertrude Stein is doing with words what Picasso is doing with

*Reprinted from the *Nation* 90 (20 January 1910): 65.

*Reprinted from *Arts and Decorations* 3 (March 1913): 172, 174. Reprinted by permission of Curtis Brown, Ltd. Copyright 1936 Harcourt Brace & Co.

paint. She is impelling language to induce new states of consciousness, and in doing so language becomes with her a creative art rather than a mirror of history.

In her impressionistic writing she uses familiar words to create perceptions, conditions, and states of being, never before quite consciously experienced. She does this by using words that appeal to her as having the meaning that they *seem* to have. She has taken the English language and, according to many people, has misused it, or has used it roughly, uncouthly and brutally, or madly, stupidly and hideously, but by her method she is finding the hidden and inner nature of nature.

To present her impressions she chooses words for their inherent quality, rather than for their accepted meaning.

Her habit of working is methodical and deliberate. She always works at night in the silence, and brings all her will power to bear upon the banishing of preconceived images. Concentrating upon the impression she has received and which she wishes to transmit, she suspends her selective faculty, waiting for the word or group of words that will perfectly interpret her meaning, to rise from her sub-consciousness to the surface of her mind.

Then and then only does she bring her reason to bear upon them, examining, weighing and gauging their ability to express her meaning. It is a working proof of the Bergson theory of intuition. She does not go after words — she waits and lets them come to her, and they do.

It is only when art thus pursues the artist that his production will bear the mark of inevitability. It is only when the *"élan vital"* drives the artist to the creative overflow that life surges in his production. Vitality directed into a conscious expression is the modern definition of genius.

It is impossible to define or to describe fully any new manifestation in esthetics or in literature that is as recent, as near to us, as the work of Picasso or of Gertrude Stein; the most that we can do is to suggest a little, draw a comparison, point the way and then withdraw.

To know about them is a matter of personal experience; no one can help another through it. First before thought must come feeling, and this is the first step toward experience, because feeling is the beginning of knowledge.

It does not greatly matter how the first impress affects one. One may be shocked, stunned and dismayed, or one may be aroused, stimulated, intrigued and delighted. That there has been an *approach* is what counts.

It is only in a state of indifference that there is no approach at all, and indifference reeks of death. It is the tomb of life itself.

A further consciousness than is already ours will need many new forms of expression. In literature everything that has been felt and known so far has been said as it has been said.

What more there may be for us to realize must be expressed in a new way. Language has been crystalized into four or five established literary forms, that up to the present day have been held sacred and intranscendant, but all the truth cannot be contained in any one or in any limited number of molds. A. E., the Irish poet, says of it:

> The hero first thought it —
> To him 'twas a deed;
> To those who retaught it
> A chain on their speed.
>
> The fire that we kindled,
> A beacon by night,
> When darkness has dwindled
> Grows pale in the light.
>
> For life has no glory
> Stays long in one dwelling,
> And time has no story
> That's true twice in telling.
>
> And only the teaching
> That never was spoken
> Is worthy thy reaching
> The fountain unbroken.

This is so of all the arts, for of course what is true of one must, to be justifiable, be true of them all, even to the art of life; perhaps, first of all, to that one.

Nearly every thinking person nowadays is in revolt against something, because the craving of the individual is for further consciousness, and because consciousness is expanding and is bursting through the molds that have held it up to now; and so let every man whose private truth is too great for his existing conditions pause before he turn away from Picasso's painting or from Gertrude Stein's writing, for their case is his case.

Of course, comment is the best of signs. Any comment. One that Gertrude Stein hears oftenest is from conscientious souls who have honestly tried — and who have failed — to get anything out of her work at all. "But why don't you make it simpler?" they cry. "Because this is the only way in which I can express what I want to express," is the invariable reply, which of course is the unanswerable argument of every sincere artist to every critic. Again and again comes the refrain that is so familiar before the canvases of Picasso — "But it is so ugly, so brutal!" But how does one know that it is ugly, after all? How does one know? Each time that beauty has been reborn in the world it has needed complete readjustment of sense perceptions, grown all too accustomed to the blurred outlines, faded colors, the death in life of beauty in decline. It has become jaded from over-familiarity, from long association and from inertia. If one cares for Rembrandt's paintings today, then how could one have cared for them at the time when they were painted, when they were glowing with life. If we like St. Marks in Venice today, then surely it would have offended us a thousand years ago. Perhaps it is not Rembrandt's paintings that one cares for, after all, but merely for the shell, the ghost — the last pale flicker of the artist's intention. Beauty? One thing is certain, that if we must worship beauty as we have known it, we must consent to worship it as a thing dead. *"Une grande, belle chose — morte,"* And ugliness — what is it? Surely, only death is ugly.

In Gertrude Stein's writing every word lives and, apart from the concept, it is so exquisitely rhythmical and cadenced, that when read aloud and received as pure sound, it is like a kind of sensuous music. Just as one may stop, for once in a way, before a canvas of Picasso, and, letting one's reason sleep for an instant, may exclaim: "It *is* a fine pattern!" — so listening to Gertrude Stein's words and forgetting to try to understand what they mean, one submits to their gradual charm. Huntley Carter, of the *New Age*, says that her use of language has a curious hypnotic effect when read aloud. In one part of her writing she made use of repetition and the rearranging of certain words over and over, so that they became adjusted into a kind of incantation, and in listening one feels that from the combination of repeated sounds, varied ever so little, that there emerges gradually a perception of some meaning quite other than that of the contents of the phrases. Many people have experienced this magical evocation, but have been unable to explain in what way it came to pass, but though they did not know what meaning the words were bearing, nor how they were affected by them, yet they had *begun* to know what it all meant, because they were not indifferent.

In a portrait that she has finished recently, she has produced a coherent totality through a series of impressions which, when taken sentence by sentence, strike most people as particularly incoherent. To illustrate this, the words in the following paragraph are strenuous words — words that weigh and qualify conditions; words that are without softness yet that are not hard words — perilous abstractions they seem, containing agony and movement and conveying a vicarious livingness. "It is a gnarled division, that which is not any obstruction, and the forgotten swelling is certainly attracting. It is attracting the whiter division, it is not sinking to be growing, it is not darkening to be disappearing, it is not aged to be annoying. There cannot be sighing. This is this bliss."

Many roads are being broken — what a wonderful word — "broken"! And out of the shattering and petrifaction of today — up from the cleavage and the disintegration — we will see order emerging tomorrow. Is it so difficult to remember that life at birth is always painful and rarely lovely? How strange it is to think that the rough-hewn trail of today will become tomorrow the path of least resistance, over which the average will drift with all the ease and serenity of custom. All the labor of evolution is condensed into this one fact, of the vitality of the individual making way for the many. We can but praise the high courage of the road breakers, admitting as we infallibly must, in Gertrude Stein's own words, and with true Bergsonism faith — "Something is certainly coming out of them!"

Tender Buttons, Curious Experiment of Gertrude Stein in Literary Anarchy
Robert E. Rogers*

There is in New York a new publishing company called simply the "Claire Marie," which issues occasionally slender books bound in pale blues and greens, oranges and light lemons. The titles are, for instance, *Sonnets from the Patagonian, Saloon Sonnets and Sunday Flutings, Sacral Dimples* and *The Piety of Fans*. These seem mad, but there is one which seems madder. It is *Tender Buttons* by Gertrude Stein.

The Claire Marie Publishing Company hopes that these will be "books for people who are tired of best sellers and of the commonplace, who are eager for the sincerely exotic, the tomorrow of literature. The poets and dramatists I shall publish will be men and women who have no quarrel with the existing order of things, who have no wish to teach or to tear down, who are concerned only with the beauty of life." But to anyone who gets in touch, even superficially with these writings, they seem to try to do for the art of literature what has already been done in painting, sculpture and music, that is, to express anarchy in art.

Boston has seen some of the paintings of Matisse and Picasso, the sculptures of Brancusi, which created such a stir of amazement and contempt last spring. It has heard too, perhaps, of the new symphonies, wild sounds produced on new and unmusical instruments, which originated lately in Italy. Boston has not pretended to try to understand them, nor to admit that there is anything to understand, not even the point of view of the perpetrators. So, in a way perhaps, these books which show the contemporary anarchy of art in the form of literature may serve as examples and explanations of the thing which has upset Paris and roused New York to a cynical interest.

To begin at the far frontiers, where literary expression as we know it jumps off into the deep waters of unintelligible derangements of words! If you open Gertrude Stein's book, *Tender Buttons*, which deals with the three simple subjects of Objects, Food and Rooms, you will find — looking at random — this:

"A Little Called Pauline. A little called anything shows shudders.

"Come and say what prints all day. A whole few watermelon. There is no pope.

*Reprinted from the *Boston Evening Transcript*, 11 July 1914, 12.

"No cut in pennies and a little dressing and choose wide soles and little spats really nice spices.

"A little lace makes boils. This is not true.

"Gracious of gracious and a stamp a blue green white bow a blue green lean, lean on the top.

"If it is absurd then it is leadish and nearly set where there is a tight head."

There are seventy-eight pages of this sort of thing. Some of the subheadings are: "A Carafe. That is a blind glass"; "Suppose an Eyes"; "Peeled pencil choke"; "Orange In." Some of the other famous lines are "Alas a dirty word, alas a dirty third, alas a dirty third, alas a dirty bird," which refers to chicken, and "Boom in, boom in, butter. Leave a grain and show it, show it, I spy," which, as the reader may have gathered, describes butter.

A WOMAN OF DEGREES

These are enough examples. Now the first thing to say about these — and most people say it — is that the woman is either a colossal charlatan or mad. But there is something else to know about her. She is a doctor of medicine and a doctor of philosophy, a brilliant scholar formerly at Johns Hopkins and Radcliffe and a student in whom William James took a great interest and for whom he prophesied a brilliant future. Furthermore, she is widely known in Europe and one of the foci of the futurist circles in Paris, where she lives. She had already done work thought remarkable, in the more usual fields of literary expression, before she turned to her "new manner."

If we consider her then as a person who is consciously working out an art form and who knows what she is about, a description of her method of work may be illuminating. She will never talk of her work herself, but a friend has given the public some hints.

"She is impelling language to induce new states of consciousness, and in doing so language becomes with her a creative art rather than a mirror of history. In her impressionistic writing she uses familiar words to create perceptions, conditions and states of being, never quite consciously before experienced. To prevent [sic] her impressions she chooses words for their inherent quality rather than for their accepted meaning." That is, she does not create new words as Edward Lear or Lewis Carroll did, quite seriously, to create new impressions by strange sounds, but she hopes to present impressions by arrangements of sounds of familiar words which suggest an emotion rather than define a fact.

"Her method of work is deliberate. She always works late at night, after reading several hours to get herself into the mood, and in the silence brings all her will power to bear on the banishing of preconceived impressions. Concentrating on the impressions she has received and which she wishes to transmit she suspends her selective faculty, waiting for the word or group of words which will perfectly interpret her meaning to rise from her subconsciousness to the surface of her mind. Then and then only does she bring her reason to bear on them, weighing and gauging their ability to express her impression. It is a working proof of the Bergson theory of intuition. She does not go after words — she waits and lets them come to her — and they do."

It is also known that the next morning after a sound sleep she has her work of the night before read aloud to her, the only way in which she can criticise what she has done. She cannot read her own work on the written page; it means nothing to her. From this we can gather that the effect must be gained through sound alone. A page read aloud, quite apart from its sense or nonsense, is really rhythmical, a pure pattern of sound, as Picasso's canvases are pure patterns of color. Some feel a curious hypnotic effect in her sentences read aloud. By complicated repetition and by careful combinations does she get the effects she wishes for. And to some listeners there comes a perception of some meaning quite other than the content of the phrases.

There is an illuminating parallel to this in the very latest of the experiments of Picasso whom Boston derided at the exhibition of last year. He strove to present, not pictures of objects, but impressions of the emotions these objects gave him. But lately he has seemed to feel in this a certain lack of complete success. So in an exhibition to open this fall in New York he will exhibit his latest work, compositions produced by combinations of actual materials, textiles and metals, bits of wood, brass, glass, ribbons and silks, nailed and glued together to form patterns.

This seems to be a still further step. He has ceased to try to represent the emotions which certain things give him; he has determined to give the public the actual things themselves, in the combinations by which he was affected, in the hope that the beholder will get the same effect.

He still, presumably, calls himself a painter, yet he has abolished the laws of painting at one fell swoop. His idea verges on photography on the one hand, on architecture on the other. It is undoubtedly anarchistic. This may help to understand Miss Stein: instead of trying to convey her impressions of facts through words selected very subtly for their meaning, she gives the exact arrangements and sounds of words which have affected her, in the hope the reader, or the listener, will get the same impression. Only, such an impression must always be weaker than that of the Picasso composition, since he uses the actuality and Miss Stein can only use words, in themselves symbols, and so inevitably lose something of the force of the impression.

How to Read Gertrude Stein   Carl Van Vechten*

The English language is a language of hypocrisy and evasion. How not to say a thing has been the problem of our writers from the earliest times. The extraordinary fluidity and even naivete of French makes it possible for a writer in that language to babble like a child; de Maupassant is only possible in French, a language in which the phrase, "Je t'aime" means everything. But what does "I love you" mean in English? Donald Evans, of our poets, has realized this peculiar quality of English and he is almost the first of the poets in English to say unsuspected and revolting things, because he so cleverly avoids saying them.

Miss Stein discovered the method before Mr. Evans. In fact his Patagonian Sonnets were an offshoot of her later manner, just as Miss Kenton's superb story, "Nicknames," derives its style from Miss Stein's *Three Lives*. She has really turned language into music, really made its sound more important than its sense. And she has suggested to the reader a thousand channels for his mind and sense to drift along, a thousand, instead of a stupid only one.

Miss Stein has no explanations to offer regarding her work. I have often questioned her, but I have met with no satisfaction. She asks you to read. Her intimate connection with the studies of William James have been commented upon; some say that the "fringe of thought," so frequently referred to by that writer, may dominate her working consciousness. Her method of work is unique. She usually writes in the morning, and she sets down the words as they come from her pen; they bubble, they flow; they surge through her brain and she sets them down. You may regard them as nonsense, but the fact remains that effective imitations of her style do not exist. John Reed tells me that, while he finds her stimulating and interesting, an entity, he feels compelled to regard her work as an offshoot, something that will not be concluded by followers. She lives and dies alone, a unique example of a strange art. It may be in place also to set down here the fact that once in answer to a question Miss Stein asserted that her art was for the printed page only; she never expects people to converse or exchange ideas in her style.

As a personality Gertrude Stein is unique. She is massive in physique, a Rabelaisian woman with a splendid thoughtful face; mind dominating her matter. Her velvet robes, mostly brown, and her carpet slippers associate themselves with her indoor appearance. To go out she belts herself, adds a walking staff, and a trim unmodish turban. This garb suffices for a shopping tour or a box party at the *Opéra*.

Paris is her abode. She settled there after Cambridge, and association with William James, Johns Hopkins and a study of medicine. Her orderly

*Excerpted from the *Trend* 7, no. 5 (August 1914): 553–57, by permission of Donald Gallup as literary trustee for the Carl Van Vechten Estate.

mind has captured the scientific facts of both psychology and physiology. And in Paris the early painters of the new era captured her heart and purse. She purchased the best of them, and now such examples as Picasso's *Acrobats* and early Matisses hang on her walls. There is also the really authoritative portrait of herself, painted by Pablo Picasso.

These two painters she lists among her great friends. And their influence, perhaps, decided her in her present mode of writing. Her pictures are numerous, and to many, who do not know of her as a writer, she is mentioned as the Miss Stein with the collection of post-impressionists. On Saturday nights during the winter one can secure a card of admission to the collection and people wander in and out the studio, while Miss Stein serves her dinner guests unconcernedly with after-dinner coffee. And conversation continues, strangely unhindered by the picture viewers.

Leo Stein happens in, when he is not in Florence, and I have a fancy that he prefers Florence to Paris. He is her brother, and their tastes in art are naturally antithetical. He believes in the painters of the "third dimension," the painters of atmosphere, and the space between objects, for thus he describes the impressionists, and he includes Peter Paul Rubens in this group. And his precise manner of grouping thought is strangely at odds with Miss Stein's piquant love of gossip, and with her strange undercurrents of ideas that pass from her through and about the place.

Mr. Stein's phrase "Define what you mean by — — —" is almost famous. It is well-known wherever he appears. Last I saw him in the Piazza Vittorio Emanuele. I sat at luncheon time on the terrace of the *Giubbi Rossi* with Mabel Dodge when he strode into view, sandals on his feet, a bundle over his shoulder, and carrying an alpenstock. He was on his way to the mountains, and, if I remember rightly, he asked me, in response to an invitation, to define what I meant by "cocktail," something singularly difficult to do in Italy.

Miss Stein's presence, as I have said before my parenthesis, is strangely dominant in these evenings and her clear deep voice, her very mellow laugh, the adjunct of an almost abnormal sense of humor and observation, remain very pleasant memories. At one time I saw her very frequently, but we talked little of her work, although we often read it.

Of all her books only *Tender Buttons*, the latest of them to appear, is generally procurable. Besides this I know of *Three Lives*, written in her early manner; *The Portrait of Mabel Dodge at the Villa Curonia*, an internationally famous monograph, published privately in Florence, and never on sale. There is a very long autobiographical work, at present, I believe, considerably longer than *Clarrisa Harlowe*, which runs through her various changes of style. There are several plays, one about me, which Miss Stein very kindly entitled, *One*. These are very short and in her very late manner. Miss Florence Bradley wished to play them in America and she may have done so in Chicago. She is now on her way to China and the she may play them there; but I have no record of performances. Miss Stein is most insistent that they be performed before they are printed, but she did allow Marsden Hartley to quote from a play about him as a foreword to his collection of pictures which was exhibited at that "little place" of Mr. Stieglitz's at 291 Fifth Avenue. There are several other short portraits, and some sketches, one of shop girls in the *Gallerie Lafayette* in Paris which is particularly descriptive and amusing. These, I think, are Miss Stein's main contributions to her complete works.

In *Three Lives* Miss Stein attained at a bound an amount of literary facility which a writer might strive in vain for years to acquire. Simplicity is a quality one is born with, so far as literary style is concerned, and Miss Stein was born with that. But to it she added, in this work, a vivid note of reiteration, a fascinatingly complete sense of psychology and the workings of minds one on the other, which at least in "Melanctha: Each as She May" reaches a state of perfection which might have satisfied such masters of craft as Turgenev, or Balzac, or Henry James.

***

The number of Camera Work for August, 1912, contains two articles by Miss Stein about her two friends, Henri Matisse and Pablo Picasso. To me they seem to bridge the period between *Three Lives* and *The Portrait of Mabel Dodge*.

***

The Portrait of Mabel Dodge made a winter amusing for those who subscribed to the clipping bureaus. The redoubtable Romeike, whom Whistler mentions, was kept busy cutting out ideas of the scriveners in Oshkosh and Flatbush about Miss Stein. To those who know Mrs. Dodge the portrait may seem to be a true one; it has intention, that is even obvious to those who do not know what the intention is. There is nothing faint or pale about Miss Stein's authority. It is as complete in its way as the authority of Milton. You may not like the words, but you are forced to admit, after, perhaps, a struggle that no other words will do.

***

And now a discussion of *Tender Buttons* seems imminent. Donald Evans, who is responsible for its publication, says that it is the only book ever printed which contains absolutely no errors. I have not Miss Stein's authority for this statement. At any rate the effect on printers and proofreaders was tremendous. I believe that even yet some of them are suffering from brain storm. *The Portrait of Mabel Dodge* was set up in Florence by compositors who, I believe, did not read English. So their trouble was less.

There are several theories extant relating to *Tender Buttons*. I may say that one I upheld stoutly for a few hours, that the entire book had a physical application, I have since rejected, at least in part. The three divisions which comprise the book in a way explain the title. They are "Food; Objects; Rooms," all things which fasten our lives together, and whose complications may be said to make them "tender."

The majestic rhythm of the prose in this book; the virtuosity with which Miss Stein intertwines her words, are qualities which strike the ear at once. And *Tender Buttons* benefits by reading aloud. Onomatopœa, sound echoing sense, is a favorite figure of speech with Miss Stein; so is alliteration which is fatally fascinating when mingled with reiteration, and Miss Stein drops repeated words upon your brain with the effect of Chopin's B minor prelude, which is popularly supposed to represent the raindrops falling on the roof at Majorka on one of those George Sand days.

The mere sensuous effect of the words is irresistible and often as in the section labelled, "Eating," or "A Seltzer Bottle," the mere pronunciation of the words gives the effect of the act or the article. On other hand, "A Little Called Pauline" seems to me perfect in the way of a pretty description, a Japanese print of a charming creature. "Suppose an Eyes" is similarly a picture, but more postery.

It would seem to me that the inspiration offered to writers in this book was an enormous incentive to read it. What writer after reading *Tender Buttons* but would strive for a fresher phrase, a more perfect similarly a picture, but more postery.

It would seem to me that the inspiration offered to writers in this book was an enormous incentive to read it. What writer after reading "Tender Buttons" but would strive for a fresher phrase, a more perfect rhythmic prose? Gertrude Stein to me is one of the supreme stylists.

In case one is not delighted, amused, or appealed to in any way by the sensuous charm of her art then, of course, there is the sense to fall back on; the ideas expressed. Here one floats about vaguely for a key to describe how to tell what Miss Stein means. Her vagueness is innate and one of her most positive qualities. I have already said how much she adds to language by it. You may get the idea of it if you close your eyes and imagine yourself awaking from the influence of ether, as you gasp to recall some words and ideas, while new ones surge into your brain. A certain sleepy consciousness. Or you may read sense through the fingers as they flit rapidly — almost word by word — through your brain. It is worthy of note that almost everyone tries to make sense out of Miss Stein just as everyone insists on making photographs out of drawings by Picabia, when the essential of his art is that he is getting away from the photographic.

Flat Prose

Anonymous*

It is not generally known, I believe, that post-impressionism has escaped from the field of pictorial art, and is running rampant in literature. At present, Miss Gertrude Stein is the chief culprit. Indeed, she may be called the founder of a coterie, if not of a school.

Her art has been defined recently by one of her admirers, who is also the subject, or victim, of the word-portrait from which I intend later to quote in illustration of my argument. "Gertrude Stein," says Miss Dodge, "is doing with words what Picasso is doing with paint. She is impelling language to induce new states of consciousness, and in doing so language becomes with her a creative art rather than a mirror of history." This, being written in psychological and not in post-impressionist English, is fairly intelligible. But it does not touch the root of the matter. Miss Stein, the writer continues, uses "words that appeal to her as having the meaning they *seem* to have [that is, if "diuturnity" suggests a tumble downstairs, it *means* a tumble downstairs]. To present her impressions she chooses words for their inherent quality rather than their accepted meaning."

Let us watch the creative artist at her toil. The title of this particular word-picture is *Portrait of Mabel Dodge at the Villa Curonia*. As the portrait itself has a beginning, but no middle, and only a faintly indicated end, I believe — though in my ignorance of just what it all means I am not sure — that I can quote at random without offense to the impressions derivable from the text.

Here then are a few paragraphs where the inherent quality of the words is said to induce new states of consciousness: —

> Bargaining is something and there is not that success. The intention is what if application has that accident results are reappearing. They did not darken. That was not an adulteration. . . . There is that particular half of directing that there is that particular whole direction that is not all the measure of any combination. Gliding is not heavily moving. Looking is not vanishing. Laughing is not evaporation.
>
> Praying has intention and relieving that situation is not solemn. There comes that way.
>
> There is all there is when there has all there has where there is what there is. That is what is done when there is done what is done and the union is won and the division is the explicit visit. There is not all of any visit.

After a hundred lines of this I wish to scream, I wish to burn the book, I am in agony. It is not because I know that words *cannot* be torn loose from their meanings without insulting the intellect. It is not because I see that this is a prime example of the "confusion of the arts." No, my

*Reprinted with permission from the *Atlantic Monthly* 114 (September 1914): 431–32. Copyright 1914 by the Atlantic Monthly Company, Boston, Mass. The omitted first page of this essay replies to a reader's remarks about "beautiful prose."

feeling is purely physical. Some one has applied an egg-beater to my brain.

But having calmed myself by a sedative of flat prose from the paper, I realize that Miss Stein is more sinned against than sinning. She is merely a red flag waved by the *Zeitgeist*.

For this is the sort of thing we are bound to get if the lid is kept down on the stylists much longer. Repression has always bred revolt. Revolt breeds extravagance. And extravagance leads to absurdity. And yet even in the absurd, a sympathetic observer may detect a purpose which is honest and right. Miss Stein has indubitably written nonsense, but she began with sense. For words *have* their sound-values as well as their sense-values, and prose rhythms *do* convey to the mind emotions that mere denotation cannot give. Rewrite the solemn glory of Old Testament diction in the flat colorless prose which just now is demanded, and wonder at the difference. Translate "the multitudinous seas incarnadine" into "making the ocean red," — or, for more pertinent instances, imagine a Carlyle, an Emerson, a Lamb forced to exclude from his vocabulary every word not readily understood by the multitude, to iron out all whimseys, all melodies from his phrasing, and to plunk down his words one after the other in the order of elementary thought.

I am willing to fight to the last drop of ink against any attempt to bring back "fine writing" and ornate rhetoric into prose. "Expression is the dress of thought," and plain thinking and plain facts look best in simple clothing. Nevertheless, if we must write our stories, our essays, our novels, and (who knows) our poems in the flat prose of the news column, — if the editors will sit on the lid, — well, the public will get what it pays for, but sooner or later the spirit of style will ferment, will work, will grow violent under restraint. There will be reaction, explosion, revolution. The public will get its flat prose, and — in addition — not one, but a hundred Gertrude Steins.

The Work of Gertrude Stein   Sherwood Anderson*

One evening in the winter, some years ago, my brother came to my rooms in the city of Chicago bringing with him a book by Gertrude Stein. The book was called *Tender Buttons* and, just at that time, there was a good deal of fuss and fun being made over it in American newspapers. I had already read a book of Miss Stein's called *Three Lives* and had thought it contained some of the best writing ever done by an American. I was curious about this new book.

*Reprinted from Gertrude Stein, *Geography and Plays* (1922; rpt. New York: Haskell House, 1967), 5–8, by permission of the estate of Gertrude Stein.

My brother had been at some sort of gathering of literary people on the evening before and someone had read aloud from Miss Stein's new book. The party had been a success. After a few lines the reader stopped and was greeted by loud shouts of laughter. It was generally agreed that the author had done a thing we Americans call "putting something across" — the meaning being that she had, by a strange freakish performance, managed to attract attention to herself, get herself discussed in the newspapers, become for a time a figure in our hurried, harried lives.

My brother, as it turned out, had not been satisfied with the explanation of Miss Stein's work then current in America, and so he bought *Tender Buttons* and brought it to me, and we sat for a time reading the strange sentences. "It gives words an oddly new intimate flavor and at the same time makes familiar words seem almost like strangers, doesn't it," he said. What my brother did, you see, was to set my mind going on the book, and then, leaving it on the table, he went away.

And now, after these years, and having sat with Miss Stein by her own fire in the rue de Fleurus in Paris I am asked to write something by way of an introduction to a new book she is about to issue.

As there is in America an impression of Miss Stein's personality, not at all true and rather foolishly romantic, I would like first of all to brush that aside. I had myself heard stories of a long dark room with a languid woman lying on a couch, smoking cigarettes, sipping absinthes perhaps and looking out upon the world with tired, disdainful eyes. Now and then she rolled her head slowly to one side and uttered a few words, taken down by a secretary who approached the couch with trembling eagerness to catch the falling pearls.

You will perhaps understand something of my own surprise and delight when, after having been fed up on such tales and rather Tom Sawyerishly hoping they might be true, I was taken to her to find instead of this languid impossibility a woman of striking vigor, a subtle and powerful mind, a discrimination in the arts such as I have found in no other American born man or woman, and a charmingly brilliant conversationalist.

"Surprise and delight" did I say? Well, you see, my feeling is something like this. Since Miss Stein's work was first brought to my attention I have been thinking of it as the most important pioneer work done in the field of letters in my time. The loud guffaws of the general that must inevitably follow the bringing forward of more of her work do not irritate me but I would like it if writers, and particularly young writers, would come to understand a little what she is trying to do and what she is in my opinion doing.

My thought in the matter is something like this — that every artist working with words as his medium, must at times be profoundly irritated by what seems the limitations of his medium. What things does he not wish to create with words! There is the mind of the reader before him and he would like to create in that reader's mind a whole new world of sensations, or rather one might better say he would like to call back into life all of the dead and sleeping senses.

There is a thing one might call "the extension of the province of his art" one wants to achieve. One works with words and one would like words that have a taste on the lips, that have a perfume to the nostrils, rattling words one can throw into a box and shake, making a sharp, jingling sound, words that, when seen on the printed page, have a distinct arresting effect upon the eye, words that when they jump out from under the pen one may feel with the fingers as one might caress the cheeks of his beloved.

And what I think is that these books of Gertrude Stein's do in a very real sense recreate life in words.

We writers are, you see, all in such a hurry. There are such grand things we must do. For one thing the Great American Novel must be written and there is the American or English Stage that must be uplifted by our very important contributions, to say nothing of the epic poems, sonnets to my lady's eyes, and what not. We are all busy getting these grand and important thoughts and emotions into the pages of printed books.

And in the meantime the little words, that are the soldiers with which we great generals must make our conquests, are neglected.

There is a city of English and American words and it has been a neglected city. Strong broad shouldered words, that should be marching across open fields under the blue sky, are clerking in little dusty dry goods stores, young virgin words are being allowed to consort with whores, learned words have been put to the ditch digger's trade. Only yesterday I saw a word that once called a whole nation to arms serving in the mean capacity of advertising laundry soap.

For me the work of Gertrude Stein consists in a rebuilding, an entire new recasting of life, in the city of words. Here is one artist who has been able to accept ridicule, who has even forgone the privilege of writing the great American novel, uplifting our English speaking stage, and wearing the bays of the great poets, to go live among the little housekeeping words, the swaggering bullying street-corner words, the honest working, money saving words, and all the other forgotten and neglected citizens of the sacred and half forgotten city.

Would it not be a lovely and charmingly ironic gesture of the gods if, in the end, the work of this artist were to prove the most lasting and important of all the word slingers of our generation!

Engineering with Words

Kenneth Burke*

Perhaps, by way of a show-down, I should begin an approach to Miss Stein's new volume, *Geography and Plays*, by admitting that I find in parts of Milton pretty much the flowering of certain modern aesthetic worries. Milton writes, for instance, "Where He now sits at the right hand of God," and the beauty of the line lies precisely in its "significant form." I say this in spite of the fact that Mr Clive Bell finds significant form a quite negligible factor in determining literary excellence. The significant form in this instance (the structural framework which appeals to us over and above the "message" of the line) is to be found in the fact that the two words "now" and "right" are unaccented in scansion, but accented in sense, so that a complexity of movement and counter-movement results. Incidentally, both of these normally unaccented words are further brought into perverse relief by the violent prominence of the "ow" and "i" sounds. But this is no doubt in the versification books, so I pass hastily on to a quotation from Miss Stein: "Point, face, canvas, toy, struck off, sense or, weigh coach, soon beak on, so suck in, and an iron."

Here, too, we have the appeal of significant form. The sentence is structurally contenting; it begins with a group of four isolated words, follows with three groups of two words, then two groups of three words, and finally a curt swing to a close. I quote one more instance, where the appeal is just as spontaneous, although more complex and difficult to analyse: "Lie on this, show sup the boon that nick the basting thread thinly and night night gown and pit wet kit. Loom down the thorough narrow."

Surely one does not have to be persuaded into liking the happy chunks of verbalism Miss Stein has given us here, the sharp ticking off of the words, with a plunge at the end like a boat grounding on thick mud. In all three of these instances we have those purely formal elements which go to make up the appeal of nursery rhymes. Here, after all the varnish, is the return to the primitive. But Milton's line has something more than Miss Stein's. The significant form is backed by subject matter, and this backing produces a heightened emotion. For, as Mr Raymond Mortimer once said in these pages, if form is sufficient to produce an emotion, subject matter is required to heighten it. Art, that is, is a process of individualization; form is general, subject matter is specific. To illustrate, if I speak of a crescendo, the reader *knows* what I am driving at, but the *crescendo* does not live for him until I play one specific assemblage of notes which forms a *crescendo*. Similarly, I get *climax* by one specific set of circumstances which fall into a climax. Which is to say, by the individualizing process of subject matter.

Now, in Milton's case, the subject matter actually contributes to the

*Reprinted from the *Dial* 74 (April 1923): 408–12.

formal element, and gives it a satisfaction beyond the mere arrangement of the vowels and the fluxes. In Miss Stein's case the satisfaction stops with the form itself. Even the nursery rhyme, by its semblance of a "message," goes farther in this particular than the quotations from Miss Stein.

We find, then, that Miss Stein's method is one of subtraction. She has deliberately limited her equipment so that she has *less* than Milton to begin with. In this matter I should say that she had ignored the inherent property of words: that quality in the literary man's medium which makes him start out with a definiteness that the other arts do not possess. That is, if the musician plays G-sharp he has prescribed no definitions; but if the literary man writes "boy" he has already laid down certain demarcations. Now, obviously, any literary artist who sets out to begin his work in a primary search for music or rhythm, and attempts to get this at the expense of this "inherent property of words" . . . obviously this artist is not going to exploit the full potentialities of his medium. He is getting an art by subtraction; he is violating his *genre*. One might, in a pious moment, name this the "fallacy of subtraction." The formula would apply to a great deal of modern art.

Miss Stein continually utilizes this violation of the *genre*. Theoretically at least, the result has its studio value. If the academies were at all alive, they would teach the arts in precisely this manner. By approaching the art-work from these exorbitant angles one is suddenly able to rediscover organically those eternal principles of art which are, painful as it may be to admit it, preserved in all the standard textbooks. Similarly, as Severini has shown us recently, cubism is (or can be) simply the first glue-eyed nosing around for the teat of classicism. The musician has always run his scales, has had his counterpoint; the student of writing, on the other hand, begins with stories or poems *about* something. It is exclusively outside the accepted channels of education that all technical research has been done in letters since God knows when. What a pity that Mallarmé was so supersensitive; for he was the man to found a really vital literary Academy.

Perhaps it has been noted with resentment that up to this point I have avoided discussing Miss Stein's use of associated ideas. I have done so because associated ideas *per se* are of no more value than are the Ozark mountains *per se*. Their encroachment into art is justified only when some sound aesthetic value is acquired thereby. And their value, it seems to me, lies precisely in the opportunity they offer for throwing into relief the *functions* of the art-work (as in the above quotations from Miss Stein's new book). A logical sequence (the perfectly lubricated novel, for instance) moves with a minimum of relief; the purpose is to conceal the form beneath the matter; the form is used to "sell" the matter. But if I wanted to emphasize, say, a transition; not try to sneak across a transition, but to throw it into relief so that the reader knew that at this moment he was going through a transition; I could get this by a chain of associated ideas, used like steps going on one direction. I should move from point to point by a *psychological* sequence rather than a *logical* sequence. To illustrate rather bluntly; let us suppose a series of nouns, running from ideas of complete stability, into ideas of inceptive motion, then gentle motion, then accelerated motion, speed, precipitancy, and finally ending in some violent cataclysm or explosion.

But this, obviously, would bring in the need of the taboo. To produce this art-form, I should have to rule out ideas of precipitancy at the beginning, and ideas of stability towards the end. The work of art, then, implies the erection of a temporary set of values, true at least for the particular problem at hand. But in the first flush of our "freedom," certain artists like Miss Stein refuse to recognize even these temporary taboos. Here is the absurdity of romanticism, or individualism; here we see carried to the extreme the tendency to take the personality of the individual as a virtue in itself; for the only unity of these associations is the unity of their having been written by one person — which is the absurdity of Dadaism. Such material may be excellent data for the psychologists; but its aesthetic value is nil, unless some further use is made of it. This further use, I maintain, is to emphasize the functional values in a work of art; and we are at least entitled to this view until someone cares to suggest another use.

At any rate, Miss Stein does get this aesthetic value at times into her sentences. And at such times they have a *raison d'être* not merely as fever charts, but also as bits of art. But here again the choppiness of her subject matter limits her achievements enormously. I think of Lycidas, and of the "programme" in the stanza sequence: the change in flux, for instance, which is acquired by the slight deviation from the stanza of

> Weep no more, woeful shepherds, weep no more

to the stanza of

> And now the sun had stretched out all the hills,
> And now had dropped into the western bay.

Miss Stein, by her short sparrow-pecks, can get a certain analytic form, the form of her sentences. But the synthetic form of paragraph or stanza, or beyond, of the art-work *in toto*, is denied her. While even her analytic form is seldom brilliant, and shows beyond a doubt that the focus of her attention is elsewhere. This, of course, results in her being diffuse. And her method leaves us with too little to feed on. One might almost say that it argues for the insignificance of significant form. Further, her book is a continual rebeginning. No sentence advances us beyond the sentence preceding. For such advances involve this synthetic form, and this synthetic form can be brought out only by a greater stability of subject matter.

(Mr Eliot, in *The Waste Land*, goes as far as the poet can go without falling into this "fallacy of subtraction." The sudden elevation from "Ta ta

Goonight, goonight" into "Good night, ladies, good night, sweet ladies" is psychological rather than logical, makes a step forward, that is, by means of an association of ideas; and it is one of the finest examples of the functioning art-work in modern poetry.)

It is, perhaps, egregious to have pursued Miss Stein with Milton throughout this review. But, at least, it is not *mal à propos*. For I have wished to bring out exactly what is sacrificed by an under-emphasis on the *selection* of subject matter, and how little is gained. For if there *is* significant form in letters, this form can only be brought out to its fullest beauty by the most cautious deviations from the norm, the logical. Which probably explains why Mallarmé, seeing one of his young admirers produce a piece of excessive violation, remarked grimly that the man had gone farther than he himself had dared after twenty years of concentration on this very problem.

Miss Stein's Stories   Edith Sitwell*

It has taken me several weeks to clarify my own feelings about Miss Stein's writings. Her work appears to have a certain amount of real virtue, but to understand or apprehend that virtue a reader would have to study Miss Stein's methods for years, and intimately; whereas this is the first book of hers that I have read. Her virtues and faults are in exact contradiction of each other. I think it is indisputable that Miss Stein has a definite aim in her work, and that she is perfectly, relentlessly, and bravely sincere. She is trying to pull language out of the meaningless state into which it has fallen, and to give it fresh life and new significance. For this purpose she uses comparatively few words, and turns them into ever-varying and new patterns till they often do, definitely, surprise us with their meaning. I imagine, however, that she was more hampered than helped by her early training. We read in the publishers' note that "she became interested in psychology and philosophy, and worked with Munsterberg and James, who both predicted a remarkable future for her. . . . Practical medicine did not particularly interest her, and soon she specialized in the anatomy of the brain and direction of brain tracts. . . ." This may account for the fact that this book, at first sight, appears to be a collection of heterogeneous words, thrown together without any respect for meaning, but only a respect for the shape and rhythm of sentences. I hope I shall not be regarded as a reactionary, but I am bound to say that I prefer words, when collected into a sentence, to convey some sense. And Miss Stein's sentences do not always convey any sense — not even a new

*Reprinted from *The Nation & The Atheneum* 33 (14 July 1923): 492.

one. It is her habit to open her mind and let words float in and out regardless of each other. What, for instance, are we to make of such a sentence as: "A clever saucer, what is a clever saucer, a clever saucer is very likely practiced and even has toes, it has tiny things to shake and really if it were not for a delicate blue colour would there be any reason for every one to differ"? This sentence, no doubt, would throw a psycho-analyst into a frenzy of excitement; and it was probably written for this purpose; but exciting psycho-analysts is not the highest aim of literature.

In a story called "Miss Furr and Miss Skene," the author repeats the following sentence, with very slight variations, for six pages — it is the whole of the story: "Helen Furr was gay there, she was gayer and gayer there and really she was just gay there, she was gayer and gayer there, that is to say she found ways of being gay there that she was using in being gay there. She was gay there, not gayer and gayer, just gay there, that is to say she was not gayer by using the things she found there that were gay things, she was gay there, always she was gay there."

Lord Tennyson could produce the same feeling of monotony with more economy of means, and with less risk of reducing his readers to the asylum.

As an example, however, of Miss Stein's method when it is successful, let us take this delicious Picasso-like landscape: "A cloud of white and a chorus of all bright birds and a sweet a very sweet cherry and a thick miss, a thick and a dark and a clean clerk, a whole succession of mantelpieces."

To sum up the book as far as is possible, I find in it an almost insuperable amount of silliness, an irritating ceaseless rattle like that of American sightseers talking in a boarding-house (this being, I imagine, a deliberate effect), great bravery, a certain real originality, and a few flashes of exquisite beauty. One feels, too, that there is a real foundation for Miss Stein's mind, somewhere deep under the earth, but that it is too deep for her to dig down to, and that she herself is not capable of building upon this hidden foundation. She is, however, doing valuable pioneer work, and I should like to take this opportunity of begging *les Jeunes* not to hamper her by imitating her, but to leave her to work out her own literary destiny.

The Spare American Emotion   Marianne Moore*

Extraordinary interpretations of American life recur to one — *The Finer Grain, In the American Grain, The Making of an American, The Domestic Manners of The Americans.* We have, and in most cases it amounts to not having them, novels about discontented youth, unadvan-

*Reprinted from the *Dial* 80 (February 1926): 153–56.

taged middle age, American materialism; in *The Making of Americans*, however, we have "not just an ordinary kind of novel with a plot and conversations to amuse you, but a record of a decent family progress respectably lived by us and our fathers and our mothers, and our grand-fathers, and grand-mothers." One is not able to refrain from saying, moreover, that its chiselled typography and an enticing simplicity of construction are not those of ordinary book-making.

By this epic of ourselves, we are reminded of certain early German engravings in which Adam, Eve, Cain, and Abel stand with every known animal wild and domestic, under a large tree, by a river. *The Making of Americans* is a kind of living genealogy which is in its branching, unified and vivid.

We have here a truly psychological exposition of American living – an account of that happiness and of that unhappiness which is to those experiencing it, as fortuitous as it is to those who have an understanding of heredity and of environment natural and inevitable. Romantic, curious, and engrossing is this story of "the old people in a new world, the new people made out of the old." There are two kinds of men and women Miss Stein tells us, the attacking kind and the resisting kind, each of which is often modified by many complex influences. Mr Dehning who was of the resisting kind, "never concerned himself very much with the management of the family's way of living and the social life of his wife and children. These things were all always arranged by Mrs. Dehning." Yet "they could each one make the other one do what they wanted the other one to be doing" – this "really very nice very rich good kind quite completely successful a little troubled american man and woman." The insufficiency of Alfred Hersland who married Julia Dehning, is shown to be largely a result of his mother's anonymity, of incompetent pedagogy, of spoiling, and of his father's impatient unconsidering wilfulness. The Dehnings were happy; the Herslands were under the impression that they too, were happy. As Miss Stein says:

> And all around the whole fence that shut these joys in was a hedge of roses, not wild, they had been planted, but now they were very sweet and small and abundant and all the people from that part of Gossols came to pick the leaves to make sweet scented jars and pillows, and always all the Herslands were indignant and they would let loose the dogs to bark and scare them but still the roses grew and always all the people came and took them. And altogether the Herslands always loved it there in their old home in Gossols.

In persons either of the resisting or of the attacking kind, contradic-tions between "the bottom nature and the other natures" result in hybrids; as in Napoleon – in Herbert Spencer – in various other kinds of nature. Disillusionment, sensitiveness, cowardice, courage, jealousy, stubborn-ness, curiosity, suspicion, hopefulness, anger, subtlety, pride, egotism, vanity, ambition – each phase of emotion as of behaviour, is to Miss Stein full of meaning. "Someone gives to another one a stubborn feeling," she says, "when that one could be convincing that other one if that other one would then continue listening," and "it is very difficult in quarrelling to be certain in either one what the other one is remembering." Of the assorting of phenomena in "an ordered system" she says, "Always I am learning, always it is interesting, often it is exciting."

There is great firmness in the method of this book. Phillip Redfern we are told, "was a man always on guard, with every one always able to pierce him." The living rooms of Julia Dehning's house "were a prevailing red, that certain shade of red like that certain shade of green, dull, without hope, the shade that so completely bodies forth the ethically aesthetic aspiration of the spare American emotion." Her mother's house was on the other hand, of a different period. "A nervous restlessness of luxury was through it all. . . . a parlor full of ornate marbles placed on yellow onyx stands, chairs of gold and white of various size and shape, a delicate blue silk brocaded covering on the walls and a ceiling painted pink with angels and cupids all about, a dining-room all dark and gold, a living room all rich and gold and red with built-in-couches. . . . Marbles and bronzes and crystal chandeliers and gas logs finished out each room."

We "hasten slowly forward" by a curious backward kind of progress. "Sometimes I like it," Miss Stein says, "that different ways of emphasizing can make very different meanings in a phrase or sentence I have made and am rereading." To recall her summary of washing is to agree with her:

> It's a great question this question of washing. One never can find any one who can be satisfied with anybody else's washing. I knew a man once who never as far as any one could see ever did any washing, and yet he described another with contempt, why he is a dirty hog sir, he never does any washing. The French tell me it's the Italians who never do any washing, the French and the Italians both find the Spanish a little short in their washing, the English find all the world lax in this business of washing, and the East finds all the West a pig, which never is clean with just the little cold water washing. And so it goes.

Repeating has value then as "a way to wisdom." "Some children have it in them." "Always more and more it has completed history in it" and "irritation passes over into patient completed understanding."

Certain aspects of life are here emphasized — the gulf between youth and age, and the bond between these two; the fact of sentimental as of hereditary family indivisibility — such that when Julia Dehning was married, every one of the Dehnings had "feeling of married living in them."

The power of sex which is palpable throughout this novel, is handsomely implied in what is said of certain uncles and cousins in the Dehning family,

> generous decent considerate fellows, frank and honest in their friendships, and simple in the fashion of the elder Dehning. With this kindred Julia had always lived as with the members of one family. These men

did not supply for her the training and experience that helps to clear the way for an impetuous woman through a world of passions, they only made a sane and moral back-ground on which she in her later life could learn to lean.

The ineradicable morality of America is varyingly exposited, as in the statement that to Julia Dehning, "all men that could be counted as men by her and could be thought of as belonging ever to her, they must be, all, good strong gentle creatures, honest and honorable and honoring." Contrary to "the french habit in thinking," "the american mind accustomed to waste happiness and be reckless of joy finds morality more important than ecstacy and the lonely extra of more value than the happy two."

There is ever present in this history, a sense of the dignity of the middle class, "the one thing always human, vital, and worthy." Of a co-educational college of the west, Miss Stein says:

> Mostly no one there was conscious of a grand-father unless as remembering one as an old man living in the house with them or as living in another place and being written to sometimes by them and then having died and that was the end of grand-fathers to them. No one among them was held responsible for the father they had unless by some particular notoriety that had come to the father of some one. It was then a democratic western institution, this college where Redfern went to have his college education.

As Bunyan's Christian is English yet universal, this sober, tender-hearted, very searching history of a family's progress, comprehends in its picture of life which is distinctively American, a psychology which is universal.

Everybody Is a Real One Katherine Anne Porter[*]

All I know about Gertrude Stein is what I find in her first two books, *Three Lives* and *The Making of Americans*. Many persons know her, they tell amusing stories about her and festoon her with legends. Next to James Joyce she is the great influence on the younger literary generation, who see in her the combination of tribal wise woman and arch-priestess of aesthetic.

This is all very well; but I can go only by what I find in these pages. They form not so much a history of Americans as a full description and analysis of many human beings, including Gertrude Stein and the reader

[*]Excerpted from *The Collected Essays and Occasional Writings of Katherine Anne Porter*. © 1970 by Katherine Anne Porter. Reprinted by permission of Delacorte Press/ Seymour Lawrence. Originally published in the *New York Herald Tribune Books*, 16 January 1927.

and all the reader's friends; they make a psychological source book and the diary of an aesthetic problem worked out momently under your eyes.

One of the many interesting things about *The Making of Americans* is its date. It was written twenty years ago (1906–1908), when Gertrude Stein was young. It precedes the war and cubism; it precedes *Ulysses* and *Remembrance of Things Past*. I doubt if all the people who should read it will read it for a great while yet, for it is in such a limited edition, and reading it is anyhow a sort of permanent occupation. Yet to shorten it would be to mutilate its vitals, and it is a very necessary book. In spite of all there is in it Gertrude Stein promises all the way through it to write another even longer and put in it all the things she left unfinished in this. She has not done it yet; at least it has not been published.

Twenty years ago, when she had been living in Paris only a few years, Gertrude Stein's memory of her American life was fresh, and I think both painful and happy in her. "The old people in a new world, the new people made out of the old, that is the story that I mean to tell, for that is what really is and what I really know." This is a deeply American book, and without "movies" or automobiles or radio or prohibition or any of the mechanical properties for making local color, it is a very up-to-date book. We feel in it the vitality and hope of the first generation, the hearty materialism of the second, the vagueness of the third. It is all realized and projected in these hundreds of portraits, the deathlike monotony in action, the blind diffusion of effort, "the spare American emotion," "the feeling of rich American living"—rich meaning money, of course—the billion times repeated effort of being born and breathing and eating and sleeping and working and feeling and dying to no particular end that makes American middle-class life. We have almost no other class as yet. "I say vital singularity is as yet an unknown product with us." So she observes the lack of it and concerns herself with the endless repetition of pattern in us only a little changed each time, but changed enough to make an endless mystery of each individual man and woman.

In beginning this book you walk into what seems to be a great spiral, a slow, ever-widening, unmeasured spiral unrolling itself horizontally. The people in this world appear to be motionless at every stage of their progress, each one is simultaneously being born, arriving at all ages and dying. You perceive that it is a world without mobility, everything takes place, has taken place, will take place; therefore nothing takes place, all at once. Yet the illusion of movement persists, the spiral unrolls, you follow; a closed spinning circle is even more hopeless than a universe that will not move. Then you discover it is not a circle, not machinelike repetition, the spiral does open and widen, it is repetition only in the sense that one wave follows upon another. The emotion progresses with the effort of a giant parturition. Gertrude Stein describes her function in terms of digestion, of childbirth: all these people, these fragments of digested knowledge, are in her, they must come out.

The progress of her family, then, this making of Americans, she has labored to record in a catalogue of human attributes, acts and emotions. Episodes are nothing, narrative is by the way, her interest lies in what she calls the bottom natures of men and women, all men, all women. "It is important to me, very important indeed to me, that I sometimes understand every one. . . . I am hoping some time to be right about every one, about everything."

In this intensity of preoccupation there is the microscopic observation of the near-sighted who must get so close to their object they depend not alone on vision but on touch and smell and the very warmth of bodies to give them the knowledge they seek. This nearness, this immediacy, she communicates also, there is no escaping into the future nor into the past. All time is in the present, these people are "being living," she makes you no gift of comfortable ripened events past and gone. "I am writing everything as I am learning everything," and so we have lists of qualities and defects, portraits of persons in scraps, with bits and pieces added again and again in every round of the spiral: they repeat and repeat themselves to you endlessly as living persons do, and always you feel you know them, and always they present a new bit of themselves.

Gertrude Stein reminds me of Jacob Boehme in the way she sees essentials in human beings. He knew them as salt, as mercury; as moist, as dry, as burning; as bitter, sweet or sour. She perceives them as attacking, as resisting, as dependent independent, as having a core of wood, of mud, as murky, engulfing; Boehme's chemical formulas are too abstract, she knows the substances of man are mixed with clay. Materials interest her, the moral content of man can often be nicely compared to homely workable stuff. Sometimes her examination is almost housewifely, she rolls a fabric under her fingers, tests it. It is thus and so. I find this very good, very interesting. "It will repay good using."

"In writing a word must be for me really an existing thing." Her efforts to get at the roots of existing life, to create fresh life from them, give her words a dark liquid flowingness, like the murmur of the blood. She does not strain words or invent them. Many words have retained their original meaning for her, she uses them simply. Good means good and bad means bad — next to the Jews the Americans are the most moralistic people, and Gertrude Stein is American Jew, a combination which by no means lessens the like quality in both. Good and bad are attributes to her, strength and weakness are real things that live inside people, she looks for these things, notes them in their likenesses and differences. She loves the difficult virtues, she is tender toward good people, she has faith in them.

An odd thing happens somewhere in the middle of this book. You will come upon it suddenly and it will surprise you. All along you have had a feeling of submergence in the hidden lives of a great many people, and unaccountably you will find yourself rolling up the surface, on the outer edge of the curve. A disconcerting break into narrative full of phrases that might have come out of any careless sentimental novel, alternates with scraps of the natural style. It is astounding, you read on out of chagrin. Again without warning you submerge, and later Miss Stein explains she was copying an old piece of writing of which she is now ashamed, the words mean nothing: "I commence again with words that have meaning," she says, and we leave this limp, dead spot in the middle of the book.

Gertrude Stein wrote once of Juan Gris that he was, somehow, saved. She is saved, too; she is free of pride and humility, she confesses to superhuman aspirations simply, she was badly frightened once and has recovered, she is honest in her uncertainties. There are only a few bits of absolute knowledge in the world, people can learn only one or two fundamental facts about each other, the rest is decoration and prejudice. She is very free from decoration and prejudice.

Tests for Counterfeit in the Arts and The Prose-Song of Gertrude Stein
Wyndham Lewis*

Tests for Counterfeit in the Arts

In the beginning was the Word should rather be, *in the beginning was Time*, according to Miss Stein (as also according to Bergson, Prof. Alexander, Einstein, Whitehead, Minkowski, etc. etc.) And she is one of the most eminent writers of what I have described as our *musical society*; that is our time-society, the highly-intellectualized High-Bohemia.

> In the beginning there was the time in the composition that naturally was in the composition but time in the composition comes now and this is what is now troubling every one the time in the composition is now a part of distribution and equilibration.

In Miss Stein's composition there is above all *time*, she tells us as best she can. As best she can, as you see; for she is not able to tell us this or anything else clearly and simply; first of all because a time-obsession, it seems, interferes, so we are given to understand. The other reason is that she is not simple at all, although she writes usually so like a child — like a confused, stammering, rather "soft" (bloated, acromegalic, squinting and spectacled, one can figure it as) child. Miss Stein, you might innocently suppose from her naïf stuttering to be, if not a child, simple, at least, in

*Reprinted from *Time and Western Man* (1927; rpt. Boston: Beacon Press, 1957), 49–51, 61–65. Copyright 1927 Wyndham Lewis and the estate of G.A. Wyndham Lewis by permission of the Wyndham Lewis Memorial Trust (a registered charity).

spite of maturity. But that is not so; though, strangely enough, she would like it to be thought that it is. That is only the old story of people wanting to be things they are not; or else, either as strategy or out of pure caprice, enjoying any disguise that reverses and contradicts the personality.

Composition as Explanation is a little pamphlet just published by the Hogarth Press. In it you have the announcement that "The time of the composition is the time of the composition." But simple as that sounds, it is only roguishness on the part of its authoress, all the while. That is her fun only. She is just pretending, with a face of solemn humbug, not to be able to get out the word; what this verbal inhibition results in is something *funny*, that will make you laugh. It is a form of clowning, in short; she will disarm and capture you by her absurdity.

But *Time*, you are told, is at the bottom of the matter; though that you could have guessed, since it has been so for a very long time, from the beginning of the present period; from the birth of Bergson, shall we say? (Bergson was supposed by all of us to be dead, but Relativity, oddly enough at first sight, has recently resuscitated him; for the *time-spacer* has turned out to be the old-timer, or timist, after all.)

Miss Stein announces her time-doctrine in character, as it were. She gives you an "explanation," and illustrations, side by side; but the explanation is done in the same way as the examples that follow it. A further "explanation" would be required of the "explanation," and so on. And in that little, perhaps unregarded, fact, we have, I believe, one of the clues to this writer's mind. It tells us that her mind is a sham, to some extent.

In doing her "explanation" of her compositions in the same manner as her compositions (examples of which she gives), she is definitely making-believe that it is impossible for her to write in any other way. She is making a claim, in fact, that suggests a lack of candour on her part; and she is making it with an air of exaggerated candour. Supposing that the following line represented a typical composition of yours: —

FugfuggFFF-fewg:fugfug-Fug-fugue-fffffuuuuuuuG

Supposing, having become celebrated for that, you responded to a desire on the part of the public to know what you were driving at. Then the public would be justified in estimating your sincerity of a higher order if you sat down and tried to "explain" according to the canons of plain speech (no doubt employed by you in ordering your dinner, or telling the neighbouring newsagent to send you the *Herald*, *Tribune*, or *Daily Express* every morning), your verbal experiments, than if you affected to be unable to use that kind of speech at all.

Every painter who has experimented in abstract design, for example, has often been put into that situation; he must often have been asked the familiar question: "But do you really *see* things like that, Mr. So-and-So?" Were Miss Stein that painter, we know now what would happen. She would roll her eyes, squint, point in a frenzy at some object, and, of course, stammer hard. She would play up to the popular ignorance as to the processes by which her picture had been arrived at, in short. She would answer "in character," implying that she was cut off from the rest of the world entirely by an exclusive and peculiar sensibility. Yet every one knows who engages in experiments of any sort, verbal or pictorial, that that is not at all the point of the matter. It is a *deliberate* adjustment of things to some formula which transforms what is treated into an organism, strange according to the human norm, though it might appear normal enough to the senses of some other animal. Normal speech, or normal vision, are not interfered with in the practitioner of these experiments, on the one hand; nor does what in the result has an abnormal appearance arise *literally* in an abnormal experience, or an experience without a normal, non-visionary, basis.

For these reasons Miss Stein's illustrations would have been much more impressive if she had not pretended, to start with, that, as to the explanation, she "could not do it in any other way." In this fact, that "explanation" and "composition" are both done in the same stuttering dialect, you have the proof that you are in the presence of a *faux-naïf*, not the real article. Miss Stein's merits elsewhere are not cancelled by this — people are often gifted without being able to lay any claim to being "sincere," as we say. But it is a little difficult to understand how she could be so stupid. Her assumption that any advantage was to be gained by this studied obscurity, where it was, after all, pointless, is that. Perhaps, however, it was only conceit.

Should my ensuing remarks sting Miss Stein into a rejoinder, then I think you would see something like the situation that would be created if some beggar shamming blindness observed a person about to disappear with his offertory box. The "blind" under such conditions would *see* at once, and rush after the robber. It is the classic test case in the everyday world of everyday sham. I am afraid, however, that Miss Stein is too cunning a stammerer to be so easily unmasked. Miss Stein's stutter in her *explanation* even of her other celebrated stutterings, is a proof, then, to my mind, that she is a homologue of the false-blind; that, in some measure, she is a sham.

The Prose-Song of Gertrude Stein

Miss Stein has certainly never had any unvirtuous and mercenary intentions of the kind besetting Miss Loos; she has never needed to be a best-seller, luckily for herself — had that been so, she would have opened our eyes, I suspect. But in her earlier books (from one of which I have quoted), she, too, became the people she wrote about, adopting their illiteracies and colloquialisms. The other main factor in her method resulted in her story taking the form of *a prose-song*.

It is in a thick, monotonous prose-song that Miss Stein characteristically expresses her fatigue, her energy, and the bitter fatalism of her nature. Her stories are very often long—all the longer, too, because everything has to be repeated half a dozen times over. In the end the most wearisome dirge it is possible to imagine results, as slab after slab of this heavy, insensitive, common prose-song churns and lumbers by.

To an Antheil tempest of jazz it is the entire body that responds, after all. The executant tires; its duration does not exceed ten minutes or so, consecutively. But it is *the tongue*—only the poor, worried, hard-worked tongue—inside the reader's head, or his laryngeal apparatus, that responds to the prose-song of Miss Stein.

At present I am referring to what I have read of Miss Stein at the *Three Lives* stage of her technical evolution. What is the matter with it is, probably, that it is so *dead*. Gertrude Stein's prose-song is a cold, black suet-pudding. We can represent it as a cold suet-roll of fabulously-reptilian length. Cut it at any point, it is the same thing; the same heavy, sticky, opaque mass all through, and all along. It is weighted, projected, with a sibylline urge. It is mournful and monstrous, composed of dead and inanimate material. It is all fat, without nerve. Or the evident vitality that informs it is vegetable rather than animal. Its life is a low-grade, if tenacious, one; of the sausage, by-the-yard, variety.

The Work of Gertrude Stein   William Carlos Williams*

Stein's theme is writing. But in such a way as to be writing envisioned as the first concern of the moment, dragging behind it a dead weight of logical burdens, among them a dead criticism which broken through might be a gap by which endless other enterprises of the understanding should issue—for refreshment.

It is a revolution of some proportions that is contemplated, the exact nature of which may be no more than sketched here but whose basis is humanity in a relationship with literature hitherto little contemplated.

And at the same time it is a general attack on the scholastic viewpoint, that mediaeval remnant, with whose effects from generation to generation literature has been infested to its lasting detriment. It is a break away from that paralyzing vulgarity of logic for which the habits of science and philosophy coming over into literature (where they do not belong) are to blame.

*Excerpted from William Carlos Williams, *Selected Essays*. Copyright 1954 by William Carlos Williams. Reprinted by permission of New Directions Publishing Corporation. Originally published in *Pagany* 1, no. 1 (January–March 1930). An early part of this essay in which Williams compares Stein with Sterne and individual paragraphs have been omitted.

It is this logicality as a basis for literary action which in Stein's case, for better or worse, has been wholly transcended.

She explains her own development in connection with *Tender Buttons* (1914) "It was my first conscious struggle with the problem of correlating sight, sound and sense, and eliminating rhythm; — now I am trying grammar and eliminating sight and sound (*transition* No. 14, Fall, 1928).

Having taken the words to her choice, to emphasize further what she has in mind she has completely unlinked them (in her most recent work) from their former relationships in the sentence. This was absolutely essential and unescapable. Each under the new arrangement has a quality of its own, but not conjoined to carry the burden science, philosophy and every higgledy piggledy figment of law and order have been laying upon them in the past. They are like a crowd at Coney Island, let us say, seen from an airplane.

Whatever the value of Miss Stein's work may turn out finally to be, she has at least accomplished her purpose of getting down on paper this much that is decipherable. She has placed writing on a plane where it may deal unhampered with its own affairs, unburdened with scientific and philosophic lumber.

For after all, science and philosophy are today, in their effect upon the mind, little more than fetishes of unspeakable abhorrence. And it is through a subversion of the art of writing that their grip upon us has assumed its steel-like temper.

What are philosophers, scientists, religionists; they that have filled up literature with their pap? Writers, of a kind. Stein simply erases their stories, turns them off and does without them, their logic (founded merely on the limits of the perceptions) which is supposed to transcend the words, along with them. Stein denies it. The words, in writing, she discloses, transcend everything.

Movement (for which in a petty way logic is taken) the so-called search for truth and beauty is for us the effect of a breakdown of the attention. But movement must not be confused with what we attach to it but, for the rescuing of the intelligence, must always be considered aimless, without progress.

This is the essence of all knowledge.

Bach might be an illustration of movement not suborned by a freight of purposed design, loaded upon it as in almost all later musical works; statement unmusical and unnecessary. Stein's "They lived very gay then" has much of the same quality of movement to be found in Bach — the composition of the words determining not the logic, not the "story," not the theme even, but the movement itself. As it happens, "They were both gay there" is as good as some of Bach's shorter fugues.

***

Writing, like everything else is much a question of refreshed interest. It is directed, not idly, but as most often happens (though not necessarily so), toward that point not to be predetermined where movement is blocked (by the end of logic perhaps). It is about these parts, if I am not mistaken, that Gertrude Stein will be found.

There remains to be explained the bewildering volume of what Miss Stein has written, the quantity of her work, its very apparent repetitiousness, its iteration, what I prefer to call its extension, the final clue to her meaning.

It is, of course, a progression (not a progress) beginning, conveniently, with "Melanctha" (from *Three Lives*), and coming up to today.

How in a democracy, such as the United States, can writing, which has to compete with excellence elsewhere and in other times, remain in the field and be at once objective (true to fact) intellectually searching, subtle and instinct with powerful additions to our lives? It is impossible, without invention of some sort, for the very good reason that observations about us engenders the very opposite of what we seek: triviality, crassness, and intellectual bankruptcy. And yet what we do see can in no way be excluded. Satire and flight are two possibilities but Miss Stein has chosen otherwise.

But if one remain in a place and reject satire, what then? To be democratic, local (in the sense of being attached with integrity to actual experience) Stein, or any other artist, must for subtlety ascend to a plane of almost abstract design to keep alive. To writing, then, as an art in itself. Yet what actually impinges on the senses must be rendered as it appears, by use of which, only, and under which, untouched, the significance has to be disclosed. It is one of the major problems of the artist.

"Melanctha" is a thrilling clinical record of the life of a colored woman in the present day United States, told with directness and truth. It is without question one of the best bits of characterization produced in America. It is universally admired. This is where Stein began.

But for Stein to tell a story of that sort, even with the utmost genius, was not enough under the conditions in which we live, since by the very nature of its composition such a story does violence to the larger scene which would be portrayed.

True, a certain way of delineating the scene is to take an individual like Melanctha and draw her carefully. But this is what happens. The more carefully the drawing is made, the greater the genius involved and the greater the interest that attaches, therefore, to the character as an individual, the more exceptional that character becomes in the mind of the reader and the less typical of the scene.

It was no use for Stein to go on with *Three Lives*. There that phase of the work had to end. See *Useful Knowledge*, the parts on the U.S.A. Stein's pages have become like the United States viewed from an airplane — the same senseless repetitions, the endless multiplications of toneless words, with these she had to work.

No use for Stein to fly to Paris and *forget* it. The thing, the United States, the unmitigated stupidity, the drab tediousness of the democracy, the overwhelming number of the offensively ignorant, the dull of nerve — is *there* in the artist's mind and cannot be escaped by taking a ship. She must resolve it if she can, if she is to *be*. That must be the artist's articulation with existence.

Truly, the world is full of emotion — more or less — but it is caught in bewilderment to a far more important degree. And the purpose of art, so far as it has any, is not at least to copy that, but lies in the resolution of difficulties to its own comprehensive organization of materials. And by so doing, in this case, rather than by copying, it takes its place as *most* human.

To deal with Melanctha, with characters of whomever it may be, the modern Dickens, is *not* therefore human. To write like that is not, in the artist, to be human at all, since nothing is resolved, nothing is done to resolve the bewilderment which makes of emotion an inanity. That, is to overlook the gross instigation and with all subtlety to examine the object minutely for "the truth" — which if there is anything more commonly practised or more stupid, I have yet to come upon it.

To be most useful to humanity, or to anything else for that matter, an art, writing, must stay art, not seeking to be science, philosophy, history, the humanities, or anything else it has been made to carry in the past. It is this enforcement which underlies Gertrude Stein's extension and progression to date.

Gertrude Stein   Edmund Wilson*

Gertrude Stein, born in Allegheny, Pennsylvania, a student of psychology and medicine who is said to have been considered by William James the most brilliant woman pupil he had ever had, published in 1909 a book of fiction called *Three Lives*. It was brought out by a small and obscure publisher and at that time attracted little attention, but, loaned from hand to hand, it acquired a certain reputation. *Three Lives*, which bore on its title-page a quotation from Jules Laforgue, was a work of what would at that time have been called realism, but it was realism of rather a novel kind. The book consisted of three long short stories — the histories of three women, two of them German servant-girls, the other a mulatto girl. What is most remarkable in these stories — especially if we compare them with such a typically Naturalistic production as Flaubert's "Un Cœur

*Reprinted from *Axel's Castle* (New York: Charles Scribner's Sons, 1931), 237–44. Only part one of this three-part chapter has been reprinted here.

Simple," in which we feel that the old family servant has been seen from a great distance and documented with effort — is the closeness with which the author has been able to identify herself with her characters. In a style which appears to owe nothing to that of any other novelist, she seems to have caught the very rhythms and accents of the minds of her heroines: we find ourselves sharing the lives of the Good Anna and Gentle Lena so intimately that we forget about their position and see the world limited to their range, just as in Melanctha's case — and this is what makes her story one of the best as well as one of the earliest attempts of a white American novelist to understand the mind of the modern Americanized negro — we become so immersed in Melanctha's world that we quite forget its inhabitants are black. And we discover that these histories have a significance different from that of ordinary realistic fiction: Miss Stein is interested in her subjects, not from the point of view of the social conditions of which they might be taken as representative, but as three fundamental types of women: the self-sacrificing Anna, who combines devotion with domination; the dreamy and passive Lena, for whom it is natural to allow herself to be used and effaced from life by other lives; and the passionate and complex Melanctha, who "was always losing what she had in wanting all the things she saw." Behind the limpid and slightly monotonous simplicity of Gertrude Stein's sentences, one becomes aware of her masterly grasp of the organisms, contradictory and indissoluble, which human personalities are.

Three Lives, though not widely circulated, exercised a considerable influence. Carl Van Vechten wrote about it; Eugene O'Neill and Sherwood Anderson read it with admiration. It is interesting to note that all three of these writers were to occupy themselves later with negro life, in regard to which Miss Stein had given an example of an attitude not complicated by race-consciousness. And Sherwood Anderson seems to have learned from her, in his own even less Naturalistic, even more dreamlike, fiction, both his recurrent repetitions with their effect of ballad refrains and his method of telling a story in a series of simple declarative sentences of almost primer-like baldness.

Gertrude Stein's next book was a long novel, *The Making of Americans*, written between 1906 and 1908, but not published until 1925. I confess that I have not read this book all through, and I do not know whether it is possible to do so. *The Making of Americans* runs to almost a thousand large pages of small closely-printed type. The first chapters show the same remarkable qualities as *Three Lives*, though in a somewhat diluted form. Miss Stein sets before us the men and women of her German-Jewish families with all the strong sense we have already admired for the various and irreducible entities of human character; and we are made, as we are in *Three Lives*, to feel life as her people feel it, to take for granted just as they do the whole complex of conditions of which they are part. But already some ruminative self-hypnosis, some progressive slow-ing-up of the mind, has begun to show itself in Miss Stein's work as a sort of fatty degeneration of her imagination and style. In *Three Lives*, the rhythmic repetitions were successful in conveying the recurrences, the gradual unwinding of life, and in the dialogue they produced the effect of the speech of slow-minded people: "I never did use to think I was so much on being real modest, Melanctha, but now I know really I am, when I hear you talking. I see all the time there are many people living just as good as I am, though they are a little different to me. Now with you, Melanctha, if I understand you right what you are talking, you don't think that way of no other one that you are ever knowing." But, though in *The Making of Americans* this sort of thing is appropriate to the patient and brooding repititousness of the German-Jewish Americans of the first and second generations, it is here carried to such immoderate lengths as finally to suggest some technique of mesmerism. With sentences so regularly rhythmical, so needlessly prolix, so many times repeated and ending so often in present participles, the reader is all too soon in a state, not to follow the slow becoming of life, but simply to fall asleep. And the further we get, the more difficult we find it to keep our mind on what we are reading: Miss Stein abandons altogether for long stretches any attempt to tell her story by reporting what her characters do and say, and resorts to a curious abstract vein of generalization:

> Some are needing themselves being a young one, an older one, a middle aged one, an older one, an old one to be ones realizing what any one telling about different ways of feeling anything, of thinking about anything, of doing anything is meaning by what that one is telling. Some are needing themselves being a young one, an older one, a middle aged one, an older one, an old one to be one being certain that it is a different thing inside in one being a young one, from being an older one, from being a middle aged one, from being an older one, from being an old one,

etc., etc. The psychological truth is still there, no doubt, but it is in a solution of about one percent to the total volume of the dose, and the volume of the dose is enormous.

This repetitious and abstract vein of the last pages of *The Making of Americans* persists still in the psychological portraits of Picasso and Matisse published in 1912:

> One was quite certain that for a long part of his being one being living he had been trying to be certain that he was wrong in doing what he was doing and then when he could not come to be certain that he had been wrong in doing what he had been doing, when he had completely convinced himself that he would not come to be certain that he had been wrong in doing what he had been doing he was really certain then that he was a great one and he certainly was a great one. Certainly every one could be certain of this thing that this one is a great one.

This is queer and very boring, like a good deal of *The Making of Americans*, but it is still intelligible. A little later, however, Miss Stein published privately another "portrait" which represented something of a new departure. In the *Portrait of Mabel Dodge*, she seems to be groping for the instinctive movements of the mind which underlie the factitious conventional logic of ordinary intercourse, and to be trying to convey their rhythms and reflexes through a language divested of its ordinary meaning.

Tender Buttons, which appeared in 1914 and was the first of Miss Stein's books to attract attention, went even further than the *Portrait of Mabel Dodge* in the direction of dislocating words from their meanings. The pieces in *Tender Buttons* are in a different vein from anything she had published before: she has here given up her long rhythms and writes pungently, impressionistically, concisely. Miss Stein had by this time gone to live in Paris (where she has remained ever since) and had become interested in the modern French painting of the generation of Picasso and Matisse, which she was one of the first to appreciate and collect; and the pieces in *Tender Buttons* — the title was supposed to describe the contents — are said to have been intended as prose still-lifes to correspond to those of such painters as Picasso and Braque. A pattern of assorted words, though they might make nonsense from the traditional point of view, would be analogous to a Cubist canvas composed of unidentifiable fragments.

> *Red Roses.* A cool red rose and a pink cut pink, a collapse and a sold hole, a little less hot.
>
> *A Sound.* Elephant beaten with candy and little pops and chews all bolts and reckless rats, this is this.
>
> *Custard.* Custard is this. It has aches, aches when. Not to be. Not to be narrowly. This makes a whole little hill.
>
> It is better than a little thing that has mellow real mellow. It is better than lakes whole lakes, it is better than seeing.
>
> *Chicken.* Alas a dirty word, alas a dirty third, alas a dirty bird.

Gertrude Stein is said, at this period, to have made a practice of shutting herself up at night and trying utterly to banish from her mind all the words ordinarily associated with the ideas she had fixed upon. She had come to believe that words had other values than those inherent in their actual meanings, and she was attempting to produce a kind of literature which should work with these values exclusively.

In *Have They Attacked Mary He Giggled — A Political Satire* (1917), she developed, however, still another genre, which at least partially left to language its common meanings — a sort of splintered stenographic commentary made up of scraps of conversation as they reverberate in the mind and awaken unspoken responses. The volumes of miscellaneous pieces which have followed — *Geography and Plays* (1922) and *Useful Knowledge* (1928) — contain examples of all her previous styles as well as several variations, including a curious kind of "play" which consists simply of long lists of phrases divided into acts. Among these, some of the satires are funny, some of the portraits rather interesting and bits of the "abstract" impressionism charming, and there are one or two really excellent short stories such as "Miss Furr and Miss Skeene," in which the repetitive rigmarole manner is admirably suited to render the monotony and insipidity of the feminine lives which are being narrated. But most of what Miss Stein publishes nowadays must apparently remain absolutely unintelligible even to a sympathetic reader. She has outdistanced any of the Symbolists in using words for pure purposes of suggestion — she has gone so far that she no longer even suggests. We see the ripples expanding in her consciousness, but we are no longer supplied with any clew as to what kind of object has sunk there.

A Note on Gertrude Stein   William Troy*

It must be recognized, first of all, that Miss Stein's new work is the most "comprehensible" and therefore, in a sense, the least characteristic work of hers that has appeared. The reason for this is twofold: it is presumably not her book at all, but the autobiography of her secretary-companion, Miss Toklas; and its subject matter is of a traditional kind. Although she cannot help falling into her own syntax and idiom most of the time, Miss Stein makes at least as great an effort to be faithful to the style of her narrator as Defoe in writing *Robinson Crusoe*. Such phrases as "awe-inspiringly" and "the house of our dreams" are intended to indicate Miss Toklas's sensibility rather than Miss Stein's own; and because this sensibility is a more familiar one most readers will have less difficulty in following it. The other reason that the book is so easy to read is that it can be enjoyed for its gossip, its fund of wit and anecdotes, its revelation of a "personality." Read in this way, it should provide inexhaustible fodder for the newspaper reviewers and abundant, if somewhat superficial, enjoyment for a large section of the reading public. Indeed, it is all too tempting to plunder some of its rarer bits for the purposes of this review; to repeat what Miss Stein has to say about Matisse, Picasso, Whitehead, Hemingway, among others; to destroy the reader's own pleasure in discovering these things for himself. For among books of literary reminiscences Miss Stein's is one of the richest, wittiest, and most irreverent ever written. In it she makes ridiculous all those who have ridiculed her for the last twenty-five years with the charge that she has had "nothing to say." She shows that she has a great deal to say of the sort that historians,

*Reprinted from the *Nation* 137 (6 September 1933): 274–75.

biographers, and literary gossipers are in the habit of saying: Miss Toklas's "autobiography" is, among other things, a critical history of modern French painting and an account of the post-war generation in American letters. But if it were only this it would be an even less characteristic book by Miss Stein than it is; others could have given us these facts, but only Gertrude Stein can give us Gertrude Stein. And the deepest interest of the book lies in the insight it gives us into the genesis of the mind and sensibility reflected in Gertrude Stein's other and more characteristic books.

There have always been only two questions about Gertrude Stein: What, precisely, has she been trying to do these many years? What, if any, is the value of what she has done? The first, which has never been satisfactorily answered, is a question that has to do not only with her method, style, and processes of composition but also with her view or "vision" of experience. The second, which cannot very well be answered before the first, is a question involving all the questions of evaluation involved in discussing any artistic work. Most of the confusion in regard to Miss Stein's work has come from the attempt to answer the second question without adequately recognizing the difficulties of the first. For Miss Stein, who happens to possess at once a highly trained metaphysical mind and an extremely refined aesthetic sensibility, offers unusual difficulties to the critic — more perhaps than any other creative writer of our time. Before disposing of her work with any real comfort it is necessary to know a great deal not only about William James and Bergson and Whitehead but also about Cézanne and Picasso and Juan Gris. Her so-called naive and primitive writing, moreover, represents such a complex synthesis of these influences that the most painstaking analysis is required to reveal them with any degree of clarity. In the end, it is much easier to turn to a "difficult" writer like Mrs. Virginia Woolf. All that will be pointed out here is that, in the general character of her mind and in its central orientation, Gertrude Stein is not nearly so isolated and eccentric a figure in American letters as is so often believed.

Before Gertrude Stein went to Paris in 1903 she had been a favorite student of James at Radcliffe, she had published a paper in the *Harvard Psychological Review*, and she had spent four years at Johns Hopkins, where her researches had been praised by Halstead and Osler. She did not take her degree there because, as she says, medicine bored her. In Paris she immediately met Matisse, Picasso, Braque, and other young painters who were busily overthrowing the "literary" painting of the previous generation in favor of an ever more abstract practice of their art. Under their inspiration she appears to have done her first literary work; *Three Lives* was written, literally, under the shadow of Cézanne. The effect of this worship of abstraction on a mind already trained in metaphysical speculation was to alienate its owner even farther from the concrete life of her own time and country. In the rue de Fleurus Miss Stein settled down to the creation of a form of writing which in style attempted to reproduce the movements of consciousness as described by James and Bergson, in form and diction to conform to the ideal of austere simplification followed by the new school of plastic artists. Like them, she hated "literature" and sought "the destruction of associational emotion in poetry and prose." Like them also, she was indifferent to the qualitative aspects of subject; she merely "rendered" people, landscapes, and events. And because her passion for "elemental abstraction" appealed to a generation that had just been through the concrete discomforts of a world war, she became in time a kind of High Priestess. Although a follower like Hemingway, remaining "nine-tenths bourgeois," never got away from the "museum smell," her non-associational prose became one of the greatest single influences on the prose of her time.

In her detachment, her asceticism, and her eclecticism, Miss Stein can only remind us of another American author who lived in Europe and devoted himself more and more exclusively to the abstract. The principal difference between Henry James (whom Miss Stein reads more and more these days) and Gertrude Stein is that the former still kept within the human realm by treating moral problems. (Miss Stein has a more absolute aesthetic ideal: "the *intellectual* passion for exactitude in the description of inner and outer reality.") Moreover, what Miss Stein has in common with James she has in common with Poe, Hawthorne, Melville, and several other important and characteristic American writers: an orientation from experience toward the abstract, an orientation that has been so continuous as to constitute a tradition, if not actually *the* American tradition. Of this tradition it is possible to see in Miss Stein's writing not only a development but the pure culmination. She has pushed abstraction farther than James or even Poe would ever have dared — to the terms of literary communication itself, "Words and Sentences." The final divorce between experience and art, which they threatened, is accomplished. Not only life but the traditional means of communication in life are "simplified" to suit the patterns which she offers in substitute.

Has Gertrude Stein A Secret?   B. F. Skinner[*]

In the *Autobiography of Alice B. Toklas* Gertrude Stein tells in the following way of some psychological experiments made by her at Harvard: —

> She was one of a group of Harvard men and Radcliffe women and they all lived very closely and very interestingly together. One of them, a young philosopher and mathematician who was doing research work in

[*]Excerpted from the *Atlantic Monthly* 153 (January 1934): 50–57.

psychology, left a definite mark on her life. She and he together worked out a series of experiments in automatic writing under the direction of Münsterberg. The result of her own experiments, which Gertrude Stein wrote down and which was printed in the *Harvard Psychological Review*, was the first writing of hers ever to be printed. It is very interesting to read because the method of writing to be afterwards developed in *Three Lives* and *The Making of Americans* already shows itself.

There is a great deal more in this early paper than Miss Stein points out. It is, as she says, an anticipation of the prose style of *Three Lives* and is unmistakably the work of Gertrude Stein in spite of the conventional subject matter with which it deals. Many turns of speech, often commonplace, which she has since then in some subtle way made her own are already to be found. But there is much more than this. The paper is concerned with an early interest of Miss Stein's that must have been very important in her later development, and the work that it describes cannot reasonably be overlooked by anyone trying to understand this remarkable person.

Since the paper is hard to obtain, I shall summarize it briefly. It was published in the *Psychological Review* for September 1896 under the title, "Normal Motor Automatism," by Leon M. Solomons and Gertrude Stein, and it attempted to show to what extent the elements of a "second personality" (of the sort to be observed in certain cases of hysteria) were to be found in a normal being. In their experiments the authors investigated the limits of their own normal motor automatism; that is to say, they undertook to see how far they could "split" their own personalities in a deliberate and purely artificial way. They were successful to the extent of being able to perform many acts (such as writing or reading aloud) in an automatic manner, while carrying on at the same time some other activity such as reading an interesting story.

II

In the experiments with automatic writing, a planchette of the ouija board type was originally used, but as soon as the authors had satisfied themselves that spontaneous writing movements do occur while the attention is directed elsewhere, an ordinary pencil and paper were used instead. The subject usually began by making voluntary random writing movements or by writing the letter *m* repeatedly. In one experiment this was done while the subject read an interesting story at the same time, and it was found that some of the words read in the story would be written down in an automatic way. At first there was a strong tendency to notice this as soon as it had begun to happen and to stop it, but eventually the words could be written down unconsciously as well as involuntarily. (I shall use Miss Stein's psychological terminology throughout.) "Sometimes the writing of the word was completely unconscious, but more often the subject knew what was going on. His knowledge, however, was obtained by sensations *from the arm.* He was conscious that he just had written a word, not that he was about to do so."

In other experiments the subject read an interesting story as before, and single words were dictated to him to be written down at the same time. These were difficult experiments, but after considerable practice they were successful. The subject was eventually able to write down "five or six" words spoken by another person, without being conscious of either the heard sounds or the movement of the arm. If his attention were not sufficiently well distracted he might become aware that his hand was writing something. The information came from the arm, not from the sound of the dictated word. "It is never the sound that recalls us. This, of course, may be an individual peculiarity to a certain extent. . . . Yet, Miss Stein has a strong auditory consciousness, and sounds usually determine the direction of her attention."

In a third group of experiments the subject read aloud, preferably from an uninteresting story, while being read to from an interesting one. "If he does not go insane during the first few trials, he will quickly learn to concentrate his attention fully on what is being read to him, yet go on reading just the same. The reading becomes completely unconscious for periods of as much as a page." Automatic reading of this sort is probably part of the experience of everyone.

The fourth and last group brings out the relevance of the experiments to the later work of Gertrude Stein. I shall let Miss Stein describe the result.

> *Spontaneous automatic writing.* — This became quite easy after a little practice. We had now gained so much control over our habits of attention that distraction by reading was almost unnecessary. Miss Stein found it sufficient distraction often to simply read what her arm wrote, but following three or four words behind her pencil. . . .
>
> A phrase would seem to get into the head and keep repeating itself at every opportunity, and hang over from day to day even. The stuff written was grammatical, and the words and phrases fitted together all right, but there was not much connected thought. The unconsciousness was broken into every six or seven words by flashes of consciousness, so that one cannot be sure but what the slight element of connected thought which occasionally appeared was due to these flashes of consciousness. But the ability to write stuff that sounds all right, without consciousness, was fairly well demonstrated by the experiments. Here are a few specimens:
>
> "Hence there is no possible way of avoiding what I have spoken of, and if this is not believed by the people of whom you have spoken, then it is not possible to prevent the people of whom you have spoken so glibly. . . ."
>
> Here is a bit more poetical than intelligible:

"When he could not be the longest and thus to be, and thus to be, the strongest."

And here is one that is neither:

"This long time when he did this best time, and he could thus have been bound, and in this long time, when he could be this to first use of this long time. . . ."

III

Here is obviously an important document. No one who has read *Tender Buttons* or the later work in the same vein can fail to recognize a familiar note in these examples of automatic writing. They are quite genuinely in the manner that has so commonly been taken as characteristic of Gertrude Stein. Miss Stein's description of her experimental result is exactly that of the average reader confronted with *Tender Buttons* for the first time: "The stuff is grammatical, and the words and phrases fit together all right, but there is not much connected thought." In short, the case is so good, simply on the grounds of style, that we are brought to the swift conclusion that the two products have a common origin, and that the work of Gertrude Stein in the *Tender Buttons* manner is written automatically and unconsciously in some such way as that described in this early paper.

This conclusion grows more plausible as we consider the case. It is necessary, of course, to distinguish between the Gertrude Stein of *Three Lives* and the *Autobiography* and the Gertrude Stein of *Tender Buttons*, a distinction that is fairly easily made, even though, as we shall see in a moment, there is some of the first Gertrude Stein in the latter work. If we confine ourselves for the present to the second of these two persons, it is clear that the hypothetical author who might be inferred from the writing itself possesses just those characteristics that we should expect to find if a theory of automatic writing were the right answer. Thus there is very little intellectual content discoverable. The reader—the ordinary reader, at least—cannot infer from the writing that its author possesses any consistent point of view. There is seldom any intelligible expression of opinion, and there are enough capricious reversals to destroy the effect of whatever there may be. There are even fewer emotional prejudices. The writing is cold. Strong phrases are almost wholly lacking, and it is so difficult to find a well-rounded emotional complex that if one is found it may as easily be attributed to the ingenuity of the seeker. Similarly, our hypothetical author shows no sign of a personal history or of a cultural background; *Tender Buttons* is the stream of consciousness of a woman without a past. The writing springs from no literary sources. In contrast with the work of Joyce, to whom a superficial resemblance may be found, the borrowed phrase is practically lacking.

IV

From this brief analysis it is apparent that, although it is quite plausible that the work is due to a second personality successfully split off from Miss Stein's conscious self, it is a very flimsy sort of personality indeed. It is intellectually unopinionated, is emotionally cold, and has no past. It is unread and unlearned beyond grammar school. It is as easily influenced as a child; a heard word may force itself into whatever sentence may be under construction at the moment, or it may break the sentence up altogether and irremediably. Its literary materials are the sensory things nearest at hand — objects, sounds, tastes, smells, and so on. The reader may compare, for the sake of the strong contrast, the materials of "Melanctha" in *Three Lives*, a piece of writing of quite another sort. In her experimental work it was Miss Stein's intention to avoid the production of a true second personality, and she considered herself to be successful. The automatism she was able to demonstrate possessed the "elements" of a second personality, it was able to do anything that a second personality could do, but it never became the organized *alter ego* of the hysteric. The superficial character of the inferential author of *Tender Buttons* consequently adds credibility to the theory of automatic authorship.

The Gertrude Stein enthusiast may feel that I am being cruelly unjust in this estimate. I admit that there are passages in *Tender Buttons* that elude the foregoing analysis. But it must be made clear that the two Gertrude Steins we are considering are not kept apart by the covers of books. There is a good deal of the Gertrude Stein of the *Autobiography* in *Tender Buttons*, in the form of relatively intelligible comment, often parenthetical in spirit. Thus at the end of the section on Mutton (which begins "A letter which can wither, a learning which can suffer and an outrage which is simultaneous is principal") comes this sentence: "A meal in mutton mutton why is lamb cheaper, it is cheaper because so little is more," which is easily recognized as a favorite prejudice of the Gertrude Stein of the *Autobiography*. Similarly such a phrase as "the sad procession of the unkilled bull," in *An Elucidation*, is plainly a reference to another of Miss Stein's interests. But, far from damaging our theory, this occasional appearance of Miss Stein herself is precisely what the theory demands. In her paper in the *Psychological Review* she deals at length with the inevitable alternation of conscious and automatic selves, and in the quotation we have given it will be remembered that she comments upon these "flashes of consciousness." Even though the greater part of *Tender Buttons* is automatic, we should expect an "element of connected thought," and our only problem is that which Miss Stein herself has considered — namely, are we to attribute to conscious flashes all the connected thought that is present?

There is a certain logical difficulty here. It may be argued that, since we dispense with all the intelligible sentences by calling them conscious flashes, we should not be surprised to find that what is left is thin and meaningless. We must therefore restate our theory, in a way that will avoid this criticism. We first divide the writings of Gertrude Stein into two parts on the basis of their ordinary intelligibility. I do not contend that this is a hard and fast line, but it is a sufficiently real one for most persons. It does not, it is to be understood, follow the outlines of her works. We then show that the unintelligible part has the characteristics of the automatic writing produced by Miss Stein in her early psychological experiments, and from this and many other considerations we conclude that our division of the work into two parts is real and valid and that one part is automatic in nature.

I cannot find anything in the *Autobiography* or the other works I have read that will stand against this interpretation. On the contrary, there are many bits of evidence, none of which would be very convincing in itself, that support it. Thus (1) *Tender Buttons* was written on scraps of paper, and no scrap was ever thrown away; (2) Miss Stein likes to write in the presence of distracting noises; (3) her handwriting is often more legible to Miss Toklas than to herself (that is, her writing is "cold" as soon as it is produced); and (4) she is "fond of writing the letter *m*," with which, the reader will recall, the automatic procedure often began. In *An Elucidation*, her "first effort to realize clearly just what her writing meant and why it was as it was," there are many fitful allusions to the experimental days: "Do you all understand extraneous memory," "In this way my researches are easily read," a suddenly interpolated "I stopped I stopped myself," which recalls the major difficulty in her experiments, and so on.

V

It is necessary to assume that when Gertrude Stein returned to the practice of automatic writing (about 1912?) she had forgotten or was shortly to forget its origins. I accept as made in perfectly good faith the statement in the *Autobiography* that "Gertrude Stein never had subconscious reactions, nor was she a successful subject for automatic writing," even though the evidence to the contrary in her early paper is incontrovertible. She has forgotten it, just as she forgot her first novel almost immediately after it was completed and did not remember it again for twenty-five years. It is quite possible, moreover, that the manner in which she writes the *Tender Buttons* sort of thing is not unusual enough to remind her of its origins or to be remarked by others. One of the most interesting statements in the excerpt quoted from her early paper is that Gertrude Stein found it sufficient distraction simply to follow what she was writing some few words behind her pencil. If in the course of time she was able to bring her attention nearer and nearer to the pencil, she must eventually have reached a point at which there remained only the finest distinction between "knowing what one is going to write and knowing that one has written it." This is a transitional state to which Miss Stein devotes considerable space in her paper. It is therefore reasonable for us to assume that the artificial character of the experimental procedure has completely worn off, and that there remains only a not-far-from-normal state into which Miss Stein may pass unsuspectingly enough and in which the *Tender Buttons* style is forthcoming.

**

VI

We have allowed for the presence of any or all of these kinds of meaning by speaking only of ordinary intelligibility. I do not think that a case can be made out for any one of them that is not obviously the invention of the analyzer. In any event the present argument is simply that the evidence here offered in support of a theory of automatic writing makes it *more probable* that meanings are not present, and that we need not bother to look for them. A theory of automatic writing does not, of course, necessarily exclude meanings. It is possible to set up a second personality that will possess all the attributes of a conscious self and whose writings will be equally meaningful. But in the present case it is clear that, as Miss Stein originally intended, a true second personality does not exist. This part of her work is, as she has characterized her experimental result, little more than "what her arm wrote." And it is an arm that has very little to say. This is, I believe, the main importance of the present theory for literary criticism. It enables one to assign an origin to the unintelligible part of Gertrude Stein that puts one at ease about its meanings.

There are certain aspects of prose writing, such as rhythm, that are not particularly dependent upon intelligibility. It is possible to experiment with them with meaningless words, and it may be argued that this is what is happening in the present case. Considering the freedom that Miss Stein has given herself, I do not think the result is very striking, although this is clearly a debatable point. It is a fairer interpretation, however, to suppose in accordance with our theory, that there is no experimentation at the time the writing is produced. There may be good reason for publishing the material afterward as an experiment. For example, I recognize the possibility of a salutary, though accidental, effect upon Gertrude Stein's conscious prose or upon English prose in general. In *Composition As Explanation*, for example, there is an intimate fusion of the two styles, and the conscious passages are imitative of the automatic style. This is also probably true of parts of the *Autobiography*. It is perhaps impossible to tell at present whether the effect upon her conscious prose is anything more than a loss of discipline. The compensating gain is often very great.

We have no reason, of course, to estimate the literary value of this part of Miss Stein's work. It might be considerable, even if our theory is correct. It is apparent that Miss Stein believes it to be important and has accordingly published it. If she is right, if this part of her work is to become historically as significant as she has contended, then the importance of the document with which we began is enormous. For the first time we should then have an account by the author herself of how a literary second personality has been set up.

I do not believe this importance exists, however, because I do not believe in the importance of the part of Miss Stein's writing that does not make sense. On the contrary, I regret the unfortunate effect it has had in obscuring the finer work of a very fine mind. I welcome the present theory because it gives one the freedom to dismiss one part of Gertrude Stein's writing as a probably ill-advised experiment and to enjoy the other and very great part without puzzlement.

One Moment Alit   Stark Young*

Mr. Paul Rosenfeld has already written of the Hartford premiere of *Four Saints in Three Acts*, and to his comment this is added, as more could well be added to this. In my opinion the production of this opera is the most important event of the theatre season: it is the first free, pure theatre that I have seen so far.

Four Saints in Three Acts has been described, reviewed and broadcast; and Miss Gertrude Stein's method of writing, with its word tricks, rhythms, buttons, anapaests and so on, its meanings submerging and emerging like a dolphin, has been well known for twenty years. The general news of *Four Saints in Three Acts* has called it the Stein opera. Since the acclaim of *The Autobiography of Alice B. Toklas* this makes better publicity, but it is, also, just. The spring and melodic fantasy of the music, the scenario, the choreography and the décor arise quite profoundly and organically from the piece Miss Stein has written. The alternations of rococo frolic and sensuous intensity are paralleled in her text. Once that is said, we must hasten to add that the actual words themselves in this opera production are a very secondary part of it. They are adapted to singing, but numbers and alphabets would not infrequently do as well. They do give Mr. Virgil Thomson a happy libretto verbally and, in an elusive manner, emotionally. But it is true of him that his gifts

*Reprinted from the *New Republic* 78 (3 July 1934): 105.

include the uncommon one of the marriage of singing and word, and that his phrases flutter and descend into the stage scene very much as the phrases of the Stein text also do. Now and then a provocative word or phrase or a sudden bloc of emotional drama draws outward to engage the ear and to elicit inquiry. But in the main the words go their way regardless. This should not trouble people who are accustomed to endless operas, with arias, quartettes or dramatic dialogues of which they understand not one word of the Italian, German and often little of the English, where it is English — I heard Caruso once when he struck a pin at Miss Farrar's waist, sing a whole air, O Cruel Pin, with exactly the same applause from the audience. Nor should it trouble people who have always known by instinct or cultivation that Mother Goose is better poetry than Longfellow — "Hickory, dickory, dock," for example, which at least lives in the ear, as compared to "Be not like dumb, driven cattle," which is born dead. And finally it can be said that, whereas often in singing you hope to be spared hearing the words, Mr. Thomson's line and phrase often make you anxious to know what the word was.

The character of the music is neither "modern" nor traditional; it releases us from any decision beyond fantasy and freedom or delight in itself. This music is melodic, though always briefly; it flits lightly, flutters, or dwells for a moment poignantly, and it is capable of many flying lyricisms. It has in it elements of jazz, pre-war melody, the ballet and, among others, something that suggests the Gregorian trimmed down shall we say to Lulli, somewhat as Titian to Watteau — at any rate there seems often present a certain finality out of France. The text itself must have left most of what we now see on the stage to be created by stage artists. Mr. John Houseman in the directing and, especially, Mr. Frederick Ashton in the choreography worked admirably. Indeed, Mr. Ashton's contribution might easily be undervalued, though almost anyone should see how the brief formal ballet of the three couples, with its kind of Galatea, sea-nymph theme, is enchanting. The décor of Miss Florine Stettheimer, in the second act a trifle monotonous, seemed perfect to the whole production. It was witty, delicious and iridescent, based on cellophane and modern painting; a sort of whimsical Victorian coquetry with the baroque that is a fresh step in stage décor. Miss Kate Lawson's costumes, not always as well executed as might be, were equally absorbing. The choice of Negro performers was very shrewd. Their relaxation, absence of prosaic, obvious analysis, and technical intuition without trained technical brittleness, were half the battle in such a venture as this. Only Miss Altonell Hines as the *commère* appeared at times to have her tongue in her cheek. The phrase "baroque fantasy" passed out by the producer as a hint to the wise is a good one for this piece of theatre art. Not the great baroque with its solemn magnificence or intellectual variation on the theme, but baroque in its unbroken air of spontaneity, its charming and capricious flights, within the key and hidden unity of the whole.

I wish I knew some way to make sure of being taken seriously when I say that *Four Saints in Three Acts* is as essential theatre the most important event of our season. Bullying clichés and fad talk would help but temporarily, but such an approach is not needed at all. This piece of theatre art is the most important for one reason because it is the most delightful and joyous — and delight is the fundamental in all art great or small — what a joke on the hardworking, hard-punching, expensive and self-evident aspect of the average musical show this whole event is! It is important because it is theatre and flies off the ground. (The only thing comparable to it in this respect is the flying wildness behind the mind of Mr. Henry Hull's Jeeter Lester in *Tobacco Road*.) It creates instead of talking about. After all, we can imagine writing a play about a professor's home, a boy's troubles, capitalists, et cetera, good matter enough, just as our legs, our blood, our hats and problems are good. But only now and then in the theatre can we hope for something of the quality of a thing in nature (a tree, a melon, a sheet of water, a flight of birds). The point in such a case is not that it is beautiful or not beautiful, but that it lives in itself, and is in essence a constant surprise; and that from it we make our conclusions and applications, deep or trivial, to art and to delight.

It is horrible to think, if *Four Saints in Three Acts* turns out to be the success, or the vogue, more or less promised by the first night's reception from both the audience and the press in New York, what imitations of it will follow. However they may miss fire, they may some of them have the prosperity with which second-hand imitations often surpass the original. Whatever happens, *Four Saints in Three Acts* cuts the theatre loose from the predictable and the repeated. The scene about the pigeons, so brief and soon gone is like some singing of little sea shells, and is a case in point. At the same moment it baffles and intrigues imitation, and in that fact precisely lies its theatre life.

The Impartial Essence   Kenneth Burke*

The repetitions and blithe blunderings that Gertrude Stein has somehow managed to work into a style make her *Lectures in America* hard for a critic to discuss. Though they have as their subject a theory of writing, they are expressed so girlishly that we are tempted not to ask how the various parts fit together.

The keystone of Gertrude Stein's literary theories seems to be her doctrine of "essence." She would get at the "essence" of the thing she is describing. She thus tends to consider literature primarily as *portraits*. She makes portraits, not only of people, but of landscapes; plays are to her

*Reprinted from the *New Republic* 83 (7 March 1935): 227.

little other than group portraits; and eventually people and landscapes become so interchangeable that a play can describe a landscape by assembling portraits of people. Hence let us, instead of attempting to follow the order of exposition in Miss Stein's book itself, build up her literary schema in our own way with "essence" as the starting point:

The essence of a thing would not be revealed in something that it does. It would be something that a thing is. The search for essence is the attempt "to express this thing each one being that one." A thing's essence is something that makes it distinct from other things; it is, as she says at another point, a thing's "melody." Since it is something that the thing *is*, action would tend to obscure it rather than reveal it. Hence:

> In my portraits I had tried to tell what each one is without telling stories and now in my early plays I tried to tell what happened without telling stories so that the essence of what happened would be like the essence of the portraits, what made what happened be what it was.

Suppose, now, that you held to such a doctrine of essence, and wanted in your writing to get down the absolute essence of each thing you wrote about. Consider the sort of problems, in both theory and methods, that might arise. In the first place, you would have to worry about resemblance. In putting down the essence of Mr. A, you would have to guard against any tendency to think of him in terms of somebody he resembled—Mr. A1. Again, since essence is something that a thing now is, you would have to guard against the tendency to think of your subject in terms of memories (an exaction which might explain in part her tendency to feel that stories or acts obscure the perception of essence). And you would now have brought yourself to the paradoxical position wherein your knowledge of your subject's past or of people like him amounts to "confusion" (a sad state of affairs upon which Miss Stein dwells at some length).

At this point you might rebel; but if you go on, as Miss Stein did at her leisure, you will find attendant considerations arising. You will talk much about getting "inside" things (perhaps thus being led to note as the primary fact about English literature the stimulus it derived from insularity). And since you, as an *outsider*, are busied with the literary task of describing things until you get *inside* them, there will necessarily hover about your theories some hint of mystic communion. In time your doctrine of essence brings you to the metaphysical problem of the One and the Many, for if you start by trying to find wherein each one is that one, you begin to find a general intermingling; and particularly as you make that outside you to be inside you, you come, through the medium of yourself, upon a kind of universal essence:

> And so I say and I saw that a complete description of every kind of human being that ever could or would be living is not such a very

extensive thing because after all it can be all contained inside in any one and finally it can be done.

How does this work out in practice? You start to write about something, to describe it, to make its portrait. You have a personal style, a set of mannerisms that suit your particular essence, and as you write you gradually get into the swing of them. When you get going, you are "excited." And since your excitement arises during your description of a thing, you may call this excitement the melody or essence of the thing. You may feel that each subject has its particular essence because you have used a particular combination of words in writing about it. But you feel the "unity" of all subjects because the quality of your excitement is the same in all cases (the way you feel when you get going), and you call this melody of yours the melody of the thing.

If the essence of external things is thus identified with the qualities of your style, you may tend to think of writing (description) primarily as a monologue act, done with little direct concern for an audience. And since this stylistic circulation about an object obliges you to consider the strategy of expression, you may arrive at the thoughts on the nature of naming that Miss Stein verbalizes as a shifty distinction between prose and poetry ("that is poetry really loving the name of anything and that is not prose").

However, you are now on the verge of a change. For the strategy of expression leads into considerations of the audience. From this point, you begin to suspect the suggestive values of narrative, since narrative unquestionably has a significant appeal to audiences. But at this point, if you are Miss Stein, you simply state that you have changed your opinion — and stop. As a kind of compromise between your initial notion of essence as non-dramatic and the fully revised notion that essence might best show itself in action, you may be grateful for her halfway metaphor: the essence is something like the engine in a car — a going without a destination.

It seems to me, however, that Miss Stein should have continued her revisionary process, until all the initial visionary assertions had been similarly modified. She might have considered, for instance, the ways in which remembrance and resemblance are inevitable; the ways in which the primary fact of English literature might be called its transcendence of insularity, etc. And then, and only then, should she have begun her book. As it stands, I maintain that it is (a) the first draft of a critical credo, (b) complicated by the co-presence of its revision, (c) further vitiated by the fact that the revisionary process was not applied to all its parts. Above all, I believe a complete revision would require her to stress (at least in this "imperfect world" of history) the *dramatic*, the *active*, the *partisan*, in direct contrast with the feature of *passivity* that is now infused through her doctrine of portrait and essence.

Gertrude Stein: A Literary Idiot   Michael Gold*

Gertrude Stein recently returned to America after an absence of many years. In Paris, where she lived as a forbidding priestess of a strange literary cult, Gertrude Stein accumulated a salon frequented by some of the outstanding names of the modern art world and acquired the reputation of a literary freak. People either gaped at her published writings, or laughed at her incomprehensible literary epigrams—"a rose is a rose is a rose."

She was looked upon by those who believed in her as the greatest revolutionist in the history of contemporary literature, and by those who scoffed as the perpetrator of a gigantic literary hoax.

As it happens, neither of the two opinions is wholly correct. Her "revolution" resembles a literary putsch, and if her writing is "a hoax" nevertheless she earnestly believes in it.

In essence, what Gertrude Stein's work represents is an example of the most extreme subjectivism of the contemporary bourgeois artist, and a reflection of the ideological anarchy into which the whole of bourgeois literature has fallen.

What was it that Gertrude Stein set out to do with literature? When one reads her work it appears to resemble the monotonous gibberings of paranoiacs in the private wards of asylums. It appears to be a deliberate irrationality, a deliberate infantilism. However, the woman's not insane, but possessed of a strong, clear, shrewd mind. She was an excellent medical student, a brilliant psychologist, and in her more "popular" writings one sees evidence of wit and some wisdom.

And yet her works read like the literature of the students of padded cells in Matteawan.

Example: "I see the moon and the moon sees me. God bless the moon and God bless me and this you see remember me. In this way one fifth of the bananas were bought."

The above is supposed to be a description of how Gertrude Stein feels when she sees Matisse, the French modernist painter. It doesn't make sense. But this is precisely what it is supposed to do—not "make sense" in the normal meaning of the term.

The generation of artists of which Gertrude Stein is the most erratic figure arduously set out not to "make sense" in their literature. They believed that the instincts of man were superior to the reasonings of the rational mind. They believed in intuition as a higher form of learning and knowledge. Therefore, many of them wrote only about what they dreamed, dream literature. Others practised a kind of "automatic writing" where they would sit for hours scribbling the random, subconscious itchings of their souls. They abandoned themselves to the mystic irrationa-

*Reprinted from *Change The World!* (New York: International Publishers, 1936), 23–26.

lities of their spirits in order to create works of art which would be expressions of the timeless soul of man, etc. The result unfortunately revealed their souls as astonishingly childish or imbecile.

The literary insanity of Gertrude Stein is a deliberate insanity which arises out of a false conception of the nature of art and of the function of language.

A leisure class, which exists on the labor of others, which has no function to perform in society except the clipping of investment coupons, develops ills and neuroses. It suffers perpetually from boredom. Their life is stale to them. Tasteless, inane, because it has no meaning. They seek new sensations, new adventures constantly in order to give themselves feelings.

The same process took place with the artists of the leisure class. Literature also bored them. They tried to suck out of it new sensations, new adventures.

They destroyed the common use of language. Normal ways of using words bored them. They wished to use words in a new, sensational fashion. They twisted grammar, syntax. They went in for primitive emotions, primitive art. Blood, violent death, dope dreams, soul-writhings, became the themes of their works.

In Gertrude Stein, art became a personal pleasure, a private hobby, a vice. She did not care to communicate because essentially there was nothing to communicate. She had no responsibility except to her own inordinate cravings. She became the priestess of a cult with strange literary rites, with mystical secrets.

In this light, one can see that to Gertrude Stein and to the other artists like her, art exists in the vacuum of a private income. In order to pursue the kind of art, in order to be the kind of artist Gertrude Stein is, it is necessary to live in that kind of society which will permit one to have a private income from wealthy parents or sound investments. With this as a basis, you can write as you please. You can destroy language, mutilate grammar, rave or rant in the name of the higher knowledge. Nobody will disturb you. And in time perhaps you can impress or intimidate a certain number of critics and win a kind of reputation.

Gertrude Stein has won the reputation. She returns home to America after an absence of thirty-one years to find herself an object of curious respect by book clubs and lecture societies, and front page news for the newspapers.

Which seems to me to be proof that with enough money and enough persistence a madman can convince a world of his sanity. Gertrude Stein appears to have convinced America that she is a genius.

But Marxists refuse to be impressed with her own opinion of herself. They see in the work of Gertrude Stein extreme symptoms of the decay of capitalist culture. They view her work as the complete attempt to annihilate all relations between the artist and the society in which he lives.

They see in her work the same kind of orgy and spiritual abandon that marks the life of the whole leisure class.

What else does her work resemble more than the midnight revels of a stockbroker throwing a pent-house party for a few intimate friends? Would it be possible to have either of these symptoms of degeneration except in a society divided into classes? Is there not an "idle art" just as there is an "idle rich"? Both do nothing but cultivate the insanity of their own desires, both cultivate strange indulgences. The literary idiocy of Gertrude Stein only reflects the madness of the whole system of capitalist values. It is part of the signs of doom that are written largely everywhere on the walls of bourgeois society.

Introduction to *The Geographical History of America*   Thornton Wilder*

This book grew out of Miss Stein's meditations on literary masterpieces. Why are there so few of them? For what reasons have they survived? What qualities separate the masterpieces from the works that are almost masterpieces? The answers usually given to these questions did not satisfy her. It was not enough to say that these books were distinguished by their "universality," or their "style," or their "psychology" or their "profound knowledge of the human heart." She thought a great deal about the Iliad and the Old Testament and Shakespeare, about *"Robinson Crusoe"* and the novels of Jane Austen — to quote the works that appeared most frequently in her conversation during the months that this book was approaching completion — and the answer she found in regard to them lay in their possession of a certain relation to the problems of identity and time.

In order to approach their treatment of identity and time Miss Stein made her own distinction between Human Nature and the Human Mind. Human Nature clings to identity, its insistence on itself as personality, and to do this it must employ memory and the sense of an audience. By memory it is reassured of its existence through consciousness of itself in time-succession. By an audience it is reassured of itself through its effect on another — " 'I am I,' said the little old lady, 'because my dog knows me.' " From Human Nature, therefore, come all the assertions of the self and all the rhetorical attitudes that require the audience — wars, politics,

*Reprinted from Gertrude Stein, *The Geographical History of America*, 43–50. Copyright 1936, renewed © 1964 by Alice B. Toklas. Reprinted by permission of Random House, Inc.

propaganda, jealousy, and so on. The Human Mind, however, has no identity; every moment "it knows what it knows when it knows it." It gazes at pure existing. It is deflected by no consideration of an audience, for when it is aware of an audience it has ceased to "know." In its highest expression it is not even an audience to itself. It knows and it writes, for its principal expression is in writing and its highest achievement has been in literary masterpieces. These masterpieces, though they may be about human nature are not of it. Time and identity and memory may be in them as subject-matter — as that existing at which the Human Mind gazes — but the absence from the creative mind of those qualities has been acknowledged by the vast multitudes of the world who, striving to escape from the identity-bound and time-immersed state, recognize that such a liberation has been achieved in these works. If then Miss Stein is writing metaphysics, why does she not state her ideas in the manner that metaphysicians generally employ?

There are three answers to this question.

In the first place, a creative metaphysician must always invent his own terms. Even though his concepts may have something in common with those of his predecessors — with such concepts as subjective, objective, soul, imagination, and consciousness — he cannot in certain places employ those terms, because they come bringing associations of (for him) varying validity and bringing with them the whole systems of which they were a part. The contemporaries of Kant complained (as the contemporaries of Professor Whitehead are now complaining) that the philosopher's terminology was arbitrary and obscure.

In the second place, Miss Stein is not only a metaphysician; she is an artist. In varying degrees artists, likewise, have always sought to invent their own terms. The highest intuitions towards a theory of time, of knowledge or of the creative act have always passed beyond the realm of "text-book" exposition. When the metaphysician is combined with the poet we get such unusual modes of expression as the myths in Plato, the prophetic books of Blake, and the difficult highly-figured phrases in Keats's letters. Miss Stein's style in this book might be described as a succession of "metaphysical metaphors." On the first page, for example, we read:

"If nobody had to die how would there be room for us who now live to have lived. We never could have been if all the others had not died there would have been no room.

Now the relation of human nature to the human mind is this.

Human nature does not know this. . . .

But the human mind can."

(Human Nature, hugging identity-survival cannot realize a non-self situation. The Human Mind, knowing no time and identity in itself, can realize this as an objective fact of experience.)

Similarly, further down we come upon the question:

"What is the use of being a little boy if you are growing up to be a man?"

(Since the Human Mind, existing, does not feel its past as relevant, why does succession in identity have any importance? What is the purpose of living in time? One cannot realize what one was like four seconds ago, four months ago, twenty years ago. "Only when I look in the mirror," said Picasso's mother, "do I realize that I am the mother of a grown-up man.")

This book is a series of such condensations, some of them, like the plays and the "detective stories" about pigeons, of considerable difficulty. These latter, it is only fair to add, have, with a number of other passages, so far exceeded the delighted but inadequate powers of this commentator. The book presupposes that the reader has long speculated on such matters and is willing and able to assimilate another person's "private language," – and in this realm what can one give or receive, at best, but glimpses of an inevitably private language?

The third reason that renders this style difficult for many readers proceeds from the author's humor. Metaphysics is difficult enough; metaphysics by an artist is still more difficult; but metaphysics by an artist in a mood of gaiety is the most difficult of all. The subject-matter of this book is grave, indeed; and there is evidence throughout of the pain it cost to express and think these things. (It is not without "tears" that Human Nature is found to be uninteresting and through a gradual revelation is discovered to be sharing most of its dignities with dogs.) But Miss Stein has always placed much emphasis on the spirit of play in an artist's work. The reward of difficult thinking is an inner exhilaration. Here is delight in words and in the virtuosity of using them exactly; here is wit; here is mockery at the predecessors who approached these matters with so cumbrous a solemnity. One of the aspects of play that most upsets some readers is what might be called "the irruption of the daily life" into the texture of the work. Miss Stein chooses her illustrations from the life about her. She introduces her friends, her dogs, her neighbors. Lolo, about whom gather the speculations as to the nature of romance, lived and died in a house that could be seen from Miss Stein's terrace in the south of France. She weaves into the book the very remarks let fall in her vicinity during the act of writing. Similarly at one period, Picasso pasted subway-tickets upon his oil-paintings; one aspect of the "real" by juxtaposition gives vitality to another aspect of the real, the created.

But why doesn't Miss Stein at least aid the reader by punctuating her sentences as we are accustomed to find them? And why does she repeat herself so often?

A great many authors have lately become impatient with the inadequacy of punctuation. Many think that new signs should be invented; signs to imitate the variation in human speech; signs for emphasis; signs for word-groupings. Miss Stein, however, feels that such indications harm rather than help the practice of reading. They impair the collaborative participation of the reader. "A comma by helping you along holding your coat for you and putting on your shoes keeps you from living your life as actively as you should live it. . . . A long complicated sentence should force itself upon you, make yourself know yourself knowing it."

The answer to the charge of repetition is on many levels. On one level Miss Stein points out that repetition is in all nature. It is in human life: "if you listen to anyone, behind what anyone is saying whether it's about the weather or anything, you will hear that person repeating and repeating himself." Repeating is emphasis. Every time a thing is repeated it is slightly different. "The only time that repeating is really repeating, that is when it is dead, is when something is being taught." Then it does not come from the creating mind, but from unliving forms. Sometimes Miss Stein's repeating is for emphasis in a progression of ideas; sometimes it is as a musical refrain; sometimes it is for a reassembling of the motifs of the book and their re-emergence into a later stage of the discussion; sometimes it is in the spirit of play.

But if this book is about the psychology of the creative act, why is it also called *The Geographical History of America*?

Miss Stein, believing the intermittent emergence of the Human Mind and its record in literary masterpieces to be the most important manifestation of human culture, observed that these emergences were dependent upon the geographical situations in which the authors lived. The valley-born and the hill-bounded tended to exhibit a localization in their thinking, an insistence on identity with all the resultant traits that dwell in Human Nature; flat lands or countries surrounded by the long straight lines of the sea were conducive toward developing the power of abstraction. Flat lands are an invitation to wander, as well as a release from local assertion. Consequently, a country like the United States, bounded by two oceans and with vast portions so flat that the state boundaries must be drawn by "imaginary lines," without dependence on geographical features, promises to produce a civilization in which the Human Mind may not only appear in the occasional masterpiece, but may in many of its aspects be distributed throughout the people.

Miss Stein's theory of the audience insists upon the fact that the richest rewards for the reader have come from those works in which the authors admitted no consideration of an audience into their creating mind. There have been too many books that attempted to flatter or woo or persuade or coerce the reader. Here is a book that says what it knows: a work of philosophy, a work of art, and a work of gaiety.

All about Ida

W. H. Auden*

Ida is not about IDA, but about Dear Ida. Who is Dear Ida? Why, everybody knows Dear Ida, but not everybody knows whom they know. Most people call the Dear Ida they know IDA, but most people do not know IDA. Then who is Dear Ida whom everybody knows? Miss Stein knows who Dear Ida is. Dear Ida lives from day to day, but a day is not really all day to Dear Ida because she does not need all day. She does not need all day because, of course, she is mostly sitting and resting and being there. Resting is what she likes best and sitting is what she does best. That is being natural, and, of course, being natural does not take all day. That is why she can only use the part of the day and night that she chooses to sit in. She stays there as long as she can, then she goes walking. Dear Ida walks in the afternoon when she is not resting. Everything happens to Dear Ida, funny things happen, husbands happen, going away happens, and Dear Ida does not know whether they are happening slowly or not. It might be slowly, it might be not. Dear Ida does not know because she does not begin, no, never, because, as Miss Stein says, if you begin, nothing happens to you. You happen. Dear Ida does not happen, Dear Ida is not funny. The only funny thing about Dear Ida is her dislike of doors. Otherwise Dear Ida is very well, very well indeed. Does Dear Ida know IDA? No, she does not know IDA, she only knows that IDA is beside her. She cannot know IDA because she thinks IDA is like what she thinks Dear Ida is like. Dear Ida does not even know Dear Ida. Only once in her life does she know Dear Ida. That is the only time Dear Ida cries. Knowing IDA beside her, and not knowing Dear Ida, like the Dear Ida she is, she thinks that IDA is Dear Ida, my twin, my twin Winnie who is winning everything and will never make me cry. When she tries to think of IDA, she can only think of her twin Winnie. When she tries to think of Dear Ida, she can only think a dog is a dog because it is always there. If Dear Ida does not know Dear Ida, who does? IDA knows. IDA is funny and is always beginning. Nothing happens to IDA. IDA does not call Dear Ida dear Ida. But Poor Ida, Lazy Ida, Bad Ida, why do you let such funny things happen to you, why don't you begin, why don't you cry? Dear Ida, you are wrong. The first of everything is not a sign of anything. Anything can be the first of everything. Perhaps ten can be a sign of something. Yes, perhaps everything after ten is a sign. I am not your twin Winnie, Dear Ida, I am IDA. If you knew this, you would not be resting. Perhaps you would be crying, but you would know IDA, and that would be as well. Most novels are Dear Ida writing about her twin Winnie, but they do not say so. O dear no, they say this is IDA writing about IDA. But it is only Dear Ida writing, and what does Dear Ida know about IDA as she sits,

*Reprinted from the *Saturday Review* 23 (22 February 1941): 8. Copyright 1941 Saturday Review Magazine Co. Reprinted by permission.

Dear Ida, and lets funny things happen and does not cry. When she writes IDA she only says, My twin Winnie who is always winning, always counting, never sitting but always crying. There is too much winning, too much counting, too much crying, too much of not resting altogether. Ida is not Dear Ida writing about her twin Winnie. Ida is IDA writing about Dear Ida. There is not too much of anything, only one hundred and fifty pages, and Dear Ida only cries once. IDA does not pretend that Dear Ida is not resting and not thinking about her twin Winnie. Dear Ida writes very often, but I do not like what she writes because it is neither about IDA nor Dear Ida, only about her twin Winnie, and that is too much. I like IDA best when she writes about IDA but she does not write about her very often. Next to IDA writing about IDA, I like IDA writing about Dear Ida.

This is what Ida is. I like Ida.

Miss Stein's Battle   Jean Wahl*

Out of the First World War there came a great American book, *The Enormous Room*, by E. E. Cummings. It had been written in a French prison. Here is a book written in a more enormous room, in the prison that was France during these years. Miss Stein's narrative of her experiences is beautiful and very moving in parts, with many marvelous simple stories. She is at her best when she creates an atmosphere of terror by little unpretentious strokes. Since "it is very funny the way everybody and anybody may feel about anything," we need not wonder to find that many funny things are also said by Miss Stein, who is not just anybody, about France and the war, which are not just anything. Sometimes we find just small talk. Nevertheless some things are said, many little things that are right, some little things that are half right, and some great things that are wrong.

Miss Stein portrays confusion: "That is that which makes a war." Undoubtedly much of this confusion really existed, probably much of it existed only in her own mind. This is what a war makes. She says she was nearly French because she had so many points of view; on the contrary these many points of view caused her to drift away from the French spirit many times. She came nearest to it when she simply rejoiced in the victories of the Americans.

She saw many collaborationists, Bernard Fay and others, all those who did not know whom they had to fear more, the Russians, the British or the Germans. Were there really so many who admired the Germans? She says the middle classes were collaborationists. But there were in every

*Reprinted from the *New Republic* 112 (19 March 1945): 396–98.

class men whose ideas were straight and some men whose ideas were wavering and crooked — the bitter and discouraged *ratés* and others. That war was not an international civil war, as has been said. The name of de Gaulle is curiously absent from the book, although Miss Stein mentions seeing the FFI cars with the Cross of Lorraine. She did not hear the radio from London, did not care to hear it, and was thus deprived of one of the important elements in the life of the average Frenchman.

She gives as reasons for praising the armistice "in the first place" that "it was more comfortable to us, who were here," and second, that the winning of the war was thus promoted. The last is certainly debatable. The following fantastic passage is almost unbelievable in its naïveté: "Pétain went up and flew the French flag upon the top of the city hall of Paris, and had a triumphal entry into his capital and, and you see the woman at Aix is right they the occupants are phantoms otherwise how could it have happened. . . . Pétain's going to Paris was really wonderful so simple so natural so complete and extraordinary, it was all that . . . it is like Verdun again it is complete and incomparable."

However, it is certain that Miss Stein does not like the collaborationists and that she does like the maquis. She knows some people who think that all maquis are terrorists and evil-doers. (I met not so many months ago an American diplomat who told the same story.) Only old grumblers and decayed aristocrats think like that, she says. She saw the courage of the young men who had to decide for themselves at eighteen or nineteen whether to go to Germany as workers or to flee. Practically unarmed, inferior in numbers, they fought without fear. And in '44 they begin to police the country and although they requisition too many cars, it is all "very French and easy. . . . Everybody is pleased." The French are not very revengeful, she says.

And she does not like the Germans: we hear of the French farmer who explains, "It is Hitler but it is not Hitler. They are always choosing someone to lead them in a direction where they do not want to go." Miss Stein seems satisfied with this psychological anomaly. And yet according to her, the Germans have a strong will to destroy. They are cruel, sadistic, she says, "to make themselves feel stronger," nearly not human, rather dead than alive. "They dream fancy-tales where everything is as it was or was not." They believe what they are supposed to believe. She uses the word "Germans," not "Nazis," showing thus an art of nondelusion, which perhaps in part she borrowed from the French peasant.

The apparent naïve improfundity of Gertrude Stein's writing does not always hide profundity. To fall into her style of writing, there are here things which are neither pleasing nor unpleasing, but also things which are more unpleasing than things which are neither pleasing nor unpleasing — for example, when she says the Jews, having an instinct for publicity, have a strong tendency to be persecuted.

The reason for this war, according to Miss Stein, is the need for hastening the slow death of the nineteenth century, a century which she characterizes as one of evolution, prayers, Esperanto, climbing, eating, superstition, realism, science and progress. The twentieth century, to which only America belongs up to now, is one of pessimism, simplicity, things just happening and Ford. We wonder what significance all this pseudo-thought of hers can have. Where is the nineteenth century which has to be killed? Not in France, she says, nor in America, but in Germany, which is nevertheless in the Middle Ages. England is in the nineteenth century, we find, but is not aware of it. Furthermore all Europe is in the Middle Ages, or in the boyhood of mankind, because we are in a war. And Miss Stein says, "What difference between life and war? There is none." Perhaps she is in the age of the Pre-Socratics with Heraclitus, the father of flux and reflux and eternal recurrence, or rather she is a Heraclitean in the nineteenth century. Like many of the intelligentsia of the dying nineteenth century, she is too intelligent and not intelligent enough.

Things as They Are   Edmund Wilson*

The Banyan Press of Pawlet, Vermont, has published, in an edition of five hundred and sixteen copies, a very early manuscript of Gertrude Stein's: a short novel, to which the author had given the title *Quod Erat Demonstrandum* but which the editor, making use of a phrase from the story, has retitled *Things As They Are*. The manuscript is dated October 24, 1903, when the author was twenty-nine, and it must have been written before *Three Lives*, the first of her published books, which came out in 1909. Like *Three Lives*, it is quite comprehensible, and it does not even show any tendency toward the Steinian repetitiousness that already appears in *Three Lives*. It is a production of some literary merit and of much psychological interest. The reviewer had occasion some years ago to go through Miss Stein's work chronologically, and he came to the conclusion at that time that the vagueness that began to blur it from about 1910 on and the masking by unexplained metaphors that later made it seem opaque, though partly the result of an effort to emulate modern painting, were partly also due to a need imposed by the problem of writing about relationships between women of a kind that the standards of that era would not have allowed her to describe more explicitly. It seemed obvious that her queer little portraits and her mischievously baffling prose-poems did often deal with subjects of this sort. Now the publication of *Things As*

*Excerpted from "Gertrude Stein Old and Young" from *The Shores of Light* by Edmund Wilson. Copyright 1952 by Edmund Wilson. Reprinted by permission of Farrar, Straus and Giroux, Inc. This selection first appeared, in slightly different form, in the *New Yorker*, 1951.

They Are comes to confirm this theory. It is a story of the tangled relations of three Lesbian American girls of the early nineteen-hundreds, told with complete candor and an astonishing lack of self-consciousness.

When one says that it is told with candor, one does not mean that it has much in common with those case-histories of Havelock Ellis that, published in his *Studies in the Psychology of Sex* between 1897 and 1910, did a good deal to clear the air. In this document of Gertrude Stein's, there is nothing in the least scandalous (unless the subject itself be considered so), and the whole thing is done with a sobriety, even an abstractness of language, that recalls the French classical novels of the type of *Adolphe* and *La Princesse de Clèves.* (The author's geometrical title was, in fact, so perfectly appropriate that one wonders why the editor should have wanted to change it.) Yet this study has behind it something of the modern scientific temper and brings us back to the brilliant young woman who, at Radcliffe, took psychology with William James and was called by him his best woman pupil, and who went through — though she did not graduate — five years of medical school at Johns Hopkins.

Gertrude Stein went to Europe in 1903, after she had dropped her medical work, and the heroine of *Things As They Are*, a college graduate named Adele, is first seen on a ship bound for Europe. She has given herself up in her steamer chair "to a sense of physical weariness and to the disillusionship [sic] of recent failures" when she is approached by a handsome girl, well-to-do and college-bred like herself, whose obvious interest in her has the result of suddenly awakening her from a "long emotional apathy." This girl, whose name is Helen, tactfully pays her court, and Adele, though with a certain passivity, more or less responds to her attentions. But Helen has another friend, Sophie, an intimate of long standing, who is also a friend of Adele's and who later explains to Adele, when they are back in the United States, the nature of her (Sophie's) relations with Helen. Adele is at first filled with horror but, goaded by Helen's challenge, eventually herself succumbs. This gives rise to something in the nature of the heterosexual ménage à trois, but with differences that come out distinctly in the report of an observant woman who is not much disturbed by emotion. The homogeneity of sex seems in some ways a stabilizing influence, yet the intrusion of a masculine element on the part of the women themselves and the difficulty they have in keeping it up are uncertain and upsetting factors. Adele will assert of Sophie that "it was not that she had the manners of a perfect hostess but the more obtrusive good manners of a gentleman," and will try to assure herself that, in her attitude toward the trusting and deceived Sophie, she has not behaved like "a cad"; but at other moments strained relations collapse into feminine cattiness and lead to bitter altercations that seem almost to reach the hair-pulling stage. This inevitably becomes faintly comic, as if one were witnessing a triangle between three mislaid empty gloves, all intended for the left hand, and one cannot be sure that Gertrude Stein is not already treating the situation with irony. One does feel some personal animus on the part of the author toward Sophie, and the triangle results in an impasse that is painful for all three of the ladies — since Helen, of whom her family disapprove and who is kept by them on short rations, is obliged to do her travelling at Sophie's expense (Europe is a necessity for all of them), and Adele, realizing at last that she cannot break up the pair, finds it too much for her pride always to be following Helen and stealing moments from her intimacy with Sophie. Yet the smiling detached Gertrude Stein is already emerging in *Things As They Are* from the perplexities and the trying adjustments of the young woman intellectual who insists that she is loyal to the middle-class virtues. You are reminded in certain passages of the comedy of Miss Furr and Miss Skeene, that touching pair of left-hand gloves who are the heroines of another story.

This latter detachment of Gertrude Stein's is seen in its beginnings in *Things As They Are*, not only in the author's tone but also in the character of Adele. Adele is self-centered and rather inert; she does not readily give herself; she likes to be alone and ruminate, to feel that she is "her own man." Helen and Sophie, with their passions and reproaches, stimulate but also annoy her; her involvement with them hampers her movements. "Much as I wanted you," she says to Helen, "I was not eager [to see you again] for after all you meant to me a turgid and complex world, difficult yet necessary to understand, and for the moment I wanted to escape all that, I longed only for obvious, superficial, clean simplicity." Her impulse, when she is faced with a problem, is not to see it through, for which Helen sometimes scolds her, but simply to drop it and go away and turn her attention to something else — as the young Gertrude Stein had declined to take William James's examination, explaining that she was very sorry but did not feel like an examination that morning. James gave her an A just the same, but she fared worse at Johns Hopkins, where her peculiar insouciance had to contend with hostile instructors who had not been convinced, in that era, that women should be admitted to medical schools. One feels, in *Things As They Are*, that Adele might have bucked Sophie if she had not so determinedly insisted on deserting the "strapped" Helen and going abroad again by herself. The mature Gertrude Stein later on — in her literary personality — went up on a high mountain, where she could dwell, when she chose, in a cloud. The already well-marked egoism of her heroine Adele is brought out by the comments of Adele's companions. It had grown, by the time of *Three Lives*, to that of the egoism of "Miss Mathilda," about whom revolve like satellites the three respectful maids, the Good Anna, Melanctha and the Gentle Lena, who give their names to the stories; and it had swollen to monstrous proportions by the time of *The Autobiography of Alice B. Toklas*, in which Miss Mathilda of Bridgepoint becomes frankly Miss Stein of Paris, an Olympian known only remotely through the impressions of an admiring high priestess.

The frustration of the young Adele, at the end of *Things As They Are*, is a matter, one feels, less of tragic loss than of failure of domination. Gertrude Stein, in her subsequent career, did partially succeed in dominating, through her salon, her collection, her wide reputation, her influence on certain writers; and in so far as she failed to carry off her pretentious claims, she seems to have concealed this—to add a third suggestion to the two I have already made to explain her later impenetrability—by putting herself, once for all, out of the reach of uncomfortable criticism. This reviewer met Miss Stein only once, but he received, in the course of that interview, an agreeable first impression of a quick and original intelligence dealing readily from the surface of the mind with the surfaces presented by life—the responses so direct and natural, the surfaces seen so unconventionally, that one did not at first feel anything wrong; but a chilling second impression of (to resort to an overworked metaphor) a great iceberg of megalomania that lay beneath this surface and on which, if one did not skirt around it, conversations and personal relations might easily crash and be wrecked. This iceberg—heavy and hard as the stone that her name brings to mind—must have been forming in an emotional solitude, and it now held her two-thirds submerged. I doubt whether the obscurity that hid it—the function of which seems to me quite different from that of Joyce or Virginia Woolf—will interest future readers as much as the limpidity of *Things As They Are*.

In any case, we must not leave *Things As They Are* without a glance at the attractive figure of the young independent girl in the costume of 1900, "the cut of whose shirt-waist alone betrayed her American origin" and of whom her friends, meeting her in Rome, exclaimed that she "looked as brown and white and clean as if [she] had just sprung out of the sea"; who liked to sit "in the court of the Alhambra watching the swallows fly in and out of the crevices of the walls, bathing in the soft air filled with the fragrance of myrtle and oleander and letting the hot sun burn her face and the palms of her hands" and who enjoyed making friends with a young Spanish girl whose language she could not speak and from whom she parted "as quiet friends part," turning again and again and "signing a gentle farewell" as long as they could see one another; who came back to "the white snow line of New York harbor," from the damp of a London winter, delighted to see the American flag, "the clean sky and the white snow and the straight plain ungainly buildings all in a cold and brilliant air without spot or stain," and who wandered for days about the Boston streets, "rejoicing in the passionless intelligence of the faces." She would be able, she must already have begun to feel, eventually to do without passion.

The Elements

Donald Sutherland*

This will be to explain as much as I understand of what Gertrude Stein did in writing.

To explain first how she began, by the leading ideas around her at the time. The work of William James and Hugo Münsterberg, with whom she studied at Radcliffe, can represent her intellectual surroundings in say 1895.

The central object of concern for James and Münsterberg and for many others at that time was the consciousness. Physiology, psychology, and metaphysics were all brought at once to bear on the consciousness as a problem. Was it a substantive entity, an epiphenomenon, a relation, a function, or what?

The consciousness had become problematical but so far it had not been displaced as the central object of concern by the subconscious or by behavior. Behavior was still a subject for ethics or the demonstration of something else.

And while the subconscious was being very much investigated it generally belonged to physiology, or brain facts, and not to mind facts, as they then made the distinction. The secondary and tertiary personalities of hysterical cases were considered conventionally as split-off parts of a total conscious personality, and rather sadly stupid. There was nothing seductive about them. The previous exaggerations of von Hartmann (1868) about the subconscious as a more gifted double of the conscious personality were standing objects of ridicule, and as for what was to come, Freud and misconstructions of Freud did not yet count at Radcliffe. In 1894 James had published a notice of one of the first articles by Freud and Breuer, on hysteria, but the *Traumdeutung* did not appear until 1900 and the great doctor in person did not burst upon New England until 1909. Before that, anything like the surrealist trust in the subconscious was hardly likely.

Gertrude Stein like everyone else investigated the consciousness, and in 1896 she and a friend named Leon M. Solomons published the results of some experiments they had made in automatic reading and writing. The purpose of the experiments was not to exploit a disreputable or at least pathological subconscious but to show that motor automatism in the normal subject with his conscious attention voluntarily distracted was capable of the elementary feats performed by the second personalities in hysterical cases. This in turn was to show that the "second personality" was an unnecessary hypothesis for explaining hysterical phenomena. Hysteria, by disordering the conscious attention, merely let the basic automatism function freely. "We *would* not, the histerique *can* not, attend

*Reprinted from *Gertrude Stein: A Biography of Her Work* (New Haven: Yale University Press, 1951), pp. 1–13, by permission of Yale University Press, copyright 1951.

to these sensations [of automatic activity]. Whatever else hysteria may be then, this, at least, seems most probable. It is a *disease* of the attention."[1]

This basic automatism was not yet thought of glowingly as the normal subconscious, and even the notion of the subliminal consciousness is treated rather briskly by Mr. Solomons and Miss Stein in passing. Out of mock deference to that theory they distinguish a "conscious consciousness."

The texts produced automatically are dealt with loftily and humorously, and all connected thought in the texts is suspected of being an interruption by the conscious consciousness. "The stuff written was grammatical, and the words and phrases fitted together all right, but there was not much connected thought. The unconsciousness was broken into every six or seven words by flashes of consciousness, *etc*. Here is a bit more poetical than intelligible.

" 'When he could not be the longest and thus to be, and thus to be, the strongest.' "[2]

This was, to the experimenters, curious enough but scarcely promising for literature. When the literary writing of Gertrude Stein came it was in full consciousness, written and to be read so. She said this and said it often but as her work did not look it she was normally not believed. The automatic passage[3] quoted above does look exactly like some of her later work. It is now not a question of belief so much as of understanding how her work was conscious and clear, objectively clear, and at the same time did not look it.

The reasons for this resemblance begin not in the question of the subconscious, whether hysterical or normal, but in the consciousness itself, as of 1895. Since the consciousness had become problematical its nature and procedures were examined very closely. It had replaced the soul and thus inherited what was left of religious and ethical concern, all the anxieties of personal identity. It was a serious matter to find the consciousness might be not only divisible but submersible. Janet's famous patient Lucie, who came in three layers, was the real Cleopatra of the late century, threatening the empire of right reason. It may seem no discovery now, but it was noticed that even the concentrated unified conscious consciousness as an observed fact or process does not move of itself in logical propositions which can be expressed in Aristotelian grammar or its extensions by subordinate clauses and ellipses and qualifications. The simple faith in reason or emotion as the base and meaning of writing, as with classicism and romanticism, was no longer possible.

The trouble was not at all confined to Radcliffe. Quite evidently the whole major literary movement of the early 20th century, with Proust, Joyce, Dorothy Richardson, Virginia Woolf, and the rest, was immensely occupied with this problem, both as a philosophical problem and as a problem of expression or form. This is common knowledge and known roughly as the stream of consciousness. James called it that but he also seems to have preferred calling it the stream of thought, which makes a difference, by including positive activity, choosing.

What will make not small but considerable differences among those novelists and Gertrude Stein is the differing conception of the contents or movements of consciousness, the conception of time or the sense of it, and the methods of forcing the words and composition to encompass or express the subject.

It makes a difference if the consciousness is thought of as in the main passively registering consecutive sensuous impressions and feelings. Out of that can be made the work of English ladies like Dorothy Richardson and Virginia Woolf, the intimate journal or a very rich and formal poetry after Keats. Again if the consciousness is taken as including at any moment a whole or partial past, as the person is his own biography, a Proust can make the most of it. If the consciousness is taken to imply at any moment a whole racial or mythological past, a Joyce can express it by sonorities of reference and verbal orchestration. And here it makes a great difference whether the literary form is extended from the logical tradition to convert the illogical material to itself, as with Richardson, Woolf, and Proust, or whether the form is directed more or less completely by the qualities and behavior of the material, or rather by the terms of the experience of the material.

What then was the consciousness and how did it operate according to James and Münsterberg? And what did Gertrude Stein make of it, having a mind of her own?

Münsterberg remained true to the consciousness as an entity in the tradition of Kant and Wundt, but James suddenly in 1895 declared that it was not an entity but if anything a relation. This created a scandal, for James had himself maintained throughout his great book, *Principles of Psychology*, published in 1890, that the consciousness was an entity. His defection from the intellectualist position in 1895 was followed gradually by more and more agreement with Bergson, and finally by the invention of pragmatism and radical empiricism. Gertrude Stein was at Radcliffe during the first and worst of the agitation, before James had fully developed his new positions. It would be neat but absurd to say that she subscribed for life to any of his old or new formulations, especially since James himself was notorious for provoking his students to do their own thinking and for insisting that ultimately one's philosophical beliefs are determined by personal temperament. Also there is the pleasant story Gertrude Stein tells, how some years later when he saw her pictures by Matisse and Picasso, in Paris, he gasped and said he had always told her she should keep her mind open. While she was a favorite pupil she was not his creature. He did not have creatures.

Still she could scarcely have helped being deeply influenced by the new crisis in the question of consciousness and the way it was put. In the

Psychology James had defined the consciousness as the passing thought, a momentary section of the stream of consciousness. The passing thought was itself the thinker. It was in itself final and simple, regardless of the time, tendencies, purposes, origins, and complications of its objects. Considering what the soul had once been, this consciousness of 1890 was not much of an entity, pared to next to nothing with Occam's razor, to the bare minimum that would explain the given phenomena; but James concluded that even that much of a substantive was not needed and the "consciousness" was a relation or a function. The word was still used in the psychological laboratory under Münsterberg, but it was more precise to speak of "attention," as being verifiable in the laboratory, and James had already said before 1890 that consciousness was equivalent to attention, or vice versa.

But for creative purposes the difference was that instead of the substantives, thought and thinker, there was now the gerund or participle: thinking. Gertrude Stein was by nature passionately given to the intellect, but all was not lost in losing the final reality of the thought and thinker. As a tough and healthy mind she could be just as ferociously excited if not more so by thinking. After all, the ways of thinking were as real as the forms of thought. The vital consequence of this new position for literature was that the consciousness was no longer a receptacle with one or many contemplated things with their qualities sitting in it at a time; the consciousness was now an activity going on. Relations were more important to it, more essential, now, than substantives. Already in his *Psychology* James had made the distinction between substantive thoughts and transitional thoughts, and declared it should be recognized that we have a definite feeling of "if" and of "and" and of "but" and of "whether," and Gertrude Stein later gave such words all their importance, but they get all their importance from the conception of consciousness as thinking in relation.

Whether or not the idea became perfectly disengaged at Radcliffe at that time in the thick of the crisis, the idea that present thinking is the final reality was to be the axis or pole of Gertrude Stein's universe, and her work from the beginning was oriented and reoriented upon that idea.

Such a persuasion is neither validated nor invalidated by what happens to fashions in philosophy or psychology. If structuralism gives way to functionalism and functionalism gives way to behaviorism and so on, it curiously makes no difference. As with the theory of humors to the Elizabethans, any philosophical or scientific theory is to an artist a working articulation of the universe, a language or an alphabet, with which to express experience. Everything depends on the eloquence, completeness, and exactitude with which the living experience is expressed by the language used. Oddly enough when theories perish as truth or as accomplishments, they often survive as a language in the arts. The only important thing for literature is whether the theory used as a language is going to look in the future like a dialect or like a diction.

At all events, the terms and objects of present thinking in average passive attention — receptivity — are, manifestly, colored by memory and anticipation and elaborate preconception, all of which makes for a general diffusion and dimness. Art can either clarify this penumbra or periphery — as Proust did — or suppress it. It is true that art can also exploit it, but such an art is journalism or one of romantic suggestion or belongs to a closed culture where the suggestions can be complete and definite.

The means of suppression or suspension are mainly a sharpening of the focus on the present, the disconnection of the object from causality and purpose. For all the Teutonic enthusiasm of his little book, *Principles of Art Education*, Münsterberg makes this function of art fairly clear. While uttering the general proposition that science is connection and art is isolation, he exhorts the public as follows: ". . . let us only once give our whole attention to that one courageous, breezy wave, which thunders there against the rock; let us forget what there was and what there will be; let us live through one pulsebeat of experience in listening merely to that wave alone, seeing its foam alone, tasting its breeze alone, — and in that one thrill we have grasped the thing itself as it really is in its fullest truth."[4]

Gertrude Stein gradually succeeded in disengaging not only substantives like waves but the relations of thinking from their scientific and pragmatical penumbra and did, later, in *The Making of Americans*, reach her element, the continuous present.

It is an interesting if idle question how it happened that she took this rather disconnected and disembodied passing thought or present thinking as hers. No doubt part of it was the intense interiority of her adolescence from which she had barely emerged on coming to Radcliffe, and part of it surely was her Jewish gift of extreme attention to abstractions. That she was personally disconnected from any native or local context is again partly a Jewish situation and partly the accident of being born in Pennsylvania, traveling in France and Austria, and living in California and Baltimore, all before turning up for college work at Radcliffe, in the deliquescence of New England and the Puritan tradition. This multiplied delocalization was not yet, I believe, the average American personal situation.

Another circumstance that could easily have inclined her to feeling the reality of such an orientation upon the exclusive present was her habit at Radcliffe of going to the opera, in the afternoon and at night. The opera as a form tends to be complete at every instant, it is in constant present activity, and it is of little or no interest what the reasons for it all are or how it will all come out. In any event Gertrude Stein kept an affection for the opera as a form and wrote a good many operas or librettos later on. She said that music was for adolescents and this could easily have been true of the music of her adolescence as performed in Boston and in late Wagner, but at least the principle of the continuous present was more or less already there in the opera form. In actual opera it was rather the prolonged present, and indeed the prolonged present was the time of her first literary work, *Three Lives*.

***

With the literary production of the time she had almost no direct connection. Swinburne and Meredith were endlessly rarefying and elaborating any casual theme and Pater had invented the hard gemlike flame, but none of it was anything radically to start from. It is very strange that when she could have started so well from Henry James she did not. Henry James had already made of his work a time continuum less of external events or things than of intellect in constant activity upon their meaning. He recognized Proust as having done very much the sort of thing that he himself was trying to do, but there is a difference. Where Proust expands by more and more particular context and elaborating more and more tenuous relationships within a universe of concrete and sensuous experience, James tended to schematize the exterior and the sensuous to mere melodrama, a mere frame or boogiewoogie bass for the real rich drama which was for him that of ethical dubiety, the considerations of terribly conscious persons.

This disembodiedness, this discontextuated activity is by no means a peculiarity of Henry James and Gertrude Stein. Its beginning may well be colonial Puritanism, in which there is little enough interest and no excitement but the interior struggle of the soul with sin. Transcendentalism and Hawthorne, Melville, Thoreau, Emerson, and even Henry Adams are all variously part of the same thing; but the pragmatic and effective suppression of the objective context, the disengagement of a single simple theme or motion, is more immediately illustrated at the end of the 19th century in America by the complete development of endless straight railroads with trestles and tunnels, by the beginning of the skyscraper, the automobile and the airplane. This peculiar American pleasure in continuous, even, present movement in less and less context did not on the whole extend to literature, not for the general public who enjoyed automobiles, western movies, airplanes, and endless aimless travel very much.

If this disengaged present thinking had these approximations in the past and these parallels in the physical world, thus coming rather naturally, how was it related to the whole person doing it, to time, to its objects and terms both interior and exterior, and so forth?

There was naturally the animal or living creature doing the thinking, and the vitality of thinking was continuous with the vitality of the person. That is to say the thinking was alive, not in a religious but in a biological way. William James talks of pulses of consciousness as Münsterberg does of pulse beats of experience. Gertrude Stein in her independent experiments on attention and fatigue in Harvard and Radcliffe students concluded that habits of attention are reflexes of the complete character of the individual. The phrase "habits of attention" is clinical for "ways of thinking."

While thinking is alive as a function of the whole creature, the whole creature is not an activity but a substantive structure. It is thought of as a complete present fact, biologically or medically, and so perfectly classifiable as a type. It is called a character, not with ethical connotations particularly, but as a shape or consistency, as definite as the ossature of a fish or a horse. Gertrude Stein made charts of the human types she described in *The Making of Americans*. If people change it is very little if at all within their lives, but by the generation or the century. Within the single individual the diffusion or concentration, the gentleness or toughness, the ways of attack or defense or dependency, of desire or strength or cowardice, do not essentially vary. In short the whole composition of the character can really be present in any moment, in the continuous present, and not as a thing remembered, not as an accumulation of personal history.

If the character does not change, if its interior and exterior history has no important influence upon it, and if it is the definition and description of types of characters and the demonstration of these types that interest the writer, the problem is one of projecting character in time without a sequence of events and all the context of irrelevant accidents. This leads naturally to repetition, the constantly new assertion and realization of the same simple thing, an existence with its typical qualities, not an event. As actually that is, on this view, what the character does, constantly asserting and insisting on its same existence from moment to moment and from day to day, the repetitions in *The Making of Americans* are an accurate expression of it.

It all differs very much from Proust, whose characters are protean and live in a perpetual metamorphosis, a sort of creative evolution, not only as families or genera but as individuals. Proust comes partly out of Bergson and impressionism, partly out of Chateaubriand and de Nerval, and ultimately out of the late classical tradition of Ovid and Apuleius. It is really extraordinary that the exotic Proustian character, "a giant in Time," saturated with incident and surrounded by depths of meaning and association, should have been perfectly convincing to educated Americans, and that *The Making of Americans*, written so rigorously on our own principles, should seem exotic and outrageous. But the educated American would still rather visit the Cloisters than the Pentagon building, which after all is to us as the Escorial is to the Spanish or Versailles to the French.

The full demonstration of the persistence, not the development, of the whole living personality through time came with *The Making of Americans* and the early portraits, but the project is already very much begun in *Three Lives*. She began writing *Three Lives* while translating the *Trois Contes* of Flaubert and while constantly looking at a portrait of a woman by Cézanne. The implications here are nearly inexhaustible, but for the moment it can be said that the difference between Gertrude Stein and Proust is the difference between Cézanne and the impressionists. The complexities of accident, light, and circumstance are reduced to a simple geometrical structure, a final existence addressed to the mind. It is tempting to take this situation also as accounting for Proust's dislike of Flaubert who in the previous century had reduced Chateaubriand to a steady present reality, but that is not my subject. Still, there is a phrase in Gertrude Stein's portrait of Cézanne, that he was "settled to stay,"[5] which expresses where she and Cézanne and Flaubert were in time, and what Proust and the impressionists and Chateaubriand were not. They were something else, with the loveliness and elegance and brilliance of being provisory, of transience, but very different.

If thinking is alive and final and continuous with the whole creature, what are its basic ways of doing? Gertrude Stein said she always had an impulse for elemental abstraction, and the primary terms of present thinking are the foundation of all her work. Whether they are to be taken as ideal existences or as procedures of thinking or as objects of thinking, they are absolutely valid so far as any human thinking goes. If Plato makes the Same and the Other objective elements in the universe, and if James talks about the feeling of sameness and the feeling of difference as events in the mind, identity and difference are for human purposes final. Relations like *if* and *and*, *in* and *out*, *up* and *down*, *left* and *right*, and so forth are final intellectual constructions. It is to them and the like that all sensations and complexities must be referred for meaning to the mind. They may involve emotion, in the sense of muscular disposition, but that is another question. They belong to the mind, as music belongs to the ear before it belongs to the possibly dancing body.

This looks perfectly natural and simple but its meaning for literary composition is a little more complicated. Most literature does not address itself directly to the final terms of present thinking but to the vague memory of complex unresolved situations and the provisory attitudes taken toward them. In short, most literature is based on sympathetic reminiscent emotion, or if you like upon anxiety, and not upon completely present disengaged thinking. This makes a difference for example between classicism and romanticism, between Mozart and Wagner, and a difference between what Gertrude Stein later called human nature and the human mind.

Notes

1. "Normal Motor Automatism," *Psychological Review*, III (1896), No. 5, 511. By permission of the American Psychological Association, Inc.

2. "Normal Motor Automatism," *loc. cit.*, p. 506.

3. In *Everybody's Autobiography* (Random House, 1937) Gertrude Stein says (p. 266) that Solomons did the reporting of these experiments, and she, being younger and docile, just

agreed, though she did not really think the writing was automatic. "We always knew what we were doing." It is difficult to say anything about it now, but most likely the distraction of attention did help at least to destroy any awareness of complexes of reference beyond the words written, and allowed the words to be treated as objects and entities rather than as signs or symbols of something else. This may have been the beginning of a word sense that became dominant in her writing much later, in 1911.

4. *Principles of Art Education* (Prang Educational Company, 1904), p. 23.

5. *Portraits and Prayers* (Random House, 1934), p. 11.

The Quality of Gertrude Stein's Creativity
Allegra Stewart*

On the basis of her first short stories in *Three Lives* and her long novel, *The Making of Americans*, Gertrude Stein has often been classified as a writer of fiction, perhaps because the great body of her work is so difficult to classify in any way at all. Since 1914, however, when she published *Tender Buttons*, most of her writing defies classification under the familiar categories of literature, although she made a few sallies into autobiography, fiction, and the essay. Her publications, to be sure, can be discriminated as poetry and prose, but she herself discarded the distinction as irrelevant. She called her psychological word-paintings of personalities and objects "portraits," and her descriptions of things moving in space (landscapes and scenes) she called "plays" and "operas." But her compositions in these literary genera are the very reverse of what one would expect, because she was always "in" her own consciousness, attempting to put into words, regardless of their associational meanings, the union of two inner realities (those of subject and object) or the marriage of outer and inner realities as it took place in presentational immediacy:

> When I see a thing it is not a play to me because the minute I see it it ceases to be a play for me, but when I write something that somebody else can see then it is a play for me. When I write other things not plays it is something that I can see and seeing it is inside of me but when I write a play then it is something that is inside of me but if I could see it then it would not be.[1]

Thus her "portraits" really leave out what everyone else can see,[2] and her "plays" make visible what nobody else can see. The portraits objectify the personality or essential nature of people and things as distilled in the alembic of Gertrude Stein's consciousness, while the plays objectify her

*Excerpted from *American Literature* 28, no. 3 (1957): 488–96. © 1957, Duke University Press.

imaginative ideas and constructions, excited by the motion and arrangement of objects in space. The portraits are impressionistic, the plays, expressionistic. Or, to put it another way, the portraits reflect her receptivity to the substantial, whereas her plays reflect the "play" of her mind with the purely phenomenal. She subjectifies the world in portraits and and objectifies the contents of her consciousness in plays.

This *bouleversement* of the portrait and the play is all of a piece with her deliberate efforts to destroy the associational meanings of words in order to express pure quality apart from the forms which carry it. Her first portraits, written in 1909, represent an abrupt break with all forms of discursive writing, and with all the conventional symbolisms of language. From the point of view of contemporary literature, her compositions were part of a general revolt against surface realism and the constricting effects upon the imagination of scientific and historical data; and her rejection of conventional plot and chronological narrative was part of the general effort to restore to reality that inwardness which had been lost to life and literature in the general materialism of thought and life in our time.

In the twentieth century, organization and mechanization have supplanted both the rationalism of the enlightenment and the extreme individualism of the romantic period, with the result that society tends to be collectivized and depersonalized and the individual lost in the statistical table of averages. To all these forces Gertrude Stein's work (like that of many of her contemporaries) paradoxically opposed an irrationalism and an impersonalism of an entirely different kind. Inevitably her writing appeared to be part of a cult of unintelligibility, or a manifestation of a new barbarism. For in a period when there seemed to be nothing that had not been explained or that could not be understood, and among sophisticates who "knew" everything and believed nothing, she was seeking to recover mystery, and to reawaken wonder.

After 1909, this affirmative effort of hers consisted chiefly of recording the motions of her own mind. Writing became for her an exercise (or ritual) in concentration, for the act of concentrating one's attention liberates consciousness from every necessity except its own autonomous activity. But the struggle for such freedom imposed upon her a stern *asceis*, requiring as it did the perception and then the verbal expression of her own inner motions, stripped of everything but presentational immediacy. Such introversion differs radically, of course, from the introspection associated with anxiety or other neurotic maladjustments.

In seeking such interior freedom, Gertrude Stein suppressed all subject matter as such in behalf of this on-going inner movement, which she tried to express without interposing any conscious purpose between her mind and its object, excluding both memory and conceptual forms. Unlike the chronological time of history and nature, the interior time of consciousness — duration, as Bergson called it — is always present time. It is in the present moment that the mind is free to act creatively and to "make" out of the "given" subject matter new objects that have no casual connections with the course of events in the external world. Gertrude Stein attempted in many different ways to record the time of duration in herself and in others as always the same, yet always different — the same because it is always present, different because it is filled with the fleeting stream of its own contents and the flux of things in chronological time. "Content without form," she was fond of saying, meaning that structures and forms should not be permitted to tyrannize over direct experience — that they are less important than the quality of life by which the forms themselves are actually distinguished.

As the activity of the individual soul alone with its "object," writing affirms the freedom and autonomy of man amid the flux of things and the determinations of space and time. Writing is "sacred," and Gertrude Stein often warned writers against trying to serve two masters, "god and mammon":

> When I say god and mammon concerning the writer writing, I mean that any one can use words to say something. And in using these words to say what he has to say he may use words directly or indirectly. If he uses these words indirectly he says what he intends to have heard by somebody who is to hear and in so doing inevitably he has to serve mammon. Mammon may be a success, mammon may be an effort he is to produce, mammon may be a pleasure he has from hearing what he himself has done, mammon may be his way of explaining, mammon may be a laziness that needs nothing but going on, in short mammon may be anything done indirectly. Now serving god for a writer who is writing is writing anything directly, it makes no difference what it is but it must be direct, the relation between the thing done and the doer must be direct.[3]

In her own struggle for directness, Gertrude Stein strained words and exerted pressure upon them, and renounced "names" (nouns), and dissected grammar. Whatever she concentrated her attention upon became isolated from all the relations in which it stood to other things. A thing-in-itself with its own existence, *sui generis*, the object entered into a process of reciprocal excitement with a knowing consciousness and became open on all sides to the understanding in contact with it. The intellectual perception of sheer existence is an act of ingatheredness, or recollection, in which the knower feels outside of time and freed from the demands of the ego. He becomes a spiritual entity whose only action is the incarnation of what it knows in the word. This, Gertrude Stein believed, is the final creative act, the mystery in which knower and known are joined in unity.

To eternize in this way a fleeting moment of life is to create a new value from what would otherwise have been carried along in the temporal flux to oblivion. Such a value need never have been realized even fleetingly, of course, because there is no necessary relation between knower and known. The conjunction between them is accidental and contingent, but the act of realization is an exchange between two finalities of experience, and no matter how trivial the object may seem to be in terms of the world's work the value of the interchange is infinite. The product of exchange serves no purpose beyond itself; its measure is devotion rather than use. In Gertrude Stein's vocabulary it is variously called a "hymn," a "prayer," a "song," a "meditation," a "master-piece" of human experience — given an immortality beyond the life of both the knowing subject and the known object, in an object totally new.

Thus Gertrude Stein could write with words "together" and "apart," dedicated to the task of resurrecting them from the smooth, dead phrases of descriptive science, surface realism, factual narrative, and philosophical abstraction: "I have of course always been struggling with this thing, to say what you nor I nor nobody knows, but what is really what you and I and everybody knows."[4] To restore to the imagination the living word, to bring back an interest in man as man, to revive an interest in the normal and the ordinary — in what everybody knows and nobody knows — such was the task she undertook. It required drastic renunciations and ascetic intellectual discipline, and it involved not being understood as well as being misunderstood.

If writing is a sacred activity, a hymn or a prayer, then the traditional classifications of literature are irrelevant. It does not matter very much what Gertrude Stein called her compositions, not only because she was not concerned with forms, but because, no matter what she wrote, it was a "piece" of an integrated consciousness, a work of the human mind absorbed in knowing. As Hegel said, the "well-known," the familiar, is never intelligibly known, since acquired knowledge is formal and not contentual.[5] Gertrude Stein had set herself the goal of discovering what knowing is, and therefore she directed her knowing against this "being-familiar" and "being well-known." In *The Geographical History of America* she maintained that hers were ordinary ideas: "That is what I mean to be I mean to be the one who can and does have as ordinary ideas as these."[6]

Whitehead once remarked that "it requires an unusual mind to undertake the analysis of the obvious. Familiar things happen, and mankind does not bother about them."[7] Gertrude Stein's analysis of the obvious, however, confronts the given in ordinary human experience with full awareness of its mystery. She raises questions as to the nature of perception, the meaning of being, the boundlessness of space and the roundness of the world, the passage of time and the nature of personality and identity, and the activities of genius. To contemplate the obvious is to confront the polarities in the universe and the contradictions in man. It is to become aware of the dualism which runs through all things.

Meditation upon these subjects has been the exercise of reflective minds in all ages, but it has been considered the work of philosophers and religious thinkers rather than of creative writers. There is a vast body of writing, however, which, while differing radically in form and content, is unclassifiable except as "meditation." Of this class are Cicero's *De Officiis*, Erasmus's *Moriae Encomium*, Pascal's *Pensées*, Traherne's *Century of Meditations*, and — to mention a sensitive modern thinker — Gabriel Marcel's *Mystery of Being*. One might say, too, that the quality of the best poetry of Wordsworth, of Yeats, and of T. S. Eliot is meditative, and that the novels of Kafka, Mann, Joyce, Hesse, and Proust are fictionalized meditations. The emergence of the meditative element in modern poetry and fiction is correlative with the secular movement in the western world, but the lyrical element itself is reflective and one need only recall such elegiac pieces as "Night Thoughts" or *The Anatomy of Melancholy* to recognize the diverse forms in which meditation upon "first and last things" has been the "object" of the writing. Hegel's *Phenomenology* and Emerson's essay on *Nature* are brought together under this mode of classification. In fact, all distinctions of form are dissolved in the masterpieces of literature, if the "object" is viewed in terms of content and not in terms of form. The actual subject matter and the personality of the mind that reflects upon it survive in the written word, stripped of all that is accidental and changing, and the written word itself becomes a "moving" power, a dynamic and living entity.

The meditative element became dominant in the writings of Gertrude Stein when she began to write portraits — in other words, at the time when she ceased to worry about communication and emphasized communion. During the writing of *The Geographical History of America*, she was concerned primarily with being, not with time and change. From *Tender Buttons* on, however, all her work is a kind of communion. She detached herself from "mechanical civilizations and the world being round,"[8] convinced that the dialectical process in time leads only from one pole to another — from communism to individualism and back again in a never-ending cycle, in which the individual is always lost in the collective or the solipsistic. The union of opposites is a creative act, but that action itself can never become the object of knowledge. To perform the act is to assert man's freedom from every necessity except that of existence itself. "The only interesting thing is that no one knows the limits of the universe," she said.[9] "You live on this earth and you cannot get away from it and yet there is a space where the stars are which is unlimited and that contradiction is there in every man and every woman and so nothing is ever settled."[10]

Like space, knowledge is infinite, but actual knowing is an individuated process within a finite world where all things change. In view of the contradiction between finite and infinite and in view of the fact that all living creatures die, the important thing is to affirm this life by living it in full consciousness — that is, by living in the present. But it is very difficult to live in the present consciously. "Somebody has to have an individual feeling";[11] "any time is the time to make a poem. The snow and the sun below";[12] but the weight of the past and the hope for, or fear of, the future prevent most people from really living in the present. "Being men is a very difficult thing to be,"[13] for the primary fact is that time passes. "After all that is what life is and that is the reason there is no Utopia."[14] Human institutions are not static and will never become so. All forms of action upon the world must consume themselves in the process except the immediate knowing of the present, but it is just as well that most people are so engaged in the struggle for existence, so occupied by the mere business of living, that they do not have time to dwell upon the mystery of existence. For they do not have the vitality to concentrate upon the present: "you have to be a genius to live in it and to exist in it and express it to accept it and deny it by creating it. . . ."[15]

Life is mysterious and can never be understood. "The only thing that anybody can understand is mechanics,"[16] but machines are neither interesting nor essential: "you cannot exist without living and living is something that nobody is able to understand while you can exist without machines it has been done but machines cannot exist without you. . . ."[17]

The modern world, overmechanized and overorganized, is an empty world, a world in which few have an individual feeling, because it has lost the sense of strangeness and mystery. To restore to it the feeling of life, writers must achieve a direct vision of the world. The novel, for example, is a dead form, because people have lost their belief in the reality of fictional characters. "I tell all the young ones now to write essays, after all since characters are of no importance why not just write meditations, meditations are always interesting, neither character nor identity are necessary to him who meditates."[18]

For Gertrude Stein, meditation is more than reflection: it is communion, participation — an act of presence. Direct, immediate — it is the only way to master the contradictions and oppositions of discursive thinking and experience and to give a content to the "now." Only through participation will the word have life, and only through the written word can life be immortalized. The written word is the one medium in which all mediation disappears. Words on the written page bear no resemblance to the things they signify, and they are therefore entirely closed to sense perception and open immediately to the inward eye. Through written words one can commune in silence across space and time by signs which in themselves need make no appeal to the senses. All other forms of expression create an object with extension in space or time that is a necessary part of them; they are bound by one or the other and therefore appeal to eye or ear. Thus, paradoxically, the written word is the most immediate of all the modes of expression. In it the writer is disembodied but enduring. "Mention me if you can," Gertrude Stein said, "because I am here."[19] She also said, "How can a language alter. It does not it is an altar."[20]

In contrast to the written word, the spoken word is mediated both by the voice and by the physical presence of the speaker. Gertrude Stein found lecturing difficult because it brought her into contact with an audience, and so she sought to isolate herself in every way possible in order that communication should not interfere with communion. When a writer is writing, "that physical something by existing does not connect him with anything but concentrates him on recognition,"[21] whereas when he is addressing, or writing for, an audience, that physical something diverts his energies and deprives his words of authenticity. Only in so far as the consciousness is concentrated upon its object — is really present to it — can there be anything created. "By written I mean made. And by made I mean felt,"[22] she said, and over and over again she defined the genius as the one who talks and listens at the same time. "One may really indeed say that that is the essence of genius, of being most intensely alive, that is being one who is at the same time talking and listening. . . ."[23] Talking and listening are not consecutive acts: they occur simultaneously in concentration, "The two in one and the one in two,"[24] "like the motor going inside the car and the car moving, they are part of the same thing."[25]

In the act of presence, by which the dualism of experience is overcome here and now, an exchange occurs, in which the objects of contemplative perception and knowing become mental phenomena. Knower and known are joined in an object — the masterpiece — through which they become intelligible to our intuition and feeling, but not to our reason. The transaction occurs in time, but it is not a time-process, and the masterpiece itself has a life beyond life. It "does nothing." Though it can be destroyed, it cannot be used. Since creative writers are contemporaries in the "continuous now," the loss of a masterpiece does not really matter because it would remain the possession of those who had known it and no one else would miss it.

The number of masterpieces is of no importance, and no one of them has any necessity either to be or not to be. They are the gratuitous acts of "presence" itself, and the witnesses to man's freedom in this world. Through them the world-and-life-negation fostered by the thought of death is overcome and the contents of time rescued from the flux. Writing thus becomes ritual, in which the writer affirms himself as one who continues to exist after his death as long as he has readers — indeed, even if he has no readers.

Notes

1. *Everybody's Autobiography* (New York, 1937), p. 193.
2. Cf. *ibid.*, p. 88, for one of her many explanations of her portrait-writing.
3. *Lectures in America* (New York, 1935), pp. 23–24.
4. *Ibid.*, p. 121.
5. *Phenomenology of Mind*, tr. J. B. Baillie (New York, 1910), I, 27–29.
6. *The Geographical History of Ameica* (New York, 1936), p. 21.
7. *Science and the Modern World* (New York, 1948), p. 5.

8. *Everybody's Autobiography*, p. 122.

9. *Ibid.*, p. 123.

10. *Ibid.*, p. 308.

11. *Ibid.*, p. 249.

12. *Ibid.*, p. 148.

13. *Ibid.*, p. 12.

14. *Ibid.*, p. 281.

15. *Ibid.*, p. 281.

16. *Ibid.*, p. 290.

17. *Ibid.*, p. 290.

18. *Ibid.*, p. 102.

19. *The Geographical History of America*, p. 155. Whitehead said (*Modes of Thought*, New York, 1938, p. 139): "We rarely mention what must be present. We do mention what might be absent."

20. *Useful Knowledge* (New York, 1928), p. 108.

21. *Narration* (Chicago, 1935), Lecture 4, p. 56.

22. *Lectures in America*, p. 165.

23. *Ibid.*, p. 170.

24. *Ibid.*, p. 180.

25. *Ibid.*, p. 170.

The Impossible
John Ashbery*

This is the latest volume in the series of the unpublished writings of Gertrude Stein which the Yale University Press has been bringing out regularly for the last decade. It will probably please readers who are satisfied only by literary extremes, but who have not previously taken to Miss Stein because of a kind of lack of seriousness in her work, characterized by lapses into dull, facile rhyme; by the over-employment of rhythms suggesting a child's incantation against grownups; and by monotony. There is certainly plenty of monotony in the 150-page title poem which forms the first half of this volume, but it is the fertile kind, which generates excitement as water monotonously flowing over a dam generates electrical power. These austere "stanzas" are made up almost entirely of colorless connecting words such as "where," "which," "these," "of," "not," "have," "about," and so on, though now and then Miss Stein throws in an orange, a lilac, or an Albert to remind us that it really is the world, our world, that she has been talking about. The result is like certain monochrome de Kooning paintings in which isolated strokes of color take on a deliciousness they never could have had out of context, or a piece of music by Webern in which a single note on the celesta suddenly irrigates a whole desert of dry, scratchy sounds in the strings.

*Reprinted from *Poetry* 90, no. 4 (July 1957): 250–54.

Perhaps the word that occurs oftenest in the Stanzas is the word "they," for this is a poem about the world, about "them." (What a pleasant change from the eternal "we" with which so many modern poets automatically begin each sentence, and which gives the impression that the author is sharing his every sensation with some invisible Kim Novak.) Less frequently, "I" enters to assess the activities of "them," to pick up after them, to assert his own altered importance. As we get deeper into the poem, it seems not so much as if we were reading as living a rather long period of our lives with a houseful of people. Like people, Miss Stein's lines are comforting or annoying or brilliant or tedious. Like people, they sometimes make no sense and sometimes make perfect sense; or they stop short in the middle of a sentence and wander away, leaving us alone for awhile in the physical world, that collection of thoughts, flowers, weather, and proper names. And, just as with people, there is no real escape from them: one feels that if one were to close the book one would shortly re-encounter the Stanzas in life, under another guise. As the author says, "It is easily eaten hot and lukewarm and cold / But not without it."

Stanzas in Meditation gives one the feeling of time passing, of things happening, of a "plot," though it would be difficult to say precisely what is going on. Sometimes the story has the logic of a dream:

> She asked could I be taught to be allowed
> And I said yes oh yes I had forgotten him
> And she said does any or do any change
> And if not I said whom could they count.

while at other times it becomes startlingly clear for a moment, as though a change in the wind had suddenly enabled us to hear a conversation that was taking place some distance away:

> He came early in the morning.
> He thought they needed comfort
> Which they did
> And he gave them an assurance
> That it would be all as well
> As indeed were it
> Not to have it needed at any time

But it is usually not events which interest Miss Stein, rather it is their "way of happening," and the story of *Stanzas in Meditation* is a general, all-purpose model which each reader can adapt to fit his own set of particulars. The poem is a hymn to possibility; a celebration of the fact that the world exists, that things can happen.

In its profound originality, its original profundity, this poem that is always threatening to become a novel reminds us of the late novels of James, especially *The Golden Bowl* and *The Sacred Fount*, which seem to strain with a superhuman force toward "the condition of music," of poetry. In such a passage as the following, for instance:

> Be not only without in any of their sense
> Careful
> Or should they grow careless with remonstrance
> Or be careful just as easily not at all
> As when they felt.
> They could or would would they grow always
> By which not only as more as they like.
> They cannot please conceal
> Nor need they find they need a wish

we are not far from Charlotte's and the Prince's rationalizations. Both *Stanzas in Meditation* and *The Golden Bowl* are ambitious attempts to transmit a completely new picture of reality, of that *real* reality of the poet which Antonin Artaud called *"une réalité dangereuse et typique."* If these works are highly complex and, for some, unreadable, it is not only because of the complicatedness of life, the subject, but also because they actually imitate its rhythm, its way of happening, in an attempt to draw our attention to another aspect of its true nature. Just as life is being constantly altered by each breath one draws, just as each second of life seems to alter the whole of what has gone before, so the endless process of elaboration which gives the work of these two writers a texture of bewildering luxuriance — that of a tropical rain-forest of ideas — seems to obey some rhythmic impulse at the heart of all happening.

In addition, the almost physical pain with which we strive to accompany the evolving thought of one of James's or Gertrude Stein's characters is perhaps a counterpart of the painful continual projection of the individual into life. As in life, perseverance has its rewards — moments when we emerge suddenly on a high plateau with a view of the whole distance we have come. In Miss Stein's work the sudden inrush of clarity is likely to be an aesthetic experience, but (and this seems to be another of her "points") the description of that experience applies also to "real-life" situations, the aesthetic problem being a microcosm of all human problems.

> I should think it makes no difference
> That so few people are me.
> That is to say in each generation there are so few geniuses
>
> And why should I be one which I am
> This is one way of saying how do you do
> There is this difference
> I forgive you everything and there is nothing to forgive.

It is for moments like this that one perseveres in this difficult poem, moments which would be less beautiful and meaningful if the rest did not exist, for we have fought side by side with the author in her struggle to achieve them.

The poems in the second half of the book are almost all charming, though lacking the profundity of *Stanzas in Meditation*. Perhaps the most successful is *Winning His Way*, again a picture of a human community: "The friendship between Lolo and every one was very strong / And they were careful to do him no wrong." The bright, clean colors and large cast of characters in this poem suggests a comic strip. In fact one might say that Miss Stein discovered a means of communication as well-suited to express our age as in their own way, the balloons (with their effect of concentration), light bulbs, asterisks, ringed planets, and exclamation marks which comic-strip characters use to communicate their ideas. In *Winning His Way*, for example, she experiments with punctuation by placing periods in the middle of sentences. This results in a strange syncopation which affects the meaning as well as the rhythm of a line. In the couplet

> Herman states.
> That he is very well.

the reader at first imagines that she is talking about a group of states ruled over by a potentate named Herman; when he comes to the second line he is forced to change his idea, but its ghost remains, giving a muted quality to the prose sense of the words.

Donald Sutherland, who has supplied the introduction for this book, has elsewhere quoted Miss Stein as saying, "If it can be done why do it?" *Stanzas in Meditation* is no doubt the most successful of her attempts to do what can't be done, to create a counterfeit of reality more real than reality. And if, on laying the book aside, we feel that it is still impossible to accomplish the impossible, we are also left with the conviction that it is the only thing worth trying to do.

An Evaluation
B. L. Reid*

It would be a great deal easier to measure Gertrude Stein if she would let us alone. It would be much easier if she would let us weigh her as a minor writer rather than a major one, or as a scientist-philosopher rather than a creative artist, or as a follower of a bypath rather than of the highroad of literature. I am suggesting, obviously, that these alternatives seem to be the essential truths about her, but she will have none of them. The critic has to cut his way through a jungle of Miss Stein's ponderous pronouncements on the subject of herself, backed by all the weight of her full assurance and supported in some degree by the evidences of her

*Reprinted from *Art by Subtraction: A Dissenting Opinion of Gertrude Stein* (Norman: University of Oklahoma Press, 1958), 168–73. © 1958 by the University of Oklahoma Press.

wholly real independence and intelligence and the acclamation of eloquent and respectable friends.

Gertrude Stein's ego is one of the great egos of all time. It is monumental; it is heroic. Flat assertion of her own genius is a leitmotiv in virtually all her books. "Think of the Bible and Homer think of Shakespeare and think of me,"[1] she says; "I am one of the masters of English prose";[2] "In this epoch the only real literary thinking has been done by a woman";[3] "in english literature in her time she is the only one";[4] "I know that I am the most important writer writing today";[5] "I have been the creative literary mind of the century."[6] She makes Miss Toklas say: "The three geniuses of whom I wish to speak are Gertrude Stein, Pablo Picasso and Alfred Whitehead. . . . I have known only three first class geniuses and in each case on sight within me something rang."[7]

I am inclined to think she gave Miss Toklas only a two-thirds chance of being right. Of course, Gertrude Stein became accustomed to the kind of carping insensitivity I am according her here, and she took it as one of the unavoidable tribulations attendant on genius. "Naturally I have my detractors," she said to Wombley Bald. "What genius does not?"[8] It may be true indeed that Miss Stein needs to be seen as a genius to be seen at all. That is, we evaluate her as a being essentially not measurable at all, as apart, unique. When we try to fit her into a context involving normality or moderate supranormality, she does not fit; there is no common yardstick; the scales refuse to function. Perhaps we must agree with Julian Sawyer's judgment of her "absolute perspicacity." If she has that, she is beyond us; we cannot know her — and the critic's job is simplified into one of awe.

If Gertrude Stein is a genius, she is one in the vulgar sense of the term: perversely elevated, isolated, inhuman. Hers is not the friendly, communicative genius of her masters, James and Whitehead, or even Picasso, pulling us gently or roughly up to the heights of their new insight. She is a genius with a tragic flaw, one curiously like the old flaw of Oedipus and Lear — the fatal combination of pride and power and blindness. We must say this with the full knowledge that Gertrude Stein seemed all her life to be trying to communicate to us, that she worked with sweat and occasional humility to make us know her mind. That, however, is her colossal blindness and her arrogance; convinced of the absolute rightness of her vision and of her literary record of that insight, she refused all moderation or compromise.

It seems to me that Miss Stein is a vulgar genius talking to herself, and if she is talking to herself, she is not an artist. It is because she does talk to herself that she offers insuperable difficulties to both reader and critic. I suggest, therefore, that she be defined out of existence as an artist. To be an artist, she must talk to us, not to the dullest or the most tradition bound or the most unsympathetic of us, but to those of us who are flexible, those

willing to be fruitfully led. There is not world enough or time enough for
Gertrude Stein's kind of writing; too much in literature is both excellent
and knowable.

What I am trying to say is that most of the confusion about Gertrude
Stein seems the result of trying to understand her in a mistaken context.
The original mistake is Miss Stein's; it happened when she defined herself
as an artist, thereby obscuring from herself and her readers the fact that
both her ends and her means pointed toward philosophy by way of
science. The whole cast and capability of her mind was scientific,
reflective, rational, philosophic. Of the truly creative ability to fabricate
and counterfeit, to excite and to move and to instruct by fact or fiction
conceived as dramatic, narrative, or lyric, she had only a rudimentary
portion, and this she studiously suppressed until it was very nearly dead.
Her works are not, properly speaking, art at all. Her aim was to "describe
reality," but description alone is not art but science. In her aesthetics she
reflects on reality as well, and it becomes philosophy.

Her "art" is one of subtraction and narrowing throughout. In her art
she does not reflect, for reflection entails consciousness of identity and
audience, an awareness fatal to the creative vision. She rules out the
imagination because it is the hunting ground of secondary talent. She rules
out logical, cause-effect relations: "Question and answer make you know
time is existing." She rules out distinctions of right and wrong: "Write and
right. Of course they have nothing to do with one another." She will have
no distinctions of true and false: "The human mind is not concerned with
being or not being true." She abjures beauty, emotion, association,
analogy, illustration, metaphor. Art by subtraction finally subtracts art
itself. What remains as the manner and matter of the specifically "creative" works of Gertrude Stein is the artist and an object vis-à-vis. This is
not art; this is science. Miss Stein would turn the artist into a recording
mechanism, a camera that somehow utters words rather than pictures.

It is vastly ironic that in a century in which the arts have been in pell-
mell flight from the camera, she, who thought herself always galloping in
the van of "contemporaneousness," has fled toward the camera. That hers
is an eccentric camera, a literal camera obscura, does not make it less a
camera. That in her early writing she was interested in what was under
the surface, in the "inside," does not make her less a photographer. There
she may be operating an X ray, but even its function is to take the picture,
not to comment upon it, clothe it, or give it life in beauty or ugliness. Hers
is still the "intellectual passion for exactitude in description."

Gertrude Stein's mistake, one must think, lies in conceiving as a
sufficient ideal the thing William James handed her as a tool, the tool of
rigidly objective scientific observation. She was conscious of this orientation toward science to some degree at one point in her work, *The Making
of Americans*; after that she thought she had lost it and embarked upon a

purely creative tack. But it seems that she never truly lost the scientific point of view. Whatever her subject, her "art" remained, within its idiosyncrasy, photographic in intention and in method.

Notes

1. Stein, *The Geographical History of America*, 81.
2. Stein, *Everybody's Autobiography*, 114.
3. Stein, *The Geographical History of America*, 182.
4. Stein, *The Autobiography of Alice B. Toklas*, 64.
5. Stein, *Everybody's Autobiography*, 28.
6. *Ibid.*, 23.
7. Stein, *The Autobiography of Alice B. Toklas*, 5.
8. Samuel Putnam, *Paris Was Our Mistress*, 137.

Gertrude Stein: Her Escape from Protective Language

William H. Gass*

It has not proved helpful to the understanding of Gertrude Stein's creative works that she wrote so much herself to justify and explain them. It has not been helpful either that her autobiographies are rich and charming or that she took such care with the rituals of genius, finally fashioning for herself a personality as eloquent and commanding as her Roman face. Of this she never tired, and she began again and again. But in her life she knew too many foolish men and women, became too willingly a legend among them, something to be seen in Paris like the Eiffel Tower. They attacked her with their admiration and she encouraged it. She gave them manuscripts to market and they handed them around as signs of their complete release from common sense. She composed their portraits and they read these aloud and had them printed on expensive paper and dropped them about like cards of visitation. Her art must have seemed an ideal medium for making known their own confusions, and I imagine it was comforting to see how all of it proceeded from one so sure, oracular, and solid. All in all she was a gesture more decisive and more meaningful than they could ever make themselves, and when they left her it was often to wobble about the world like Mabel Dodge, enshrining foolishness. They would receive their portraits and they would write to say how pleased their friends were, how delighted. "Am I really like that, Gertrude? how very wonderful to be!"

Her stories, poems, and plays lie beside the mass of modern literature

*Excerpted from *Accent*, 18, no. 4 (Autumn 1958): 233–40.

like a straight line by a maze and give no hold to the critic bent on explication. Art to be successful at nearly any time dare not be pure. It must be able to invite the dogs. It must furnish bones for the understanding. Interest then has sought the substitutes that she provided for it. There has been prolonged and largely malicious gossip about her and her circle and those famous friendships that finally faded. And there have been all those horrid little essays whose titles she might have enjoyed arranging into piles: The Notion of Time in Gertrude Stein, repeated again and again. Only a few people, and nearly all of them are writers, have done as Donald Sutherland advises in his book about her (the advice comes too late for Mr. Sutherland to have taken it):

> Forget all this talk about her work and do not prepare to have an opinion of your own to tell. Simply read her work as if that were to be all.[1]

Gertrude Stein has mostly been, therefore, an anecdote and a theory and a bundle of quotations. The advice of Mr. Sutherland is certainly simple but it seems too hard. Once admired by a few without judgment, she is now censured by many without reason, and that perplexity her work and person have created, as Coleridge noted the connection, has contained sufficient fear to predispose some minds to anger.

B. L. Reid, whose book is the most recent attack,[2] makes all the customary substitutions. He describes it, with an easy presumption of its power, as "an essay in decapitation" and he genuinely believes that it destroys her reputation. On the other hand, Mr. Reid insists, Gertrude Stein has no literary reputation. She is "effectively dead as a writer" and "nobody really reads her." The critics have ignored her and all the important essays about her can be lightly ticked across the fingers of a single hand. As a result she occupies her present literary position by default. It is Mr. Reid's intention, apparently, to drag Miss Stein from the dizzy height to which ignorance, calumny and neglect have raised her. But there have been a "sizable flurry" of books about her; Yale is unaccountably printing her previously unpublished work; and while no one reads her "everybody continues to talk knowingly and concernedly about her." Mr. Reid must have been standing on this shore of his confusion when he subtitled his book "a dissenting opinion," for these words imply the presence in it of a carefully composed and calmly judicial argument, fashioned to overcome an opposition equally deliberate and well-defined, while his book is, in fact, a muddled and angry piece of journalese whose only value lies in how well it expresses the normal academic reaction and how superbly it contains and how characteristically it uses those malicious inferences fear lends so readily to anger.

The first of these inferences is double-jointed. It permits Mr. Reid to malign Miss Stein's work by maligning Miss Stein, and her work, of course, is the major source of evidence against her.

He begins his book with an anthology of critical exclamations, nearly all violent, amid which he tries to find his place as an impartial judge, one who will refrain from the mindless flattery or the vulgar abuse Miss Stein customarily receives. Too many critics, he complains, disturbed by the degree of their feelings, fail to bed their conclusions safely on a text and try to make their points by shouting. But Mr. Reid's claim to objectivity and scholarship is sheer pretense, a rhetorical stance that he assumes to aim his blows, most of which follow a feint toward generosity.

> There is no point in vilifying Gertrude Stein. She is the victim of her pathology rather than her villainy. (205)
> . . . one cannot, of course, impugn her sexuality. Dark suspicions are certainly possible, but I am more inclined to attribute her literary attitude toward sex to that pathological ability to compartmentalize her mind that I have called near schizophrenic. (74)
> If Gertrude Stein is a genius, she is one in the vulgar sense of the term: perversely elevated, isolated, inhuman. (170)

As Mr. Reid proceeds, like a warrior given courage by his own noise, he enlarges his anger, showing he can make his points as loudly as anybody.

> It is finally just to say that Gertrude Stein's true position is anti-literary, anti-intellectual, and often antihumane and antimoral. Her whole orientation is ruthlessly egocentric. (191)

Not satisfied with this list of crimes, Mr. Reid goes on to "document" what he repeatedly calls Miss Stein's schizophrenic pathology by complaining that she once confessed that anything in oil on a flat surface could hold her attention ("indiscriminate ingestiveness"), that she described a fire once as "one of those nice American fires that have so many horses and firemen to attend them" ("antihumane and egocentric"), that she referred to war as a form of dancing ("monumental detachment"), that she liked to arrange buttons and hunt hazel nuts ("enormous patience with triviality"), enjoyed Burma Shave rhymes ("unproductive catholicity") and never learned to speak French perfectly ("ivory tower").[3]

If in the first instance Mr. Reid replaces Miss Stein's work with Miss Stein, in the second he substitutes her critical writings for her creative ones. And these he systematically misreads. In a book that is heavily marbled with quotation, there are only a few examples from her creative work and even these are used for autobiographical purposes. There is not a single analysis of any of her stories, poems, and plays. Mr. Reid gives no concrete evidence of having read them, and surely this is the critic's first responsibility.[4]

The critical essays show Miss Stein at her best, Mr. Reid says, but he brings to their explication the willful literal-mindedness of an investigating congressman. He is so intent upon conviction that he often misses the tone of her language,[5] fails to follow the directions in the context,[6] supplies no historical background for her remarks,[7] blurs essential distinctions,[8] and is prevented from dealing justly with some of the ideas he does understand because he regards them, having come from Miss Stein, as peculiar and mad, even though they may be (and are) characteristic of an entire movement in modern literature that begins at least as far back as Gautier's preface to *Mademoiselle de Maupin* and contains many of the most important literary figures of our time. One example of his way of reading should be enough.

In *The Geographical History of America* Miss Stein writes:

> It is only in history government, propaganda that it is of any importance if anybody is right about anything. Science well they never are right about anything not right enough so that science cannot go on enjoying itself as if it is interesting, which it is. . . . Master-pieces have always known that being right would not be anything because if they were right then it would not be as they wrote but as they thought and in a real master-piece there is no thought, if there were thought then there would be that they are right and in a master-piece you cannot be right, if you could it would be what you thought not what you do write.
> Write and right.
> Of course they have nothing to do with one another.[9]

And Mr. Reid declares that this passage makes the "full antimorality and anti-intellectualism of her position abundantly clear."[10] On a page following, Mr. Reid quotes Miss Stein again:

> . . . master-pieces exist because they came to be as something that is an end in itself and in that respect it is opposed to the business of living which is relation and necessity.[11]

This displays "the full preciosity, the distasteful hermetic quality" of her anti-intellectualism.[12] I cannot understand what is precious, distastefully hermetic or anti-intellectual about thinking that the values of master-pieces are intrinsic, or that they constitute a system in themselves or that they are composed for their own sakes, nor is there anything about the Kantian language Miss Stein uses that gives any strength to that impression.

It is clear from the opinions Mr. Reid expresses here and there that Miss Stein's work embodies principles that upset his whole notion of art, but he is so far from grasping what these principles are that he prefers to linger without, talking about her talk about it, where there is safety. And he is naturally upset that anyone should admire these mad babblings or their complacent author or that the English language should absorb any of the qualities of her absurd style. If only she hadn't written *Three Lives*; if only she hadn't insisted on the Picassos when she and Leo split their spoils;[13] if only she hadn't written all these compelling aphorisms or hadn't put together phrases that fasten themselves in the memory like great lines of verse (one wants to laugh at the pigeons on the grass, and does, but the pigeons aren't disturbed and fail to fly); if only William James had thought less highly of her or if Hugo Munsterberg hadn't called her "an ideal student";[14] if she had lost her wit and magnetism and gone strange as her writing did, and if her lectures had failed and the soldiers had been bored and if her writing had continued in its obscurity and hadn't, at the close of her life, clarified again and become strong at the end; if she hadn't been so sure of herself, so tough and so consistent; if, really, she hadn't written *Yes Is for a Very Young Man* or "The Coming of the Americans"; then it might be easier to dismiss her as a fraud or a neurotic lady with too much leisure, as a lesbian or a Jew or just another of the wild ones, or as a genius, even, destroyed by ego; Mr. Reid wouldn't have felt any need to write his book. Certainly he would not have felt, against all the facts, so alone with his anger, in the camp of "dissent" — with most of the world on his side.

The writings of Gertrude Stein became a challenge to criticism the moment they were composed and they have remained a challenge. This challenge is of the purest and most direct kind. It is wholehearted and complete. It asks for nothing less than a study of the entire basis of our criticism, and it will not be put off. It requires us to consider again the esthetic significance of style; to examine again the ontological status of the artist's construction; to try to fix, if we can, the location of value in the work; to state, once more, the relation between the artist's vision, his medium, and his effect. None of the literary innovators who were her contemporaries attempted anything like the revolution she proposed, and because her methods were so uncompromising, her work cannot really be met except on the finest and most fundamental grounds. *Finnegans Wake*, for instance, is a work of learning. It can be penetrated by stages. It can be elucidated by degrees. It is a complex, but familiar compound. One can hear at any distance the teeth of the dogs as they feed on its limbs. With Miss Stein, however, one is never able to wet one's wrists before cautiously trusting to the water, nor can one wade slowly in. There the deep clear bottom is at once.

In *Things As They Are*,[15] Gertrude Stein's first story, the pressures that shaped her style show plainly. The novel is a psychological analysis of the relationship among three women, one of whom, Adele, is clearly the author, and it is equally transparent that the fiction is a stratagem against the self to take its secrets, for the novel has no other subject than the strength and character of its author's sexuality and the moral price she must pay if she wishes to indulge it. Such an intimate inquiry might have been lurid, should at least have been interesting, but is remarkably dull instead. The self is revenged and keeps its secrets.

The language of *Things As They Are* is not very promising. It is abstract, monotonous, pompous, vague. Circumlocution, euphemism, pedantry bring the story to its knees. Its rhythms are held back; they go with stilted care. Even those passages in which Miss Stein permits herself

to touch the air are afraid, and the mark of the graduate essay is
everywhere.

> One usually knows very definitely when there is no chance of an
> acquaintance becoming a friendship [sic] but on the other hand it is
> impossible to tell in a given case whether there is. (15)

The characters cannot pay one another compliments without getting them
up like letters of recommendation.

> Adele you seem to me capable of very genuine friendship. You are at
> once dispassionate in your judgments and loyal in your feelings; tell me
> will we be friends. (15)

The wit is weary and rhetorical.

> "You were very generous," she said "tell me how much you do care for
> me." "Care for you my dear" Helen answered "more than you know and
> less than you think." (15)

Thought is not permitted any real precision but, held off by the shame and
intimacy of the subject, merely apes it. The result is protective speech.
One way in writing of not coming near an object is to interpose a kind of
neutralizing middle tongue, one that is neither abstractly and imperson-
ally scientific nor directly confronting and dramatic, but one that lies in
that gray limbo in between, composed of the commonest words because its
objects are the objects of everyday, and therefore a language that is simple
and unspecialized, yet one whose effect is flat and sterilizing because its
words are held to the simplest naming nouns and verbs, connectives,
prepositions, articles and pronouns, the tritest adjectives of value, a few
adverbs of quantity and degree, and the automatic flourishes of social
speech — good day, how do you do, so pleased. This desire to gain by
artifice a safety from the world — to find a way of thinking without the
risks of feeling — is the source of the impulse to abstractness and simplicity
in Gertrude Stein as it is in much of modern painting where she felt
immediately the similarity of aim.[16]

Protective language names, it never renders. It replaces events with
speech. It says two people are in love, it does not show them loving. Jeff
and Melanctha talk their passion. Protective language, then, must be
precise, for in a world of dangerous objects which by craft of language
have been circumvented, there remains a quantity of unfastened feeling
that, in lighting elsewhere, will turn a harmless trifle into symbol. Name a
rose and you suggest romance, love, civil war, the maidenhead. The
English language is so rich in its associations that its literature tends to be
complex and carry its meanings on at many levels. Conrad, who, as Ford
remarks, wanted to write "a prose of extreme limpidity," often bitterly
complained that English words were never words; they were rather
instruments for exciting blurred emotions.[17] Protective speech must cut off
meanings, not take them on. It must find contexts that will limit the

functions of its words to that of naming. Gertrude Stein set about discovering such contexts.

Notes

1. Sutherland, Donald. *Gertrude Stein: a Biography of Her Work.* Yale University Press, New Haven (1951), p. 200.

2. Reid, B. L. *Art by Subtraction: a Dissenting Opinion of Gertrude Stein.* University of Oklahoma Press, Norman (1958).

3. Strangely Mr. Reid makes little use of Wyndham Lewis, who attacked Miss Stein in *Time and Western Man*, and he does not seem to know Katherine Anne Porter's essay, "The Wooden Umbrella," which is one of the most rhetorically effective personal attacks in modern literature.

4. What should we think of someone who undertook to estimate the achievement of Henry James by reading the prefaces and *The Middle Years*, examining some of the letters, and studying Percy Lubbock?

5. Her remark about the nice American fires, for instance, p. 193.

6. *Ibid.* War is dancing.

7. As, for example, her allusions to Shelley in the discussion of God and Mammon, Reid, chapter 3.

8. Between the artist as artist and the artist as citizen, soldier, friend, etc. See below.

9. *Geographical History*, pp. 198–99. Reid, p. 76. In other words: It is fortunate for science that its methods give only probable and fallible results, for absolutes halt inquiry. Only politicians and propagandists need absolutes. The purpose of art is not the enunciation of such Truths or their discovery, but rather that of presentation and rendering. Masterpieces do not depend upon being True but upon being faithful and exact, for if they depended upon being True, how many of them would there be?

10. Reid, *ibid.* What is evident in this passage is the stumbling in the style, but Mr. Reid never complains about bad writing in this sense.

11. *What are Masterpieces*, p. 90. Reid, p. 78.

12. Reid, *ibid.* Compare F. M. Ford: "The one thing you can not do is to propagandise, as author, for any cause. You must not, as author, utter any views: above all you must not fake any events. . . . It is obviously best if you can contrive to be without views at all: your business with the world is rendering, not alteration." *Joseph Conrad.* Duckworth, London (1924), p. 208. Ford does not mean that an author, as a private person, ought to have no opinions. He means what Stein means, that write and right have nothing to do with one another. This may be a mistake but it can scarcely be evidence of pathology.

13. Leo didn't want them. He wanted the Renoirs, as he didn't care much for Picasso. He always said that Gertrude knew nothing about painting. *The Flowers of Friendship*. Edited by Donald Gallup. Knopf, New York (1953), pp. 86, 91.

14. *Ibid.*, p. 4.

15. Written in 1903 and called, significantly, *Quod Erat Demonstrandum*, no effort was made to publish it until it was "discovered" among her things and sent to Louis Bromfield for his opinion in 1931. He found it "vastly interesting" but thought publication would be difficult. (*The Flowers of Friendship, op. cit.*, pp. 249–50.) It was retitled and published by The Banyan Press, Pawlet, Vermont, in 1951. The quotations that follow were taken purposely from the same scene.

16. Mr. Reid very frequently complains of the flat effect of this language and comments on its evasiveness.

17. Ford, *op. cit.*, p. 214. In Reid see ch. 7.

Gertrude Stein as Post-Modernist:
The Rhetoric of *Tender Buttons*   Neil Schmitz*

> We are all trying, with different methods, styles, perhaps even preju-
> dices, to get at the core of this linguistic pact . . . which unites the
> writer and the other, so that—and this is a contradiction which will
> never be sufficiently pondered—each moment of discourse is both
> absolutely new and absolutely understood.
>
> —Roland Barthes

Although she is still barely noted in most studies of modern narrative—Wayne Booth accords her a single reference in *The Rhetoric of
Fiction*—Gertrude Stein's meditations on the subject, particularly those
rendered in *Composition as Explanation* (1926) and *Lectures in America*
(1935), have become increasingly luminous in the past several decades.
Her attack on the formal coherence of the novel as a false ordering of
experience, on literary structure itself, no longer seems merely apologetic,
a rationale for her eccentric style, her inability to work within established
forms, but rather a lucid penetration of the *episteme* underlying traditional narrative, an attempt to create, in Roland Barthes' words, "a new
status in writing for the agent of writing."[1] She is, in brief, as perplexing as
Alain Robbe-Grillet and William Burroughs, both of whom have similarly
chosen to inhabit the "continuous present" in narration, releasing their
subject from the unities of plot and character. Yet Gertrude Stein's
research into the problematics of narrative, for all its remarkable presci-
ence, was not based on a comprehensive survey of the post-Jamesian novel;
she drew up her critique (as Melville had in *Pierre*) from her own
experience as a writer. Her primary text is invariably the *mythos* of her
style, the tale repeatedly told in her criticism of its labored genesis in her
early fiction and subsequent realization in the lyric intensity of the
portraiture and plays. It was in this period (1903–1914), as she struggled to
find her voice, that she began to extrude the referential content of story
from her narrative and replace it with the drama of writing itself, the
experience of language.

Tender Buttons, the most innovative and enigmatic of Gertrude
Stein's major works, is not only the *Ursprache* in this history but also a
significant event in our history, a discerning response in 1914 to the
exemplary despair John Barth describes in *Lost in the Funhouse* (1968): "I
see I see myself as a halt narrative: first person, tiresome. Pronoun sans
ante or precedent, warrant or respite. Surrogate for the substantive;
contentless form, interestless principle; blind eye blinking at nothing."[2] In
Tender Buttons the umbilical cord that fastened *Three Lives* and *The*

*Reprinted from the *Journal of Modern Literature* 3, no. 5 (July 1974): 1203–18. © 1984,
Temple University.

Making of Americans to the fiction of Flaubert and Proust is cut without remorse, the stuttering discourse of the experimental portraits refined, the radiant *I* of the writer assumes its commanding presence "sans ante or precedent." If only in the light of Barth's Beckett-like soliloquies, the agonized isolation from which so many contemporary writers speak, "crying out for nothing," as Robbe-Grillet puts it, the feat of Gertrude Stein's contented subjectivity, her sense of stylistic liberation in *Tender Buttons*, deserves close scrutiny. In its own modest scope, a triptych of domestic objects, food and rooms, *Tender Buttons* seems deliberately minor in its conception, a bibelot, but this frame is deceptive, an order immediately disordered. The elusiveness of her style, this consternating discourse which refuses to be still for the act of formal analysis, challenges both Literature and Knowledge, not with the flamboyance of Dadaist manifestoes, but with the visceral stamina of "Song of Myself." My purpose in this essay is to establish the meaning of Gertrude Stein's mode in her text, the core of its linguistic pact, and to set that mode within the context of contemporary narrative. There is no other way to engage *Tender Buttons*. The wrenched turn her disjunctive prose gives the reader's trained sensibility leads him nowhere but *in medias res*, into her time on her terms.

A Carafe, That Is a Blind Glass

A kind in glass and a cousin, a spectacle and nothing strange a single hurt color and an arrangement in a system to pointing. All this and not ordinary, not unordered in not resembling. The difference is spreading.

Glazed Glitter

Nickel, what is nickel, it is originally rid of a cover.
    The chance in that is that red weakens an hour. The change has come. There is no search. But there is, there is that hope and that interpretation and sometime, surely any is unwelcome, sometime there is breath and there will be a sinecure and charming very charming is that clean and cleansing. Certainly glittering is handsome and convincing.
    There is no gratitude in mercy and in medicine. There can be breakages in Japanese. That is no programme. That is no color chosen. It was chosen yesterday, that showed spitting and perhaps washing and polishing. It certainly showed no obligation and perhaps if borrowing is not natural there is some use in giving. (p. 9)[3]

To take the terms of this language seriously, one must first set aside John Malcolm Brinnin's notion that *Tender Buttons* is "wholly a product of the cubist dispensation."[4] The influence of Picasso's discoveries, his disavowal of representation in art, is readily apparent in Gertrude Stein's discourse, but this perspective, while it describes the experimental provenance of the text, tends to reduce *Tender Buttons* to the status of an exercise. "What she wanted to do in her emulation of the cubist painters," Michael J. Hoffman writes in *The Development of Abstractionism in the Writings of Gertrude Stein*, "was to develop, exclusive of the inherent symbolic nature of words, a written art form without a mimetic relationship to the external world except through certain suggestive devices."[5] Although Hoffman finally abandons this approach, citing the qualitative difference in media, he does not relocate the basis of his interpretation. The result is a reading of the text that ultimately dismisses itself, white on white. Similarly the attempt to analyze *Tender Buttons* as a psychological experiment begins by necessarily amputating the element of its style. B. F. Skinner's suggestion that it is a specimen of automatic writing represents the dead level of this approach. "All the traditional functions of words and grammar mean nothing," Hoffman observes, "once language is used as a plastic material rather than as a communicative symbol."[6] For Hoffman the language of *Tender Buttons* predicates nothing but itself, words as objects, "this is this," and thus discloses a chaos beyond its mute signs. The primary device in Gertrude Stein's style is the *non-sequitur*. Failing to find narrative logic, causal sequence, and linear duration, he finds abstraction, Mallarmean space. Failing to locate a stable center within *Tender Buttons*, the *primum mobile* of its themes, he establishes his own center outside its language and then circumlocutes his mystification.

What this criticism fails to note is that Gertrude Stein begins in her text (if not in her title) by challenging the primacy of *its* assumptions, *its* intelligiblity, this "epistemic discourse" which, as Jacques Derrida remarks, "absolutely requires . . . that we go back to the source, to the center, to the founding basis, to the principle, and so on."[7] It is in part her attempt to manifest the arbitrariness of such discourse that makes *Tender Buttons* so densely significant, so paradoxically rhetorical, a long and sustained piece of lyrical persuasion. Gertrude Stein's writing of her experience *does* follow; it records, moment by moment, the play of her mind with the world before her. But since the writer is not fixed, writing from a position, from a clarifying knowledge of the nature of things, and since the world (carafes, cushions, umbrellas, mutton, celery) is also in process, presenting only phases and attributes in their time and place of existing, nothing can be named and then classified, given as real. Everything is contingent, changing as it moves and the mind moves. To write in this mode of perception, Gertrude Stein constantly presses against the order of language those elements of syntax and signification that provide philosophical and scientific discourse with its stability. Judged by its criteria, she is indeed senseless. The copula of its sentence is an axiom rigorously denied in *Tender Buttons*.

She begins, as it were, in that mythical third world Borges devises in *Labyrinths*, the world of Tlön. "The world for them," he writes, "is not a concourse of objects in space; it is a heterogeneous series of independent acts." In this hemisphere each "mental state is irreducible: the mere fact of naming it — i.e., classifying it — implies a falsification. From which it can be deduced that there are no sciences on Tlön, not even reasoning." Tlönian discourse, however, is intensely reasoned. It is Borges' sport to evince the lucidity of its craziness. For the inhabitants of Tlön think in the terms of post-Einsteinian physics and their fluent participial language is an appropriate cognition. "They know that a system is nothing more than the subordination of all aspects of the universe to any one such aspect."[8] Hence the past is at best a "present memory." Tlön confirms the flux of phenomena and makes no effort to contain it. Robbe-Grillet's *Last Year at Marienbad* similarly proposes a "world without a past, a world which is self-sufficient at every moment and which obliterates itself as it proceeds."[9] The successive entries in *Tender Buttons* constitute a passage not unlike the movement of Robbe-Grillet's frames on a screen. Each utterance is discrete, an independent act, yet contiguous: "a kind in glass / and a cousin, / a spectacle / and nothing strange / a single hurt color / and an arrangement in a system to pointing." For Gertrude Stein the "blind glass" of the world, Melvillean whiteness, is the postulate not of chaos but freedom, freedom from the snare of categories. Just as in the Borgesian Tlön there is no word for moon, only the verb, to moonate, the carafe in *Tender Buttons* is not there in *esse* but here in *percipi*, an "arrangement in a system" presented to changing points of view and different states of mind. Thus the denotated world collapses, its tables and orders break up, awash in process, and concurrently syllogistic discourse breaks down. Words as buttons fastening side to side, signifier to signified, become tender, pliable, alive in the quick of consciousness. "And the thing that excited me so very much at that time and still does," Gertrude Stein later wrote of *Tender Buttons*, "is that the words or words that make what I looked at be itself were always words that to me very exactly related themselves to that thing the thing at which I was looking, but as often as not had as I say nothing whatever to do with what my words would do that described that thing."[10]

Decentered and unstructured, at large in this visual plenum, Gertrude Stein's writing becomes play, "writing what you are writing" and not "what you intended to write."[11] It serves no end but itself, necessarily denies the factor of its being read, and yet because the field of its play is language, not graphic abstraction, this writing does not seal itself off from meaning. The casing of the old discourse remains; the track of the nominative sentence, never precisely followed or exactly fulfilled, is always there. Structure is evoked by the triadic division of *Tender Buttons*, the nature of the catalogue. The text itself is set within an interrogative framework, a refrain of questions, persistent calls for identification, for naming. "Nickel, what is nickel, it is originally rid of a cover" (p. 9); "Cloudiness, what is cloudiness, is it a lining, is it a roll, is it melting" (p. 38). Yet these aspects of writing exist only to be overcome, surpassed. They constitute an old skin (to borrow D. H. Lawrence's figure) or set from which the writer struggles and against which surprise is created. If the questions set up the expectations of logical discourse, the middle term, the container, is never given. Spaces hover before and after each utterance. What we look for in those ellipses is the coherent and stable object, the object riveted to a past from whence (tagged and labeled), it can be realized, but like "cloudiness" the object is a word shimmering with connotations.

Indeed this contraposed rhetoric (arguing against demonstration and conviction) with its absent punctuation, its paratactical leaps, its unpredictable stops and starts, draws the reader into an intense awareness of its phrasing, forces him to listen as well as read. As one follows Gertrude Stein's analysis of the impertinence of preconceptions in *A Seltzer Bottle*, the prose sizzles with sibilance.

> Supposing a certain time selected is assured, suppose it is even necessary, suppose no other extract is permitted and no more handling is needed, suppose the rest of the message is mixed with a very long slender needle and even if it could be any black border, supposing all this altogether made a dress and suppose it was actual, suppose the mean way to state it was occasional, if you suppose this in August and even more melodiously, if you suppose this even in the necessary incident of there certainly being no middle in summer and winter, suppose this and an elegant settlement a very elegant settlement is more than of consequence, it is not final and sufficient and substituted. This which was so kindly a present was constant. (p. 16)

Where is the bottle specified by the entry's heading? "This which was so kindly a present was constant." Invariably the entries under specific headings confound the pat image or preconception given by the sign. Similarly her sentences assert with vigor but without context, without origin. Under *Glazed Glitter*: "There can be breakages in Japanese. That is no programme. That is no color. It was chosen yesterday, that showed spitting and perhaps washing and polishing" (p. 9). These referentless pronouns boldly determining clauses serve as synoptic conclusions to swallowed paragraphs, dense instantaneous reveries that are unspoken, submerged by the rapidity with which she articulates the quick turns of her attention. The reference is as private as the unknowable being of the objects listed in *Tender Buttons*. What was chosen yesterday can only be surmised. The text exists in the same sense that the carafe exists, not as a hidden entity embedded in tropes, a core of facts, but only in her emergent discourse. One must read as she writes. "So then," she declares elsewhere in *Objects*, "the order is that a white way of being round is something suggesting a pin and is it disappointing, it is not, it is so rudimentary to be analyzed and see a fine substance strangely, it is so earnest to have a green point not to red but to point again" (p. 11). Affirming the subjectivity of her language, the perspective we can not possibly know, that "white way of being round," she nonetheless paradoxically affirms the transparency of her discourse and entices the reader into her own absorbed presence. What we witness, the rhythm of our own reading broken, is her struggle with the taxonomical habits of perception.

Commonplace objects are no longer in their common places. *A Long Dress* is palpably sensed, but first as pure electrical energy (its crackle "makes machinery") and then as a pastiche of colors. The entry under *Malachite* gives us no green stone but a spoon. A moralizing spoon. "The sudden spoon is the same in no size. The sudden spoon is the wound in the decision" (p. 22). Against the distinctive quality of decorative malachite, the paperweight, Gertrude Stein invokes the apparent uniformity of spoons, tablespoons and teaspoons in their sets, but the "sudden spoon" properly regarded, seen in its singularity, is as rare as the piece of malachite. If what we see is always in relation, *this, not this, because*, here the ground of identification is destroyed. The spoon so conceived will no longer fit in its sized groove. And without grooves, defined places, decision is indeed made vulnerable. Those vexing absences where there should be presences (the pronoun's reference) become, in short, openings through which one glimpses the quotidian world, bizarre as a New Guinea rain forest, coalescing in Gertrude Stein's consciousness.

As one moves through *Objects* into the second section, *Food*, it becomes increasingly clear that the text folds back on itself. For if her style disjoins the factitious modalities of verisimilitude and negates their logic, it also resumes, pieces together its own alogical coherence. Certain motifs nebulously emerge and then constellate into discernible patterns. References to dirt and cleanliness recur. The notion of change and exchange is constantly registered. In both cases there is typically sexual allusion. In *A Substance in a Cushion* she writes: "Callous is something that hardening leaves behind what will be soft if there is a genuine interest in there being present as many girls as men. Does this change. It shows that dirt is clean when there is a volume" (p. 10). The relativity of perspective is therein whimsically established, but more importantly she begins in this passage to play with the word "dirt" itself. The darting vision that deftly situates four petticoats under the singular heading *Petticoat*: "a light white, a disgrace, an ink spot, a rosy charm" (p. 22), and later places a pun in Alice B. Toklas' pump: "A shallow hole rose on red a shallow in and in this ale less" (p. 26), simultaneously explores the carnality of language, the change and exchange of multiple meanings words assume in discourse. Certain entries are anatomically graphic. *Nothing Elegant* offers: "If the red is rose and there is a gate surrounding it, if inside is let in and there places change then certainly something is upright" (p. 13). In *Red Roses* and the subsequent *In Between* the tableaus are strictly visual and provocatively ambiguous. "A cool red rose and a pink cut pink, a collapse and a sold hole, a little less hot" leads directly to *In Between*:

> In between a place and candy is a narrow foot-path that shows more mounting than anything, so much really that a calling meaning a bolster measured a whole thing with that. A virgin a whole virgin is judged made and so between curves and outlines and real seasons and more out glasses and a perfectly unprecedented arrangement between old ladies and mild colds there is no satin wood shining. (p. 24)

What the words turn up (the phallic bolster on the bed) is genially extended (made virgins) as mere data. The writer becomes in effect polymorphously perverse, noting in *A Feather* its "mounted reserves and loud volumes," then describing with no significant break *A Brown*: "A brown which is not liquid not more so is relaxed and yet there is a change, a news is pressing" (p. 25). The free and unerring play of dream language, linking opposites, reconciling the profane and the sacred, loosely enters conscious discourse. Indeed dirt, excrement, is the nexus through which the pulsations of matter record their visible changes — solids liquefying, outside becoming inside, then reverting. For Gertrude Stein it is, humorously, the fundamental rhythm of life, one's consummate metaphor. That love's mansion is pitched near the place of excrement does not excite her disgust or menace her conception of passion.

The final entries in *Objects* are thus striking not only in their stylistic anticipation of the language in *Finnegans Wake* but in their candor as well. *Book* sounds the note of a quarrel ("Book was there, it was there. Book was there.") that deepens into a remonstrance vaguely suggestive of sexual jealousy:

> Suppose a man a realistic expression of resolute reliability suggests pleasing itself white all white and no head does that mean soap. It does not so. It means kind wavers and little chance to beside beside rest. A plain.
>
> Suppose ear rings that is one way to breed, breed that. Oh chance to say, oh nice old pole. Next best and nearest a pillar. Chest not valuable, be papered. (p. 28–29)

The estrangement is resolved in lovemaking, a scene rendered with Rabelaisian vigor.

This Is This Dress, Aider

Aider, why aider why whow, whow stop touch, aider whow, aider stop the muncher, muncher munchers.

A jack in kill her, a jack in, makes a meadowed king, makes a to let. (p. 29)

Richard Bridgman's reading of this passage in *Gertrude Stein in Pieces* is prudishly evasive. "Although sexual experience may form the metaphorical base for this bizarre conclusion," he argues, "one may also take it to be a dramatization of the death of conventional literary practice."[12] The punning is far too evident. *This is this Dress, Aider* is saturated with correlative meanings, most of them as pat as the joke in "Rub her coke," the terse entry for *Peeled Pencil, Choke. Aider* is an infinitive that contains its own object, Ada, the name Gertrude Stein had given Alice B. Toklas in an earlier portrait. "Certainly," she wrote there, "this one was loving this Ada then."[13] In any event, the infinitive calls twice: Ada to help and to help Ada. And since the distress is passion, the rhythm of that call is true: *aider* is mutual. The sequence ends in orgasm. "A jack in kill her" leaves both satiated, the king "meadowed" and "a to let." In "to let" is a's submission, the sign of her absence, and no less significantly their toilette, love's prosaic aftermath. *Objects* comes round to this ultimate pause, this anecdote in which self and style are fused, writer and lover conjoined.

Food, the middle section of *Tender Buttons*, begins with *Roastbeef* and a lyrical hymn to mutability. "In the inside there is sleeping, in the outside there is reddening, in the morning there is meaning, in the evening there is feeling." The sentences slowly rise and fall, move along the cadence of breathing, circling through a continuum that is finally reduced: "This makes sand" (p. 33). Here, and in the subsequent *Mutton* and *Breakfast*, the paragraph appears in volume for the first time in the text, enabling Gertrude Stein to sound beneath the compounding of questions, the report of sensations, a musical resonance. It is as though the entire entry, this Shakespearean witches' brew of words (with Blakean echoes) were a single incanted word, some variant *OM* with its unitary meaning—*this exalts being.* "Lovely snipe and tender turn, excellent vapor and slender butter, all the splinter and the trunk, all the poisonous darkning drunk, all the joy in weak success, all the joyful tenderness, all the section and the tea, all the stouter symmetry" (p. 35). *Roastbeef* is filled with assertions "not claiming anything." It is, in its fashion, a complex round ("Supposing there is a bone, there is a bone. Supposing there are bones. There are bones.") sung in waiting for the main course. "Please be the beef, please beef, pleasure is not in wailing," she writes late in the entry. "Please beef, please be carved clear, please be a case of consideration" (p. 37).

As in *Objects*, one must recognize in *Food* the sinuous immediacy of Gertrude Stein's discourse. "A sudden slice," she notes under *Breakfast*, "changes the whole plate, it does so suddenly" (p. 41). Into such notations erupt occasions of speech: "Alas, alas the pull alas the bell" (p. 53), the name fittingly turned into an impatient lament. Here the items are rendered not as objects extended in space, as were the umbrellas and boxes in the first section, but as things being done, prepared and served. Veal is washed, vegetables are cut, sausages placed, things stew and boil. "A white egg and a colored pan and a cabbage showing settlement, a constant increase," Gertrude Stein begins in *Milk*, observing then: "Cooking, cooking is the recognition between sudden and nearly sudden [simmer and boil] very little and all large holes" (p. 47). Over these menial tasks streams revery, those small *recherches du temps perdu* that occur when one is so engaged: "A tiny seat that means meadows and a lapse of cuddles with cheese and nearly bats, all this went messed" (p. 48). The salad is arranged. One waits for the sauce. There are several headings for potatoes, "real potatoes" that are sliced and the potato as a base for cheese or butter. *Chicken* is presented in four events, but only as a *jeu d'esprit*. Compared to a pheasant, it is a "peculiar third," then a "dirty word," and finally "alas a dirty bird" (p. 54). Throughout these entries the prose bustles with movement. Neologisms are formed, outrageous puns occur, brief metrical spurts of melody intervene. Like the potato, words and phrases have several states, can be sliced and cooked, changed in character. *Eating* spills into mock prayer: "Eel us eel us with no no pea no pea cool, no pea cool cooler . . ." (p. 56), and "a no since, a no since when" (p. 58) strays comically from nuisance / nonsense.

The parallel between food and the cooking of food (this clamorous activity) and the apprehending and expression of experience is obvious. *Orange In* succinctly affirms Gertrude Stein's measured achievement: "Pain soup, suppose it is question, suppose it is butter, real is, real is only, only excreate, only excreate a no since" (p. 58). Pain soup is simply marvellous. Surely it is what we are served as the first course in life. In *Mutton* we are reminded that "A letter which can wither, a learning which can suffer and an outrage which is simultaneous is principal" (p. 38). But the question, the supposing, one's restless imagination, attacks the real in its withering letters and makes it "only." The admonition to excreate proposes her style, the necessary risk of "no since." *Food* concludes with *A Centre in a Table*, with "some sum." A folder is on the table replacing food at its center. The rituals of eating are transformed into the organic process of writing: "Cod liver oil pressed is china and secret with a bestow, a bestow reed, a reed to be a reed to be, in a reed to be" (p. 59). Having broken through the constraints of representation ("real is only"), the restrictions imposed on conception by formal discourse, she turns to the narrative itself, to "re letter and read her." The body of her own experience is here in the body of this text.

In *Rooms*, then, she circles back to the topic of her style, to what is in the folder on the table. We are told immediately to distrust the "use" of centers, to proceed without the governance of structure. "Act so that there is no use in a centre," she writes. "A wide action is not width" (p. 63). The center is nowhere but in the *now* of utterance, always redistributing itself in the duration of discourse. As a dimension to be attained, a *telos*, width is not out there, but widening (writing) exists. Structure is momentary *con*struction made and unmade by the writer pushing into the silence of the next moment. Gertrude Stein understood the Bergsonian concept of Being endlessly drawing its existence from the past, not as revised summary or altered copy, but as a "free adaptation" of all the resources of the past. Yet this supple movement in writing, she realized, occurred within the containment (rooms) of language. In *Food* there is a remark that indicates her awareness of the problems imposed by her style: "A sentence of a vagueness that is violence is authority and a mission and stumbling also certainly also a prison" (p. 38–39). The weight of that equivocation is deeply felt in *Rooms*. In this third and final section, which constitutes something of a conspectus, the question of her "authority," the nature of one's "prison," is eloquently restated. "Then tender and true that makes no width to hew is the time that there is question to adopt" (p. 63). Her stylistic strategies are passed in review, not systematically, but seductively, as demonstrated values. "Is there pleasure when there is a passage," she asks, "there is when every room is open" (p. 65). To a large extent, *Rooms* is an account of the freedom won in the writing of *Tender Buttons*.

To open her discourse, as we have seen, Gertrude Stein began first of all with the basic units of written discourse: the word, parts of speech, grammar and syntax. These she loosened; the structure, any sentence in her text, follows the diversions of her sense of the thing seen. The proper noun is stripped of its property, loses its fixed position both in space and the lexicon.

> If comparing a piece that is a size that is recognized as not a size but a piece, comparing a piece with what is not recognized but what is used as it is held by holding, comparing these two comes to be repeated. Suppose they are put together, suppose that there is an interruption, supposing that beginning again they are not changed as to position, suppose all this and suppose that any five two of whom are not separating suppose that the five are not consumed. Is there an exchange, is there a resemblance to the sky which is admitted to be there and the stars which can be seen. Is there. That was a question. There was no certainty. (p. 67)

And yet (this large yet) Gertrude Stein argues her style assumes its particular cogency in this "no certainty." "Fitting a failing," she continues, "meant that any two were indifferent and yet they were all connecting that, they were all connecting that consideration." Discourse is most properly an interrogation of the fleeting mystery of the thing to be said. Her faith in language is indeed compelling. She is bluntly solipsistic in *Tender Buttons*. The mysterious referent (her style's most conspicuous feature) is ultimately the historical person of Gertrude Stein, the dark side of the moon, the unknown subject whose experience places her on those points from which she supposes. Given that esoteric "vagueness," she contends nonetheless that we are most understood when we are most subjective. In her spontaneous leaps over formal rules, the sudden passages opened in her syntax, the writer is strikingly manifest. The power struggle of interpretation ceases when everything to be said is said at once. There are no interdictory personae coiled in this narrative striving to retain suspense by retaining information. The blank that confronts Barth's narrator in *Lost in the Funhouse* looms with dread immensity because in part an impatient reader is on its other side waiting for the blank to be brilliantly filled. In *Tender Buttons* this "dogged, uninsultable" *You* has no bearing on the *I* of the writer. Here it is the writer who is "dogged, uninsultable," who professes the multifarious integrity of her consciousness, who writes it forth.

In later works, *The Geographical History of America or The Relation of Human Nature to the Human Mind* and *Four in America*, she would theorize, almost in Emersonian terms (the Me and the Not/Me), about the distinction between the writer's self and the authorial person, mind and nature. In *Tender Buttons* she simply reposes in the paradox. "What I experience or portray," Walt Whitman wrote in the preface to the 1855 edition of *Leaves of Grass*, "shall go from my composition without a shred of my composition. You shall stand by my side and look in the mirror with me."[14] Gertrude Stein's stance in *Tender Buttons* is somewhat analogous. In fact, Whitman's hortatory note in "Song of Myself" is the note on which she concludes her discourse. The linearity of traditional writing has come to mean death:

> A line in life, a single line and a stairway, a rigid cook, no cook and no equator, all the same there is higher than that another evasion. Did that mean shame, it meant memory. Looking into a place that was hanging and was visible looking into this place and seeing a chair did that mean relief, it did, it certainly did not cause constipation and yet there is a melody that has white for a tune when there is straw color. This shows no face.

The cook as writer, relief from the constipation of writing blocks, the step by step of discursive prose—these images from the earlier sections are brought forward to underscore the prowess of her style. And then, with passion, the questions are resumed:

> Why is there education, there is education because the two tables which are folding are not tied together with a ribbon, string is used and string being used there is a necessity for another one and another one not being used to hearing shows no ordinary use of any evening and yet there is no disgrace in looking, none at all. This came to separate when there was simple selection of an entire pre-occupation. (p. 71–72)

The world systematized and tabulated by discursive language (system upon system, one string after the other) begins to collapse when the arbitrary basis of language (usage) is scrutinized. The lyrical interludes in *Rooms* become the consummate rhetoric of *Tender Buttons: what* becomes *why*, a forcing of language beyond its tolerances.

> Why is a pale white not paler than blue, why is a connection made by a stove, why is the example which is mentioned not shown to be the same, why is there no adjustment between the place and the separate attention. Why is there a choice in gamboling. Why is there no necessary dull stable, why is there a single piece of any color, why is

there that sensible silence. Why is there the resistance in a mixture, why is there no poster, why is there that in the window, why is there no suggester, why is there no window, why is there no oyster closer. (p. 69–70)

The alogical demands of the child upon the word, his *reductio ad absurdum*, is here reinstated with a new and powerful validity — not as a game of riddles, but as the outcry of a captive losing the grace of his freedom, compelled to relocate his consciousness (eat his pain soup) in the containing rooms of language and thenceforth speak his world within the rule of prescriptive grammar and proper diction. But if this fall from innocence is necessary, the subsequent imprisonment is not. For language, properly viewed, does not contain nature; it is a part of nature. "Why is the name changed," Gertrude Stein asks derisively. "The name is changed because in the little space there is a tree, in some space there are no trees, in every space there is a hint of more, all this causes the decision" (p. 71). The knowledge of the primer, a knowledge of labels, is discarded. Having begun in its title with an oxymoron, *Tender Buttons* ends with a lyrically extended oxymoron, a rebellious figure of speech that mocks the predicative assumptions of language: "The care with which the rain is wrong and the green is wrong and the white is wrong, the care with which there is a chair and plenty of breathing. The care with which there is incredible justice and likeness, all this makes a magnificent asparagus, and also a fountain" (p. 78). It is this same care that makes *Tender Buttons* wrong.

"Every writer born," Barthes declares in *Writing Degree Zero*, "opens within himself the trial of literature, but if he condemns it, he always grants it a reprieve which literature turns to use in order to reconquer him." For Gertrude Stein there is no reprieve. By virtue of her style, style in Barthes' poetic sense, she remains outside the entrapment of formal writing, resistant to the pull of those "ancestral and all-powerful signs which, from the depths of a past foreign to him, impose Literature on him like some ritual, not like a reconciliation."[15] In *Four in America* she herself distinguished two primary modes of composition: "writing what you are writing" and "writing what you intended to write." These modes were not absolute; they represented a bias, an intention, but in her distinction she placed herself emphatically within the former. Narrative thus becomes what it is in *Tender Buttons*, the telling of what happens in each successive moment of its happening. And in such narrative art one's singular resource is style as Barthes describes it:

Style is almost beyond it [Literature]: imagery, delivery, vocabulary spring from the body and the past of the writer and gradually become the very reflexes of his art. Thus under the name of style a self-sufficient language is evolved which has its roots only in the depths of the author's personal and secret mythology, that subnature of expression where the first coition of words and things takes place, where once and for all the great verbal themes of his existence come to be installed.[16]

Writing, so conceived, is a constant calling-forth of those themes, a questioning of not merely the thing seen but the word or words that fit it, the words that connect the consideration. It is also in a Faulknerian sense a "relinquishment," a submission to the depths of one's nature, a letting-go, but not, as Skinner argues, writing in a trance. For the trial of literature is also constant in *Tender Buttons*. Its structures and forms, its very language, constrain the writer — they are always the first part of the question.

With what seems now remarkable clairvoyance Gertrude Stein saw in 1914 the situation of modern narrative, the "blind alley" writers like Barth and Beckett deplore. This essay began with the suggestion that her writings, particularly *Tender Buttons*, constituted something of a matrix (the pun is redeemable), a strenuously experimental canon in which all the vexing questions that make contemporary literature so problematic are brilliantly asked. But this can perhaps be put differently now: after *Tender Buttons* she ceased to ask the technical question about story and character so desperately current in modern writing. Yet in this withdrawal from the instrumentality of narrative, her refusal to employ any language other than her own, she did not, curiously enough, abandon the sociopolitical realm, rise, as Barthes puts it, "above History." Both Richard Brautigan and Donald Barthelme, writing on the different coasts of American experience, reflect in their fiction (*In Watermelon Sugar, City Life*) elements of the immediate and restless discourse Gertrude Stein brought to maturity in *Tender Buttons*. If the questions posed in *Tender Buttons* seem mild when placed against the frantic staccato of the questions in Burroughs' *The Ticket That Exploded*: " 'What is sex? What is word? What is color?' "[17] they are nevertheless the same questions. In a century stifling in its systems, overfed with information, overwhelmed by plans and planning, relentlessly tracked and scheduled, Gertrude Stein's gentle reminder, "Nothing aiming is a flower" (p. 76), remains an arduous lesson.

Notes

1. Roland Barthes, "To Write: Intransitive Verb?" in Richard Macksey and Eugenio Donato, eds. *The Languages of Criticism and the Sciences of Man*, (Johns Hopkins, 1970), p. 144. An early recognition of Gertrude Stein's innovative theories occurs in E. M. Forster's *Aspects of the Novel* (1927), but Forster, while granting Gertrude Stein "noble motives," objects that the "time-sequence" cannot be destroyed without destroying fiction. *Vide Aspects of the Novel* (Harcourt, Brace, Jovanovich, 1954), pp. 41–42.

2. John Barth, *Lost in the Funhouse* (Doubleday, 1968), p. 35.

3. Gertrude Stein, *Tender Buttons* (New York: Haskell House reprint of 1914 Edition, 1970).

4. John Malcolm Brinnin, Introduction to *Selected Operas and Plays of Gertrude Stein* (University of Pittsburgh Press, 1970), p. xii.

5. Michael J. Hoffman, *The Development of Abstractionism in the Writings of Gertrude Stein* (University of Pennsylvania Press, 1965), p. 162.

6. Hoffman, p. 191.

7. Jacques Derrida, "Structure, Sign, and Play," in *The Languages of Criticism and the Sciences of Man*, p. 257.

8. Jorge Luis Borges, *Labyrinths* (New Directions, 1964), pp. 8–10.

9. Alain Robbe-Grillet, *For A New Novel, Essays on Fiction* (Grove Press, 1965), p. 152.

10. Gertrude Stein, *Writings and Lectures 1909–1945*, Patricia Meyerowitz, ed. (Penguin, 1971), p. 115.

11. Stein, p. 294.

12. Richard Bridgman, *Gertrude Stein in Pieces* (Oxford University Press, 1970), p. 130.

13. Gertrude Stein, *Geography and Plays* (Boston, 1922), p. 16.

14. Walt Whitman, *Leaves of Grass* (Norton Edition, 1968), p. 717.

15. Roland Barthes, *Writing Degree Zero* (Beacon Press, 1970), pp. 86–87.

16. Barthes, p. 10.

17. William Burroughs, *The Ticket That Exploded* (Grove Press, 1968), p. 145.

The Steinian Portrait

Wendy Steiner*

The three texts published here for the first time are examples of the portrait, a genre central in Gertrude Stein's theoretical and artistic development.[1] The portrait forces upon its writer the problems of what an individual is and how he can be artistically represented so that his uniqueness and non-fictional status will be apparent, felt by the reader. These two issues, the one psychological, the other aesthetic, indicate as well the two major fields of interest of Stein's life. It was the combination of scientific, descriptive psychology and technical artistry required by the portrait genre that caused her to keep returning to it, from the early days of her writing (1908) to the very end of her career (1946). The one hundred and thirty-two resulting texts are a remarkable document of the growth of a creative mind, and more importantly, of the limitations and possibilities inherent in the portrait form.

Stein's interest in psychology seems to have begun with her studies under William James at Radcliffe. Indeed, it would be accurate to state that her basic notions about character, time, and language (the three problematic factors for her in portrait-writing) are all derived from the teachings of the great pragmatic philosopher and psychologist. Unlike the concepts of character implicit in literary portraits up to the twentieth century—the individual as a static configuration of physical or spiritual traits, as determined by a "ruling passion" or an "overruling accident," as defined by his social status or occupation—the conception which Stein inherited from James treated the individual as a dynamic process. For James the essential way to conceive of one's identity was

*Reprinted from the *Yale University Library Gazette* 50 (July 1975): 30–40.

to think ourselves as thinkers. This attention to thought as such, and the identification of ourselves with it rather than with any of the other objects which it reveals, is a momentous and in some respects a rather mysterious operation.[2]

This operation is particularly momentous when applied to verbal portraiture, a genre sprung from the much older art of visual portraiture. In painted portraits the easiest and commonest way to render a subject present is to imitate[3] his appearance on a canvas. This approach is facilitated by the correspondence between the static quality of painting and the static notions of character outlined above. However, since writing uses a temporal, dynamic medium rather than a spatial, static one, iconicity in literary portraiture had never been a possibility. The importance for portraiture of James's notion of character as thought process, then, lies in the new matching of medium to represented object, which opens the way for a truly iconic literary portraiture. The adjustment of the concept of the individual to the medium of expression so as to produce iconicity was the program behind the development of all of Stein's writing.

James discusses as well the problem of how we come to know ourselves, *i.e.*, the mode of our thinking about ourselves. He defines identity as a special case of knowledge problem. The way we come to know ourselves, or any other object, is through feelings of sameness which surround thoughts of the same thing. Identity is thus a function of memory and of our ability to see resemblances. Now, feelings of sameness are one of the many sorts of associations accompanying thought which James called "psychic fringes," and the presence or absence of mental fringes is the distinguishing feature of James's two different modes of thought—"acquaintance" and "knowledge-about."

> . . . the difference between those [states of mind] that are mere "acquaintance," and those that are "knowledge-*about*" . . . is reducible almost entirely to the absence or presence of psychic fringes or overtones. Knowledge *about* a thing is knowledge of its relations. Acquaintance with it is limitation to the bare impression which it makes.[4]

Clearly then, the sense of one's identity is "knowledge about" oneself.

If we juxtapose Stein's first notion of identity to James's notion, the similarity between the two becomes apparent. Identity for Stein is "recognition, you know who you are because you and others remember anything about yourself . . . I am I because my little dog knows me."[5] And if identity is based on remembrance and comparison, other people's identity is based on the same factors. One knows others by seeing the connection between all the separate "instances" of them. Further, this sameness in difference can be extended to the sphere of the relations among people. Not only does one know someone by discovering the sameness beneath the variations in his appearance, but one recognizes him as belonging to a character type by seeing the basic similarity underlying the differences among people. As Stein puts it:

> Every one then is an individual being. Every one then is like many others always living, there are many ways of thinking of every one. . . .
>   Every one is one inside them, every one reminds some one of some other one who is or was or will be living.[6]

This conception of identity as "knowledge-about," with its insistence on memory and comparison, leads Stein to see the "bottom nature" of the individual as a *shared* nature:

> I see a very certain thing in my way of seeing kinds in men and women, that I am really understanding the meaning of the being in them.[7]

Now if this individual — simultaneously a thinker and an object of thought — is to be imitated in the temporal medium of language, it becomes crucial to understand how time functions in relation to thought. And again, Stein's ideas in this respect can be traced back to the teachings of William James. His conception of time in thought can be summarized as follows. First, thought is in essence temporal; it "goes on."[8] Secondly, thought is constantly changing, and at the same time it is continuous. It is a continuous succession of "now"s.[9] But, thirdly, thought cannot be perceived as "now"s, for as soon as we consider our thought, memory comes into play and every moment is seen against the background of the moments surrounding it. Therefore,

> the unit of our perception of time is a duration. . . . It is only as parts of this *duration-block* that the relation of *succession* of one end to the other is perceived. . . . We are constantly conscious of a certain duration — the specious present — varying in length from a few seconds to probably not more than a minute, and . . . this duration (with its content perceived as having one part earlier and the other part later) is the original intuition of time.[10]

By terming the duration in thought a "specious present," James was placing a truth value on the notion of time as a continuous succession of "now"s. Stein embraced this "authentic" notion of time as the mode proper for the imitation of the individual in verbal portraiture and in fact for the imitation of all perception in writing. The name she first gave to her presentation of time was the "prolonged present," later modified in various ways to become the famous "continuous present." The importance of the notion for Stein may be seen in her insistence that it was operating from the very start of her experimental writing:

> In beginning writing I wrote a book called *Three Lives* this was written in 1905. I wrote a negro story called *Melanctha*. In that there was a constant recurring and beginning there was a marked direction in the direction of being in the present although naturally I had been

accustomed to past present and future, and why, because the composition forming around me was a prolonged present.[11]

Stein related the notion of the prolonged present to the nature of the individual in a seemingly logical way. If the individual is a succession of sames in different contexts and times, and if time is a succession of constantly changing "now"s, then the way to represent the individual is as a sequence of virtual repetitions. Sentences or phrases can serve as "authentic nows," the small variations among which would then stand for the differences accompanying perceptions of the same — the subject's "bottom nature." Repetition[12] is thus a crucial factor in character representation and in the perception of others: "Repeating is a wonderful thing in being, everything, every one is repeating then always the whole of them."[13] Stein saw this essential repetition of character as a property of everyone, a "rhythm of personality":

> I began to get enormously interested in hearing how everybody said the same thing over and over again with infinite variations but over and over again until finally if you listened with great intensity you could hear it rise and fall and tell all that there was inside them, not so much by the actual words they said or the thoughts they had but the movement of their thoughts and words endlessly the same and endlessly different.[14]

However logical this linkage of identity to the "authentic now" might appear, it is founded on a contradiction. The notion of identity, as we have seen, is a product of "knowledge-about," while the "authentic now," James had stressed, could never be held onto by thought. Identity depends upon comparison and memory, while the entrance of these factors into time perception immediately leads to the construction of a "specious present." Thus, where Stein had deliberately matched her presentation of the individual to "authentic" time perception in an attempt to create iconicity, she had ended up with a contradiction and a blockage of the correspondence so necessary for mimesis. Stein's realization of this problem and her accommodation of the concept of the individual to the "authentic now" marked the boundary between the first two phrases of her portraiture, and occurred in approximately 1911. It is the earliest group of portraits (1908–13) — including the famous portraits of Matisse and Picasso[15] — that are characterized by the notion of the individual as Jamesian "identity" with a "bottom nature" relating him to the other members of his character type.

In this early phase of portraiture, Stein began to develop a particular approach to language. Characteristically for her this approach owes much to the theories of James. Throughout his *Principles of Psychology* James treats language as a direct reflection of thought. Implicit in his discussion of language, then, are the mimetic possibilities for a verbal portraiture defining the individual as a thinker or an object of thought. Significantly,

James explains the difference between "acquaintance" and "knowledge-about" in terms of the sentence: "the grammatical sentence expresses this [difference]. Its 'subject' stands for an object of acquaintance which, by the addition of the predicate, is to get something known about it."[16] In most simple terms, then, grammatical relations represent knowledge relations. By attaching a portrait subject's name to some activity or state in a sentence predicate, one establishes knowledge about him, and hence reveals his identity. Stein makes a great deal of the relation between identity and the sentence:

> I like the feeling the everlasting feeling of sentences as they diagram themselves.
>   In that way one is completely possessing something and incidentally one's self.[17]

James went on to associate the parts of speech with different modes of thought — the "substantive" and the "transitive":

> *for a state of mind to survive in memory it must have endured for a certain length of time.* In other words, it must be what I call a substantive state. Prepositional and conjunctival states of mind [along with verb states] are not remembered as independent facts.[18]

Nouns and adjectives, creating the resting-places of thought, are the currency of memory and are invariable in form as well. Because of this, James goes on, they are mimetically inadequate to "now" — perception. Verbs, conjunctions, prepositions, adverbs, and pronouns — the "transitive" parts of speech — all change either their form or their referent, and thus are mimetically adequate to thought.

These ideas about language blossomed forth some years later in Stein's essay, "Poetry and Grammar,"[19] perhaps the most passionate depiction of the parts of speech to be found in English writing. Here the noun becomes the great villain in the play of writing, for it dissipates the "now" by evoking classes of objects and hence comparison and memory, and by remaining static in form and referent:

> A noun is a name of anything.
>   . . . things once they are named the name does not go on doing anything to them and so why write in nouns.
>   . . . As I say a noun is the name of a thing, and therefore slowly if you feel what is inside that thing you do not call it by the name by which it is known. Everybody knows that by the way they do when they are in love and a writer should always have that intensity of emotion about whatever is the object about which he writes.[20]

Transitive words, on the other hand, have the happy faculty of being "mistaken," of keeping thought dancing among several referents and temporal vantage points:

> Nouns and adjectives never can make mistakes can never be mistaken but verbs can be so endlessly, both as to what they do and how they agree or disagree with whatever they do. . . .
>
> Besides being able to be mistaken and to make mistakes verbs can change to look like themselves or to look like something else, they are, so to speak on the move and adverbs move with them and each of them find themselves not at all annoying but very often very much mistaken. . . . Then comes the thing that can of all things be most mistaken and they are prepositions. Prepositions can live one long life being really being nothing but absolutely nothing but mistaken and that makes them irritating if you feel that way about mistakes but certainly something that you can be continuously using and everlastingly enjoying.[21]

The result of this reflection on the parts of speech was an early style dominated by transitive or relational language and built on incremental repetitions. One work of this period, for example, "A Portrait of One: Harry Phelan Gibb," is one hundred and forty-one words long, but contains only eighteen different words. It uses only one finite verb, "is," either as a copular or as part of a present progressive tense with a present participle. It has no nouns, adverbs, or adjectives (except for the demonstrative adjective, "that," which has enormous potential for mistakes); it has only one preposition, "in," one pronoun, "he," one coordinating conjunction, "and," and one subordinating conjunction, "that," which invariably introduces a noun clause after "saying," "hoping," and "knowing." These participles/gerunds appear in profusion, along with indefinite pronouns such as "some one" and "something."[22] This is a style of extreme redundance and lack of concreteness. It is perhaps the most widely known of Stein's numerous solutions to the problem of imitating perception in language.

However, as we have already pointed out, there is a contradiction inherent in Stein's early adjustment of character to time and language. As Stein wrote,

> The thing one gradually comes to find out is that one has no identity that is when one is in the act of doing anything.
>
> . . . At any moment when you are you you are you without the memory of yourself because if you remember yourself while you are you you are not for purposes of creating you.[23]

Her solution to this problem, also implicit in James's thought, was to conceive of the individual not as a function of "knowledge-about," but of "acquaintance." The individual was to be experienced as raw perception, as sensory data unconnected with anything, past or to come. Memory and comparison with their concomitants, identity and typologizing, were not to be operative in the second phase of portraiture, but were to be replaced by the notion of the subject as "entity," *being*, with the verbal force of the gerund in ascendance:

> . . . I had to find out inside every one what was in them that was intrinsically exciting and I had to find out not by what they said not by what they did not by how much or how little they resembled any other one but I had to find it out by the intensity of movement that there was inside in any one of them.[24]

Stein tried to express this "movement" in the second-phase portraits (1911–25, with less frequency in the years following) by disrupting syntax and the normal semantic functioning of words, so as to destroy the conventional Jamesian knowledge relations within the sentence. Stein's combining of words in such a case militates against the reader's combining them into a meaningful sequence. Words tend to become intransigently isolated objects, rather than elements cooperating to create a pattern of meaning. As a result, in this phase Stein does not hesitate to use nouns and adjectives, since any part of speech could be successfully de-semanticized by severe syntactic disruptions. The most concrete nouns are reduced to their palest dictionary meanings by this technique. We might point to the first sentence-paragraph of "Simon" as an example of such verbal strategies.

However, analyses of such portraits[25] indicate that a careful scrutiny of the text and factual information about the portrait subject can usually explain the most arcane formulations. These early second-phase portraits thus seem to work on the assumption that the reader will have an immediate experience of the subject as "acquaintance" through a normal reading of the portrait, but will be able to discover "knowledge about" him by subjecting the text to analytic scrutiny. The evocation of the subject before our consciousness takes place on the level of the reading, while the predication made of him is reserved for another mode of cognition. Thus, Stein forces the reader in this second phase to be both a naive and a critical reader, and to have a temporally mixed perception of the subject.

Part of the motivation behind the isolation of words from each other in anti-syntactic sequences can be traced to Stein's growing interest at this time (ca. 1911–13) in the nature of visual perception. Immediacy of perception, she thought, could be established by creating a direct correspondence between the sensory aspect of the word — its sound — and the visuality of the object:

> I began to wonder at about this time just what one saw when one looked at anything really looked at anything. Did one see sound, and what was the relation between color and sound, did it make itself by description by a word that meant it or did it make itself by a word in itself.[26]

The answer, of course, was that "it made itself by a word in itself," the word seen as a concrete sensory object. Such ideas eventually led Stein into experiments with synesthesia, where the moving force of her portraiture was at times a rollicking, at times a rapturous word play. "Grace Yves de

Longevialle" is a case in point of this second-phase tendency. The first fourteen lines of it are built on a set of sound variations around the sequence "Grace is the name of a man," while the last eight lines take up a new set of associations motivated by homonyms, rhymes, and other sound correspondences.[27]

Within the second phase of Steinian portraiture, then, are the difficult two-level portraits such as "Simon," the portraits dominated by sound-play such as "Grace Yves de Longevialle," and a number of portraits written as mini-dialogues while Stein was particularly interested in drama. After approximately 1925 the first two of these possibilities continued to appear in Steinian portraiture, but two other approaches developed as well. One of these was the "appreciation,"[28] a comparatively conventional sort of depiction of the subject, from the point of view of the historical development of the portrait genre. No attempt is made in these charming pieces to produce iconic writing, and they read very much like *The Autobiography of Alice B. Toklas.*

The other new kind of portrait emerging after 1925 grew directly out of Stein's radically mimetic program. Disappointed with the synesthetic writing in which sound had become an end in itself rather than a way of establishing a direct connection to the visual object, and aware of the contradiction implicit in the presence of "knowledge-about" within the earlier two-level portraits, Stein again developed a new approach. She eliminated the secondary level of analytic "knowledge-about" and the pure sound play, so as to transform the portrait into a kind of equivalent for its subject, but one that would not refer to that subject in any of the ways language normally does. The portrait was to become a kind of "text-object"[29] aiming at the same degree of "movement" and life within it that its subject had.[30] Stein described this third-phase notion of the portrait in discussing what she considered to be one of the most successful texts of its type, "George Hugnet":

> It really does not make any difference who George Hugnet was or what he did or what I said, all that was necessary was that there was something completely contained within itself and being contained within itself was moving, not moving in relation to anything not moving in relation to itself but just moving. . . .[31]

By treating the subject as a mode of self-enclosed movement, and by producing a similar mode of movement in the portrait, Stein felt that there would be no discrepancy between the temporal mode of the work and that of its subject; language would be functioning in a purely mimetic manner.

However, the effect of these portraits of "self-enclosed movement" is, in fact, anti-iconic. The only connection between the text and its subject that the reader can "know" comes through the title, and at a certain point the title begins to appear purely ornamental. When we consider, too, that one of these portraits, "Bernard Faÿ," later occurs bereft of its title as part of the text of "Sentences" in *How To Write*,[32] the portrait-status of such works comes into question. Paradoxically, by trying to fulfill the requirements of the mimetic literary portrait without any compromises, Stein ended up by severing the bond between subject and text, and thus eliminating the possibility of the reader's perceiving the text as a portrait. The difficult third-phase portraits represented a theoretical and practical dead-end to portraiture.

We might conclude by summarizing the major trends of the three phases of Stein's portraiture. From 1908 to 1913 she produced the typologizing, repetitive portraits of the first phase, in which a contradiction existed between the mode of the portrait subject and the temporal mode of representation of this subject. Then came the two-level style of the second phase, in which the subject was presented as the "raw perceptual data" of "acquaintance," and only became organized into "knowledge-about" through careful analysis on the part of the reader. This style was first seen in 1911, dominated Stein's portraiture until approximately 1925, and appeared with less frequency after that. Finally, Stein came to the "self-enclosed movement" of the third phase, in which the portrait was designed as a "text-object" which was to imitate its subject by its own "movement." These phases are echoed in the rest of Stein's writing as well, but it is the condensed quality of the portrait and its definitional combination of referential and aesthetic norms that present these stylistic developments in the most graphic way.

Notes

1. The present article is a condensation of some of the findings of my doctoral dissertation, "Gertrude Stein's Portrait Form" (Yale University, 1974). Restrictions of space have necessarily led to a simplification of some of the issues involved, but it is hoped that this essay will serve as an introduction to Stein's theory of portraiture as well as a help to the reader's appreciation of the portraits themselves.

2. William James, *The Principles of Psychology* (New York, 1890), p. 296.

3. Throughout the discussion I am using the terms "imitation," "mimesis," and "iconicity" to refer to the state of signification in which the sign vehicle resembles its referent. *Cf.* C. S. Peirce, *Collected Writings*, Vol. IV (Cambridge, Mass., 1966), pp. 359–361.

4. James, *op. cit.*, p. 296.

5. "What Are Master-Pieces and Why Are There So Few of Them" in *What Are Masterpieces* (Los Angeles, Calif., The Conference Press [1940]), p. 84.

6. *The Making of Americans* ([Paris, Contact Editions, 1925]), p. 212.

7. *Ibid.*, p. 230.

8. James, *op. cit.*, p. 225.

9. *Idem.*

10. *Ibid.*, pp. 609–610, 642.

11. *Composition as Explanation* (London, Hogarth Press, 1926), pp. 16–17.

12. Actually, Stein called her technique "insistence" rather than "repetition" in order to stress the difference in each repeated phrase created by gradually cumulating context. See

"Portraits and Repetition" in *Lectures in America* (New York, Random House [1935]), pp. 166–169.

13. *The Making of Americans*, p. 207.

14. "The Gradual Making of *The Making of Americans*" in *Lectures in America* (New York, Random House [1935]), p. 138.

15. "Matisse" and "Picasso" in *Portraits and Prayers* (New York, Random House [1934]), pp. 12–20. (I am of course referring to the first of Stein's portraits of Picasso.)

16. James, *op. cit.*, p. 222.

17. "Poetry and Grammar" in *Lectures in America*, p. 211.

18. James, *op. cit.*, pp. 643–644.

19. This lecture was written in 1934 as one of the *Lectures in America*, but the concept of language it describes was clearly at work in the earliest portraits.

20. "Poetry and Grammar" in *Lectures in America*, pp. 209, 210.

21. *Ibid.*, pp. 211–212.

22. For a full analysis of this portrait, see my "Gertrude Stein's Portrait Form," pp. 144–150.

23. "What Are Master-Pieces," in *What Are Masterpieces*, pp. 84, 85–86.

24. "Portraits and Repetition," in *Lectures in America*, p. 183.

25. See my "Gertrude Stein's Portrait Form," pp. 150 *ff*.

26. "Portraits and Repetition," p. 191.

27. Unfortunately it is impossible in this space to analyze any of the three "new" portraits in detail.

28. *e.g.*, "Duchess de Rohan — A Writer," "The Life of Juan Gris," "Picabia."

29. The parallel to the cubist term, *tableau-objet*, is intentional here. See my "Gertrude Stein's Portrait Form," Chapter IV.

30. The "Portrait de Madame Langlois" is almost surely of this type, although a complete analysis would be necessary to determine this.

31. "Portraits and Repetition," p. 202.

32. (Paris, Plain Edition, 1931), see pp. 129–130, 131, etc.

Weininger and *The Making of Americans*

Leon Katz*

It is a significant mistake that Stein remembered starting *The Making of Americans* in 1906 and finishing it in 1908.[1] As with many of her inaccurate reflections, this one was patently false and yet bore a kind of truth that explains its error. For from the spring of 1906, when she took up work on the novel in earnest, she pursued her original purpose of showing "the old world in the new or more exactly the new world all made out of the old"; but in the summer of 1908 the book suddenly began to develop explicitly and in earnest the understanding of personality first used in

*Excerpted from *Twentieth-Century Literature* 24, no. 1 (Spring 1978): 8–17.

Melanctha, and which had implied, when it was being used most authentically in *Melanctha*, a contradiction of the fictional form itself. When this understanding of character description was brought to its logical conclusion in the last chapter of *The Making of Americans*, Stein had moved outside the conventions of communicative literary art—a development in her writing which, because its continuity has not been apparent, has come to symbolize the capricious and irresponsible side of twentieth-century art.

The transition from the realistic and thoroughly conventional first novel to the unique manner of the second followed inevitably from the fixed allure that psychological schematizing held for her, but the catalyst that led to so sudden and dramatic a change in the novel's purpose and method in the summer of 1908 was a book that fell into her hands during the previous winter.

It was probably Leo Stein who first picked up a copy of Otto Weininger's *Sex and Character*[2] in a bookshop, though, as in the case of buying pictures, it is a debatable question whether Leo himself or he and Gertrude together first came across the book and bought it.[3] In any case, they were among the first of their acquaintances to read it, and for the rest of the winter until they set off for Florence in May of 1908, the book was the center of violent discussion. After the first enthusiasm, they sent copies to everyone, even to old friends in America.[4] Leo felt that Weininger was an example of pure genius, and since he was meeting regularly with Roché about once a week during that winter for hours-long discussions of set subjects, they used Weininger's book for a while as their focus, and as Leo adumbrated, Roché interlarded his copy of the book with Leo's notes and comments. Leo responded for a time to Weininger's antifeminism, and at the peak of his interest in him, declared that if one could take women's minds off their wombs, they might be helped to some kind of development after all.[5] But his interest in this project passed, and he returned soon to his more comfortable preoccupations with questions of consciousness and of art.

Gertrude's response to Weininger left more permanent impress on her; the book confirmed and extended a variety of her own current beliefs, but most importantly of all, prodded her toward emulating Weininger's systematization of psychology. From the beginning, she avoided Leo's invitations to point-by-point discussion of the book, and though she shared his enthusiasm for it entirely, she felt that once Weininger started his premises rolling, the rest of his elaborate argument followed normally and without surprise, needing neither discussion nor elaboration.[6] Regarding the book as a major contribution to the study of character, she felt Weininger's work corroborated her own. He clarified problems of description and explanation on which she had been foundering and suggested almost limitless descriptions of relations among the mass of people she was using for the character studies in her notebooks. The surge of renewed speculation finally broke the confines of the fictional frame to which she was still clinging in the novel, and to use up the new possibilities, and the quantities of notes that were accumulating, she started several studies of characters, the most important of which were *A Long Gay Book, Many Many Women,* and a work published as *Two: Gertrude Stein and Her Brother,* but which is in fact an analysis not of Gertrude but of her sister-in-law Sarah Stein and of Leo.[7]

Weininger's book was ostensibly nothing more than a violent anti-feminist tract basing its argument on a definition of the psychological differences between "maleness" and "femaleness," and pushing its argument into the outer reaches of the absurd by equating the highest individual possible with the "total male" and the lowest with the "total female."[8] Except for a noticeable change in Stein's tone in analyzing men and women after reading Weininger—she adopted his vocabulary and his animus against women freely during the early months of his influence on her writing[9]—and her tentative borrowing of Weininger's basic distinction between male and female for the basic distinction used for her own system,[10] this part of Weininger's animadversions had little permanent interest for her. His book was fundamentally concerned, however, with much more interesting and useful matters, and these Stein either availed herself of for the first time or used to bolster the direction in which her own views and interests had already been tending.

The nature of his influence must be carefully defined, since Stein's way of absorbing influence was aberrant and unusual. That the book was of major importance in the framing of the "system" Stein organized at this time is evident, but there is little point in looking for logical extensions of Weininger's notions in her work, or even for the presence of his ideas in their own logical context. Her relations with books and ideas were neither disciplined nor conscientious. Unlike Leo, whose reading in philosophy and psychology kept abreast with his interests in art and in letters, Stein appears to have read little but narrative during these years, with almost the single exception of Weininger's book; nor was she habituated to precise comprehension of close philosophic reasoning. It is even possible to suspect that her reading Weininger at all is largely a reflection on the blunt, dogmatic, unshaved, and unqualified clarity of his reasoning. Stein would easily have been held by his flamboyant way of sweeping aside, in compact and violently lucid paragraphs, centuries of common belief. The very qualities of his writing that caused him to be dismissed and laughed at (Freud thought he was mad) would have been the ones to awaken startled interest in her, and a host of tangential ruminations.

Tangential rumination was her way. Leo's and Roché's cognition over and burrowing through the connective tissue of Weininger's elaborate thesis was avoided by Stein, who was interested in new suggestions only if they could be woven into the fabric of her own beliefs. The evidence of the extent to which she carried such assimilation does her no credit. Though she speaks of Weininger as a genius in the notebooks[11] and quotes fragments of his book at length,[12] she actually writes in one entry, "That thing of mine of sex and mind and character all coming together seems to work absolutely."

The aspect of Weininger's thesis that would have struck her immediately was his orientation toward the problem of a science of psychology. Like Nietzsche, Weininger believed psychology to be the "queen of the sciences," but experimental psychology as he knew it in Germany and Austria, and as Stein had known it in America at the Harvard Psychological Laboratory, was for Weininger not merely a superficial but an irrelevant approach to true psychological inquiry.

> If anything is to be gained in the future there must be a demand for a really psychological psychology, and its first battle-cry must be: "Away with the study of sensations."[13]
>   This unlimited science of character . . . will be more than a sort of policy of the motor and sensory reactions of the individual, and in so far will not sink so low as the usual "results" of the modern experimental psychologists, which, indeed, are little more than statistics of physical experiments. . . . The two most intelligent of the empirical psychologists of recent times, William James and R. Avenarius, have felt almost instinctively that psychology cannot really rest upon sensations of the skin and muscles, although, indeed, all modern psychology does depend upon study of sensations.[14]

Stein, having come to the same conclusion about experimental psychology in the course of her work at Harvard, had already anticipated Weininger's substitute for it: a "broad and deep characterology," at the heart of which would *not* be "a complex system of coordinate lines" signifying the "particular determinants" for the description of each individual, for this would only result in, as Weininger put it, "a mosaic psychology" — a psychology which defines character by a mosaic of typifying adjectives. It is true that both Weininger and Stein, in their separate but wholly parallel endeavors in creating a characterology, expended a good deal of energy in trying to "determine the exact point occupied by an individual on the line between two extremes, and multiply this determination by discovering it for a great many characters"; still, beyond this preliminary charting of terms, the essence of Weininger's search lies in the attempt to discover and describe "the single and simple existence" in a man, his "character" in this "unlimited" sense, which "is not something seated behind the thoughts and feeling in the individual, but something revealing itself in every thought and feeling." "This existence, manifest in every moment of the psychical life, is the object of characterology."[15] Stein had already, both in *Melanchtha* and in *QED*, attempted to describe the operation of a "ruling force" — not *in* character, but *of* character — the sense in which the "whole man is manifest in every moment of the psychical life, although, now one side, now the other, is more visible";[16] she had already attempted to inform her string-of-adjectives descriptions of her characters in those works with some principle of wholeness which she thought of as their pulse, their "timing," their rhythm. Weininger was now to make her goal explicit for her: to achieve a synoptic vision of the ego of each character so inclusive that the character's every act and sensation could be observed in its whole relevance to the complete field of his ego. The observer, passing beyond the need to separate one "aspect" of personality from another — a separation which he can accomplish only by the trick of abstraction — would seize on his wholeness, and in that way know in each character "the last touch of [his] human being."

This was precisely the intention Stein first fully recognized in herself during her wrestlings with Annette Rosenshine's woes, and Weininger's fixing of the problem — coming as it did in the midst of her work with Annette — became a kind of call to action in both her messianic psychological activity and her writing.[17] Weininger certainly did not have the effect of changing her intention in her writing, but rather of suppressing all others — all general themes, all ethical precepts, all plans for the narrative, in favor of this single pursuit.

There was no further writing done of any other kind; all of *The Making of Americans* written after 1908, and all of the portraits and short works written through 1911, are "characterological" and nothing else, either diagramming relations among many or setting down synoptic visions of one.

Weininger's psychology, beginning as it does from philosophic premises, is itself not worked out in *Sex and Character*, but merely anticipated.[18] His explosion is *toward* a psychology of character, and lays the basis for both the fundamental typology through which distinctions of character may be described and the ultimate conception of the nature of character which transcends the "mosaic" of typologies.

The typology itself begins with a basic distinction between male and female, as representing, not "types" in human being, but factors. He posits bisexuality in all human beings, whereby the basic sexual nature of a single human being is made up of maleness and femaleness in varying proportions. Human relations in love, in friendship, in hostility, are predicted on the basis of instinctive pairing of opposite "types" — that is, those whose sexual natures complement one another (producing love) and those whose sexual components are similar (producing hostility or indifference).

The opacity and mathematical rigidity of this system is extraordinary. Weininger even went so far as to express his "Laws of Sexual Attraction" in formulae such as

$$A = \frac{K}{a-b} f^t$$

where f^t is an empirical or analytical function of the period during which it is possible for the individuals to act upon one another, what may be called the "reaction-time"; whilst K is the variable factor in which we place all the known and unknown laws of sexual affinity [etc., etc.][19]

But Weininger's naïve scientism is a little mitigated by his detailed enumeration of the factors either belonging to or attending on the two sexual natures, although his violent dogmatism is given even more free play in these enumerations: everything good is male, everything bad is female.

It is important to understand the distinction, though, that some of these characteristics are *components* of the sexual bases, while others are merely attendant on them. Further, some "factors" that contribute to the description of human being are not present at all in one of the ideal types. "Femaleness," for example, not being capable of conceiving of the good, cannot be spoken of as either ethical or unethical; it is merely nonethical. Nor can it be spoken of in terms of lying and telling the truth, for it cannot conceive the truth.[20]

The descriptive attributes of male and female are further particularized in relation to the categories of mind, religion, ethics, existence, individuality, [21] and so on. All these categories are subsequently mirrored in Stein's system; even when she breaks away from the basic separation of types into male and female, her own two basic types continue to be examined in relation to Weininger's categories.

A further problem concerning sex in relation to character is elucidated by Weininger and in turn provides matter for Stein's own system. Since no ideal male or female exists, in a proper psychology both must be treated merely as fictions, valuable as descriptive terms but not to be confused with the actual facts of human being. The error of psychology has always been, says Weininger, that it has been diverted into endless attempts to describe such unrealities as ideal types, but a true characterology must describe actual human beings and the relations among them, not the relations of descriptive terms to one another. Experimental psychology fails in this task because the observations it makes through experimental and statistical methods can never be better than the descriptive categories within which it is making them, and not being grounded in a thoroughly and conscientiously explored philosophy of character, it endlessly confuses even its primitive, unsophisticated descriptive terms with observable instances of human being.[22]

The characterology to which Weininger is looking forward, then, is to meet the practical problem of description with greater refinement of terms and a more precise elaboration of its philosophic justification than had ever before been attempted. And since his own book is merely a preliminary excursion into the philosophy of psychology, and far from a model exercise in psychologizing itself, he confesses that the refinement of psychological terms will have to be far greater than he himself provides in his own work. Nevertheless, he offers examples in his book of the kind of categorizing that is to be done.

Beginning with the assertion that the male-female component in each human being is at the base of his character, the problem of description is that of working out the precise relation of a man's "temperament" and "mind" to his sexual base. To do this intelligibly, various "ideal" combinations of maleness and femaleness must be used as categories. Weininger uses common and recognizable character roles to name artificially fixed points along the line of gradation from total male to total female and matches up these "ideal" fixed points for man and woman by pairing "roles" that are equivalent for each of them. The female prostitute, for example, is equivalent to the male politician; both, as sexual types, are located near the extreme of total femaleness, exhibiting the same self-negating urges of servility, lack of memory, and moral apathy.[23] Since the book is an antifeminist tract, Weininger concentrates on enumerating female roles to attack woman; men's roles are named sparsely.

Stein's system is noticeably afflicted by this imbalance in her source. Her names for female roles include all of Weininger's suggestions, and her additional terms are consistent in kind with his originals. His enumerated female roles are prostitute, mother, servant, saint, and masculine woman.[24] Stein's variations on these are prostitute, "mother of all," servant girl, and "genuine masculine."[25] Weininger's "saint" disappears as a group in her system except for a single instance: Alice Toklas is called by either her own name or St. Theresa's, though the original significance of "saint" is gone. In Weininger, saints exemplify hysteria in women; in Stein, "St. Theresa" is an instance of self-effacing devotion akin to, and allied to, the femininity of the prostitute.[26] Stein adds four women's roles to Weininger's: the "lady," the "mistress," the "sister," and the "spinster." These are juxtaposed in subgroups and combinations such as the "mistress prostitute," the "lady masculine," the "pseudo-masculine,"[27] and so on.

In establishing male groups — finding little to go on in Weininger — her inability to cope for long with a logical scheme betrays her. After striking obvious parallels to some of Weininger's female groups, she adds whimsical and privately suggestive names for male groups that are inconsistent as classification with the other terms and among themselves. They are unhappily as consistently banal, too, as the names she inherited. The list runs: "Bazarofian," man-of-the-world, Anglo-Saxon, masculine prostitute, adolescent, old tabby, fanatic, and primitive soul. One additional large group — idealist — is divided into four subgroups, depending upon what one is being idealistic about: intellect, beauty, romance, or power.[28]

But more significant than any of the terms and categories that Stein took from Weininger — and the aspect of his work that apparently struck her most forcibly — was his immensely pertinent resolution of her original twin problem: the conscious feeling of dissociation from the cosmos (in her phrase, the loss of the "feeling of everlasting") and that contemporary description of men as bundles of "factors" and causative patterns which leads to a loss of one's sense of uniqueness (in her phrase, that "each one is one").[29]

Since Weininger's interests are fundamentally ethical and metaphysical, his psychology of "character" moves unswervingly toward the definition of "ultimate" human being, which is defined in terms of consciousness. Ultimate self-consciousness embraces absolute memory, absolute self-comprehension, and truth; and ultimate cosmic consciousness embraces absolute identification and unqualified relation of the self with the universal and the eternal. For Weininger, therefore, the completed individual is one whose consciousness — and therefore whose true existence — has moved outside of time and has thereby conquered it.[30]

The importance of this notion for Stein can hardly be overestimated. It appears at length in her work first in the portrait of David Hersland, but later in her work — in her speculative writing of the 1930s — this notion of the "completed individual" continued to be the basis of her repeated attempts to lay to rest her nineteenth-century dilemmas concerning loss of uniqueness and "everlasting." The concept of the completed individual, "outside of time," became in fact the unifying locus of her thought from the beginning to the end of her writing.

William James's *The Will to Believe* was merely a disappointment to her hope that it, at least, might mitigate her large metaphysical desperations.[31] Whatever logic exists in her speculative writing rests on her denial of pragmatism and her conscientious attempt to shore up against its ruins minimal certainties on the basis of Weininger's Kantian idealism. The whole incrustation of Stein's ideas and feelings in her writings from 1908 to the end of her life derives from Weininger's envisioning of the highest "type" of human being — the only true individuality — in terms of his achieving the promise of immortality by escaping from the contingency of time. Her later discussions of human nature as opposed to the human mind, of genius, of memory, of the hopelessness of "human nature" (for her, the "diagrammed" aspects of human being) achieving "entity" out of itself, and her notion that the "human mind" alone and of itself can effect and know its own "entity" — all these discussions elaborate the basic definition in Weininger of the steps whereby the ultimately human redeems itself from the "mosaic" of factors currently accounting for human existence. And Stein follows Weininger's system of values to its end by insisting that this victory over time is achieved only by means of those qualities and capabilities of mind and spirit that belong to the genius or to the saint alone. In her writing of the 1920s and 1930s, the relevance of saints to her thought, the meaning of works such as "Saints and Singing," the meaning, in *The Mother of Us All*, of Susan B. Anthony's "You may be married to the past one, no one can be married to the present one, the one, the one, the present one,"[32] the rationale of her insistence on her own genius (apart from its basis in personal idiosyncracy), may be looked for in her emulation of Weininger's unqualified and unlimited individuality, incapable of being known to others but capable only of being self-known, and the consequence to human being of such a creature coming to fruition.

Her enthusiasm for this new conception was first expressed in her revision and enlargement of the portrait of David Hersland in the novel. In the first version of the novel, he was to be merely "singular" as a Westerner—and in terms of the first version, that was eminence enough. Now, in the 1908 notes for revision, his "singularity" is given Weiningerian dimensions. Make "David completed individual," she instructs herself, and further, "must realise my hero by making him go through my development."[33] Understood in this light, does this mean that David was to be the "genius" of Weininger's description? No, he was to be merely the character in the book who might have been, the only character of whom one might properly say that he should have been, and failed. None of the other characters have sufficient "being" to be worthy of such a failure—neither their success nor their failure is on a par with his. As in the original plan of the book, he remains a defeated man, trapped by his longing for death.

To give his failure further distinction, Stein added her own imagined characterization of Weininger himself, when she made the shocking discovery of his suicide.[34] After that discovery, everything fitted anew: her own "sense of failure" at twenty-nine (that is, in 1903, her desperate "suicidal" year after the abortive May Bookstaver affair); Leon Solomon's "suicide" when he "chose" cancer and, more verifiably, chose to undergo a fatal operation at the age of twenty-nine; and finally Weininger's suicide after his brilliant achievement, especially relevant since that achievement rested so largely on the intellectual comprehension and expression of the victory the "singular" individual is capable of winning over death. Weininger, a Jew, could be understood, then, to have suffered from what Stein thought of as the inevitable failure of Jews: that they "run themselves by their minds."[35] And David, in the 1908 revision, so acquired one of his subtlest dimensions. Beyond his longing to discover why he should be alive—a cripplingly laborious activity in itself—he "runs" himself and his inquiry "by his mind," and so shares in the tragic mistakes of Weininger the man; but all the while he is making this error as a man, he is moving toward the discovery of and in part becoming the embodiment of, the individual envisioned by Weininger the philosopher.

Notes

1. Title page, *The Making of Americans* (Paris: Contact Editions, 1925). All subsequent complete editions are offsets of this edition. *The Making of Americans* will hereafter be appreviated as *MA*.

2. Otto Weininger, *Sex and Character* (London: William Heinemann; New York: G. P. Putnam's Sons, 1906).

3. Alice B. Toklas, interviews, and Henri Pierre Roché, interview. From November of 1952 to February of 1953 Toklas adumbrated and orally annotated the "Notebooks" out of her store of memories for about eight hours a day, four days a week. . . . For information on Roché see *The Autobiography of Alice B. Toklas* (New York: Harcourt, Brace and Co., 1933), pp. 54–55, 123.

4. Letters, E. L. Erving to GS, December 14, 1908, and May 3, 1909; Marion Walter to GS, 1909. All letters referred to in this article are part of the Gertrude Stein Collection, the Yale Collection of American Literature, the Beinecke Rare Book and Manuscript Library, Yale University.

5. Roché, interview.

6. Toklas, interviews.

7. Gertrude Stein, *Two: Gertrude Stein and Her Brother, and Other Early Portraits (1908–1912)* (New Haven: Yale Univ. Press, 1951). *A Long Gay Book* and *Many Many Women* were published in *Matisse Picasso and Gertrude Stein* (Paris: Plain Edition, 1933).

8. Weininger, pp. 5–10.

9. See especially *NB*-DB, passim. . . .

10. *NB*-DB, p. 16.

11. *NB*-A, pp. 15, 16; *NB*, Note #49.

12. Weininger's quotation from Kant's *Anthropology*, p. 161, is in turn quoted by GS in an unassigned fragment. Two other unassigned notes quote passages from *Sex and Character*.

13. Weininger, p. 83.

14. Ibid., pp. 81–82.

15. Ibid., p. 83.

16. Ibid.

17. Gertrude's and Sarah Stein's sessions with Annette Rosenshine, during which they alternately attempted to cure their patient of her neuroses (Sarah with Christian Science and Gertrude with her own aggressive brand of psychological analysis), is recounted in Annette Rosenshine's unpublished memoirs, "Life's Not a Paragraph," deposited in the Bancroft Library, University of California at Berkeley.

18. Weininger, p. ix.

19. Ibid., pp. 37–38, 195.

20. Ibid., p. 130.

21. Ibid., Ch. IX.

22. Ibid., pp. 82, 84.

23. Ibid., p. 228.

24. Ibid., pp. 8, 17, 214–35, 272, 277.

25. The concurrent *NBs*, *NB*-DB and *NB*-ⓒ, detail these types.

26. *NB*-D, pp. 4, 6, 8, 9, 10, 15; *NB*-E, p. 11.

27. *NB*-DB, *NB*-Ⓑ, *NB*-ⓒ and *NB*-J.

28. *NB*-DB, pp. 8, 9, 10, 11, 13, 17, 18; Note #45.

29. Refrain used in *Many Many Women*, published in *Matisse Picasso and Gertrude Stein*, pp. 119–98.

30. Weininger, pp. 136–37:

Memory only fully vanquishes time when it appears in a universal form as in universal men.

The genius is thus the only timeless man — at least, this and nothing else is his ideal of himself; he is, as is proved by his passionate and urgent desire for immortality, just the man with the strongest demand for timelessness, with the greatest desire for value. . . . His universal comprehension and memory forbid the annihilation of his experiences with the passing of the moment in which each occurred; his birth is independent of his age, and his work never dies.

31. The most considerable misunderstanding involves the importance of the influence of William James. (The influence of William James's "practical and radical empiricism" is thoroughly argued by Frederick J. Hoffman, *Gertrude Stein*, Univ. of Minnesota, Pamphlets on American Writers, No. 10 [Minneapolis: Univ. of Minnesota, 1961].) Gertrude, during the writing of *The Making of Americans*, was in full flight from James and from pragmatism. Her personal admiration for James and her continuing interest in him is evident in several notebook entries: *NB-A*, p. 1; *NB-B*, p. 1; *NB-H*, p. 3; *NB-J*, pp. 12, 13, 15; but her revolt from his teaching is one of the important bases of the whole book.

32. "Saints and Singing, A Play," published in *Operas and Plays* (Paris: Plain Edition, 1932); "The Mother of Us All," in *Last Operas and Plays* (New York: Rinehart & Co., 1949), p. 75.

33. *NB-MA*, p. 23.

34. Toklas, interviews.

35. *NB-A* p. 1.

Gertrude Stein and the Problems of Autobiography

James E. Breslin*

When *The Autobiography of Alice B. Toklas* was published in 1933, the book soon became, as Gertrude Stein both hoped and feared, a critical and popular success. Stein earned celebrity and a substantial amount of money, both of which depressed her. *The Autobiography*'s subsequent literary reputation might have cheered her up, however, for Stein's critics — with the notable exception of her best critic, Richard Bridgman[1] — have generally either ignored or rejected *The Autobiography*. B. L. Reid dismissed it as "chitchat," and many readers find it merely anecdotal and gossipy.[2] Certainly, readers who approach it with expectations shaped by the revival of confessional writing in the 1960's are apt to reject it as too reserved. Stein herself had somewhat different misgivings about the book, stating in *Everybody's Autobiography* (1936) that the earlier work had dealt with what had happened instead of "what is happening."[3] Yet *The Autobiography*'s charming, playful, anecdotal surface has distracted its readers from its real complexity; it provides not — as Stein seems to have thought — a mere submission to the conventions of autobiography but an intense and creative struggle with them.

*Reprinted from the *Georgia Review* 33, no. 4 (Winter 1979): 901–13. © 1979 by the University of Georgia. Reprinted by permission of the *Georgia Review* and James E. Breslin.

In many ways the autobiographical act is one at odds with, even a betrayal of, Gertrude Stein's aesthetic principles. Her essay "What Are Master-pieces and Why Are There So Few of Them" offers a concise statement of those principles: "The minute your memory functions while you are doing anything it may be very popular but actually it is dull," Stein warns; her desire to live and write in a continuous present thus turns her against the necessarily retrospective act of autobiography.[4] But Stein's opposition to the conventions of her genre runs even deeper than this, because her commitment to a continuous present forces her to reject the notion of identity altogether. "Identity is recognition," she writes: "I am I because my little dog knows me" (pp. 146–47). Identity, an artificial construction based on the perception of certain fixed traits that allow my little dog or anyone else to imagine that they know me, stresses repetition, which is, according to Stein, antithetical to creativity. Identity "destroys creation" (p. 147) — as does memory; both, carrying the past over into the present and structuring by repetition, are ways we have of familiarizing the strangeness, the mysterious being, of others. Masterpieces de-familiar-ize; they derive from "knowing that there is no identity and producing while identity is not" (p. 151). In part Stein is warning against self-imitation, and she quotes Picasso as saying that he is willing to be influenced by anyone but himself; but she is also stressing that to live in a continuous present, to *be* rather than to *repeat*, one must constantly break down identity. But can there be an *auto*-biography in which "there is no identity"? Or, to put the question somewhat differently: autobiographies are customarily *identified* as acts of *self*-representation, but Stein is challenged to refashion the form to show that she eludes or transcends the category of self or identity.

At the same time her belief in a continuous present sets Stein against the kind of narrative that we are accustomed (again) to find in auto-*bio*-graphy. "What is the use of being a boy if you are going to grow up to be a man?" she asks in "What Are Master-pieces" (p. 150). Like remembering and identifying, narrating — telling, say, the story of a girl becoming a woman — such narrating represents a linear sequence of time, not an ongoing present. In addition, remembering, identifying, and narrating all view things in relation to other things (e.g., girl in relation to woman), instead of viewing a thing as what Stein calls an "entity" (p. 149) — a thing existent in and for itself. A masterpiece, transcending linear time and recognizable identity, is itself an "entity," not, as Eliot had said, a revision of the literary tradition but an absolute act of creation. The fact that the early works of Cubism derive from such absolute acts of creation explains why, as we are told in *The Autobiography*, they are so strange, almost physically painful to look at — and yet must be looked at intently: the viewer must struggle to get beyond mere recognition, the comfortably familiar. But autobiographies are hardly absolute acts of creation; they are historical, referring to persons and events that clearly existed out there, in reality, prior to their representation in language. Finally, Stein holds that any concession to—or even consciousness of—an audience undermines creativity; as soon as a writer begins to think of him/herself in relation to an audience, he or she "writes what the other person is to hear and so entity does not exist there are two present instead of one and so once again creation breaks down" (p. 148). But if we now find it problematic to think of even a lyric poem as autotelic, how can we imagine an autotelic autobiography? Can Stein create an autobiography without identity, memory, linear time? And if she did, could we bear to read it? In some ways *Everybody's Autobiography*, dealing with "what is happening" instead of what had happened, comes closer to these aims; but what makes *The Autobiography of Alice B. Toklas* so interesting is that it admits the conventions of memory, identity, chronological time—in order to fight against and ultimately to transcend their deadening effects.

When she was asked to write her autobiography, Stein replied, "Not possibly,"[5] and it is easier to imagine her writing an essay called "What Are Autobiographies and Why Are None of Them Master-pieces" than it is to imagine her writing her own autobiography. Of course, she did not write her own autobiography; she wrote *The Autobiography of Alice B. Toklas*. Or did she? Some writers have speculated that Alice B. Toklas wrote her own autobiography or at least substantial parts of it.[6] But perhaps the most important point about this debate is that it seems to have been generated not just by an extraliterary curiosity about the book's composition, but by an actual literary effect the book has on its readers—namely, the effect of raising questions about just whose book it is.

I will return to this issue; for the moment, assuming (as I have been) Stein to be the book's author, I want to suggest how she took up the formal challenge of autobiography by recalling a young man named Andrew Green, who appears briefly in the third chapter of *The Autobiography*. Andrew Green "hated everything modern." Once while staying at 27 rue de Fleurus for a month he covered "all the pictures with cashmere shawls"; he "could not bear" to look at the strange, frightening paintings. Significantly, "he had a prodigious *memory* and could recite all of Milton's Paradise Lost by heart" (my emphasis). "He adored as he said a simple centre and a continuous design." Green *has* an identity, so much so that his character can be fixed in a single, brief paragraph. Gertrude Stein does not have an identity; in attempting to represent her "self" she created in *The Autobiography of Alice B. Toklas* a book with an elusive center and a discontinuous design.

Even the title page of the current Vintage edition—*The Autobiography of Alice B. Toklas* BY Gertrude Stein—is enough to suggest that the center of the ensuing text may be difficult to locate. The original Harcourt edition made the same point in a more subtle way: both the cover and the title page print only a title—*The Autobiography of Alice B. Toklas*—but no author's name is given. The frontispiece (facing the title page), however, is a Man Ray photograph which shows Stein in the right foreground, seated at a table, but with her back to the camera and in dark shadow; Alice B. Toklas stands in the left background, but she stands in light and framed by a doorway. The photograph, with its obscure foreground and distinct background, has no clear primary subject — like the book that follows; the seated Stein, however, is writing, and the possibility is raised that *she* may be the author of the book, an uncertainty not resolved for the reader of this edition until its final page — when "Toklas" tells us that Stein has in fact written *The Autobiography*. Moreover, the book's style blends the domestic particularity, whimsical humor, and ironic precision of Toklas with some of the leading features of Stein's writing — e.g., stylized repetition, digression, a language that continually points up its own artifice. The reader is not certain who it is he is listening to; nor is he meant to be. Richard Bridgman has shown that "Stanzas in Meditation," written at the same time as *The Autobiography*, is at least partly about writing *The Autobiography*, and the poem strongly suggests that our uncertainties were an intended effect: "This is her autobiography one of two / But which it is no one . . . can know."[7]

But most readers are more like Andrew Green than Gertrude Stein; they don't like to dwell in uncertainties, and so most discussions of *The Autobiography* begin by assuming the character of Stein to be its easily identifiable center, and they proceed to discuss this character as if it were not mediated for the reader by a perspective that is to *some* degree external to it. Yet, even if we proceed along these lines, the character of Stein turns out to be an elusive and enigmatic "center." Stein, Toklas tells us, sought in her writing to give "the inside as seen from the outside" (p. 156); that is one reason she creates herself through the external perspective of Toklas. What she means by "the inside" can be clarified through *The Autobiography*'s account of Picasso's famous portrait of Stein; it was with this painting, we are told, that Picasso "passed from the Harlequin, the *charming* early italian period to the *intensive struggle* which was to end in cubism" (p. 54; my emphasis). Stein emphasizes the "intensive struggle" that went into the painting of the portrait itself. During the winter of 1907 Stein patiently posed for Picasso some eighty or ninety times, but then he abruptly "painted out the whole head." "I can't see you any longer when I look, he said irritably" (p. 53). At this point both Stein and Picasso left Paris for the summer, but the day he returned "Picasso sat down and out of his head painted the head in without having seen Gertrude Stein again." In the enigmatic sentence, "I can't see you any longer when I look," what is the referent of "you"? On the one hand, it is not the external, literal Stein, recognizable to her little dog or a realistic novelist. That is why, when Stein later cuts her hair short, Picasso, at first disturbed, can conclude that "all the same it is all there." He was not striving for a realistic mimesis, as Stein stresses in her account of Picasso's difficulties with what turned out to be the least realistic feature of the portrait, the face. On the other hand, Picasso was not trying to evoke the inner, subconscious depths of Stein, of the sort that might fascinate a psychological novelist; in fact, Toklas later claims that Stein had no subconscious (p. 79).

In the painting itself Stein's body is solid, massive, weighty, sculptured; the simple, severe lines of the eyebrows, nose and mouth, the slightly uneven eyes create a stylized, mask-like face. She inhabits an abstract space, her eyes conveying an almost fierce attentiveness, but she is calm, at rest, even serene. Picasso's Stein seems a regal, perhaps deific, figure, but the earth colors of her dress, blending with the tan background, modify the austerity of the face and the monumentality of the body to create warmth and to humanize Stein. The portrait is thus an instance of what Stein herself called "elemental abstraction" (p. 64); the "you" painted by Picasso is, therefore, not a personality, a recognizable identity, but an entity — Stein's being, awesome, serene, strange, mysterious yet human. Like Picasso's portrait, *The Autobiography* gives the inside by way of the outside; it plays down psychology and sticks to the surface, recording externals (objects, acts, dialogues) in a way that clearly manifests deliberate and idiosyncratic acts of selection and stylization. Such admitted artifice annoys many readers who, with simpler models of self and autobiography, demand a fuller intimacy and deeper psychology of their autobiographers. But Stein's stylization of the surface reveals the "you" that Picasso, having looked so long and intently, could no longer see when he looked. *The Autobiography*, in short, gives us Gertrude Stein being.

To envision *this* Stein required an "intensive struggle" and at many points Picasso was urged by friends — among them Andrew Green — to stop with the "beauty" of what he had so far accomplished, but Picasso, turning his back on his audience, went on. In this way, renouncing a "charming" for a more severe and difficult work, Picasso produced a masterpiece. Compare Picasso's heroic struggles with the facility of a Vallaton:

> When he painted a portrait he made a crayon sketch and then began painting at the top of the canvas straight across. Gertrude Stein said it was like pulling down a curtain as slowly as one of his swiss glaciers. Slowly he pulled the curtain down and by the time he was at the bottom of the canvas, there you were. The whole operation took about two weeks and then he gave the canvas to you. First however he exhibited it in the autumn salon and it had considerable notice and everybody was pleased. (p. 51).

Vallaton's scrupulously predetermined works are the comic opposites of Picasso's adventurous and difficult acts of discovery. Vallaton's paintings pleased everybody, whereas at first only "the painter and the painted" admired Picasso's portrait of Stein. Creative works thus demand an intensive struggle from both creator and audience. "The pictures were so strange that one quite instinctively looked at anything rather than at them just at first," Toklas recalls of her first evening in Stein's atelier (p. 9), and even in recollection, some twenty-five years later, this difficulty is reexperienced: Toklas comes to describe the paintings (about which the reader is very eager to hear) only slowly, almost resistingly, after several digressions. Gertrude Stein can rest her head against a rock and stare at the Italian noonday sun; but like a masterpiece or the sun, Stein herself is hard to look at directly — another reason for the mediation of Toklas — and even Toklas approaches her, too, very slowly. Stein is first mentioned on page 5 where Toklas reports of their first meeting only that "I was impressed by the coral brooch she wore and her voice,"and that "a bell within me rang" certifying that Stein was a genius. The reader expects the first meeting between the two women to be related with ample circumstantial and emotional detail; instead, only two rather oddly selected details are given, then a long leap is made to a perception of Stein's genius, though the playful tone makes it hard for us to be sure exactly how seriously we are to take this claim. The scene is deliberately simplified; circumstantial and psychological detail are eliminated — to foreground the powerful, strange presence of Stein and the intuitive powers of Toklas.

Stein is next glimpsed obliquely, through objects associated with her — again, as if her presence were too powerful to be looked at directly. Toklas remembers from her first visit to the atelier "a large table on which were horseshoe nails and pebbles and little pipe cigarette holders" which she later found "to be accumulations from the pockets of Picasso and Gertrude Stein" (p. 9). Without any clear associational values, these objects at once invite and frustrate psychological speculation, as the stylized surface of *The Autobiography* so often does; we are tempted to "identify" Stein but are shown that we can't. Resisting metaphorization, these simple objects nevertheless provide humanizing detail (like the earth colors of Picasso's portrait) before the mythologizing of Stein that follows just a few sentences later.

> The chairs in the room were also all italian renaissance, not very comfortable for short-legged people and one got the habit of sitting on one's legs. Miss Stein sat near the stove in a lovely high-backed one and she peacefully let her legs hang, which was a matter of habit, and when any one of the many visitors came to ask her a question she lifted herself up out of this chair and usually replied in french, not just now.

In this Gertrude Stein — sitting "peacefully" in a high, hard, uncomfortable chair, dispensing regal gestures of denial — the reader confronts a presence of profound, contemplative calm, a figure very like the one in Picasso's portrait. The first image points toward the Stein who, later, finds it restful to stare at the midday sun or at those disquieting paintings that Andrew Green covered with cashmere shawls; it also points toward the later mysterious, sibylline Stein who makes enigmatic pronouncements, who lives in a world of "hidden meanings" (p. 15) and who does not explain things to the reader or even to Toklas, leaving the adventure of discovery to us; it is this Stein who dismisses Pound as the "village explainer" (p. 200). But in this first representation of Stein, as throughout *The Autobiography*, the external perspective of Toklas, sticking to the observable surface, suggests the inside while leaving it mysterious. As a result, Stein is not created as a realistic, psychologically complex character; she is, rather, an abstraction, a deliberate simplification — a mythical figure whose peaceful self-sufficiency allows her to transcend external circumstances.

The *Autobiography* of Benjamin Franklin records the attempt to create an identity through acts of will; *The Education of Henry Adams* records the breakdown of a similar attempt and the dissolution of the very idea of identity. *The Autobiography of Alice B. Toklas* takes the process one step further; the book shows us not someone striving to create a self, but someone who *exists* calmly in a world without any external orders. Again and again the book shows us Stein existing "peacefully" under circumstances that are often far more stressful than uncomfortable chairs. Even Picasso, the character closest to her equal, is "fussed" when he arrives late for a Stein dinner party; looks "sheepish" when he wrests his piece of bread back from Stein, who has accidentally picked it up; or becomes embarrassed when Stein mentions the possibility of his seeing Fernande after they have temporarily separated. Stein, on the other hand, seems to possess an inner stillness that allows her to respond to external pressures with serenity, sometimes even with good humor. When World War I starts while she is visiting London, Stein is concerned but not alarmed about the fate of her writings, all copies of which are back in Paris. Later, after her return to Paris, during an air raid, she calmly quiets an Alice B. Toklas who is so frightened her knees are literally knocking together; and in *The Autobiography*'s final chapter Stein enters the confused and diminished Paris of the postwar era with the same equanimity she had shown during the many crises of the war. Most impressive, however, is the cheerful confidence with which she meets the frugality, frequent disorder, and the public antagonism of the early years of her career. Stein remains steadfastly committed to her work, in spite of her difficulties in finding publication — and in spite of journalistic ridicule when her writing does appear. When *Three Lives* is privately printed, her publisher sends to 27 rue de Fleurus a young man, who questions her knowledge of English; Stein laughs — as she often does at moments when we expect her to be angry or embittered — and her response is contrasted with that of Matisse, two pages earlier, whose feelings are "frightfully" hurt by newspaper ridicule of his art school.

Yet the Stein of *The Autobiography* is by no means as easy to pin down as this discussion of her so far implies; rather, the book frustrates any attempt to fix Stein in a simply identity. In *Everybody's Autobiography*

Stein admires paintings which move rather than being about movement and which seem to come out of the "prison" of their frames — as if the subject were alive, truly existing (*EA*, p. 312). Stein's own aesthetic theory, as we have seen, made her acutely aware that by attempting to incarnate her being in language in an autobiography, she was running the risk of merely fixing, of limiting and deadening, herself. But the pressures of autobiography, among them the pressure of language itself, constitute another set of external circumstances to which Stein calmly responds with a playful sense of adventure. The result is that *The Autobiography of Alice B. Toklas* presents a Gertrude Stein who keeps stepping out of the frame, as if she were alive, truly existing. The "psychology" of her character may be a simplified one, but a reader who tries to delineate this character in a careful way finds him/herself speaking in contradictions; and these very contradictions are what make the character of Stein remain mysterious, elusive — alive.

Gertrude Stein liked to sit and pose for Picasso and other artists, but she also liked the long walks home afterwards through the darkening Paris streets. Stillness and motion are one set of contraries that create the character of Gertrude Stein. Andrew Green, resisting the challenge of modernity, of the moment, remains anxiously fixed and static — neither at rest nor in motion. But alongside the oracular Stein who can sit peacefully in a hard, high-backed chair, we must place the Stein who, in a recurring phrase, "goes on." "Keep your mind open," William James had told her at Radcliffe (p. 78), and the willingness to move into new experience — or "liveliness" — becomes a standard against which all characters are measured in *The Autobiography*. Fernande feels "heavy in hand" (p. 14) and seems "indolent" (p. 19); Matisse is "very alert although slightly heavy" and, later, virile but without "life" (p. 37). In contrast with both of these Picasso is "quick moving but not restless" (p. 12); Stein herself is lively and adventurous, not heavy nor indolent; she may move slowly, but she moves forward — although not restlessly. Not long after Gertrude Stein and her brother arrive in Paris, they begin to buy Cézannes, small ones at first. But "having gone so far," they "decided to go further, they decided to buy a big Cézanne and then they would stop" (p. 33). But even then they go on and later Stein — unlike her brother, another casualty to modernity — goes on to Picasso. This commitment to process explains why Stein "loves objects that are breakable": "she says she likes what she has and she likes the adventure of a new one" (p. 88). In fact, so committed is Stein to ongoing movement that when driving her car "she goes forward admirably, she does not go backward successfully."

But even this account of the contradictions in Stein's character simplifies it, for each side of the rest/motion opposition generates, in turn, its own oppositions. Stein may be calmly self-possessed, but she also has an "explosive temper" (p. 11); she enjoys the novelty of fresh experience, yet she is upset if asked to do something suddenly (p. 221). The important point, however, is that these various features are not presented as the odd twists and turns within a complex yet ultimately unified character; they are the unresolved contradictions of Gertrude Stein's being. She resists all our attempts to frame her as surely as that odd assortment of objects from the pockets of Picasso and Stein resist our efforts to find meaning in them: they just *are*.

Contradictions similarly proliferate when we examine the book's theories about and actual practice of writing. At times Stein speaks of her own work as if it were based on a very simple model of art as representation. Real life sources are given for characters in her fiction; Picasso's cubism is given a realistic basis in Spanish landscape and architecture (p. 90) and Stein speaks of art as the "exact reproduction of an inner or an outer reality" (p. 211). Yet in the same paragraph Stein asserts that "events" ought not to be "the material of poetry and prose"; her writing is often described as the making of sentences, as if it were more construction that representation; and she elsewhere affirms distortion and abstraction in art. Anyone who reads *The Autobiography* looking for a "key" to Stein's fictional works — and many do, as Stein knew they would — will be just as frustrated as the one who reads it looking for the "key" to Stein's private psychology. "Observation and construction make imagination," Stein says (p. 76), as if she were demystifying the imagination, making it a matter of perception and craft, but Stein, of course, *goes on*: "Observation and construction make imagination, that is granting the possession of imagination," and imagination and Stein herself remain playfully mystified. Oracular and witty, Stein is a sibylline presence, no village or even a Parisian explainer.

The oppositions in Stein's "theorizing" reappear in the writing of the book itself, which continually offers contradictory clues about what *kind* of book it is. Its anecdotal manner, its preoccupation with recognizable, real figures, its concern with "the heroic age of cubism" give it the quality of a memoir, as if it were presenting a true historical record. Yet it is *The Autobiography* OF *Alice B. Toklas* — BY Gertrude Stein: the book is marked at once as an autobiography and a fiction (since it is the autobiography of someone other than the author). An ingenuous sentence at the end tantalizes us in the same way: "I am going to write [the autobiography] for you," Stein tells Toklas. "I am going to write it as simply as Defoe did the autobiography of Robinson Crusoe" (p. 252). But how simply was that? Not even this sentence is very simple; it is one written by the (likely) actual author, Stein, imputed to the fictive author, Toklas, who is reporting something said by the character Stein to the character/author Toklas; the sentence, moreover, compares the autobiography of a fictional character (Robinson Crusoe) with that of a character who was real, at least until Stein started writing her autobiography for her. Throughout, *The Autobi-*

ography's whimsical, self-interrupting, repetitious, stylized prose marks it as a piece of admitted and self-conscious artifice. The book is an historical memoir; the book is a fictional construct.

To put it another way, *The Autobiography* continually points up the disparity between actuality and its representation, but it does so without irony, without lamenting the insufficiency of either reality or of literary fictions. The book's narrative method simultaneously acknowledges chronological time and the power of writing to play freely with that time; again Stein does not privilege either one over the other. "Moving is in every direction," Stein writes in *Narration*.[8] Just the chapter titles in *The Autobiography* ("Before I Came to Paris," "My Arrival in Paris," "Gertrude Stein in Paris — 1903–1907," "Gertrude Stein Before She Came to Paris," "1907–1914," "The War," and "After the War — 1919–1932") are enough to suggest that the book both establishes and breaks a forward movement toward the time of its composition. Yet this overall movement is further complicated by the book's local texture — partly by its numerous portraits (which halt temporal progression) and partly by Toklas' wandering style of narration, its constant excursions backward and forward in time. For it is not accurate to speak, as I just did, of the book's forward movement toward the time of its composition, because we listen to Toklas in the *act* of recollection; and Toklas, no Vallaton proceeding along pre-designed lines, moves by playful, free association — thereby liberating herself from chronological order while still accepting its reality. Another temporal dimension of *The Autobiography* is thus the continuous present of its telling. The book's multivalence, its moving in all directions, can also be seen in its ending. In the foreground of the final chapter we have Toklas writing in the present; she is writing about "After the War — 1919–1932," and by looking backward to this period she carries the book's narrative forward into the post-war era and acknowledges the reality of historical time. One feature of this period that is emphasized is Stein's increasing literary success, which might seem to provide the book with a happy conclusion until we remember that, for Stein, recognition is as much reason for self-doubt and suspicion as it is for gratification, and Toklas equally emphasizes the postwar decline from "the heroic age of cubism." At the same time Stein, fixated neither by success nor by nostalgia for an heroic past, is shown searching for the source of a new creative idea she believes has entered painting; the source may be the work of Francis Rose, but this is not certain. With "her never failing curiosity" (p. 250) the adventuresome Stein remains in a continuous present, an entity.

At *The Autobiography*'s close, the narrative catches up with itself or at least with its beginning, as we learn of the genesis of the book and that Stein is its author. In the original edition this final page of the text was followed by a photograph of the first page of the manuscript. *The Autobiography* ends by folding back on itself; and a reader is invited to reread the book in light of the revelation that Stein is its author. Lest this revelation make the reader too comfortable, he or she is also, as we have seen, assured of the book's Defoe-like simplicity in a way that warns of its complexity and deviousness. At the end *The Autobiography* circles back on itself as if it were an autonomous verbal reality. Yet the book's conclusion also reveals Stein to be on a quest that is not completed; the book's ending is also open. The end of the book closes off and frames a life at the same time that it breaks out of its frame, its artificial closure, to affirm the ongoing process of the author's life. At its close, as throughout *The Autobiography*, moving is in all directions.

Gertrude Stein complained to Matisse that "there is nothing within you that fights itself" (p. 65); that is why he lacks life. Through its contradictions *The Autobiography of Alice B. Toklas* fights itself and so achieves creative life. The problems of the book—many of which are versions of the problem of referentiality, the relation of the work to external reality—are the problems and contradictions of autobiography itself, problems that make the genre such a difficult one for both theoretical and practical criticism. How can we deal with the tension between historical truthfulness and aesthetic design in autobiography? Or with the splitting of the author into character and writer? Or with the difficulties of ending an autobiography, given that the author's life is likely to go on? Stein deliberately raises and foregrounds these difficult questions, not in order to solve or answer them, but to play with them and to make the ways in which the genre fights itself into her book's energizing principles. Her relation to autobiography parallels what she says the relation of a genius to time must be: he or she must "accept it and deny it by creating it" (*EA*, p. 281). By renouncing a simple center and a continuous design, by exploring the formal dilemmas of the genre, Gertrude Stein at once accepted, denied, and created autobiography.

Notes

1. Richard Bridgman, *Gertrude Stein in Pieces* (New York: Oxford Univ. Press, 1970), pp. 209-37.

2. B. L. Reid, *Art by Subtraction* (Norman Univ. of Oklahoma Press, 1958), p. 186.

3. *Everybody's Autobiography* (New York: Vintage Books, 1973), p. 303. Hereafter cited as *EA*.

4. "What Are Master-pieces and Why Are There So Few of Them," in *Writings and Lectures, 1911-1945*, ed. Patricia Meyerowitz (London: Owen, 1967), p. 150. Subsequent citations in the text are to this edition.

5. *The Autobiography of Alice B. Toklas* (London: Arrow Books, 1960), p. 251. Subsequent citations in the text are to this edition.

6. Bridgman, pp. 209-17.

7. Bridgman, pp. 213-17.

8. *Narration* (Chicago: Univ. of Chicago Press, 1935), p. 19.

Guardians and Witnesses:
Narrative Technique in Gertrude
Stein's *Useful Knowledge*
Elizabeth Fifer*

In *Useful Knowledge* (1928),[1] a collection of previously unpublished shorter pieces written between 1914 and 1926, Gertrude Stein makes the case for "redress" and "excess" (p. 200) in our sexual and imaginative lives. The composite text is a dramatic collage of changing styles, alternating between distinct voices and various roles. Its most inventive bursts of free rhythms invariably give way to tight rhyme schemes and exact meters. Surprising juxtaposition is its most basic resource, resonance and fluidity its basic procedures. Of twenty-one short works collected, none provides a constant narrator. Instead, Stein continues her earlier practice of role-playing,[2] evaluating her own relationship with Alice B. Toklas, and attempting a first experimental autobiography, whose sequel, *The Autobiography of Alice B. Toklas*, would appear in 1933. In that book, she would use another entire personality as a mask. In *Useful Knowledge*, the language itself functions both as primary vehicle and disguise, simultaneously concealing and revealing her purposes. It is as if her extreme need to speak the unspeakable forced its way into a new channel—a way to both say and unsay at once.

In *Useful Knowledge*, Stein takes special delight in submerging her questions and lists, with their extensive sexual puns, into a distanced scientific and philosophic language. As in a philosophic inquiry, the questions asked are often "leading questions," which sharply narrow and carefully determine their response. Yet in another sense they also provide Stein with a release and a way to go forward—a technique that cuts through the themes of the book and allows her to step in and manage her own, and her audience's, perception. By using leading questions and other philosophic "proofs" to convince us her suppositions are correct, she balances between oppositions and creates extremes to dramatize all the sides of her argument. She addresses herself to a novice who needs instructions, hence the title, but she remains intensely conscious that her words will be overheard by a disapproving general audience, composed of guardians and witnesses, internal as well as external, bound to local values and traditional social behavior.

As often occurs in such situations, Stein develops a sort of secret code which the novice might understand while the guardians may not.[3] "Would it seriously threaten anyone to be cowardly to offer to write and say something" (p. 9) she asks. Here, as elsewhere, Stein's words bounce back and forth between crazy mirrors, interchanging positives and negatives. Therefore, "not to be cowardly" is as much what Stein means to say as "to be cowardly." And, of course, since she is being "cowardly" to use a code at

*Reprinted from the *Journal of Narrative Technique* 10 (Spring 1980): 115–27.

all, she can draw attention to her own fears. This code is often arbitrary. She may put in one negative and take out another, or reverse the statement and say the opposite of what she wants the reader to hear. Though this procedure is frustrating to some, it is an important technique for Stein herself — it shocks her out of her normal syntax and helps her to locate new forms while remaining at least partially hidden and protected. No wonder that she continually worries and assesses the clarity of her symbolic language, which validates her claims to being a teacher — worrying "can you tell them this bliss?" (p. 107) and asking "how can a language alter?" (p. 108)[4] as well as questioning the appropriateness for her purpose of the "disguise" of philosophic reasoning, "how can you reason about that?" (p. 110) and of her Socratic questioning (with a pun on the hymen), "can be wisdom be curtained" (p. 108). She asks of the initiate and of her presumably disapproving audience, "is it necessary to change?" (p. 20).

Her basic problem, stated through repetition, can be summed up in her statement "what is the difference and why do you marry?" (p. 164) — what are the differences between homosexual love and heterosexual love, and what are the necessities of both? The role-playing of man and wife generates much of Stein's metaphor, and energizes her thematic preoccupations with dominance and submission, and freedom of sexual expressiveness. When she speaks to the question of whether she has hidden anything she hopes to reveal, she "invents" a phrase that includes a pun on lovemaking, "do we secrete anything?" (p. 14).

To help her say many things in many voices, all at once or almost at once, Stein creates different distinct metaphorical fields in which her work as a whole operates. One such important field of meaning is the general analogy between the nuclear family and the homosexual marriage; another is the general analogy she creates between the body and geography. Stein has often associated "natural images" with sexuality, but in *Useful Knowledge* the pattern is especially clear. She begins coyly, telling us the book is about "romance" and "owning the earth just as pleasantly as ever." She plays on this analogy successfully throughout, but its sexual significance — "arousing the land" (p. 166) — must be inferred by the novice. In terms of the audience at large, she remains at least partially disguised — hiding behind the sense of passion she links to the general idea of any ownership or possession. This possessing, as we will see, is usually by a member of the family group.

Much of the "geography" of Stein's sexuality has to do with dominance, "conquering territory." *Useful Knowledge*'s writer roams over the body, a previously unexplored map, and takes it over, disregarding danger, recording the new cartology with an almost exultant sense of duty.

> Explorer . . . occupies successively the places . . . he recognizes . . . so that he will later be able to make maps of the region which he has traversed . . .
>
> (p. 32)

The section "Wherein the South differs from the North" extends this metaphor by associating Stein herself with the warmer more emotional South and Alice B. Toklas with the colder more intellectual North. But the piece is also a dialogue of id and super ego, of the free-speaking sexual prophet and the censor, both resident in Stein's personality. When the two speakers finally unite ("North and South nestles," p. 29), Stein's conciliatory "there is no need for opposition" (p. 23) can be understood as being only a partial truth. Duality is central to her procedure, as her purpose is to conquer the guilt in both the regions of the body and the mind:

> It is in the interest of the North that this is told, it is in the interest of the South that this is told.
>
> (p. 34)

These maps are puzzles, mazes, dangerous journeys. Their very inaccessibility only emphasizes their fragile and vulnerable nature. Even so, the explorer might enjoy the difficulty of the terrain.

After the delights of discovery, Stein tells the novice the land must be claimed as an extension of the explorer's self, as family, that it must be owned as well as recorded. "Can you give me the regions?" (p. 78) she asks, and "we commence to supplant" (p. 164). This territory, once entered, must be made safe from the incursions of other lovers-artists-travellers. It must be claimed by the family group. Like the imagery of geography, imagery of family relations provides Stein with an important and highly charged field.[5] Mother, father and sibling to her beloved, Stein is metamorphosed into all possible roles. In this way, Stein alters the family to suit her own requirements. Speaking to the novice, she uses the intimacy of familiar associations to play upon the incestuous implications of lesbian love, as well as reflecting, in a distanced, humorous way, mostly for the benefit of the wider audience, on her own complex family history and on the acceptability of her present conduct. In "Business in Baltimore,"[6] Stein's persona marvels on the jumbled chaos of the family tree when a lesbian relationship both parallels and displaces the nurturing love of mother and of sibling:

> Placed and placing should a daughter be a mother. Placed and placing should a mother be a sister altogether.
>
> (P. 74)

By untangling the new relationships with the meticulous detail of the anthropologist, she can use its metaphors to simultaneously reveal and conceal her own relationships:

> Can you love another mother?
>
> (p. 111)

By considering her relationship in terms of the family, Stein finds metaphorical and explicit ways of displacing, describing, and admitting to guilt. As with much of *Useful Knowledge*, fearful autobiographical material, specifically dealing with the early part of her stay in Paris (for example, moving Alice into her apartment in 1909, which led to Leo Stein's departure in 1913), resurfaces for further assimilation. Darker images point to her suspicion of family hostility, and of the inevitable rejection implied in choosing the lover over the nuclear family: "In the shadow of our brother we have eaten" (p. 104). Other "shadowy" references surround the choice, not only of the ways that parents and siblings might disapprove, but even more, of the reaction of the outside world. But the wider her imagined audience, the more she feels called upon to reveal, and then to defend, and then to conceal, her repudiation of conventional morality.

The following passage reflects the kind of complexity Stein continually builds into her code about homosexual love:

> If we mean mother and daughter, black and black caught her, and she
> offers it to me. That is very very right and should out below and just so.
>
> (p. 92)

The reference to the family directs her into a private reference about guilt ("black and black caught her"). Her generalized "it" includes love, both physical and spiritual. Her affirmative phrase "very right" disguises the suggestion of orgasm, which, though not mentioned, "should out below and just so." "it . . . should out below" both in birth and in some private hell in which such sexual feelings are justly punished, but mostly in her writing itself, which follows "below" in the text itself.

If both the natural imagery and the family imagery function to re-tell and to conceal her autobiography, these purposes are reinforced by Stein's innovative narrative techniques. By switching pronouns around and using rhyme and rhythm to deliberately give the feeling of nursery-rhyme nonsense language, the compressed biographical and erotic materials that she records will be subsumed under the strangeness of the stylistic presentation. Thus, though Stein keeps pointing out the changing landscapes and recasting her biography in terms of geographic journeys, it is moving Alice into her apartment with herself and her brother in 1909 that she is most concerned with, though this is never directly mentioned. She prefers to dwell on her move from America to France seven years earlier. Stein, simultaneously a political and a sexual exile, now seems to challenge the language itself, though she still retains fierce American and heterosexual loyalties.[7]

> Why don't you visit your brother with a girl he doesn't know and in the
> midst of emigration we have wishes to bestow we gather that the West is
> wet and fully ready to flow we gather that the East is wet and very
> ready to say so.
>
> (p. 84)

Again, everything functions as a form of sexual disguise—the wishes she wants to "bestow" are specifically sexual, everything is a combination of command and seduction. Her direct experience all but disappears, only to reappear in the guise of a specific private symbol which, by its presence in seemingly unrelated neutral material, points the reader toward the interpretation she intends. In the following passage, her mention of "cows," already an emblem for sexual experience, specifically orgasm[8] in her work, provides just such a key. The "he" is, again, Stein herself:

> He originally cultivated cows. After that he joined himself to all of them and after that he was as helpful as he could be . . . after that he was nearer . . . he had made what was to be attended to. That does make the difference.
>
> (p. 133)

"Cows," "joined," "nearer," "made," "attended to," and "make" are all neutralized erotic references — "attending to" them makes the difference. In "Emily Chadbourne" (a friend of Stein's, also "I'm a lie" . . . "had borne") Stein is like land up for barter, but she is "not a saleable surface," not the romantic ideal for her times, and the choices for such women are few. "A surface that is too rigid is ruined, a surface that is loosed is smiling, a surface that is mine is mind" (p. 88). The tremendous eclipse of personal information behind terse all-encompassing metaphorical statements about the freedom, ownership, and cohesion of her body, encodes her experience, both physical and spiritual. Her body, literally scattered throughout the book, demands a reader who is also a lover — "a surface that is missed is widowed" (p. 88).

As Stein's speaker is the surface of the land, enjoying the tilling of the beloved, she is also the text in the knowing hand of the reader, and the elements of nature, enjoying the primal experience of love, that the earth recounts with an "organic wit" (p. 153). In extended musings about the effects of the "weathers" of love upon her, she arouses her readers, and deepens their response, as she moves deftly from one kind of sexual image to another. A typical meditation begins in rain, associating emotion and moisture, and ends by describing the feeling of orgasm, all in terms of nature and the natural elements.

> I don't like rain. I don't mean that thunder scares me. You know very well what I mean. I mean that sometimes I wish I was a fish with a settled smiling center. I think it is an ugly word.
>
> (p. 11)

Stein interjects her direct statement ("you know very well what I mean"), the voice of her revelatory self, to help the reader — and herself, writing the passage — to recognize what her submerged subject is. Instead of feigning innocence about her admission, she chides the reader for not recognizing it sooner. Once she has achieved this focus, her private "natural" associations (the fishy smell of the vagina, the clitoris as "settled, smiling center") can be introduced. As usual, negative and positive are switched — the passage moves from denial of sexual desire to its full expression, though ending with a filip in the direction of conventional morality. What word is ugly? It is, of course, the one she does not use.

Stein's major imagery is particularly vital because it often achieves synesthesia in its punning effects. Thus, "repeated leopards" (p. 13) both puns on the sound of "leap on" and on the visual eroticism of the leaping cats, who were the beasts of Dionysius. When she counts "pansies" and lives in a "fruit house" (pp. 142; 157), even a list of states will become erotically charged. "Kansas" will become "can's ass," while "Indiana" will become "In Diana," in the virgin, even though Stein is ostensibly remembering the home states of certain World War I doughboys.[9]

The book's title lends resonance to Stein's methods. Her creation of a "how to" manual integrally relates both her sexuality and her experimental writing. Both display the same reticence and versatility of style. As Stein tells us, "I learned to correct snatches" (p. 12). The closer Stein is to sexual meaning, the more fanciful her technique, the more vivid her imaginative associations, the more developed her need for narrative disguise. Innovative sexuality demands innovative narrative.

> What a cake. What a kindness.
> What a smell. What a shame.
> What a sight. What a sound.
> What a universal shudder.
>
> (p. 12)

Only a reader knowledgeable of Stein's actual sophistication can fully appreciate this text's mocking edge. And as if even such a cryptic manner might still be too direct, she immediately fuses the compromising material in this passage with the kind of automatic denial the reader has come to expect.

> I will not be coerced. But I was.
> I was coerced. I see it.

Her abrupt truths and graphic descriptions are thus deflected by her tactful evasions and apologies. In this latter mode, learning is not spontaneous, but based on rote memorization, the student learning to "copy all the special ways of sitting" (p. 8). Finally, the art of the text lies in the interaction between revelation and concealment — "the emphasis can be where you like" (p. 12). Her attitudes toward sexuality are offered — but each passage is its own epigrammatic maze, which the reader must traverse at his own peril.

The nonsense argument, so difficult to refute or even to respond to in a coherent way, is useful to Stein as an effective means of disarming her audience. It is the centerpiece for much of the stylistic virtuosity displayed throughout *Useful Knowledge*. Its mystery, its obsessive motifs of guilt and its autobiographical content, its sexual puns, are all reduced to a childlike doggerel, the broken flow of "inappropriate" sections that disguise circular affirmations of her difficult "information." Her whole manner informs the reader that she does not mean to argue her points at all, merely to display and conceal the virtuosities of a stylized verbal dance. Without any specific reference to homosexuality, she can argue simultaneously for and against it.

> It is a disease. Is there any way to stop it. There is a way and that way was the way that was shown to be their way. Dear things.
>
> (p. 9)

Such circular argument is bound in contradiction. The basic insolubility becomes indissoluble—each half requires the other, even after the two halves are joined and the seams of the joint erased. In nonsense, Stein can use her dilemma against itself, and explore the options of not answering to the antithesis in her formulations. In terms of Freud's theoretical constructs, Stein both "blocks" and "denies"—she represses the manifest meaning, and, when it appears, she rejects it, but in such an obvious way as to show she recognizes both her surface and her "deep" meanings.

The problem or contradiction that Stein brings up most often, stated simply, is that she isn't "supposed" to be married to another woman—which parallels, in terms of her own writing, her realization that she isn't "supposed" to use nonsense to communicate. "I don't think you can say that this is too natural" (p. 11). Nonsense is composed of sense plus a negation of that sense, and Stein controls her sexual and artistic rebellion, creates a pattern for her writing, from the idea of sense merged in nonsense, the wise man in the company of the fallen. If she begins by affirming her "fall from decency," she can then deny her very affirmation, going with the social standard, in an argument that is always circular and contradictory: "This is the way it has to be . . . and not to do it again . . . she has absolutely promised never to mention birds" (p. 139).[10]

Of course, the negation can be most completely fused with its opposite when one is actually imbedded in the other. Then the very denial becomes, like a kind of absence or a kind of silence, a reason to suspect "hidden" meanings. The nonsense code requires denial of any involvement or intention, while nevertheless remaining involved in the content.

Stein's rhyming is a central vehicle for this "nonsense" technique, providing its own dizzying and hypnotic circularity. The rhyming in *Useful Knowledge* pervades and lulls, giving Stein more energy for revelation, because rhyme, like denial, takes her ever forward, into the trance of unexpected truth. Like an ecstatic shaman, Stein riffles through her improvisational cards until they begin to make sense:

> History is told, will he be a great man will he learn to fan, can fanning be fun, can we satisfy a nun, can we seize what is won, can a tall man hold a gun . . .
>
> (p. 109)

In this passage, history and the idea of the great man—Stein liked to think of herself as Caesar—spring-boards the text into erotic fantasy. The question the "run" poses is: can a person learn to satisfy himself outside the accepted norms? Stein "invents" the image of "fanning" for masturbation, neutralizes the "I" with a "we," replaces the "lover" with a "nun," but includes her code word for sexual mastery, "seize," which reminds her of "Caesar." "Caesar" reappears at the end, in the form of a direct hint to the initiated, as a "tall man" instead of as a "short woman," holding the offending organ, a "gun" that goes off with the explosion of orgasm, which is also, as always, the pen of the writer, forcing truth into the text.

If the rhythmic and rhyming sections of *Useful Knowledge* offer Stein an effective disguise, they also work emotively, submerging the reader in Stein's subtext, where the same idea can be stressed repeatedly, with short variations, enforcing its intensity, convincing both reader and writer of the inevitability of the actions described. The section below resembles the "in wed led" section of *Four Saints in Three Acts*:[11]

> In heights and whites in whites
> and lights, in lights in sizes,
> in sizes in sides and in wide, or
> as wise or wiser. This is not to
> be the first to know.

> (p. 66)

If readers notice any transformation in this paragraph, she writes in the last lines above, they will not be the first to know it. Knowing about "in sides," as she indicates by punning, will make them "as wise or wiser" than she — though no one will be the "wiser," since she has written about this in nonsense.

Nonsense and the nonsense rhyme protect Stein's content against disapproving censors, internal and external:

> I like it descriptive. Not very descriptive.

> (p. 79)

> This is the use of a guardian, where it is guarded it is as well guarded as ever.

> (p. 154)

Paradoxically, as she meditates on the idea of constraint, constriction, censorship, her own fears of being revealed provide a way to go on, a method of underlining those themes that she might otherwise suppress. In this, she is very much like the school-child whose enthusiastic erasures only attract attention.

Stein's discussion of guilt always has a double edge. Underneath her denial, an affirmation waits to push through. Underneath her affirmation, yet another negation waits. If she cannot show all sides of her feelings directly, the suppressed point of view surfaces to torment and mock her. Where she speaks of the traditional sex roles, the whole attitudinal tone is childlike, assuring, but her childish nonsensical style often parodies her message. Rhyme and nonsense provide Stein with a mysterious cloak of "silliness." Stein uses the suggestive power of nonsense rhyme to project her problems against a backdrop that seems non-existent, impossible, laughable, and therefore not threatening, "the scene of the future."

> The scene of the future.
> Can you wish that jelly
> Can you wish that jelly
> Can you wish that jelly
> be eaten with cream.
>
> (p. 105)

If Stein creates circularity with her rhyming nonsense, she also injects mystery that unravels itself, mystery always ready to reveal an answer, even if that answer is just the reverse of the answer already given. "Nobody knows how open and how closed it is. Nobody knows. It could be taught" (p. 136). The more she immerses her writing in this medium, the more she appears to resemble Lear's fool. Mystery gives a too-blatant subject subtlety and humor, which somehow purges the eroticism of its profane quality, softens it, makes it easier to accept, as if laughter sanctified the act.

It is for this reason that Stein often narrates autobiographical sections in nonsense runs that sound like a mixture of half-formed stories and babytalk:

> I come suddenly to be there and
> to be exciting. It was worse than
> money.
> Alright I will be natural.
> B is for birthday baby and blessed
> S is for sweeties sweeties and sweetie.
> Y is for you and U is for me and we are
> as happy as happy can be.
>
> (p. 12)
>
> Is reading painful?
>
> (p. 13)

After her revelation in her first sentence, her second blends remorse and desire. Sex, or "it," is "worse," or even greater in its effect on her, than money, and the possession of money. By speaking of being "natural," she gives a customary wave in the direction of respectability, but by far the longest section in this patterned run is the famous sentimental baby-rhyme to Alice B. Toklas.[12] The last question, "is reading painful," could be considered as a separated "follow-up" to the pattern. Her persona can avoid the "pain" caused by the uninitiated reading something shocking or unacceptable, and in this way she can avoid feeling this pain herself. There is only a small portion of her audience, internal and external, that "understands" the "useful knowledge" she here offers. Though she only uses key words as touchstones to invoke her whole information system, the reader must actively grapple with the content and recreate it. In this way, she outmaneuvers the passive audience of guardians and witnesses. Stein's persona, like an oracle, will only come forth with a garbled prophecy at a certain kind of command. She often stops to remind the novice of this, and to compress and to catalogue, to reprise the knowledge she has offered, though covertly, in her persona of teacher: "We know about blame and circles and now we know about considerably added currents. The currents that come there. Where did you say. Call me louder" (p. 165).[13]

Family reference, like geographical reference, can lead both to fantasy and resolution, especially when incorporated in Stein's nonsensical lyricism. In "An Instant Answer or a Hundred Prominent Men," for instance, alliteration releases a sensuality that compels Stein first to revelry and then to self-consciousness:

> How often do we dream of daughters.
> Can you color it to satisfy the eye,
> can you. Can you feel this as an
> elaborate precaution. Can you. Who
> won Mrs. Kisses. Who won you.
>
> (p. 145)

As the irrational and the aesthetic converge in linguistic playfulness, they also remind her of the need for chameleon changes, protective coloring "to satisfy the eye" in the retelling of her own courtship — "can you feel this as an elaborate precaution?"

Of course in this chaos or jumble of family members, in the exchange of one for the other, the nature and function of sexuality becomes diffuse. In terms of the family romance[14] identity has fragmented — from the central core of the nuclear family, her identity has become diffuse. Stein continually reflects on role displacement and the complexities of sexual differentiation under her revolutionary system.

> If to have and to turn over
> the edge and to have returned
> a mother to a father makes it
> as a mixture of later. Not late
> at all. To them both.
>
> (p. 59)

She deftly combines the two ideas, of "turning over" her sexual identity with "going over the edge" into the madness of switched identities and "returning," somehow, at least in terms of her own definition. She has been transformed, changed from a "mother" into a "father," since Stein thinks of herself and Toklas as a couple in a conventional marriage — and this discovery of her true self is not too late to give satisfaction "to them both." Stein's ability to transcend the expected limits is extended through the mysterious nature and function of her erotic and literary activity, a style in which "they" "reinstate the act of birth" (p. 96) but "we" "do not recognize an heir" (pp. 166–7).

The persona can step in and out of the roles of teacher, philosopher scientist, family member, farmer or explorer, as if they were a series of Chinese boxes. In each case, she rehearses her unequivocal duties as the subjects for her art, in order to lead the novice on while the speaker remains hidden from her internal and external guardians. Her very need for secrecy forces Stein into a new and strangely powerful language, brimming with sexuality, but contained by an equally surprising prudence. Thinking of her "exercises," both sexual and literary, she says of herself:

> He does not elaborate exercises.
> There are witnesses there.
>
> (p. 146)

Notes

1. (New York: Payson and Clarke, Ltd.; rpt. American Alpine Club, 1972). The only organizational requirement of *Useful Knowledge* was that the publisher should "make it all the short things she (Stein) had written about America," *The Autobiography of Alice B. Toklas*, in *Selected Writings of Gertrude Stein*, ed. Carl Van Vechten (New York: Random House, 1945), p. 227. The pieces in this book range from her Mallorcan experiences to her post-war preparation for the autobiographies she would publish during the next decade. In this, the period before she would achieve fame as a best-selling author, Stein was deeply concerned about the theory of her artistic practice. She was searching for uniqueness in a highly experimental period and she was analyzing her writing, obsessed with exploring the shock of ambiguities "built into the language," Richard Bridgman, *Gertrude Stein in Pieces* (New York: Oxford University Press, 1970), p. 163.

2. As in *Geography and Plays* (1922).

3. Encoding in Stein's work is discussed both by Catharine Stimpson (*Critical Inquiry*, Vol. 3, No. 3, "The Mind, the Body, and Gertrude Stein"), and by Linda Simon (*The Biography of Alice B. Toklas* [New York: Doubleday, 1977], "Appendix: A Word About Caesars and Cows"). In his *World Within the Word* (New York: Knopf, 1978), William Gass observes, "The manifest texts contain a coded commentary on the covert texts," p. 92.

4. Also, language is not a god displayed upon an altar, to be worshipped only in one form (for the reverse, see *Useful Knowledge*, p. 108).

5. Gass has noted that Stein "lacked a locale which might help to define her and a family she could in general accept," p. 73.

6. The city where Stein spent her years as a graduate student in medicine at Johns Hopkins (1897–1901) and where she had relatives.

7. This presents a central paradox of Stein's writing and life: although she loved America and was proud of it, attesting to that love in her autobiographies and histories (*The Autobiography of Alice B. Toklas*, *Everybody's Autobiography*, and *Wars I Have Seen*), Stein chose to live her life abroad; similarly, although she was a lesbian, she both thought of and spoke of herself as a man in a conventional marriage and gravitated to the men she invited to her salon, leaving Alice to sit with the wives.

8. See Bridgman, pp. 151–2, and Simon's "Appendix."

9. James Mellow, *Charmed Circle* (New York: Praeger, 1974; rpt. Avon, 1975),

" 'Wherein Iowa Differs from Kansas and Indiana' [was] prompted by her discussions with American doughboys," p. 341.

10. At once a neutral reference and a bawdy reference; Stein expects the knowledgeable reader to remember earlier uses in folklore while the naive reader would just see a non-sequitur.

11. "In wed in dead in dead wed led in led wed dead in dead in led in wed in said in said led dead . . ." *Selected Writings*, p. 609.

12. Mellon calls this "doggerel sentiment," p. 269, but misunderstands its intention.

13. A possible gloss on this passage might be that the blame attached to the "circles" of the female body creates "considerably added currents" in her lovemaking. "Call me louder" could refer both to the attraction of the forbidden, which calls her "louder" than accepted behavior, and also to the need for the reader to use greater understanding in "calling" Stein's meaning from the text.

14. "The later stage in the development of the neurotic's estrangement from his parents . . . might be described as 'the neurotic's family romance,' " Sigmund Freud, *Collected Papers*, *Vol. 5* ed. James Strachey (New York: Basic Books, 1959), p. 75.

Gertrude Stein and Modern Painting: Beyond Literary Criticism

Marianne De Koven*

Gertrude Stein's writing was undoubtedly influenced by the modes of modern painting she helped to discover and promulgate, particularly cubism. A good deal of Stein criticism has explored this influence, attempting to account for her perennially resistant radical work by discovering in it direct adaptations to literature of cubist technique.[1] Though this notion of borrowed technique is problematic, comparisons of Stein's work to modern painting can be helpful in adjusting our vision to writing which continues to appear strange. Moreover, Stein's pre-World War I work *is* very similar to cubist painting of the same period. They share an orientation toward the linguistic or pictorial surface, a movement in and out of recognizable representation; both shatter or fragment perception and the sentence (canvas), and both render multiple perspectives. Useful as these analyses of Stein's writing as literary cubism have been in helping us approach her work, we should not overrate their reliability in accounting for its specific linguistic shapes.

Cubism, or rather modern painting in general, was certainly crucial to Stein, but crucial as a spur to her daring rather than a source of technique. In "Pictures," one of the six *Lectures in America* of 1934,[2] Stein makes Cézanne the original muse of her career:

And then slowly through all this and looking at many many pictures I came to Cézanne and there you were, at least there I was . . .

*Reprinted from *Contemporary Literature* 22, no. 1 (Winter 1981): 81–95.

> The apples looked like apples the chairs looked like chairs and it all had nothing to do with anything because if they did not look like apples or chairs or landscape or people they were apples and chairs and landscape and people. They were so entirely these things that they were not an oil painting and yet that is just what the Cézannes were they were an oil painting. They were so entirely an oil painting that it was all there whether they were finished, the paintings, or whether they were not finished. Finished or unfinished it always was what it looked like the very essence of an oil painting because everything was always there, really there. . . .
>
> This then was a great relief to me and I began writing. (pp. 76–77)

Stein felt relief at the discovery of an art that was simultaneously pure form and quintessential content—pure paint on canvas, yet also the essence of its subject—a precarious balance she herself achieved in *Three Lives*, with its stylized prose surface simultaneously focusing attention on itself and rendering the abstract "rhythm" or "pulse," the psychological essence, of character.

Looking at Cézannes seemed to liberate Stein's literary energy in a way that no amount of reading could do (Stein considered herself in danger of reading everything in print). We can say, then, that the greatest, or at any rate most interesting influence of modern painting on Stein's work lies in the way its relatively loose strictures on meaning, on the range and significance of content, expanded the possibilities of literature for a writer of her radical propensities. Stein went beyond any other major early modern writer in English: she continues to be the least read giant of twentieth-century literature, primarily because her radical work cannot be read in the normal way. It subverts the kind of coherent, referential meaning we are trained to expect in literature; hence it resists the standard critical method of interpretation, or thematic synthesis. Thematic synthesis—reading whose end is to discover coherent, referential, transcendent meaning in a text—does not allow for the experience of fecund incoherence which Stein's experimental writing offers us in place of orderly sense.[3]

In her experimental period (approximately 1911–1932, encompassing *Tender Buttons*, most of *Geography and Plays* and six of the eight volumes of the Yale Edition of the Unpublished Writings of Gertrude Stein,[4] *Portraits and Prayers, Useful Knowledge, Lucy Church Amiably, Four Saints in Three Acts, How to Write*) Stein substitutes for coherent meaning and referentiality the primacy of surface—the ascendency of the signifier—and also an order of meaning between conventional coherence and utter unintelligibility: meaning multiplied, fragmented, dedefined, unresolved. This order of meaning represents a genuinely oppositional—that is, antipatriarchal and antilogocentric—alternative mode of signification.

What does it mean to differentiate between "unintelligible" and "incoherent"? "Unintelligible" connotes the utter absence of readable meaning, while "incoherent" suggests meaning which is present and readable, but incapable of resolution into conventional order or sense. Stein's experimental writing, or the ideal instance of it, is incoherent rather than unintelligible. Meaning is present, but it is multiplied, fragmented, unresolved: "A bottle that has all the time to stand open is not so clearly shown when there is green color there. This is not the only way to change it. A little raw potato and then all that softer does happen to show that there has been enough. It changes the expression."[5] This incoherence represents an order of meaning which our overwhelming valorization of coherent, referential sense in literature generally prevents us from recognizing.

To clarify this notion of incoherence, we might look at Noam Chomsky's idea of "degrees of grammaticalness."[6] Chomsky establishes three "degrees of grammaticalness" by differentiating among utterances which are strictly or conventionally grammatical (first degree), "semi-grammatical" (second degree), and totally ungrammatical (third degree). Chomsky's explanation of his distinctions is relevant to the argument here: "In short, it seems to me no more justifiable to ignore the distinctions of subcategory that give the series "John plays golf," "golf plays John," "John plays and," than to ignore the rather similar distinctions between seeing a man in the flesh, in an abstract painting, and in an inkblot" (p. 385).

Chomsky makes his most powerful case for these degrees of grammaticalness by listing examples.:

> First degree: a year ago; perform the task; John plays golf; revolutionary new ideas appear infrequently; John loves company; sincerity frightens John; what did you do to the book, bite it?

> Second degree: a grief ago; perform leisure; golf plays John; colorless green ideas sleep furiously; misery loves company; John frightens sincerity; what did you do to the book, understand it?

> Third degree: a the ago; perform compel; golf plays aggressive; furiously sleep ideas green colorless; abundant loves company; John sincerity frightens; what did you do to the book, justice it? (p. 386)

Phrases of the second degree such as "a grief ago," "colorless green ideas," and "John frightens sincerity" are strikingly similar to Stein's successful experimental writing, particularly in the 1911–1914 style of Tender Buttons, "Susie Asado," "Preciosilla," and "Portrait of Mabel Dodge at the Villa Curonia." Moreover, phrases of the third degree such as "a the ago," "perform compel," and "golf plays aggressive" are very similar to the unsuccessful writing that resulted from Stein's experiments in the late twenties and early thirties with unrelated successions of single words (see particularly How To Write). As Chomsky shows, the difference between the second and third degrees is precisely their relative accessibility to reading through purposive articulation of meaning; or, as Chomsky puts it, through deviation from conventional grammar in the second degree as opposed to utter negation of it in the third. The second degree undermines or fragments coherent meaning and subordinates meaning altogether to the linguistic surface (we notice the strangeness or freshness of the verbal combinations themselves — the words "stand out" *as words* — before we register consciously their dedetermined, unresolved meanings), and yet, unlike the third degree of totally unintelligible phrases, these "deviant utterances" retain significant connections among the meanings of their words. Without such articulations of meaning in a literary work, we would be unable to read it.

Not so a canvas, as abstract impressionism testifies: unlike words, painted shapes are not necessarily signs, and therein lies the danger of calling Stein's experimental writing literary cubism. Chomsky's degrees might seem at first to buttress rather than undermine the cubist analogy. We can certainly accommodate cubism very readily to the second degree: while it retains "readable" shapes — bits of a face, a hand, a table, a violin — it fragments them, multiplies them, flattens them toward the surface of the canvas, makes them incoherent.[7] But a painted shape, unlike a word, has only two potential degrees of meaning: referential or abstract. Either it refers recognizably to an anterior object, something we might say the painting is "of," or it has only the emotional, spiritual suggestiveness of musical tones, along with its formal, compositional significance, as in abstract expressionism. Words, on the other hand, may or may not be used in an intentionally referential way — to say something coherent about a particular subject — but they always retain the lexical meanings they carry in the language. The meanings of the words in a piece of writing need not refer to a theme or topic which the writing is "about," yet they are nonetheless understandable, which enables us to read the writing. This sentence from *Tender Buttons* is readable, though it has nothing to do with its ostensible subject, "Lunch": "Luck in loose plaster makes holy gauge and nearly that, nearly more states, more states come in town light kite, blight not white."[8] Can we say that this sentence is "about" lunch, or "about" anything at all — that it has coherent, referential meaning? But we cannot deny that it is replete with multiple, unresolved lexical meanings. On the other hand, a section of a cubist canvas containing no representational shapes has no "readable" meaning whatsoever: it has only the emotional, "aesthetic" suggestiveness of its formal configurations. Part of a cubist painting fragments and multiplies its subject (a person, a still life, a landscape); the rest is abstract. Stein's writing is never abstract, and its multiplied, fragmented signification generally ignores its nominal subject. A reader unfamiliar with Stein criticism might be in the best position to recognize that fact: a first reading of *Tender Buttons* seldom suggests any immediate connection between the actual writing and its ostensible subject, while it is clear at first glance that cubist compositions are structured around the fragmentation of their representational elements (contrast the above sentence from "Lunch" with Picasso's 1910 portrait of Daniel-Henry Kahnweiler).[9]

Even when such a representational connection is evident in Stein's writing, as in "A Purse" ("A purse was not green, it was not straw color, it was hardly seen and it had a use a long use and the chain, the chain was never missing, it was not misplaced, it showed that it was open, that is all that it showed")[10] or in "Susie Asado" ("A lean on the shoe this means slips slips hers"),[11] discovering that connection has little to do with accounting for the effect the writing produces on the reader:[12] a stimulating, perhaps infuriating sense that these phrases almost make sense, that they hover close to coherence, yet remain insistently, even perversely, beyond it. This writing forces us to relinquish our conventional expectation of coherent sense, to embrace instead an open-ended text which we ourselves have as much responsibility for writing as the author. In S/Z, Roland Barthes calls such writing *scriptible* or writerly:

> Why is the writerly our value? Because the goal of literary work (of literature as work) is to make the reader no longer a consumer, but a producer of the text. Our literature is characterized by the pitiless divorce which the literary institution maintains between the producer of the text and its user, between its owner and its customer, between its author and its reader. This reader is thereby plunged into a kind of idleness — he is intransitive; he is, in short, *serious*: instead of functioning himself, instead of gaining access to the magic of the signifier, to the pleasure of writing, he is left with no more than the poor freedom either to accept or reject the text: reading is nothing more than a *referendum*.[13]

Meaning in cubist painting has very much to do with representation; meaning in Stein's experimental writing does not. Instead, it has to do with language, with writing. Not only the effect of Stein's work on the reader and its linguistic structures, but also its larger significance as an alternative literature can best be understood by referring it to theories of writing.

In *Of Grammatology*,[14] Jacques Derrida describes and dismantles the cultural hegemony of sense, order, and coherence in writing that Stein's work overthrows. He attacks this hegemony as logocentrism: the ascendancy not only of speech (over writing) as self-presence, Derrida's preoccupation, but of rationality, linearity, and hierarchical order — of the "transcendental signified" or logos — over the free play of the signifier. The ascendancy of the transcendental signified makes all language, and particularly all writing, a mere "secondary representation" of an anterior, absolute meaning or truth, a constraint which painting can more readily evade. It is easy to see the connection between this transcendental signified (God, truth, ideal form, "principle of principles," etc.) and the coherent, referential meaning, the thematic synthesis we expect in literature. Like

1 or the logos itself, statements of thematic content grant the text value or legitimacy by translating it to a "higher," or transcendent, order of meaning: what was merely a piece of writing becomes a statement about life.[15]

For Derrida, experimental writing like Stein's points toward a cultural order beyond logocentrism. As the characteristic writing of logocentric culture, the conventional text is "linear," not only in its treatment of time, but, quite literally, in its structure of successive lines, which reflects and endorses the fiction of smoothness and coherence, the step-by-step accumulation and integration of "evidence" on which thematic synthesis, and, more generally, transcendent order and truth, depend. This linearity is not innocent. It has been instituted at the expense of repressing what Derrida calls "pluridimensionality," which is, as we have seen, the central feature of Steinian experimental writing. As Derrida puts it, nonlinear writing has re-emerged in the modern period, and this re-emergence is both a challenge to logocentric hegemony and a glimpse or harbinger of a possible cultural order beyond it. Or, to paraphrase him more precisely, nonlinear writing has one face inevitably turned back toward, or trapped within, the only cultural order we know, but the other face pointing toward the future, in what he calls a "suspense between two ages of writing" (p. 87):

> The enigmatic model of the *line* is thus the very thing that philosophy could not see when it had its eyes open on the interior of its own history. This night begins to lighten a little at the moment when linearity — which is not loss or absence but the repression of pluri-dimensional symbolic thought — relaxes its oppression . . . Not that the massive reappearance of nonlinear writing interrupts this structural solidarity; quite the contrary. But it transforms its nature profoundly. The end of linear writing is indeed the end of the book, even if, even today, it is within the form of a book that new writings — literary or theoretical — allow themselves to be, for better or for worse, encased. (p. 86)

Derrida claims not the appearance but the reappearance of nonlinear writing. He postulates a "past of nonlinear writing," not naturally superseded so much as systematically suppressed by logocentric linear writing:

> We have seen that the traditional concept of time, an entire organization of the world and of language, was bound up with it (the linearity of the symbol). Writing . . . is rooted in a past of nonlinear writing. It had to be defeated, and here one can speak, if one wishes, of technical success; it assured a greater security and greater possibilities of capitalization in a dangerous and anguishing world. But this was not done *one single time*. A war was declared, and a suppression of all that resisted linearization was installed. And first of what Leroi-Gourhan calls the "mythogram," a writing that spells its symbols pluri-dimensionally; there the meaning is not subjected to successivity, to the order of logical time, or to the irreversible temporality of sound. This pluri-dimension-

ality does not paralyze history within simultaneity, it corresponds to another level of historical experience, and one may just as well consider, conversely, linear thought as a reduction of history. (p. 85)

The rationale of this suppression is clear when we link logocentrism with patriarchy. Derrida himself makes this connection, calling Freudian thought "phallogocentric," but it is not one of his primary emphases. It is, however, a primary emphasis in the work of the French feminist critic Julia Kristeva. Along with other writers such as Luce Irigaray and Hélène Cixous,[16] Kristeva builds on the work of Derrida and also of the psychoanalyst Jacques Lacan to arrive at a profound feminist theory of culture and writing.

While Derrida uses "suppression" (political/historical) and "repression" (psychological) interchangeably, Kristeva consciously incorporates, through Lacan, the Freudian notion of psychic repression. Repression is coincident with the Oedipal phase, which in turn is coincident with the acquisition of symbolic language. What for Derrida is a suppressed cultural/historical past of nonlinear writing is for Lacan a repressed psychological past of presymbolic language. Symbolic language is simply language as we commonly conceive it: primarily a way to make and order communicable meaning. We are accustomed either to forget or to ignore, except in the restricted areas of learning theory and developmental psychology, the presymbolic state of language we all experience before we consolidate our competence in symbolic language. Presymbolic language, like experimental writing and in opposition to symbolic language, is characterized by the ascendancy of the signifier: the play of intonation, rhythm, repetition, sound association. Symbolic language is similar to Derrida's logocentric writing: both encompass the ascendancy of hierarchical order, sense, reason, and the signified.

Crucially, Kristeva, again through Lacan, links the acquisition of symbolic language in the individual with the Freudian acquisition of culture, which take place at the resolution of the Oedipal crisis by means of capitulation to the father.[17] The acquisition of culture, in human society as we know it, is the institution of what Lacan calls the "Rule of the Father," or patriarchy. To enter or acquire culture is to embrace simultaneously the symbolic order of language and the "Rule of the Father." For Lacan, the two are inseparable, and both come at the cost of repressing, again simultaneously, presymbolic language and the omnipotent, magical unity of the self with the outer world of which presymbolic language is the expression. The symbolic language of the father is, in fact, a compensation for that lost omnipotent unity: a means of dominating and controlling the newly alienated outer world.[18] In Lacan's theory, the repression concomitant with acquisition of symbolic language—the repression of the ascendent signifier—creates and wholly constitutes the unconscious: the content of the unconscious is the "autonomous" or "supreme" signifier.[19]

The French feminist theorists of female "différence" reverse this formulation. For them, the content of the unconscious, repressed by the institution of the "Rule of the Father" or patriarchy (and, therefore, by the institution of Derridean logocentrism) is the female: the pre-Oedipal hegemony of the mother, which is concomitant with presymbolic language and with Derrida's pluridimensionality. Irigaray and Cixous, most closely associated with the polemic for female "différence," argue for the restoration of the repressed female, a restoration which would, in Lacan's analysis, accomplish the Freudian goal of "making conscious the unconscious." The means for achieving this restoration would be a new women's language, yet to be, or in the process of being, invented.

For Julia Kristeva, the restoration of the repressed female unconscious, a goal hardly restricted to women, is already accomplished in the experimental writing of the avant-garde. Kristeva's work demonstrates the clear connection between Lacan's symbolic language and Derrida's logocentrism, and inversely, between Lacan's repressed presymbolic language and Derrida's suppressed past of nonlinear, pluridimensional writing, a supp-repressed past which is both cultural/historical and psychological. Kristeva makes brilliant use of Chinese culture in *About Chinese Women* as a concrete instance of her theoretical synthesis.[20] She looks at Chinese culture and sees that

> in ancient history but also throughout the history of Chinese socialism and up to the present, the role of women, and, consequently, that of the family, have a particular quality in China which is unknown in the monotheistic West. . . . the *otherness* of China is invisible if the man or woman who speaks here, in the West, doesn't position him/herself some place where our capitalist monotheistic fabric is shredding, crumbling, decaying. But where? . . . Women. We have the luck to be able to take advantage of a biological peculiarity to give a name to that which, in monotheistic capitalism, remains on this side of the threshold of repression, voice stilled, body mute, always foreign to the social order. (p. 14)

Kristeva's focus in this book is the contrast she sees between Western monotheistic patriarchy and Chinese culture, which, despite a phase of intensely absolutist patriarchy (the Confucianism which instituted footbinding) still retains traces of an early matrilinear cultural order, particularly in its metaphysics and in its language. In Western culture,

> by establishing itself as a symbolic principle of community — paternalistic, moralistic, beyond ethnic consideration, beliefs and social loyalties, monotheism represses — along with paganism — the greater half of agrarian civilizations and their ideologies: women and mothers. . . . No other civilization, therefore, seems to have made the principle of sexual difference so crystal clear: between the two sexes there is a cleavage, an abyss, which is marked by their different relationships to the Law (religious and political) . . . without this gap between the sexes, without this localization of the polymorphic, orgasmic body, laughing and

> desiring, in the other sex, it would have been impossible, in the symbolic
> sphere, to isolate the principle of One Law — One, Purifying, Transcen-
> dent, Guarantor of the ideal interest of the community. In the sphere of
> reproductive relations . . . it would have been impossible to insure the
> propagation of the race by making it the only acceptable end of
> *jouissance*. (pp. 18–19)

Kristeva's "One, Purifying, Transcendent Guarantor of the ideal interests
of the community" is manifestly Derridean logocentrism; the *jouissance* of
the female then becomes Derrida's suppressed past of nonlinear, pluridimensional writing. Like Roland Barthes, in *The Pleasure of the Text*,[21]
Kristeva locates this pluridimensional *jouissance* in the radical or experimental text, but unlike Barthes she does so by connecting it to the early
experience of the "mother's body." The *jouissance* of the "polymorphic,
orgasmic body, laughing and desiring" is defined and repressed as the
female "other" by patriarchal culture. The rebellion of that repressed
other, which releases *jouissance*, takes place in experimental writing.
Again, while paternal, symbolic language is sensible, orderly, clear, and
dominated by anterior meaning, the presymbolic language of the mother,
which experimental writing liberates, absorbs and employs, being a "pre-
sentence-making disposition to rhythm, intonation, nonsense; makes nonsense abound within sense: makes [one] laugh" (pp. 29–30).

Though cubism also subverts hierarchical order, sense, and coherence, and though, as we will see, Stein and Picasso share and express a
common vision, the revolution in painting, unlike that in writing, was able
to flourish well within the boundaries of patriarchal/logocentric culture.
Painted shapes are not signs: they are not at the core of symbolic thought
as words are. Pluridimensionality or incoherence in painting does not
threaten hierarchical, linear thought as incoherence in writing inevitably
does.

Nonetheless, the relative unimportance of content in modern painting did liberate Stein as literature itself never could from the compulsion
of conventional (patriarchal, logocentric) writing to make coherent sense.
Stein's closest creative affinity was with Picasso, and she is notorious for
finding reasons to avoid and dislike most of the other great modernist
writers (usually attributed, in part correctly, to her jealousy and insecu-
rity): Pound was a "village explainer, excellent if you were a village, but if
not, not";[22] Eliot was solemn and fussy in his ultimately fruitless negotia-
tions to publish her in *Criterion*; Joyce was one of the "incomprehensibles
whom anybody can understand,"[23] a remark which Stein attributes to
Picasso. Stein considered herself and Picasso neither incomprehensible nor
easy to understand. They both cultivated simplicity, transparency. Their
"difficulty," unlike that of Pound, Eliot or Joyce, lies in learning to look at
(read) them in the right way, and vanishes when one embraces the
unfamiliar mode of vision they require.

Their shared vision is the subject of Stein's 1938 book on Picasso.[24]

Stein makes no mention of similarities in technique; instead, she says again and again that (she and) Picasso embody a new vision of reality in their art, the "twentieth-century" reality or "modern composition" that Stein devotes a good deal of her theoretical work to explaining and championing. It is through shared vision more than through shared technique that Stein and Picasso are most profoundly linked:

> One must never forget that the reality of the twentieth century is not the reality of the nineteenth century, not at all and Picasso was the only one *in painting* who felt it, the only one. More and more the struggle to express it intensified. (pp. 21-22; my emphasis)

> The surrealists still see things as every one sees them, they complicate them in a different way but the vision is that of every one else, in short the complication is the complication of the twentieth century but the vision is that of the nineteenth century. Picasso only sees something else, another reality. Complications are always easy but another vision than that of all the world is very rare. That is why geniuses are rare, to complicate things in a new way that is easy, but to see the things in a new way that is really difficult, everything prevents *one*, habits, schools, daily life, reason, necessities of daily life, indolence, everything prevents *one*, in fact there are very few geniuses in the world. (p. 43; my emphasis)

> To-day the pictures of Picasso have come back to me from the exhibition at the Petit Palais and once more they are on my walls, I can not say that during their absence I forgot their splendor but they are more splendid than that. The twentieth century is more splendid than the nineteenth century, certainly it is much more splendid. The twentieth century has much less reasonableness in its existence than the nineteenth century but reasonableness does not make for splendor. (pp. 48–49)

Crucially, Stein does not say she was doing the same thing as Picasso; she certainly does not say she adapted Picasso's techniques. She does say "I was alone at this time in *understanding* him, perhaps because I was expressing the same thing in literature, perhaps because I was an American and, as I say, Spaniards and Americans have a kind of *understanding of things* which is the same" (p. 16; my emphasis).

Stein is pointedly aware in *Picasso* that writing and painting are different means for expressing this twentieth-century vision, their mutual "understanding of things." The terms she uses to describe the difference tell us clearly that she could not have seen herself adapting or translating into her own medium techniques that belong to Picasso's: "The painter does not conceive himself as existing in himself, he conceives himself as a reflection of the objects he has put into his pictures and he lives in the reflections of his pictures, a writer, a serious writer, conceives himself as existing by and in himself, he does not at all live in the reflection of his books" (p. 4):

He commenced to write poems but this writing was never his writing
. . . it was not for him to decide every moment what he saw, no, poetry
for him was something to be made during rather bitter meditations, but
agreeably enough, in a café. . . . As I have said Picasso knows, really
knows the faces, the heads, the bodies of human beings, he knows them
as they have existed since the existence of the human race, the soul of
people does not interest him, why interest one's self in the souls of people
when the face, the head, the body can tell everything, why use words
when one can express everything by drawings and colors. (pp. 46–47)

Stein is touching here upon the very difference between words and
paint that she is accused of ignoring or attempting to obliterate: that
words are inevitably signs while painted shapes need not be. To call Stein's
writing "literary cubism," to accommodate it to a critical vocabulary
developed for painting, is to overlook that central, defining difference:
unlike paintings, Stein's experimental work is neither representational nor
abstract. If a painting has readable meaning, that meaning is referential,
representational. If a painting does not have representational meaning, it
is abstract; it has no strictly readable meaning. Stein's writing has
readable meaning, and therefore is not abstract, but since it is seldom
"about something" – it generally has no coherent thematic content – it is
not referential, or representational. Its meaning consists rather of the
connections among the lexical meanings of its words. Painting has nothing
in its semantic repertoire comparable to lexical meaning, and it is precisely
at that level that Stein's experimental writing operates. Because it has
lexical meaning, it is able to challenge patriarchal/logocentric thought as
pictorial radicalism cannot do.

In her recent book on Stein's portraits, Wendy Steiner uses the fact
that writing is not painting – that words are signs while paint need not
be – to condemn Stein's fully experimental writing. She is able to do that
because she begins with the assumption that Stein's radical work is literary
cubism. Her argument runs as follows: 1) Stein's experimental writing is
literary cubism, but 2) because writing is a second-level sign system it
cannot really adopt a form indigenous to painting, a first-level sign
system, therefore 3) the writing fails. More typically, analyses of Stein's
work as literary cubism simply ignore the fact that words are signs, that
their mode of signification need not be referential (representational), and
thereby ignore the center of her writing: the creation of culturally
alternative modes of literary meaning.

Notes

1. See, for example, Mabel Dodge, "Speculation, or Post-Impressionism in Prose," *Arts
and Decoration*, 3 (1913), 172–74; L. T. Fitz, "Gertrude Stein and Picasso: The Language of
Surfaces," *American Literature*, 45 (1973), 228–37; Samuel H. McMillan, "Gertrude Stein,
the Cubists, and the Futurists," Dissertation, University of Texas, 1964; Marilyn Gaddis Rose,
"Gertrude Stein and the Cubist Narrative," *Modern Fiction Studies*, 22 (1976–77), 543–55;

Wendy Steiner, *Exact Resemblance to Exact Resemblance: The Literary Portraiture of Gertrude Stein* (New Haven: Yale Univ. Press, 1978); Wylie Sypher, *Rococo to Cubism in Art and Literature* (New York: Random House, 1963); William Wasserstrom, "The Sursymameri-cubealism of Gertrude Stein," *Twentieth-Century Literature*, 21 (1975), 90–106. The most recent treatment of Stein's work from this point of view, and a sophisticated, persuasive argument, is Marjorie Perloff, "Poetry as Word-System: The Art of Gertrude Stein," *American Poetry Review*, 8, No. 5 (1979), 33–43.

2. *Lectures in America* (New York: Random House, 1935).

3. See, for example, Allegra Stewart's interpretation of *Tender Buttons* as a mandala, in *Gertrude Stein and the Present* (Cambridge, Mass.: Harvard Univ. Press, 1967).

4. Those six are *Bee Time Vine and Other Pieces* (1913–1927), *As Fine as Melanctha* (1914–1930), *Painted Lace and Other Pieces* (1914–1937), *Stanzas in Meditation and Other Poems* (1929–1933), *Alphabets and Birthdays*, and *A Novel of Thank You*. Also from this period come portraits such as "Portrait of Mabel Dodge at the Villa Curonia," "Susie Asado," "Preciosilla," "Guillaume Apollinaire," "The Completed Portrait of Picasso," "A Valentine to Sherwood Anderson," "Lipschitz," "George Hugnet," and many others.

5. "Portrait of Mabel Dodge at the Villa Curonia," in *Selected Writings of Gertrude Stein* (New York: Random House, 1946). p. 528.

6. Noam Chomsky, "Some Methodological Remarks on Generative Grammar," *Word*, 17 (1961), 219–39; reprinted as "Degrees of Grammaticalness," in *The Structure of Language: Readings in the Philosophy of Language*, ed. Fodor and Katz (Englewood Cliffs, N. J.: Prentice-Hall, 1964), 384–89. Future references will be to the latter edition.

7. See, for example, Winthrup Judkins, "Toward a Reinterpretation of Cubism," *Art Bulletin*, 30 (December, 1948), 275–76.

8. "Food," *Tender Buttons*, in *Selected Writings of Gertrude Stein*, p. 488; subsequent references will be to this edition.

9. Oil on canvas, 39⅝ × 28⅝ inches, Art Institute of Chicago, gift of Mrs. Gilbert W. Chapman in memory of Charles B. Goodspeed.

10. "Objects," *Tender Buttons*, p. 469.

11. *Selected Writings of Gertrude Stein*, p. 549.

12. I do not contend here, or elsewhere in this article, that the discoveries of interpretive criticism are invalid; only that they are generally tangential to the crucial issues of linguistic signification that Steinian experimental writing raises.

13. Roland Barthes, *S/Z*, trans. Richard Miller (New York: Hill and Wang, 1974), p. 6.

14. Jacques Derrida, *Of Grammatology*, trans. Gayatri Chakravorty Spivak (Baltimore: Johns Hopkins Univ. Press, 1974).

15. Susan Sontag made a version of this argument in "Against Interpretation," *Against Interpretation* (New York: Farrar, Straus & Giroux, 1961).

16. See Hélène Cixous, "Sorties," in *La Jeune Née* (Paris: Union Générale d'Editions, 10/18, 1975); Luce Irigaray, *Speculum de l'autre femme* (Paris: Editions de Minuit, 1974) and *Ce Sexe qui n'en est pas un* (Paris: Editions de Minuit, 1977). Extracts from these are published in translation in *New French Feminisms*, ed. Elaine Marks and Isabelle de Courtivron (Amherst: Univ. of Massachusetts Press, 1980). See also Elaine Marks, "Review: French Literary Criticism," and Carolyn Greenstein Burke, "Report from Paris: Women's Writing and the Women's Movement," both in *Signs*, 3 (1978), 832–42, 843–55.

17. This argument, of course, focuses on the universal aspect of the Oedipus complex rather than on the admittedly crucial differences for the two genders.

18. See also D. W. Winnicott, *Playing and Reality* (New York: Basic Books, 1971).

19. See particularly "The Agency of the Letter in the Unconscious or Reason since Freud" and "The Signification of the Phallus" in *Écrits: A Selection*, trans. Alan Sheridan (New York: Norton, 1977), pp. 147–78, 281–91.

20. Julia Kristeva, *About Chinese Women*, trans. Anita Barrows (London: Marion Boyars, 1977). Subsequent references will be to this edition. Kristeva's argument for the persistence of an early matrilinear cultural order in Chinese society, which I do not give here, is premised on the presence of presymbolic, pre-Oedipal modes of signification in Chinese language.

21. Roland Barthes, *The Pleasure of the Text*, trans. Richard Miller (New York: Farrar, Straus & Giroux, 1975).

22. Gertrude Stein, *The Autobiography of Alice B. Toklas* (New York: Random House, 1933), p. 200.

23. *Autobiography*, p. 212.

24. Gertrude Stein, *Picasso* (New York: Scribners, 1940). Subsequent references will be to this edition.

The Somagrams of Gertrude Stein

Catharine R. Stimpson*

"Behind thoughts and feelings, my brother," wrote Nietzsche in "The Despisers of the Body" in *Thus Spake Zarathustra*, "there is a mighty lord, an unknown sage—it is called Self; it dwelleth in thy body, it is thy body." But when we represent the body, we must transmute our dwelling into a ghost-ridden, ghost-written language. Soma must become a somagram.

The somagrams of Gertrude Stein—hers and ours about her—illustrate this well-worn axiom. They reveal something else as well: attempts—hers and ours—to fix monstrous qualities of the female body. Like all monstrosities, we despise them, and thus, we seek to fix, to repair, them. However, like all monstrosities, we also need them, and thus, we seek to fix, to stabilize, them. We often toil in vain.

For those who would represent her, Stein's body presents an alarming, but irresistible, opportunity. For her body—the size of it, the eyes, nose, sweat, hair, laugh, cheekbones—was at once strange, an unusual presence, and special, an invigorating one. Increasingly indifferent to "feminine" norms of dress, style, and action, Stein herself appeared to behave as if that strangeness—like her writing itself—was more special than strange, at once original and right.

Mixing attraction and repulsion, the representers of Stein often choose to stress Stein's size. Clearly, she was fat, but her fatness is also a signifier valuable because capacious enough to absorb contradictory attitudes towards the female body. In a complementary act, Stein's representers also note how thin Alice B. Toklas was. They make the women, partners in life, counterparts in proportion. So doing, they sharpen divisions within Stein's domestic union.

*This essay is included by permission of the author. ©1984, Catharine R. Stimpson. It originally appeared in *Poetics Today*, 6, nos. 1–2 (1985): 67–80, and is reprinted here in slightly altered form.

For Stein's admirers, weight is a sign of life. She is, in all ways, outsized. Poignantly, in some photographs of her when she was tired and dying, she is much thinner. For Mabel Dodge Luhan, Stein's body is attractively exceptional rather than ludicrously freakish:

> Gertrude Stein was prodigious. Pounds and pounds and pounds piled up on her skeleton — not the billowing kind, but massive, heavy fat. She wore some covering of corduroy or velvet and her crinkly hair was brushed back and twisted up high behind her jolly, intelligent face. She intellectualized her fat, and her body seemed to be the large machine that her large nature required to carry it.
> Gertrude was hearty. She used to roar with laughter, out loud. She had a laugh like a beefsteak. She loved beef. . . . (Luhan 1935, 324)

Picasso, in his 1906 portrait, the most famous visual representation of Stein's body, drapes immense breasts, buttocks, hips, and thighs in dark cloth. However, the face and body are powerful. Because the browns and oranges of the sitter's clothing blend with the browns and oranges and dark blues of the background, the body seems at home, in place.

For more ambivalent admirers, Stein's fatness is a fact that they, and she, must transcend. Saying that Stein weighed two hundred pounds; less impartially judging that ugly; and then equating beauty and erotic love, Alfred Kazin states: "Stein and Toklas were certainly not beautiful, so their physical love for each other is all the more impressive." (Kazin 1977, 33). A chatty biography for children begins with an unhappy adolescent Gertrude wishing that she "weren't so large," and gazing enviously at the "slender grace" of her more flirtatious, and feminine, friends. However, this Gertrude consoles herself by being "different in more important ways" as well. Splitting lively mind from lumpy body, Gertrude reminds herself that her mind is "quicker" than that of those friends (Wilson 1973, 1).

Stein's detractors reverse the response of her genuine admirers. To them, her physical fatness is nothing less than proof of a hideous cultural and psychological overrun. She is nothing less than ". . . (a) . . . ten-ton granite American expatriate" (Corke 1961, 370). At their most hostile, such detractors — men and women alike — go on to comment on Stein's Jewishness. Katherine Anne Porter, whose stiletto persistently flicked out at Stein, sneered at her as ". . . a handsome old Jewish patriarch who had backslid and shaved off his beard" (Porter 1952, 43). Inevitably, detractors of Stein's body conflate her mind and body. They then disdain and fear her work. They seek to neutralize the threat to a dominant ideology of the well-spoken Christian lady that her potent combination of nature and culture offers: the body that she lived in; the family religion she more or less abandoned; the writing she never abandoned.

In a subtle maneuver, to picture Stein as fat also deflected the need to inscribe her lesbianism fully and publicly. One could offer a body, but not an overtly erotic one. One could show some monstrosity, but not too much. Although people refer to such "mannish" characteristics of Stein's as her sensible shoes, no one spoke openly of her lesbianism until after her death in 1946. Her friends protected her desire for privacy. Her detractors evidently found the taboo against mentioning lesbianism stronger than their desire to attack. Moreover, a popular icon of the lesbian, which *The Well of Loneliness* codified — that of a slim, breastless creature who cropped her hair and wore sleek, mannish clothes — did little to reinforce an association between the ample Stein and deviancy. She may have cropped her hair, with Toklas as her barber, but she wore flowing caftans and brocaded vests and woollen skirts.

After her death, Stein's lesbianism became more than a pronounceable, permissible subject for investigation. In the 1960s, in the women's movement and the gay movement, it stimulated celebration. In popular culture, her lesbianism evoked crass, but affectionate, jokes, as if it were odd but fun. In *The National Lampoon*, for example, "Gertrude Steinbrenner," a "Lesbo Boss," who looks like a hybrid of George Steinbrenner and Picasso's Gertrude Stein, buys the New York Yankees and feistily brings her team into the modernist movement. Her cubist field has eight bases; Diaghilev inspires her uniforms (Barrett 1982).[1] Significantly, in the same period, critics begin to reinterpret her Jewishness. It no longer deforms her, but rather, like her sexuality, gives her the subversive perspectives of marginality.

Stein was, of course, far more than the fat lady of a Bohemian circus. She was a serious modernist, whose formal experiments were as radical as those of any other modern writer, if not more so. The fact that her work provokes so much ridicule and anxiety, which often masks itself as ridicule, is one mark of her radicalism. Not even Stein's most ardent detractors can dismiss her — try though they might. Confronting such an alliance of body and literary activity, people, whether supporters or detractors, drew on two mutually contradictory sets of metaphors to depict her. The incompatibility of these sets itself reflects the difficulty, which Stein ultimately transcended, of having such a body devoted to such a cultural task.

The first set of metaphors domesticates Stein. Meant to praise, and to honor the monstrous lesbian as crafter, they also re-place her securely within women's traditional domain of the home. Because Stein's fatness also evokes the association of the fleshy female body with fertility, a Venus von Willendorf, this taming language has an added resonance. In 1922, Sherwood Anderson, one of her most loyal friends, wrote effusively of meeting her in Paris the year before:

> In the great kitchen of my fanciful world in which I have, ever since that morning, seen Miss Stein standing, there is a most sweet and gracious aroma. Along the walls are many shining pots and pans, and there are innumerable jars of fruits, jellies and preserves. Something is going on in the great room, for Miss Stein is a worker in words with the same loving touch in her strong fingers that was characteristic of the women in the kitchen of the brick houses in the town of my boyhood. She is an

American woman of the old sort . . . who cares for the handmade
goodies. (White 1972, 24)

In the same year, Man Ray took his famous photograph of Stein and Toklas
at 27 rue de Fleurus. Toklas, in a low chair, and Stein, in an easy chair, sit
on either side of the fireplace. Between them is a wooden table, above
them paintings. Toklas wears a dress with ruffled collar and sleeves. The
vaster Stein is clad in habitual items from her wardrobe: woolly socks,
sandals, a blouse with a broach at the throat, a flowered jacket.[2] Indeed,
several of the most widely circulated photographs of Stein frame her at
home—in Paris or in the country.

The second set of metaphors inverts such cozy portraits of Stein at
home by the range. In them, she is beyond society and social control;
beyond ordinary sexuality, and therefore, beyond the need for sexual
control. If the first set of metaphors drains monstrosity of its threat
through enclosing it, the second does so through casting it out and away
from daily history. In part, these metaphors transmogrify Stein into a
sacred monster — to be sought after by some, cursed by others. Describing
Stein after a walk in the Tuscan hills, Mabel Dodge Luhan oracularizes
her:

> . . . when she sat down, fanning herself with her broad-brimmed hat
> with its wilted, dark brown ribbon, she exhaled *a vivid steam around
> her* (italics mine). (Luhan 1935, 327)

In 1920, a head of Stein that Jacques Lipchitz sculpted — with a topknot of
hair, high cheekbones, narrow oval eyes — helped to create a linkage
between Stein and Buddha. Sinclair Lewis, as insult, called her "Mother
Superior." Moving between polarities, Sherwood Anderson

> . . . was the first of several hundred people to liken her to a monk. Some
> religious quality about her unadorned habiliments brought to mind not
> so much a nun as a monk. There was something sexless about her, too, a
> kind of dynamic neuter. She was a robe surmounted by a head, no more
> carnal than a portly abbot. (Rogers 1948, 39)

Such distancing metaphors also eject Stein back into time past. With
suspicious frequency, her viewers compare her to a Roman emperor or
well-born citizen. In Picabia's portrait of 1933, she stands—in a striped,
toga-like robe. Two years later, an interviewer wrote:

> The hair is close-cropped, gray, brushed forward or not brushed at all
> but growing forward in curls, like the hair of Roman emperors. (Preston
> 1935, 187)

Physically, her strong bones, and that hair, made such an identification
plausible. Psychologically, she seemed Roman in the persistence and ease
of her will — especially, in a conjunction of metaphors, when she was at
home. As Roman, Stein could also be "mannish," without any direct
declaration of lesbianism.

Hemingway's is the saddest engagement with the Roman metaphor. In his memoirs the now-alienated man, who was once surrogate son and brother, took revenge on Stein. He first remembers being responsive to her body. Describing it, he performs one of his standard rhetorical moves: rummaging through a number of non-Anglo-Saxon cultures for tropes to express pleasure. Stein has beautiful eyes, a "German-Jewish" face, "immigrant hair," and the face of an Italian peasant woman (Hemingway 1964, 14). Centering his erotic recall on his relationship with Stein, Hemingway refers to Toklas only as "the friend." However, Hemingway centers his bitterness on that friend. For, he tells us, the relationship with Stein ended, although not formally, when he once went unexpectedly to 27 rue de Fleurus. He overheard Toklas speaking to Stein "as I had never heard one person speak to another; never, anywhere, ever." (118). Given Hemingway's experience, his adverbial stresses seem disingenuous. Despite this, he goes on to tell of hearing Stein beg "Pussy" for mercy. In his shock, he strips both women of their bodies and reduces them to invisible, but scarring, voices. His final word for Stein tries to restore the power of which the scene has denuded her: she is again "Roman" (119).

Stein's somagrams of her body partially resemble and reinforce the patterns of representation I have outlined. For example, in the erotic celebrations of her relationship with Toklas, she famously, and notoriously, acts out the part of "Caesar."[3] Whether they resemble her representers or not, her somagrams are never radically visceral or visual. She is no physiological blueprinter. In her salon, she also ". . . frowned on anything that smacked of vulgarity" (Mellow 1974, 324). She might voyeuristically provoke gossip and displays, but she believed in discretion. To measure her reticence one might compare her to Apollinaire in 1909. She was writing "Ada," the lyrical portrait about her growing relationship with Toklas, and "Miss Furr and Miss Skeene," a witty short story about a disintegrating relationship between two other women. Neither has any explicit sexual detail whatsoever. Meanwhile, Apollinaire was publishing and endorsing the first anthology of the works of deSade.

Nevertheless, during her career, Stein's somagrams became freer and more flexible—as she became less monstrous to herself. Her happiness with Toklas diluted the guilts and stains of a homosexuality that violated the "decent" norms of the heterosexual bourgeois family to which Stein had once been committed. She was increasingly confident of herself as a writer—even boisterously so. So doing, she became more sympathetic to women's aspirations and talent (DeKoven 1983, 137). Though Stein was never a public feminist, during the 1920s she began to cut the cord she and Western culture had tied between masculinity and towering creativity.

Her body also enlivens her writing—be they somagrams or not; be they lyrics, meditations, or diary-like notations. For texts read as if her voice were in them; as if she were speaking and dictating as much as writing. Unlike a Charles Olson, Stein lacks a theory about the relationship of the poetic line to the human breath. Nevertheless, she illustrates that "The best writing is energized by speech, and the best speech surges forward like a wave . . . In poetry, writing is not the same as speech, but is transformed by speech . . ." (Vernon 1979, 40). Once, when Stein was objectifying mutton in *Tender Buttons*, written in 1911, but not published until 1914, she mused and teased, "A sign is the specimen spoken" (Stein 1971, 182). Stein's work is liveliest when read and heard; when our own o/aural talents lift her words from the page and animate them in an informal or formal, private or public, theatrical environment.

Stein's somagrams became freer and more flexible in at least two entwined ways, which in turn entwine psychology and rhetoric. First, she modified her motives for being discreet when she wrote about the female body. In the first decade of the twentieth century, she was fearful of what she might say, of what she might confess — to herself and others. She disguised her own lesbian experiences through projecting them onto others or through devising what William Gass, one of her most scrupulous and sensitive critics, has called her "protective language":

> . . . a kind of neutralizing middle tongue, one that is neither abstractly and impersonally scientific nor directly confronting and dramatic, but one that lies in that gray limbo in between. . . . (Gass 1972, 89)

Perhaps her fear was never wholly to disappear. Still, Stein was later to see the body as but one element in a larger physical, emotional, social, linguistic, and metaphysical universe.[4] Even in *Q.E.D.* (1903), Stein wrote about women's bodies as signifiers of psychic and national types: the body of Helen Thomas demonstrates the American version of an "English handsome girl"; that of Mabel Neathe the American version of an older, decadent Italian aristocracy; that of Adele (based on Stein herself) the values of a young, hearty, middle-class woman. In *Q.E.D.*, too, the lesbian triangle of Helen, Mabel, and Adele is less an erotic intrigue (though Adele's introduction to erotic experience matters) than an arena of power plays. For Stein, I believe, too great a preoccupation with the body would grossly swell its importance. Though some inhabitants of the twentieth-century might be skeptical, such a belief is legitimate, not a prude's rationalization of sexual repression. Stein once said that sex, like violence, was the root of much emotion. Nevertheless, it was but part of a whole; sexual passion was less than passion conceived as "the whole force of man."[5]

> Literature — creative literature — unconcerned with sex is inconceivable. But not literary sex, because sex is a part of something of which the other parts are not sex at all. (Preston 1935, 191)

Throughout her writing, Stein so places the female body that it merges with, and gives way to, other activities. For example, in 1940, in *Ida*, Stein has a passage about Ida's adolescence. She simultaneously alludes to menstruation and slides away. The double process of allusion and slippage both evokes the body and dissipates its presence:

> And so Ida went on growing older and then she was almost sixteen and a great many funny things happened to her. Her great-aunt went away so she lost her great-aunt who never really felt content since the orange blossoms had come to visit her. And now Ida lived with her grandfather. She had a dog, he was almost blind not from age but from having been born so and Ida called him Love, she liked to call him naturally she and he liked to come even without her calling him. (Stein 1971, 340)

In her blurring, the boundaries of gender identity themselves decompose. Female and male become fe/male. "Arthur angelic angelica did spend the time," Stein gossips (Stein 1975, 39). As she wipes out punctuation marks, she makes it equally possible that someone is telling Arthur about Angelica; that angelic Arthur is spending time with Angelica; that angelic Angelica is spending time with Arthur; that two angels are spending time together; or that Arthur and Angelica are one heavenly creature.

Invariably, inevitably, the body fuses with writing itself. Stein merges herself with her work, and that unity with the world. Look at "Sacred Emily," a 1913 piece in which Stein first said, "Rose is a rose is a rose." Its first line is "Compose compose beds" (Stein 1922, 188). Multiply punning, the line refers to gardens and to flowering beds; to making beds, that site of sleep and sex; to making beds musical, and to making beds a language game. Even in "Lifting Belly," Stein's most ebullient record of her life with Toklas, sexual tension, foreplay, and climax interweave with other, fragmenting sensations and phenomena to create ". . . a tense we might call 'present sensual . . .' " (Retallack 1983, 251). The phrase "Lifting belly" becomes both a repetitive synecdoche for a repeated, repeatable sexual act and a generalized metonymy for Stein's life at large. Because the poem has such a successful decentering device, almost any group of lines, pulled out at random, inflects the "present sensual" tense:

> Lifting belly is a credit. Do you care about poetry?
> Lifting belly in spots.
> Do you like ink.
> Better than butter.
> Better than anything.
> Any letter is an alphabet.
> When this you see you will kiss me.
> Lifting belly is so generous.
> Shoes. (Stein 1980, 48)[6]

Indeed, in Stein's more abstract writing, the body disappears into language utterly, or becomes an example of a linguistic category. Kisses may illustrate, not the body in action, but a problematic grammatical class: the noun.

Stein's second demonstration of a freer, more freeing, more flexible sense of women's bodies is her growing ability to represent the body as a site of pleasure. In her work in the first part of the twentieth-century, the experience of eros, for heterosexual and homosexual women alike, breeds frustration, anxiety, and guilt — particularly for more vulnerable and powerless women. For heterosexual women, eros is inseparable from a fated, dutiful maternity. No matter what their sexuality, women's bodies are mortal. In *Three Lives*, Good Anna dies after an operation; Melanctha dies in a home for poor consumptives; Gentle Lena dies, worn out after three pregnancies, giving birth to a fourth child, itself still-born.

Then, in 1909, Stein began to write of sexuality with pleasure (Schmitz 1983, 194–96). To be sure, she continued to remember sexual trauma and unhappiness. In *How To Write*, published about thirty years after Stein's wretched entanglement with May Bookstaver, she has a long, broody paragraph about Mabel Haynes, Stein's rival for May's allegiance, and about Mabel's subsequent career as wife and mother (Stein 1975, 222). Stein could also write ambivalently about sexuality. In *Tender Buttons*, she ends her first section, "Objects," with "This Is This Dress, Aider." "Aider" puns on "To aid" and "Ada," that surrogate name for Toklas. Only two lines long, the meditation replicates the rhythms of an act that seems at once richly pleasurable and violent. Stein, in *Tender Buttons* and elsewhere, was to become more and more skillful in imitating the rhythms of an act in order to name it without resorting to, and consorting with jaded old nouns. "This Is This Dress" ends: "A jack in kill her, a jack in, makes a meadowed king, makes a to let" (Stein 1971, 176). The act seems to be sexual, but it may, of course, also be anything that follows a pattern of building and releasing tension. The last three words, for example, may allude to "a toilet," which, in turn, may be the process of getting dressed, or of going to the bathroom, or of both.

To be sure, too, Stein never lost her sense of the body's fragility. In the 1930s, she was, as if it were a minor obsession, to work and rework the stories of two mysterious, sinister deaths near her country home. In one, Madame Pernollet, a hard-toiling hotelkeeper's wife in Belley, has died — five days after falling onto a cement courtyard. In the second, a Madame Caeser (that Roman word again) had been living with a Madame Steiner (another extension of Stein's own names). However, an Englishwoman has interrupted their idyll. After some complications, she is found dead. Despite the fact that she has two bullets in her head, she is declared a suicide. As if to compensate for such a sense of fragility, and to declare her own power over the body, Stein, in the 1930s, was to give the author herself the power to destroy. In *Everybody's Autobiography*, she notes, with aplomb:

> . . . Give me new faces new faces new faces I have seen the old ones . . .
> Having written all about them they ceased to exist. That is very funny if
> you write all about any one they do not exist any more, for you, and so
> why see them again. Anyway that is the way I am. (Stein 1973, 118)

In spite of such strong residual memories and perceptions, Stein's eventual delight in the female body spins and rushes through her work, inseparable from her pleasure in food, or a dog, or the landscape, or a French hat. "It is very pretty," she writes, "to love a pretty person and to think of her when she is sleeping very pretty" (Stein 1975, 359). Because she is happy as both carnal participant and observer, as both actor and audience, she sites/cites her body, and that of her partner/s, in a "magic theater" (Fifer 1979, 473). However, the celebration of the body is more than a performance. Inverting the puritanism that Stein never fully escaped, the celebration of the body can be ethically charged as well. For it becomes ". . . at its climax a celebration of the capacity we have for emotion, for 'care,' the tenderest mode of human feeling and behavior" (Secor 1982, 304).

Given this, Stein's coding of sexual activities ceases to be a suspect evasion and becomes, instead, a privileged, and a distinguished, "anti-language." The anthropologist, M.A.K. Halliday, writes of anti-languages as the speech of anti-societies, "set up within another society as a conscious alternative to it" (Halliday 1976, 570). The anti-language has several purposes: to display a speaker's abilities, to preserve secrecy, to act out a "distinct social structure" (572); to socialize people into that structure. In brief, the monsters speak up within, and for, their lair. Halliday writes, not of homosexual anti-societies, but of criminal underworlds, prisons, and vaudeville. Nevertheless, Stein and Toklas, in their own home and the social circles they inhabited, were citizens of a homosexual anti-society. For that home, and for those circles, Stein, as part of her vast experiments, uttered an anti-speech that has become more public as the dominant society has become less hostile to her subjects.

Whether or not her anti-language is "female" as well is a far more perplexing matter. In 1976, Ellen Moers rightly suggested that Stein deploys landscape to project and to represent female sexuality. So doing, she extends a female literary tradition (Moers 1976, 254). Stein does often resort to nature to emblemize female sexuality; female being; and her own creativity. In one of her later presentations of self-as-writer, Stein brought together two complementary quasi-natural metaphors: the fountain, traditionally masculine, and the womb, invariably feminine.

> Technique is not so much a thing of form or style as the way that form or style came and how it can come again. Freeze your fountain and you will always have the frozen water shooting into the air and falling and it will be there to see — oh, no doubt about that — but there will be no more coming . . . You cannot go into the womb to form the child; it is there and makes itself and comes forth whole — and there it is and you have made it and have felt it, but it has come itself. . . . (Preston 1935, 188).

Stein also belongs to the history of women writers as women writers for reasons other than her landscape imagery. They include her cultural marginality; her interest in domesticity; and her teasing of patriarchs and of gender relations. Moreover, her lesbianism — the sexual deposition of her body, her choice of a woman as lover/companion — helped to give her the distance she needed to reform English literature and the homely security she needed if she were to be such an intrepid pioneer.[7]

The question of a women's tradition provokes yet another query: that of its causes. Clearly, a common history and culture, not a common psychobiology, can determine a women's tradition. When Stein adapted George Eliot's landscape metaphors, even as she devised her own, she could have done so because she had read and admired Eliot as a precursor; because she had read and admired Eliot's texts as texts that were, in part, *about* women's experiences. However, since Moers' work in the mid-1970s, attempts to adjectify Stein's work as "female" have entangled that work far more deeply with Stein's femaleness as femaleness, as an elemental condition, inseparable from the body.

Some of these efforts derive from critics who owe a strong theoretical allegiance to United States radical feminism. As they construct the world, they profoundly genderize it. Knowing, thinking, writing — all are dualistic, male or female. Two such critics claim:

> Patriarchal expressive modes reflect an epistemology that perceives the world in terms of categories, dichotomies, roles, stasis, and causation, while female expressive modes reflect an epistemology that perceives the world in terms of ambiguities, pluralities, processes, continuities . . . complex relationships. (Penelope and Wolfe 1983, 126).

For them, Stein, a woman deep within the process of creation, is a prophet of a female expressive mode emerging fully in the late twentieth-century.

Other critics genderize the world less radically. They reflect the influence of a liberal United States feminism that fears casting "femaleness" and "maleness" in the eternal bronze of an essential. Nevertheless, they, too, deploy contemporary theories of the female to place Stein as a writer. Subtle, supple, finely intelligent, Marianne DeKoven adapts the theories of Kristeva and Derrida to distinguish between two languages: our conventional, patriarchal speech, and an experimental, anti-patriarchal speech. The former celebrates the triumph of the male over the female; the post-Oedipal over the pre-Oedipal; the father's dictionary over the mother's body; meaning over things; the linear over the pluridimensional — in brief, the signified over the signifier. For DeKoven, Stein is the great, subversive experimental writer in English. Rejecting the repressions of patriarchal language, locating herself in the psychosocial position of women, loving the play of the signifier, Stein necessarily reclaims the mother's body as well (DeKoven 1983).

I admire such ideas, and resist them. Elsewhere I have tangled with my general ambivalence about "female" writing.[8] Let me now think more particularly of Stein. To begin — she was a fresh, brilliant, thoughtful literary theoretician. To be sure, in her theory and practice, she praised the spontaneous, the immediate "flow" of language from writer to page. Nevertheless, banks of theory line that flow; rocks of theory interrupt it; bridges of theory cross it. For better or worse, Stein is utterly impure: linear as well as pluri-dimensional; "male" as well as "female;" the fountain as well as the womb.

Given this, one might argue that Stein clinches the case for Kristeva (Kristeva 1980). First, like male avant-garde writers, Stein reaches back and down into pre-Oedipal speech. She shows how pre- and post-Oedipal mix — how the semiotic and the symbolic — play off and against each other. Studies of the ways in which children actually acquire language render suspect the terms "pre-Oedipal" and "post-Oedipal" and a picture of childhood that transforms children into boys and girls whose primary schooling in language is first with the mother's body and then with the father's rule. Of course the sex of the parent still matters to the child. A mother's voice, for example, has a different frequency than that of a father. Nevertheless, in the acquisition of language, infants may share a mentality and competence that transcends sex and gender — be it their own, or that of the parents. A characteristic of that mentality and competence is the sheer earliness at which they adopt, and adapt, rules.

First, at ten to twelve months, children demonstrate a "holophrastic speech," single word utterances used to express complex ideas about their environment (Dale 1972). Next, at about eighteen to twenty months, they progress to two-word utterances: a "pivot word" that appears in the same position in every phrase; an "open word" that changes. Next, children do more word combinations; formulate noun phrases; and differentiate classes of modifying words. Even as infants, children are regulatory, rule-making, rule-analyzing creatures who seek to combine creativity with patterns, self with laws, needs with necessities. As a leading linguist writes:

> It is striking how little difficulty a child has with any of the general mechanisms of language: the notion of a sentence, the establishment of word classes and rules for combining them, the concept of inflections, the expression of a wide variety of meanings, and more. All are present from a very early age . . . As impressive as the complexity of child language is, it appears to be outstripped by the uses to which a child wants to put it . . . the child is above all attempting to express his own ideas, emotions, and actions through whatever system he has thus far constructed. . . . (Dale 1972, 50)

In brief, when Gertrude and her brother Leo were little, they grasped, grappled with, and broke the rules of language *as children*, each with his or her individual being. As they grew up, they entered an adult world. As Stein knew, it gave men more power than women — including greater power over and within the female body. Because of this, we can legitimately call this world "post-Oedipal." Stein's sense of her own monstrosity in this world—as a sexual being, as a marginal cultural citizen—influenced her writing, and her somagrams. Laboring with language in this world, Stein came to believe that women were in many ways more capable than men. Women could assume power over and within language; over and within their bodies. Resiliently, she transformed the monstrous into pleasure and into art. Because of this, we can call her a visionary of the "post-post-Oedipal."

If we do so, however, we must limit our Oedipal vocabulary to a way of talking about historical experience and various social uses of language. Stein's texts warn us against going on to genderize grammar itself. Her literary language was neither "female," nor an unmediated return to signifiers freely wheeling in maternal space. It was instead an American English, with some French twists and a deep structure as genderless as an atom of platinum. It could bend to patriarchal pressures, or, lash against them. It could label and curse monsters, or, finally, respond to a monster's stubborn and transforming will.

Notes

1. See, too, the cartoon strips of T. Hachtman, first in the *Soho News* and then gathered in Hachtman 1980. My thanks to Albert Sonnenfeld for bringing the Barrett piece to my attention.

2. The best collection of reproductions of paintings, photos, and sculptures of Stein is in Hobhouse 1975.

3. The translation of Stein's private sexual language begins with Bridgman 1970. It continues with Simon 1977; Stimpson 1977; Fifer 1979; Stimpson 1984.

4. My position modifies that of Wilson 1952. He believes that Stein's denial of her sexuality was greatly responsible for much of the opacity of her prose. See, too, Phelps 1956.

5. To adopt Stein's terms, the body may belong to the realm of "identity," not the more significant realm of "entity."

6. Note that "shoes" puns on "choose" and "chews."

7. Secor 1982, DeKoven 1983, and Schmitz 1983 persuasively analyze Stein as an antipatriarchal writer. I am writing a longer work on Stein that will treat her as an antipatriarchal writer, with strong moorings to the patriarchy.

8. For more comment, see Jardine 1981 and Stimpson forthcoming.

References

Barrett, Ron. 1982. "A Portrait of Gertrude Steinbrenner." *National Lampoon*, July, 70–73.
Bridgman, Richard. 1970. *Gertrude Stein in Pieces*. New York: Oxford University Press.
Corke, Hilary. 1961. "Reflections on a Great Stone Face." *Kenyon Review* 23, No. 3 (Summer). 367–89.
Dale, Philip S. 1972. *Language Development: Structure and Function*. Hinsdale, Ill.: Dryden Press.
DeKoven, Marianne. 1983. *A Different Language: Gertrude Stein's Experimental Writing*. Madison: University of Wisconsin Press.

Fifer, Elizabeth. 1979. "Is Flesh Advisable? The Interior Theater of Gertrude Stein." *Signs: Journal Of Women in Culture and Society* 4, No. 3 (Spring). 472–83.

Gass, William. 1972. "Gertrude Stein: Her Escape from Protective Language." In *Fiction and the Figures of Life*. New York: Vintage Books, 79–96.

Hachtman, T. 1980. *Gertrude's Follies*. New York: St. Martin's.

Halliday, M. A. K. 1976. "Anti-Languages." *American Anthropologist* 78, No. 3 (September). 570–84.

Hemingway, Ernest. 1964. *A Moveable Feast*. New York: Charles Scribner's Sons.

Hobhouse, Janet. 1975. *Everybody Who Was Anybody: A Biography of Gertrude Stein*. New York: G.P. Putnam's Sons.

Jardine, Alice. 1981. "Pre-Texts for the Transatlantic Feminist." *Yale French Studies* 62. 220–36.

Kazin, Alfred. 1977. "Gay Genius and the Gay Mob." *Esquire* 88, No. 6 (December). 33–34, 38.

Kristeva, Julia. 1980. *Desire in Language: A Semiotic Approach to Literature and Art*, ed. Leon S. Roudiez. New York: Columbia University Press.

Luhan, Mabel Dodge. 1935. *European Experiences*. Vol. 2 of *Intimate Memories*. New York: Harcourt, Brace and Co.

Mellow, James R. 1974. *Charmed Circle: Gertrude Stein and Company*. New York: Praeger Publishers, 528.

Moers, Ellen. 1976. *Literary Women: The Great Figures*. Garden City, New York: Doubleday and Co.

Penelope, Julia, and Susan J. Wolfe. 1983. "Consciousness as Style: Style as Aesthetic." In *Language, Gender and Society*, ed. Barrie Thorne, Cheris Kramarae, and Nancy Henley. Rowley, Ma.: Newbury House Publishers, 125–39.

Phelps, Robert. 1956. "The Uses of Gertrude Stein." *Yale Review* 45, No. 4 (June). 603.

Porter, Katherine Anne. 1952. *The Days Before*. New York: Harcourt, Brace and Co.

Preston, John Hyde. 1935. "A Conversation." *Atlantic Monthly* 156 (August). 187–94.

Retallack, Joan. 1983. "High Adventures of Indeterminacy." *Parnassus* 11, No. 1 (Spring/Summer). 231–62.

Rogers, W.G. 1948. *When This You See Remember Me: Gertrude Stein In Person*. Reprint. New York: Avon Books, 1973.

Schmitz, Neil. 1983. *Of Huck and Alice: Humorous Writing in American Literature*. Minneapolis: University of Minnesota Press.

Secor, Cynthia. 1982. "Gertrude Stein: The Complex Force of Her Femininity." In *Women, The Arts, and the 1920s in Paris and New York*, ed. Kenneth W. Wheeler and Virginia Lee Lussier. New Brunswick: Transaction Books, 27–35.

Simon, Linda. 1977. *The Biography of Alice B. Toklas*. Garden City: New York: Doubleday and Co.

Stein, Gertrude. 1922. *Geography and Plays*, with a foreword by Sherwood Anderson. New York: Something Else Press, 1968 reprint.

1971. *Writings and Lectures* 1909–1945, ed. Patricia Meyerowitz. Baltimore: Penguin Books.

1973. *Everybody's Autobiography*. New York: Vintage Books, originally published 1937.

1975. *How to Write*, with a new preface and introduction by Patricia Meyerowitz. New York: Dover Publications, originally published 1931.

1980. *The Yale Gertrude Stein*, ed. Richard Kostelanetz. New Haven and London: Yale University Press.

Stimpson, Catharine R. 1977. "The Mind, the Body, and Gertrude Stein." *Critical Inquiry* 3, No. 3 (Spring). 489–506.

1983. "Feminism and Feminist Criticism." *Massachusetts Review* 24, No. 2 (Summer). 272–28.

Forthcoming. "Gertrice/Altrude." In *Mothering the Mind*, ed. Ruth Perry. New York: Holmes and Meier.

Vernon, John. 1979. *Poetry and The Body.* Urbana: University of Illinois Press.
White, Ray Lewis. 1972. *Sherwood Anderson/Gertrude Stein, Correspondence and Personal Essays*, ed. Ray Lewis White. Chapel Hill: University of North Carolina Press.
Wilson, Edmund. 1952. *Shores of Light.* New York: Farrar, Straus and Young, 575–86.
Wilson, Ellen. 1973. *They Named Me Gertrude Stein.* New York: Farrar, Straus and Giroux.

Beyond the "Talent of Knowing": Gertrude Stein and the New Woman

Elyse Blankley[*]

Long before Gertrude Stein blossomed as a literary iconoclast in Paris, she was a successful American college girl in the 1890s, a time when women strove to master the western intellectual tradition in order to equal their male peers at Harvard or Princeton.[1] In later years Stein would savor the memory of her distinguished undergraduate performance as William James's Radcliffe protégée. But her intellectual achievements did not, and could not, make her sympathetic to the New Woman's crusade for sex equality through education. Stein distrusted the college girl's naive belief that complete parity with men would be won on the battlefield of books: she recognized that intellectual mastery does not automatically bestow the bearer with cultural privilege and power. The New Woman was, in short, derivative; and since Stein wanted to be an original, she had to rid herself of the eager New Woman in order to become her own woman. In her earliest fictions, Stein would work to efface from her imagination the college girl who dines on a diet of western (patriarchal) culture's words. The real revolution of the word would begin with Stein herself.

There was a time, however, when Stein rallied to the college girl's cause. Speaking before a group of Baltimore women on the value of a college education for women, Stein in 1898 seemed the complete New Woman, fresh from her promising first year in medical school and four brilliant years at Harvard as the star undergraduate psychology student of Hugo Münsterberg and William James. She was the perfect candidate to lecture other women on intellectual trailblazing and economic independence. A college education, Stein explained, "does not tend to unsex but to rightly sex a woman"; because the university-educated female can make her own living, her "sex desire is a much purer one as it is not marred by being a means of obtaining a livelihood."[2] With this statement Stein accomplished two things: she assured her audience that education, contrary to popular belief, would not "unsex" or turn women against their so-called natural role as breeders; furthermore, by suggesting that women

*This essay was commissioned for this volume and appears in print here for the first time.

need not form heterosexual relationships based exclusively on the economic trade-off of man as provider and woman as breeder, Stein subtly implied that university women need not form heterosexual relationships at all, if indeed so many are predicated on the financial dependence from which the college woman is freed (Stein's own nascent lesbianism made this latter issue a necessity, not just a theoretical option). The New Woman's sexual desire could be said to be "purer," then, both within and outside of the traditional heterosexual alliance.

Stein's speech borrows heavily from Charlotte Perkins [Stetson] Gilman's *Women and Economics*, as Stein herself admits, and her acceptance of Gilman's ideas, which had been published the same year, suggests that Stein agreed with the major feminist issues of the day. Her Baltimore presentation voices opinions held by many of her female contemporaries, including those of Martha Carey Thomas, the Bryn Mawr president who insisted vehemently that "sex solidarity" was an intellectual woman's only hope in the losing battle between ambitious careers and marriage.[3] Were the Baltimore speech our only document on which to base a quick sketch of young Stein and her politics, we would describe her as intellectual, dedicated, independent, and above all, feminist.

But a conflicting picture of Stein emerges from other biographical details. If we may believe the testimony of one of her Cambridge classmates, Stein "wasn't interested in clothes or suffrage or politics. . . ."[4] Moreover, her feminist Baltimore speech would, in essence, be completely renounced in *The Autobiography of Alice B. Toklas*, in which Stein defends her decision to leave the Johns Hopkins School of Medicine in 1902: though her close friend and feminine classmate Marion Walker might plead, "But Gertrude Gertrude remember the cause of women," Stein would coolly reply, "You don't know what it is to be bored."[5] She was pleased with her decision to snub the cause of women in favor of the demands of her own fierce independence, which ironically excluded her from the ranks of New Women who so desperately wanted her to succeed and hence to serve as a model. The Baltimore speech survives as an artifact from Stein's heady college days, showing us how Stein at one time in her life embraced — with whatever originality or clarity — the New Woman. In contrast, *The Autobiography* reveals Stein's later concern with establishing the difference between these two selves. Indeed, Stein and Marion Walker, although the best of friends, disagreed "violently" for more than four decades about the cause of women: "Not, as Gertrude Stein explained to Marion Walker, that she at all minds the cause of women or any other cause but it does not happen to be her business."[6]

What happened to be Stein's business, of course, was Stein. Her self-absorption might be compatible with Margaret Fuller's ideal of the "free spirited individual," but it clashed with the Carey Thomas/Bryn Mawr spirit of the 90s that insisted upon the general advancement of women, united by a common goal to compete with men.[7] Whenever Stein does refer to her university days, the evidence is always summoned to buttress the personal Stein myth of the "brilliant young woman who throws over a promising medical career for literature," complete with testimony from the legendary William James. The emphasis falls on Stein the individual, not Stein the New Woman among others. Catharine R. Stimpson speculates that Stein had to reject the New Woman's idealized figure (a fantasy blend of wife, mother, and liberally educated helpmate) in order to begin her lonely assault on "a male world too strong for most women."[8] But the college girl's liberated education was itself at fault and would have paralyzed Stein in Paris had she followed its tenets: she had to erase the New Woman's image because it still functioned within the intellectual paradigms established by men.[9] In her struggle with Miss Bruce, Martha Hersland, and Nancy Redfern (three characters in her earliest works), Stein would kill the New Woman, just as Virginia Woolf had to kill the Angel in the House. Stein's demon was, as we shall see, every bit as dangerous for her artistic career as its winged sister was for Woolf's; in order to engender herself through language, Stein had to sacrifice the college girl on the altar of her imagination. For almost a decade, seated at her renaissance table and cloaked in dark flowing robes, Stein performed the literary rites of exorcism that would bring about her own rebirth/ renaissance in Paris.

Nowhere is Stein's contempt for the Carey Thomas philosophy of female equality/superiority more clearly revealed than in *Fernhurst*, an early novella composed in 1905 and later incorporated into *The Making of Americans*. Before beginning *Fernhurst*'s thinly disguised fictional account of the M. Carey Thomas/Mary Gwinn/Alfred Hodder scandal at Bryn Mawr in the mid-1890s, Stein offers her reader an essay condemning the modern college girl's hope that her education will make her man's equal. It is wrong, says Stein, that contemporary young women pass through an athletic childhood and a liberated college education "as if there were no sex and mankind made all alike and traditional differences mere variations of dress and contour."[10] Stein singles out the false promise of the New Woman's liberal education:

> I have seen college women years after graduation still embodying the type and accepting the standard of college girls — who were protected all their days from the struggles of the larger world and lived and died with the intellectual furniture obtained at their college — persisting to the end in their belief that their power was as a man's — and divested of superficial latin and cricket what was their standard but that of an ancient finishing school with courses in classics and liberty replacing the accomplishments of a lady. (4)

Although the narrator concedes that some women "must do a piece of the man's work" (4), most are unqualified or unwilling to make the rough transition between learning and action, between sexless theory and sex-dominated practice:

> I have heard many graduates of this institution [Fernhurst] proclaim this doctrine of equality, with a mental reservation in favor of female superiority, mistaking quick intelligence and acquired knowledge for practical efficiency and a cultured appreciation for vital capacity and who valued more highly the talent of knowing about culture than the power of creating the prosperity of a nation. (5)

What use are intelligence and acquired knowledge to dreamy girls who will not/*can* not share in the power of creating culture? Because there is so little connection between the philosophy of sex equality and its praxis, Dean Helen Thornton's glorious vision "of a people to remake and all sex to destroy" (7) is doomed to fail. Stein asks acidly, "I wonder will the new woman ever relearn the fundamental facts of sex" (4) — the facts, that is, governing the distribution of power between the sexes in a world where educated women's intellectual standards are mismatched with their limited arena of real participation in culture.

While it is hard to imagine a stronger indictment of the New Woman, it is curious that Stein, a woman who benefited from eight years of university education, would mount the attack.[11] Stein, moreover, was directly touched by the largesse of M. Carey Thomas's missionary feminist spirit because Thomas's money was in part responsible for the admission of women to The Johns Hopkins School of Medicine.[12] Yet Stein chose to lay bare with unflinching honesty the shortcomings of Thomas's philosophy, despite its dramatic impact on women's higher education. In turning her back on the college girl's utopian visions of the woman of the future, Stein was revising her 1898 opinion that education can "rightly sex" a woman. If indeed her so-called education amounts to nothing more than a glorified finishing school course, then the New Woman is rightly sexed not for herself but for the man whose pleasure she is designed to enhance. His university achievements lead him to the "affairs of the big world" (7) — hers, to a stale mental parlor where she sits imprisoned by her "intellectual furniture."

Stein underscores her distrust of the New Woman's academic pretensions in *Fernhurst*'s first meeting between Janet Bruce and the Redferns:

> . . . Redfern wandered up to a window where the Dean Miss Bruce and Mrs. Redfern were standing looking out at a fine prospect of sunset and a long line of elms defining a road that led back through the village of Fernhurst through the wooded hills behind, purple in the sunset and beautiful to look at. Redfern stood with them looking out at the scene.
> ———— ———— ———— [sic]
> said Miss Bruce quoting the lines from the *Iliad*. Mrs. Redfern listened intently, "Ah, of course you know Greek" she said with eager admiration. Miss Bruce made no reply. . . . (12–13)

Although the lines in Greek are not directed at any specific person standing at the window, Janet Bruce's scholarly quotation from *The Iliad* does reestablish the intense intellectual tone set by her absorbing and deliciously arcane discussion with Philip Redfern a few minutes earlier. Their private conversation had been interrupted by the demands of the more general group discussion in progress, but Miss Bruce's Greek now seeks to recover the flavor of that intensely intellectual tête-à-tête with Philip. Interestingly, Nancy Redfern, not Philip, responds to Miss Bruce's Greek, unwittingly uniting the two women against Philip's silent failure to acknowledge Miss Bruce's mastery of the language that is traditionally considered one of the most difficult of all intellectual disciplines.

It is perhaps inevitable, though, that Philip would make no comment on the Greek because it could not possibly have meant the same thing to him that it did to Miss Bruce and Nancy Redfern. In the nineteenth century, Greek was the final and most difficult wall for an aspiring female scholar to scale before storming the bastion of male intellectual superiority.[13] Not surprisingly, it strikes a responsive chord in Nancy Redfern, who sees it as her key to complete parity with Philip. But Nancy foolishly mistakes intellectual achievement for sexual equality, and at *Fernhurst's* end she is a pathetic figure, spurned by Philip and self-exiled in Germany, studying Greek "so that she may become worthy of [Philip's] companionship" (48). Janet Bruce's intellectual advantages no more help her "win" Redfern than Nancy's Greek will help her "win" him back. Greek, Stein would say, has nothing to do with the fundamental facts of sex.

Stein's indictment of the classics and the inherited tradition cuts still more deeply in *Fernhurst*. In the passage quoted above, the lines of Greek are absent; Leon Katz says that "Miss Stein never filled in the lines from the *Iliad* in the manuscript of *Fernhurst*" (13n), and we may assume she would have done so later had she not completely excised the passage from *The Making of Americans*. Stein would likely have had to go to some trouble for those Greek lines, since she herself never studied the language. But the blanks are more eloquent than the Greek would have been because they speak for Stein's cavalier attitude toward the classics that supposedly formed the backbone of any rigorous university curriculum. It is as if Stein were saying, "Fill in the blanks with anything you like. It's all Greek to me." Naive women like Janet Bruce or Nancy Redfern might cling to the classics as their ticket to equality, but for Stein, Latin was only a tiresome requirement that had to be satisfied before she could receive her Radcliffe degree.[14]

How this runs counter to the widespread modernist obsession with the inherited tradition! For writers like Joyce, Pound, and Eliot, who threaded their works with copious classical references, the ancient world became the measuring rod with which modern man might judge the decline of life in the twentieth century. Although young writers like Hemingway, Fitzgerald, Malcolm Cowley, and E. E. Cummings might also share Stein's disdain of "inherited traditions,"[15] these writers can be counted among the heirs in the 1920s of a revolution in literary sensibility begun by Stein as early as 1905. Indeed, Stein's "revolt" was the more radical because of her gender: as a woman, she did not share the same male privilege to rebel against the intellectual tradition, a privilege vouchsafed by the understanding that western intellectual thought is every *man's*, to embrace or to scorn at will; in contrast, practically no one in late nineteenth-century America questioned a woman's exclusion from that tradition and hence from the luxury of spurning it. Thus Stein was boldly dismissing an intellectual legacy to which she, a second generation New Woman, had just recently been granted access.

If Stein's disdain of tradition separates her from the male giants of modernist literature, it also sets her apart from some important female peers as well. H. D., May Sinclair, Olive Schreiner, and Virginia Woolf all felt obliged to learn Greek. Woolf's obsession which began in her teens and which resulted in her being tutored at home by Janet Case, continued throughout her life to be of central importance to Woolf as a writer and a thinker.[16] In her essay "Professions for Women," she observes:

> Though I flatter myself that I killed [the Angel in the House] in the end, the struggle was severe; it took much time that had better have been spent upon learning Greek grammar; or in roaming the world in search of adventures.[17]

To Woolf, Greek was a woman's key to the man's intellectual world outside the home, and any women with a mastery of classics had already begun to take hold of that world. Stein would applaud Woolf's urge to roam the world but scoff at her passion for ancient linguistics; as a university-educated woman, she might easily have studied the classics, but she remained nonetheless indifferent to the glorious rigors of classical scholarship for which a young Virginia Stephen had had to struggle in private.[18]

While the girls of Bryn Mawr and Radcliffe were digesting the lessons of the past in order to take their place in society as women of the future, Stein had learned to trust the voice within herself: "How can you read a book how can you read a book and look. / I have no book. / I look," said Stein in 1922.[19] In America she had read many books, passively placing herself, in theory, beside the generations of male university graduates who had preceded her. But the fundamental differences of sex still separated the women schooled passively in theoretical equality and the men who actively shaped the society that continued to suppress women. In Paris, Stein stopped "reading" the lessons of the past and began "looking" — she made her transition, that is, from the American college girl schooled in possibilities to the American expatriate woman actualizing those possibilities far from the theoretical dreams of her female peers. America "made me . . . [Paris is where] I made what I made": Stein, for so long the direct object of America, now found the power to act as her own subject in France.

The New Woman could never have pleased Stein, who had no desire to be an imitation man in a man's world. Nor, however, could Stein simply speak with a woman's voice, for one senses her dissatisfaction with the purely matriarchal pose, estranged as it is from the power at patriarchal culture's center. Stein had long envisioned herself enshrined in history's pantheon of genius: "Think of the Bible and Homer think of Shakespeare and think of me," she suggests in *The Geographical History of America.*[20] But how would she, a woman who lacked the metaphorical penis of power and creation, place her work in the company of these singularly male masterpieces? Her solution was a strategy of such revolutionary proportions that even the most radical alternatives proposed by her New Woman feminist peers seemed tame by comparison: instead of parodying the *patria*'s worn-out linguistics, Stein started afresh by taking English back to the Word, to the Logos. If Parnassus was the Greek playground of Apollo and the muses, then what better occupation for Stein in Montparnasse than playing God with language?

By the time Stein wrote the extraordinarily daring *Tender Buttons* in 1913, she had begun to revolutionize the mother tongue that she had carried away from the fatherland ten years before. Stein, literally an "expatriate" in Paris, was artistically shaping a distinctly "ex-patriate" vision (in the word's original Latin sense of "away from the father"). But before she could become the verbal anarchist of *Tender Buttons*, she had to write *The Making of Americans* and *Fernhurst*, not just because these works prepared her technically for *Tender Buttons*'s later innovations but also because they helped her discover her power as an artist by letting her confront her own internalized images of female powerlessness that may have prevented her from writing all her later experimental work. Before Stein could sail with authority into uncharted literary seas, two of her college girl doppelgängers—Nancy Redfern and Martha Hersland—had to act out the dangerous submissive female fantasies that still threatened Stein during these crucial early years in Paris.

Nancy Redfern, Stein's *Fernhurst* version of Martha Hersland in *The Making of Americans*, is a free-spirited western college woman whose candor and naïve moral integrity make her a mirror-image of young Gertrude Stein at Radcliffe. Nancy's pathetic beaten figure at the story's end differs dramatically from her initially exuberant character—a contrast so marked that one wonders whether Nancy is the same woman at all or merely a player acting out a poorly realized part in an essentially triangular drama. But one aspect of Nancy's submissive transformation carries Stein's trace: she, like Stein, leaves America and expatriates herself to reforge a new personal identity. The similarities between Nancy and Stein quickly diverge, however; by succumbing to the false promise of Greek and the male intellectual tradition, Nancy acts out a doomed version of the New Woman, whose troubling image still haunted Stein, fresh from eight years at the university. Nancy Redfern, struggling in exile to learn a dead language so that she may become a true citizen of the patriarchal intellectual community, fades in the rarefied but etiolated atmosphere of ancient Athens; Stein, however, expands in the life-giving linguistic possibilities that she creates in Paris. As she would later say in *How To Write*, "Grammar is in our power": she had found the strength to mount a frontal attack on an inherited linguistic system. She had also discovered that "grammar" — *Stein* grammar — is one source of her power to change language: "grammar" is indeed "in" (contained within, part of) our "power."[21]

Like a Prince Charming come to rouse Sleeping Beauty, Stein began shaking language from the torpor in which time and familiarity had placed it. Her famous line "Rose is a rose is a rose is a rose" exemplifies her interest in revivifying language, not to resurrect old ghosts but to transform language in new contexts. As she explained the "rose" phrase during her 1934 American tour, "I think that in that line the rose is red for the first time in English poetry for a hundred years."[22] For Stein, the spell that holds language in suspended animation cannot be broken unless language is forcibly torn from its timeworn patterns. To this end, she introduces her poem "Patriarchal Poetry" (1929) with a string of long repetitive sentences interrupted by the word "spell":

> As long as it took fasten it back to a place
> where after all he would be carried away, he would
> be carried away as long as it took fasten it back
> to a place where he would be carried away as long
> as it took.
> For before let it before to be before *spell* to be
> before to be before to have to be to be for before
> to be tell to be to having held to be to be. . . .[23]
> [emphasis mine].

The poetry of the patriarchy is naturally a study of the past — "their origin and their history," as Stein says later in the poem (115). Although her language spirals in a series of long incantatory repetitions and rhymes that suggest a movement backward in time, Stein is not trying to locate herself somewhere in this vast cultural snail shell of history that the patriarchy carries on its back; rather, she is moving further back in time, "before spell," where she can "be" and "tell." This is Stein's formula for releasing herself from the burden of the past (including its inherited intellectual and linguistic traditions) by returning language to the free-form primordial mélange in which each word vibrates with the energy it possessed before the spell was cast and language fixed.

Moreover, Stein attributes her discovery of the world/word before "spell" to the fact that she is a woman. "Why is it that in this epoch the only real literary thinking has been done by a woman," she asks in *The Geographical History of America*.[24] She answers that question indirectly in *How To Write*:

> Analysis is a womanly word. It means that they discover there
> are laws.
> It means that she cannot work as long as this.[25]

Analysis ultimately leads anyone ("they" — but especially women here) to laws — that is, things broken down into their component parts will yield a pattern or system governing the whole, in the way that logical Aristotelian discourse, for example, leads to the laws or truths that underlie and govern rational human discourse. Stein finds this process "womanly," not because analysis as a mental discipline is inherently female but because the discovery of laws that *limit* is a particularly female condition. When woman, according to Stein, discovers the laws governing language and culture, she does not find what men perceive as absolute and universal "Truth" but an external system placed on her and restricting her: "she cannot work as long as this" is the "law" that would try to short-circuit Stein, and its unconditional finality resembles Charles Tansley's admonition to Woolf's Lily Briscoe that women "can't paint, can't write."

Women are placed outside the law by culture because men, not women, make those laws, as French feminist Luce Irigaray observes.[26] But their exclusion from the law — the patriarchal order — also gives women the potential for putting that Law into a unique perspective. Had Stein heeded the New Woman's exhortation to study Greek, learn the Law, she might have lost the viewpoint that allowed her to disregard the "laws" governing language. In order to escape the law of the father, she shunned the New Woman and spun the unique Steinian thread that guided her through history's linguistic labyrinth back to the world/word before "spell," a world where she could "be" and "tell."

One final secret self and image of female submission had to be recognized, however, before Stein could break free to the world before "spell." Martha Hersland, a woman caught in the binds of family and culture, is the fictional good girl serving Daddy at home while the real girl (Stein) writes her way out of that prison. Martha's story is borrowed from Nancy Redfern, with the exception that after her failed marriage with Philip, Martha returns home to California to nurse her ailing elderly father, the man whom she has always distrusted and feared.[27] Only geography separates Martha and Nancy; both characters are essentially the same passive woman sinking in different spots of the cultural quicksand that awaits them. The girl learning Greek and the girl waiting on a demanding patriarch are split images of Milton's daughters who, patiently reading Greek to their imperious blind father, personify western culture's ideal of the woman as man's ministering angel and helpmate.[28] Writers like the Brontës created powerful female characters to act out their authors' internalized feelings of rage against the *patria*; Stein, on the other hand, modeled two submissive handmaidens who would act by proxy in the roles that she no longer wished to play. Moreover, Martha and Nancy may even have helped Stein assuage her guilt at turning away from the role of Daddy's domestic slave or eager intellectual disciple.

It is interesting to note that David Hersland, Martha's father and the unmistakable fictional descendant of Daniel Stein (Gertrude's real father), is also a clear forerunner of another boorish and demanding fictional Daniel/father, Daniel Webster in Stein's play *The Mother of Us All* (1946), a blustering deaf pedant who trips on his own language despite his disclaimer that "there have been men who have stammered and stuttered but not, not I."[29] Webster is both reincarnation and evolutionary refinement of the earlier David/Daniels; moreover, he suggests another father/Webster, Noah Webster, the monolithic father of the dictionary who represents the final threat to a scribbling daughter trying to subvert that institutionalized codification of language. By writing *The Making of Americans*, Stein was both exiling herself from these crippling fathers and preparing for her war on words and on Webster's dictionary. Indeed, before *The Making of Americans* was completed, she had lobbed a missile in the enemy's direction by composing several linguistically revolutionary portraits and prose poems.[30] *The Making of Americans* was the long apprentice piece that hastened Stein's maturation as a modern artist and helped her clarify her goals as a writer. Martha Hersland, trapped in *His*land, let Stein create her own life in Paris.

One other aspect of Martha's story helps shed light on Stein's "expatriation," or movement away from the father: I am referring to the umbrella with which Martha is associated on two key occasions in *The Making of Americans*. As a very young child, Martha one day threatens to throw her umbrella into the mud because of feelings of anger, fright, and despair evoked presumably by some childish quarrel with her friends, who have gone on ahead without her. When she does finally thrust her umbrella into a puddle "in a movement of triumphing" (394), her gesture registers both empty frustration and childish defiance: its "triumph" announces young Martha's first confrontation with the laws of parental authority, which say that little girls should keep their umbrellas for protection from the rain.[31] Later in the novel, Martha witnesses another curious scene involving an umbrella, and this event also carries unmistakable although different Freudian overtones: a man hits an angry, pleading woman with an umbrella in public, and the scene "was for [Martha] the ending of the living I [Stein] have been describing that she had been living. She would go to college, she knew it then and understand everything and know the meaning of the living and the feeling in men and women" (424). This altercation between a man and woman (his wife? a relative? a prostitute?) hints at more than Stein's sexual and emotional awakening away from home; it also introduces Martha to the brutality of the symbolic phallus (umbrella) turned against women. Prior to this incident, young Martha had but dimly recognized the relationship between sex and power in culture. College life clarified Martha/Stein's understanding of the "fundamental facts of sex" — more specifically, the knowledge that one sex holds power and uses it, quite frequently, against the other.

The umbrella that young Martha throws down and the umbrella used to beat the woman in the road coalesce symbolically in another powerful stylus — the pen — that Stein in exile picks up for good at the age of twenty-nine. When young Martha/Stein throws away her umbrella, the gesture is an empty triumph that leaves her defenseless without even an umbrella/weapon with which to confront man on an equal footing in a public place. (The fencing metaphor is not as strained as it may seem: what was literary modernism if not a series of symbolic duels publicly waged on the pages of little magazines in New York, London, and Paris?) The umbrella signifies power, which takes its symbolic place under the sign of the phallus, the inevitable symbol of power in a patriarchal, indeed a phallogocentric culture, to borrow Derrida's term from *Spurs*. The umbrella/pen does not truly become Stein's tool until she has physically separated herself from the *patria* and psychically wrestled (through Martha and Nancy) with the *patria's* lingering demands. By 1921, when Stein fashions herself as "Little Alice B's" husband, she had become her own phallic pillar dancing across the page: "To be a roman and Julius Caesar and a bridge and a column and a pillar and pure how singularly refreshing."[32] And again: "Lifting belly is so round. / Big Caesars / Two Caesars / Little seize her / Too. / Did I do my duty / Did I wet my knife. / No I Don't mean whet."[33] The phallus is not merely appropriated from the father; it is transformed from the violent weapon/umbrella turned against women to the playful sexual agent, the knife that is "wet," not "whet."

With the expropriated pen in hand, Stein stretched her linguistic expatriation to the limit: the result in 1913 was *Tender Buttons*, which remains one of Stein's most hermetic pieces. Here words create their own *raison d'être*, triumphantly emerging as verbal usurpers that subvert the voice and the underlying linguistic structure of the composition by jamming the syntactical circuits with unfamiliar choices. The audience becomes an enslaved participant in this subversion as soon as it sets its eyes on Stein's prose because the calm omniscient voice narrating these verbal vignettes is at once compelling and mocking, seductive and manipulative.[34] The voice tempts the reader with a promise of perfectly sensible, foursquare prose, and yet everywhere that expectation is overturned.

Stein knows that her audience is trained to respond to an authorial omniscient voice and a rule-bound grammatical/syntactical system. By undermining these two arbiters of meaning, Stein mocks both the system and the audience so dependent on such a system; she offers us, says Neil Schmitz, both "a criticism of definitive discourse and a liberation from it."[35] Whether we as readers throw up our hands in disgust, meekly beg the author for a "clue," or rise above the chaos by creating/interpreting a new order based, for example, on Freudian associative principles, our response is determined by Stein's failure to give us the meaning we demand or expect. We have passed through the looking glass to a world that is neither neatly reversed nor clearly inverted — to a world through whose verbal relativity we grope, lured onward by only one constant, *Stein*: herself now become the Word, the Logos.

Tender Buttons became Stein's mark and manifesto, her dissertation (or perhaps we should say, her anti-dissertation), which bestowed upon her no formal degree but the infinitely more subtle initials of influence. Although she was not to enjoy widespread acclaim until *The Autobiography of Alice B. Toklas* was published in 1934, by the mid-20s Stein's early works had helped shape the literary development of Anderson, Fitzgerald, Wilder, and Hemingway, all of whom would later change or had already begun to alter the course of twentieth-century letters. Even Joyce was not immune to Stein's "little sentences." Indeed, the sweeping and fundamental linguistic changes suggested by *Tender Buttons* are echoed in Joyce's final work; but where Joyce's encyclopedic *Finnegans Wake*, the universal dictionary of language, is actually an index of fathers (Sterne, Aristotle, Shakespeare, Vico, etc.) sustained and upheld by a monumental cross-referencing of western civilization, Stein's work refers back to no one but herself.

From her Parisian salon, Stein presided over a virtual Stein University, an ad hoc literary school whose texts were Stein's own plays and poems: the anti-canon. Here at last was a college whose teachings might bestow the "power of creation"; Carey Thomas's charges would have to make do with the "talent of knowing" (*Fernhurst* 5). No less ambitious than her counterpart at Bryn Mawr, Stein charted a revolutionary and most singular course toward capturing the power and influence that would never automatically be granted the American college woman for having mastered western culture's intellectual menu. To this end, she demanded that her college's "student body" remain exclusively male,[36] encircling herself with admiring men while Alice amused the wives of genius in the kitchen. As sole doyenne of her private university, Stein was more than "making it in a man's world": she herself created a world and then schooled her pupils who, already enjoying the cultural privileges afforded them by virtue of their sex, could spread the world/word according to Stein and guarantee that Stein's influence on twentieth-century American literature might some day be, as a recent evaluation by Richard Kostelanetz claims it is, "unmatched by any other modern author."[37]

Perhaps the New Woman's revolution was too young to be of value to Gertrude Stein, for whom the college girl would always be derivative and powerless. Stein achieved the kind of success that her university peers had hoped its generation of educated women might earn, yet she did so without the guidance of the New Woman. By sacrificing that shadow self in her early works, Stein found the power to become her own literary progenitor — the mother and father of us all.

Notes

1. In 1897, the year of her graduation from Radcliffe, Stein was part of the second generation of New Women to profit from the expanded opportunities for women in American higher education. See Phyllis Stock, *Better Than Rubies: A History of Women's Education* (New York: Putnam, 1978), 190–91.

2. Gertrude Stein, ["The Value of a College Education for Women."] TS. The Cone Collection Archives, The Baltimore Museum of Art. I am grateful to The Baltimore Museum of Art for permission to quote from this manuscript.

3. Roberta Frankfort, *Collegiate Women: Domesticity and Career in Turn-of-the-Century America* (New York: New York University Press, 1977), 32–33.

4. Quoted in John Malcolm Brinnin, *The Third Rose* (Boston: Little, Brown & Co., 1959), 28.

5. Gertrude Stein, *The Autobiography of Alice B. Toklas* in *Selected Writings of Gertrude Stein*, ed. Carl Van Vechten (New York: Vintage Books, 1972), 18.

6. Stein, *Autobiography of Alice B. Toklas*, 78.

7. Frankfort, *Collegiate Women*, 30.

8. Catharine R. Stimpson, "The Mind, the Body, and Gertrude Stein," *Critical Inquiry* 3, no. 3 (Spring 1977): 497.

9. Part of Stein's quarrel with the New Woman also rests with the latter's moral insincerity, a theme explored with devastating effect in *O.E.D.* I wish, however, to focus in this essay on Stein's need to reject the New Woman's naive belief in a traditional [male] education's potential for neutralizing gender barriers.

10. Gertrude Stein, *Fernhust, Q.E.D., and Other Early Writings* (New York: Liveright, 1971), 4.

11. To be sure, part of Stein's early revulsion from the Bryn Mawr New Woman also stemmed directly from her emotional near-collapse over a muddied triangular love affair with May Bookstaver and Mabel Haynes, two Bryn Mawr graduates (for a complete account of this chapter in Stein's life, see Leon Katz, "Introduction," in Gertrude Stein, *Fernhurst, Q.E.D., and Other Early Writings* [New York: Liveright, 1971], i–xxxiv). When Stein censures the American college woman in *Fernhurst's* introduction, however, she aims to undermine the entire feminist academic community and its hopes for equality through education.

12. Richard Bridgman, *Gertrude Stein in Pieces* (New York: Oxford Press, 1970), 34 and note.

13. In the 1870s, Wellesley, Vassar, and Smith required Greek for entrance in order to insure academic excellence in a world where successful men were "always grounded in the classics" (Louise Schutz Boas, *Woman's Education Begins: The Rise of Women's Colleges* [New York: Arno Press, 1971], 258).

14. Brinnin, *Third Rose*, 33–34.

15. Malcolm Cowley, *Exile's Return: A Literay Odyssey of the 1920s* (1956; rpt. New York: Penguin, 1976), 115.

16. See, for example, Virginia Woolf, "On Not Knowing Greek," in *The Common Reader*, First Series (New York: Harcourt, Brace, and World, 1953), 24–39.

17. Virginia Woolf, "Professions for Women," in *The Death of the Moth and Other Essays* (New York and London: Harcourt Brace Jovanovich, 1974), 238.

18. Compare Woolf's breathless admiration of Cambridge classical scholar Jane Harrison (the "J———H———" of *A Room of One's Own*) with Stein's mocking scorn of Harrison in her poem "Crete." Woolf, *A Room of One's Own* [New York: Harcourt Brace Jovanovich, 1957], 17; Stein, *Bee Time Vine and Other Pieces* [New Haven, Conn: Yale University Press, 1953], 172–73.

19. Stein, *Bee Time Vine*, 7.

20. Gertrude Stein, *The Geographical History of America* (New York: Random House, 1936), 81.

21. Gertrude Stein, *How To Write* (1931; rpt. New York: Dover, 1975), 73.

22. Brinnin, *Third Rose*, 337–38.

23. Gertrude Stein, "Patriarchal Poetry," in *The Yale Gertrude Stein*, ed. Richard Kostelanetz (New Haven, Conn: Yale University Press, 1980), 106.

24. Stein, *Geographical History of America*, 182.

25. Stein, *How To Write*, 32.

26. Luce Irigaray, quoted by Diana Adlam and Couze Venn in "Women's Exile: Interview with Luce Irigaray," *Ideology and Consciousness* 1 (Summer 1978): 66.

27. Gertrude Stein, *The Making of Americans* (New York: Something Else Press, 1966), 135.

28. For a detailed and useful discussion of Milton's daughters as imaged in nineteenth-century British and American fiction and poetry by women, see Sandra M. Gilbert and Susan Gubar, *The Madwoman in the Attic: The Woman Writer and the Nineteenth-Century Literary Imagination* (New Haven, Conn: Yale University Press, 1979), 214–21.

29. Gertrude Stein, *The Mother of Us All*, in *Last Operas and Plays* (New York and Toronto: Rinehart and Co., 1949), 75–76.

30. These poems include "A Man," "Five or Six Men," *Two Women*, "Men," "A Kind of Women," and "A Family of Perhaps Three" [from the chronology established by Bridgman, 365–66]. Among dozens of titles, these are both representative and revealing, showing both a depersonalized interest in human nature reduced to its lowest common (or uncommon?) denominator — gender — and a heightened awareness of that final schism dividing family, culture, and literature. As a woman working to escape the *patria*'s restrictions, Stein had become hypersensitive to sex.

31. Richard Bridgman interprets this scene similarly, viewing it as Martha's specific sexual challenge to the people who should be watching out for her moral welfare: i.e., "If you will not take care of me, I shall do something bad. I shall throw my protection in the dirt" (Bridgman, 15).

32. Gertrude Stein, "A Sonatina Followed by Another," in *Bee Time Vine*, 13.

33. Gertrude Stein, "Lifting Belly," in *Bee Time Vine*, 83.

34. Pamela Hadas calls this voice the "ordering power in the tone of *Tender Buttons* . . . that leads us on in reading." From Pamela Hadas, "Spreading the Difference: One Way to Read Gertrude Stein's *Tender Buttons*," in *Twentieth Century Literature* 24, no. 1 (Spring 1978): 63.

35. Neil Schmitz, *Of Huck and Alice: Humorous Writing in American Literature* (Minneapolis: University of Minnesota Press, 1983), 26. See also Schmitz, 160–98, for a brilliant analysis of *Tender Buttons* as a pivotal work in Stein's break from the father.

36. One notable exception to this rule was poet Mina Loy, who admired Stein immensely and wrote an exegesis of her work as a letter to Ford Madox Ford in two issues of the 1924 *Transatlantic Review*.

37. Richard Kostelanetz, Introduction to *The Yale Gertrude Stein* (New Haven and London: Yale University Press, 1980), xxx.

The Writer in the Theater:
Gertrude Stein's *Four Saints in Three Acts*

Jane Bowers*

I

Gertrude Stein approached drama as she did every genre: She examined the genre's conventions, found them inadequate, and proceeded to redefine the genre as she worked within it. By the time she began writing *Four Saints in Three Acts* in 1927, Stein had grappled with the redefinition of drama in over sixty plays.[1]

Reading these plays, one can see that Stein rejected the conventional definition of drama as articulated later on, for example, by Eric Bentley. According to Bentley:

> The drama everyone agrees presents character in action. Human actions become "an action" in the drama when they are arranged effectively, when that is, they are given what we can recognize as a proper and praiseworthy structure.[2]

Stein's earliest plays, the dialogue plays of 1913 to 1919, lack that arrangement of action which convention sanctions as the "proper and praiseworthy structure" of drama. Not only did Stein eliminate a pattern of action from these plays, she also minimized isolated actions, thereby defying another convention of drama which J. L. Styan has called "the primacy of occasion." Styan writes:

> Both in the conception and in the communication of drama, the picture must always anticipate the words, and by generalized impressions the spectator is powerfully prepared for the specific and incisive focus of the words.[3]

Stein's plays assert, not the primacy of occasion, but the primacy of language — in the dialogue plays, the primacy of spoken language. Although speech is the primary activity in Stein's dialogue plays, Stein's speakers are never characters. Susanne Langer has stated that "a character in a play stands before us as a coherent whole."[4] This Stein's speakers never do. They are never characterized, either by habits or speech or through coherent portrayal. Stein's dialogue plays make for strange theater since, in them, dialogue fails to fulfill its conventional dramatic function as a secondary phenomenon — secondary to action and to character.

Ultimately, however, Stein was not content with unconventional dialogue as a solution to the problems she experienced with conventional

---

*This essay was written specifically for publication in this volume and is included here by permission of the author.

drama. It was all very well to eliminate structure and action from her plays, but the elimination of characters was more problematic. Dialogues must have speakers, and once language becomes attached to living people, the playwright loses control of it as a medium. No matter how assiduously the playwright avoids characterization, speech is a characterizing act. Through gesture, through tone, through personality, the speaker/actor can reinstate the very elements of drama which Stein tried to eliminate, especially since the language of her dialogue plays is mimetic. By imitating conversation, Stein was automatically creating an opportunity for the speaker to mimic a living person, to become a character. As Andrew Kennedy points out:

> A dramatist cannot leave behind the "living speech" of his age in the radical way in which an abstract artist can leave the human figure out of his canvas or his sculpture. The "living language" keeps pressing with peculiar tenacity on the "shaping imagination" of the dramatist.[5]

II

For Gertrude Stein, the conflict between the "living language" and the "shaping imagination of the dramatist" was but an extension of the conflict she experienced in all her writing between the demands of the living (those she wrote about and those she wrote to) and the shapes her imagination perceived and produced. This conflict she saw as an extension of the opposition in all human beings between what she called "human nature" and "human mind."

Briefly, human nature is that part of us which is easily recognized and known, our surface selves, including our names and physical characteristics, the appurtenances, qualities, and actions by which we can be identified as social beings, and which change with time and pass out of existence with our deaths. The human mind is more difficult to recognize and to know, and Stein had a correspondingly difficult time describing and defining it. She found it easier to determine what the mind is not than to say what it is. The most she could assert was that the human mind is the irreducible element in every person, the essence of one's individuality, and that the human mind is unchanging and timeless.

Language is the expressive vehicle of both nature and mind, but, as Stein came to feel, written language better represents the mind than does spoken language. In *The Geographical History of America* she writes:

> . . . but this I do know that the human mind is not the same thing as human speech . . . writing has nothing to do with human speech with human nature and therefore and therefore it has something to do with the human mind.[6]

Although writing can "have something to do with" the human mind, not all writing does. According to Stein, writing which is concerned with the social activities of human beings does not reflect the mind; neither does writing which imitates human speech. Stein laments, "I wish I could say that talking had to do with the human mind I wish I could say so. I wish I could."[7] But she cannot and she does not.

Nevertheless, Stein notes repeatedly in *The Geographical History* that "the human mind does play" and conversely that "human nature does not play." The mind may well play, but can its play also be "a play"? A play is writing, a record of the mind's play, but in performance the writing becomes speech. In the plays she wrote between 1920 and 1937, Stein tried to reconcile writing and performance so that her writing could be performed, and so that in performance, the words would be as much a reflection of her mind as they had been when she wrote them down. Her first step was to eliminate dialogue and to replace it with what she later called "landscape," creating plays in which language represents, not speech, but thought. *Four Saints in Three Acts* is one of these landscape plays.

The idea of a play as landscape evolved out of Stein's belief in the connection between the mind and the land. Stein believed that one's mind is shaped to some extent by one's place of birth and that the geography of a country determines the characteristics of its citizens. Thus she could call the record of her meditations on human nature, human mind, and play, *The Geographical History of America*, because she saw a correspondence between the contours of her mind and the contours of her country of origin. As her title indicates, she equated the history of her thoughts with the geographical history of her birthplace. So it is with her landscape plays. They record the play of the mind; they too are a kind of geographical history, a landscape. When we see them, we see the shape of the land, the geography of the mind which created them.

III

There are two groups of landscape plays: the lyrical landscapes (1920–1923) and the static landscapes, beginning with *Four Saints* in 1927 and including twenty-eight plays written between 1927 and 1937. In the lyrical landscapes, Stein uses language as a kind of vocal gesture, emphasizing its rhythmic, lyric, and expressive qualities. In these texts Stein persists in the word plays and metatextual musings by which she typically expressed her mind, but the sensuality and lyricism of Stein's language in these plays has far more impact (especially in performance) than the intellectual exercise of her mind. Stein's mental activity is overwhelmed in these plays, left behind by the musical thrust of her language.

Stein had always distrusted the melodiousness of language and her facility at expressing it. Of the work of this period, she writes:

> . . . I found that I was for a little while very much taken with the beauty of the sounds as they came from me as I made them. This is a

thing that may be at any time a temptation. This temptation came to me a little after the Saint Remy period when I wrote Saints in Seven, Four Religions, Capital Capitals . . . [it] resulted in . . . an extraordinary melody of words and a melody of excitement in knowing that I had done this thing. . . . This melody for a little while after rather got the better of me . . . I did begin to think that I was rather drunk with what I had done. And I am always one to prefer being sober. I must be sober. It is so much more exciting to be sober, to be exact and concentrated and sober. So then as I say I began again.[8]

Stein's playwriting "began again" with *Four Saints*, after a four-year hiatus and with much reluctance. The idea of collaborating on an opera was Virgil Thomson's, not Gertrude Stein's. Shortly after meeting Stein in February or March 1926, Thomson, who had long admired her works, set one of her 1913 portraits, "Susie Asado," to music. Stein knew nothing of this until he brought her the score on New Year's Day 1927. He followed this presentation, in February of the same year, with the composition of the music for "Preciosilla" (also a 1913 portrait), and in April with *Capital Capitals* (a 1923 play).

One of Thomson's special interests was English musical declamation. He was sensitive to the musical rhythms of speech, possibly because of his early choir and glee club training. In *The Musical Scene* he writes about the connection between music and language:

> . . . way back in the mind, where music gets born, it has a closer concordance with language and with gesture than it can ever possibly have with the obscure movements of the viscera or with states of the soul.[9]

In Gertrude Stein, Thomson saw a writer who was as aware as he of the affinities between music and language, and whose writing was, as Thomson describes it, with particular reference to *Capital Capitals*, "closer to musical timings than to speech timings."[10] Thomson explains his intentions in setting Stein to music as follows:

> My hope in putting Gertrude Stein to music had been to break, crack open, and solve for all time anything still waiting to be solved, which was almost everything, about English musical declamation. My theory was that if a text is set correctly for the sound of it, the meaning will take care of itself. And the Stein texts, the prosodizing in this way, were manna. With meanings already abstracted, or absent, or so multiplied that choice among them was impossible, there was no temptation toward tonal illustration. . . . You could make a setting for sound and syntax only, then add, if needed, an accompaniment equally functional.[11]

Thomson accomplished his intentions with "Susie Asado." The music complements the words, the musical declamation closely following Stein's language — its "sound and syntax." The piano accompaniment matches the simplicity of Stein's vocabulary and the discontinuity of her syntax. What Stein heard in "Susie" was the articulation of the music she knew to be inherent in her writing. She also heard that the music did not overpower the words, that the words led and the music followed.

In "Preciosilla" Thomson tried a different tactic. The music is not complement, but contrast to the text. For Stein's text, Thomson devised a formal musical arrangement (an old-fashioned one at that), dividing it into recitative and aria. John Cage describes the effect of this juxtaposition of music to words thus: "The words remind us that we are living in the twentieth century; the music convinces us that we are listening to a baroque cantata."[12]

Whether Thomson arranged his music as a reflection of Stein's text or in opposition to it, his belief in the affinity between music and language was tempered by his sense of the limitations of both media, limitations which keep them from achieving identity, limitations which mean that music has something to contribute to language and language to music in any vocal composition. In discussing *Four Saints*, Thomson addresses the difference between music and language:

> What gave this work so special a vitality? The origin of that lay in its words, of course, the music having been created in their image. Music, however, contains an energy long since lost to language, an excitement created by the contest of two rhythmic patterns, one of lengths and one of stresses. A pattern made up of lengths alone is static, and the stuttering of mere stresses is hypnotic. But together, and contrasted, they create tension and release; and this is the energy that makes music sail, take flight, get off the ground. By applying it to the text of Gertrude Stein, I had produced a pacing that is implied in that text, if you wish, but that could never be produced without measured extensions. Speech alone lacks music's forward thrust.[13]

Thomson associates music with directional movement — "forward thrust," "sail," "take flight," "get off the ground" — and language with rhythmic patterns which he describes as "static" and "hypnotic." For Stein, who was worried that the "implied" musical "pacing" of her prose would overwhelm the intellect with the beauty and excitement of melody, Thomson's theories could only have been reassuring. Even more reassuring, no doubt, was the practical application of his theories to her texts. No matter how melodic, how rhythmically compelling she judged her texts to be, Thomson's music was more melodic, more rhythmic. By comparison her language seems flat and static.

Despite such reassuring observations, Stein was uncomfortable with the prospect of writing an opera libretto. Ordinarily a prolific writer, she now labored slowly, spending at least a month to produce the first five pages of printed text and expressing in these pages her dread of the endeavor. Her hesitancy is understandable. When she and Thomson first discussed their collaboration, Thomson had set a direction which Stein would have found difficult to follow. According to Thomson, he and Stein came to the following understanding:

> The theme we chose was of my suggesting; it was the working artist's working life, which is to say, the life we were both living. It was also my idea that good things come in pairs. . . . This dualistic view made it possible without going in for sex unduly, to have both male and female leads with second leads and choruses surrounding them. . . . I thought we should follow overtly, however, the format of classical Italian opera, which carries on the commerce of the play in dry recitative, extending the emotional moments into arias and set-pieces. And since the eighteenth-century *opera seria*, or basic Italian opera, required a serious-mythological subject with a tragic ending, we agreed to follow that convention also.[14]

Thomson's expectations seem to have inhibited Stein. But his removal to the south of France in April 1927, and, on his return, Stein's removal to her summer home at Bilignin freed Stein to pursue her own course unencumbered by her collaborator's presence.

Thomson could not have known how far from his conception of a traditional opera with a serious subject and a tragic ending Stein's libretto was moving because he never saw the libretto until a month after Stein finished writing it. Beyond their initial discussion of subject, form, and theme, and a few letters which reported Stein's progress to Thomson without detailed reference to the particulars of that progress, the libretto was written without consulting the composer.[15] After she completed the libretto to her own satisfaction, she sent it off to Thomson with permission to do with it what he would to make it musical and stageable. The artistic collaboration between Thomson and Stein was largely Thomson's collaboration with the *fait accompli* of the Stein text, just as it had been when he set to music those texts which Stein had written before she knew him.

Although Stein graciously relinquished her text, after its completion, to those who would turn it into a musical performance, she had created an active role for herself in that performance as the author of the libretto. She included, in the libretto itself, the writer and the act of writing. The process of composition is as palpable as the procession of saints in Act III.

Stein makes herself and her creative process manifest during performance by giving herself most of the lines. As Richard Bridgman has pointed out, "almost two-thirds of the text is composed of authorial statement and commentary."[16] Thomson obscured this fact by parceling out the authorial commentary to two figures of his invention (called "commere" and "compere") who behave like stage directors but whose lines are addressed less to the business of staging than to the business of writing. Notwithstanding Thomson's adjustments, the first quarter of the libretto is a running commentary on the writing process. This commentary consists of self-criticism, self-encouragement, progress reports, plans and preparations for writing, and discussions of the ease or difficulty of writing.

As the play begins, the writing task seems difficult indeed. Stein's assignment is to write a libretto, but she soon states her preference for narrative. To resolve her conflict she postpones the primary task and proposes instead a narrative as a preparation for *Four Saints*. The libretto begins:

> To know to know to love her so.
> Four saints prepare for saints.
> It makes it well fish. . . .
> Four saints prepare for saints. . . .
> In narrative prepare for saints.
>
> . . . .
>
> A narrative of prepare for saints in narrative prepare for saints. Remain to narrate to prepare two saints for saints.[17]

At the bottom of the first page of text Stein does indeed begin a narrative of "What happened today." This narrative, set in the past tense, tells of a trip to the country on a beautiful day and of a visit (presumably later in the day) from a "he," who "said he was hurrying" *(O&P,* 12). The visitor's rather confusing conversation is reported using the narrative convention of indirect discourse. At the end of the visitor's long speech (a one-sentence paragraph) there appears a short sentence: "This is how they do not like it" *(O&P,* 12), which has no connection to the speech which precedes it (except a spatial one) but seems instead to be an evaluation of the narrative with which Stein was preparing for saints. "They do not like it" and, accordingly, the format of the text changes from lengthy paragraphs, suitable to narrative, to a succession of single lines, and from a narrative of what happened to an invitation to "Imagine four benches separately." To "imagine four benches" is to move outside the text, not back in time to a world of which the text is a report, but forward, to a world which the text is going to create—a movement from narrative to play-writing.

Shortly thereafter Stein urges herself to begin the play. "Begin three saints. Begin four saints" *(O&P,* 12–13). But beginning is no easy task and more narrative, more indirect discourse follow. Again Stein urges, "Imagine imagine it imagine it in it" *(O&P,* 14). Finally Stein commits herself to the play, reiterating the title, "Four Saints in Three Acts"; setting a scene, "A Croquet Scene"; invoking the central character, "Saint Therese"; and listing the other characters, twenty-one saints in all. Stein then begins Act One, in which she imagines "Saint Therese in a storm at Avila" and "Saint Ignatius not there" *(O&P,* 15). But Saint Therese is silent. When she is asked "If it were possible to kill five thousand Chinamen by pressing a button would it be done," she does not answer; she is not "interested"

(*O&P*, 16). Having gotten Saint Therese on the stage, what was Stein to do with her? What words was she to put in Saint Therese's mouth? Stein tries again: "Repeat First Act" (*O&P*, 16). Stein spends a great deal of time now setting the scene, but she does finally have Saint Therese speak, after a preparatory announcement: "Saint Therese about to be . . . Saint Therese. Nobody visits more than they do visits them Saint Therese" (*O&P*, 16). As if satisfied with what she has accomplished, Stein announces her intention to "Enact end of an act" (*O&P*, 17), although Act One continues for five pages.

Once Stein has her principal saints on stage and speaking, she drops the role of writer/editor and assumes the role of writer/director. Rather than discussing the text that has been written or urging herself to write more of it, Stein begins to deal with the written text as a plan for performance. However, it is a plan which is never settled because we are meant to see the writing and the performance as simultaneous acts.

Among the cast of characters are a Saint Plan and a Saint Settlement. Planning and settling are mentioned at intervals, often when Stein or her saints are having difficulty deciding how the plan is to be settled. Stein and company pose many questions about the project they are working on. They ask: How much of it is finished? How many saints are there in it? How many acts? How many nails? How many floors? How many doors? How many windows? These questions become refrains, often repeated because seldom answered satisfactorily. "It is easy to measure a settlement," says Saint Therese (*O&P*, 30), but when she is asked how much of it is finished, she is unable to answer. The matter is not settled; therefore the measurement is not easy to make.

The question of how many saints are in the play has several answers, all of which skirt the issue:

> Saint Therese. How many saints are there in it.
> Saint Therese. There are very many many saints in it.
> Saint Therese. There are as many saints as there are in it.
> Saint Therese. How many saints are there in it.
> Saint Therese. There are there are there are saints saints in it . . .
> [Stein then names seven saints, which is hardly a complete list.]
>
> · · ·
>
> Saint Cecelia. How many saints are there in it.
> Saint Therese. There are many saints in it.   (*O&P*, 28)

The only way to know how many saints are in it is to see them and to count them. Accordingly, in the last scene, Stein specifies that the saints ("All Saints") be lined laterally to the left and right of Saint Ignatius for our perusal. As the opera ends we can count the saints and answer one of the questions posed in the text.

As for the number of acts, the title promises us three, but the title, written first, cannot possibly measure the libretto, which has not yet been written, or the performance, which has not yet been given. In fact, the libretto has four named acts, but there are three first acts, two second acts, two third acts, and one fourth act, making a total of eight acts. The only certainty regarding the number of acts in the opera is that which is obvious at the end—"Last Act. / Which is a fact." No matter how many acts there are in it, the opera is certain to finish. Only when it is finished will we know how many acts there were in it, just as the number of doors, windows, floors, and nails in a house cannot be counted until the building is complete, for even the most carefully laid plans can be changed.

Like any sound structure, *Four Saints* is certainly preplanned. The written texts exists and it is the plan which the performance follows. We are made to feel, however, that the plan is being created in our presence, as the performance proceeds. So, for example, Stein will make a statement, "Who settles a private life," which is then supposed to be echoed by an actor—"Saint Therese. Who settles a private life." This pattern recurs regularly. It appears that the performers have no lines except those they are fed by the writer during the performance.

The fact that *Four Saints* abounds in conditionals adds to our sense of the tentativeness of the plan. For instance, Stein writes, "Saint Ignatius might be very well adapted to plans and a distance" (*O&P*, 25). Because of such conditional statements, the libretto seems always to be in process. As might be expected, uncertainty is most intense in the first half of the libretto. As the libretto takes shape, it leaves fewer questions unanswered, fewer conditions unfulfilled. In act one, however, almost nothing has been determined.

For example, it takes Stein five pages to consider how best to dispose the principal saints on the stage. The matter is never decided because Stein's deliberations are a series of contradictions. She begins by repeating four times that Saint Therese is seated. She then immediately contradicts herself. "Saint Therese is not seated. . . ." This direction is repeated, and then, as if to reconcile the contradictory directions, Stein adds, "Saint Therese not seated at once" (*O&P*, 16). Presumably, Saint Therese is to begin by standing and is then to sit. "Saint Therese once seated. There are a great many places and persons near together. Saint Therese seated and not surrounded." (*O&P*, 16). Just as Saint Therese's placement seems resolved, another dilemma is introduced. Saint Therese is to be "very nearly half inside and outside outside the house." Stein specifies that "the garden" too is "inside and outside of the wall." While a garden can quite easily be split in two, a person cannot. Saint Therese, then, is neither in nor out, but somewhere in between. Poised on a threshold, she is, as Stein says, "About to be" (*O&P*, 16), ready to take her place, but not quite in it. As for Saint Ignatius, Stein tells us that he "could be" and finally "is standing." At this point, when the disposition of Saint Therese and Saint Ignatius seems set, Stein launches into a passage which epitomizes the text in process:

Saint Therese seated and not standing half and half of it and not half
and half of it seated and not standing surrounded and not seated and not
seated and not standing and not surrounded and not surrounded and not
not not seated not seated not seated not surrounded not seated and Saint
Ignatius standing standing not seated. Saint Therese not standing not
standing and Saint Ignatius not standing standing surrounded as if in
once yesterday. In place of situations Saint Therese could be very much
interested not only in settlement Saint Settlement and this not with with
this wither wither they must be additional. Saint Therese having not
commenced.   (*O&P*, 17)

Saint Therese, who was about to be, has not yet commenced and Saint
Ignatius is standing and not standing at the same time. The question of
whether the two saints are to sit or to stand is not decided.

A secondary effect of the conditional suggestions and the contradictory directions is to immobilize the actors and the opera. Like Saint
Therese, who is half in and half out, the whole libretto is suspended in a
kind of limbo. It consists entirely of preparation, beginning with a
narrative which prepares for a libretto, followed by a libretto which
prepares for a performance, and ending with the opera's only certainty,
the last act. Between the preparatory narrative and the last act, Stein's text
works to counteract its own momentum and that of the music and the live
production which was eventually to usher it into the theater. No matter
how we approach this text, whether we hear it in performance, or read
Stein's retrospective comments on it, or focus only on the text, its form and
its themes, we will come to the same conclusion: that everywhere we look
we find stasis.

Critics reviewing performances of *Four Saints* have almost always
noticed that the Stein text is at once musical and static, energetic and
immobile. Kenneth Burke noted "a private playfulness . . . a deliberation
which too often makes her [Stein's] lines elusive," but at the same time
found that this deliberate "nonsense of Stein's has established its great
musicality . . . Even as nonsense it sings well." Stark Young, writing for
the *New Republic*, saw the duality of the text as based, on the one hand,
on its "unbroken air of spontaneity, its charming and capricious flights"
and, on the other, on "the hidden unity of the whole." In reviewing the
1952 production, Brooks Atkinson saw a contrast between the "form and
style" of the libretto, which he found "admirable," and "the content" and
"emotional values" which he found "unsatisfying," "full of a feeling of
aimlessness," "repetitious," and "desultory." Reviewing the same production in the *New York Journal American*, Miles Kastendieck described
Stein's libretto as both "a state of mind" and as an "experience in sound."
Gilbert Seldes gave the most insightful explanation of the obvious division
in Stein's libretto: "Unlike most words for opera, they carry, from time to
time, a charge of emotion, and the great difficulty of Miss Stein's method

is that she interferes with the very emotion she creates."[18] Each of these critics is responding to the stasis he senses in what is normally a temporal medium, language. Each seems to recognize that Stein had a plan which worked against the natural energy and musical momentum of her prose.

Stein's plan began with her inspiration for the principal saints. Stein later explained that she imagined Saint Therese as being like the photographs she saw in a store window, of a girl becoming a nun — still shots, one following another, the immobilization of a process by dividing it into the frozen moments of its unfolding. Stein refers to this image of Therese's saintly development within the libretto:

> Saint Therese could be photographed having been dressed like a lady and then they taking out her head changed it to a nun and a nun a saint and a saint so. . . ."   (O&P, 17)

Saint Ignatius is also transfixed by Stein's suggestion that he be a porcelain statue, which she later explained referred to an actual figurine, again in a store window, which she imagined to be Saint Ignatius.

Saint Therese, the photograph, and Saint Ignatius, the statue, are represented in a libretto where even the syntax of the sentences tends toward a kind of suspended animation. The sentences in *Four Saints* remind us of a record which has caught the phonograph needle in one groove.

> Saint Therese. How many are there in this.
> Saint Chavez. How many are there in this.
> Saint Chavez. How many are there in this.   (O&P, 33)

Or, the sentences seem like circles, ending where they began: "Saints all saints all saints" (O&P, 29); or like a kind of mirror writing where the words coming into the text are immediately reflected in reverse order:

> Saint Ignatius. Withdrew with with withdrew. . . .
> Saint Ignatius. Occurred withdrew.
> Saint Ignatius. Withdrew occurred.   (O&P, 33)

Some sentences seem to pivot around a center, the words held in place by a kind of centrifugal force of syntax: "Saints all in all Saints" (O&P, 29).

Within her stalled sentences Stein minimizes or manipulates grammatical indicators of activity. Verbs are often eliminated and sentences replaced by noun phrases, like the familiar "pigeons on the grass." The preferred verb form is the participle, most often used as a verbal, as in "Saints not found. / Saint Therese unsurrounded . . ." (O&P, 24). The effect of the verbal is to immobilize the subject, who is the passive recipient of the action, the inactive center of movement. At one point Stein asks, "What is the difference between a picture and pictured" (O&P, 21). The difference is that the former is a noun and the latter a participial adjective, and further that one refers to form and the other to content. But both words (noun and verbal) focus on the immobilized object (the picture) rather than the activity (picture-making). Even when the subject is the actor, not the receiver, Stein avoids placing the activity in time by using participles, as in "Saint Therese seated. / Saint Ignatius standing" (*O&P*, 17). The participle pictures the subject in a steady state. Activity has neither beginning nor end. By using verbs as adjectives, Stein forces the performance into a series of tableaux, in which action is transformed into a quality, with no reference to time.

When Stein does refer to time in the play, it is to render it a meaningless measurement. For instance, memory, which is normally a present evocation of a past event or entity, is used in the following passage with an apparent disregard for its temporal function:

> It is very easy in winter to remember winter spring and summer it is very easy in winter to remember spring and winter and summer it is very easy in winter to remember summer spring and winter it is very easy in winter to remember spring and summer and winter.
>
> (*O&P*, 13)

It is possible in *one* winter to remember a winter gone by, but as the passage stands, it states that one remembers "winter in winter." One cannot, however, remember something one is "in." One must be out of and past winter to remember it. The passage causes temporal confusion. Is winter past or is it present?

The following passage also presents a temporal impossibility:

> In the morning to be changed from the morning to the morning in the morning. A scene of changing from the morning to the morning.
>
> (*O&P*, 25)

Change, like memory, is a function of time. To change is to move from one form of identity to another, from the past (before the change) to a different time (after the change). Change cannot occur without the passage of time. Therefore, there cannot be a change from the morning to the morning. If time does not change, then nothing can change. Such instances of temporal confusion, temporal impossibilities, and temporal absurdities are only reflections in miniature of the larger time warp created by the libretto itself.

I have said that in *Four Saints* Stein makes the writing process a part of the performance. In doing this, she blurs the temporal distinction between writing and performance. The composition of the libretto is antecedent to its performance. The same can be said for staging and rehearsal. But Stein conflates the time of writing (past), the time of planning (past), the time of rehearsal (past), and the time of performance (present). She also synchronizes these activities so that they occur at the same rate of speed. Because the sensual stimuli of performance (music, action, and language sounds) move at a faster tempo than the conceptualizing activities (writing and planning), Stein immobilizes the former in order to accommodate the latter. We come to feel that all of these activities occur simultaneously in a very slow-moving present.

The Thomson arrangement and the Maurice Grosser production obscured the purpose and meaning of the libretto by disguising the authorial voice and by ignoring the improvisational illusion which Stein created. The actual performance of *Four Saints* emphasized the sensuality and musicality of the text. Of course, the play does have its musical side. As the play proceeds, Stein allows her language to become more lyrical and provides arias for the singers. But Stein never relinquishes her hold on the text, never withdraws as the playwright or librettist usually does. "When this you see," she writes, "Remember me" (*O&P*, 47). Even when she allows the text to become a song, Stein, the writer, is its singer. We must not ignore the fact that the arias in this opera are passages of unassigned text. Even "Pigeons on the Grass" is a Stein song, although Thomson and Grosser had Saint Ignatius sing it. This is how the aria appears in Stein's original text:

Scene II

Pigeons on the grass alas.
Pigeons on the grass alas.
Short longer grass short longer longer shorter yellow
grass pigeons large pigeons on the shorter longer yellow grass
alas pigeons on the grass.
If they were not pigeons what were they. He had heard
of a third and he asked about it it was a magpie in the sky.
on the grass alas and to pass the pigeon on the grass
alas and the mapgie in the sky on the sky and to try and to try
alas on the grass the pigeon on the grass the pigeon on
the grass and alas. They might be very well very well very well
they might be they might be very well they might be very well
very well they might be.
Let Lucy Lily Lily Lucy Lucy let Lucy Lucy Lily Lily
Lily Lily let Lily Lucy Lucy let Lily. Let Lucy Lily.

(*O&P*, 36)

With the repetition of "alas," Stein reminds us, even in this celebration of sound, that the writer is present. "Alas" could very well be "Alice."[19] By singing to Alice (the witness to the writing and the companion of the writer), Stein once again draws creation and performance together.

IV

Four Saints is a representation of the mind of Gertrude Stein, and Gertrude Stein sees to it that the representation is brought into the theater. In that sense, this opera is a landscape, a rendering of the mind's geography. Stein had previously used other painting genres as metaphors for her writing. In her verbal still lifes, Stein's purpose was to portray the static in a temporal medium. The subject was a cloak, a roast beef, a carafe; the poem portraying the subject was a still life. In the verbal portrait, Stein's purpose was to portray the temporal subject in a temporal medium. The subject was a person; the poem portraying the person was a portrait. In her landscapes, Stein tried like any landscape painter, to capture the transient. But it was not the subject itself which she wished to immobilize. The subject, the mind, was already a landscape, already a timeless entity. However, the medium through which she was trying to represent the mind, language, and specifically language in the theater, was inevitably time-bound. Her solution was to make the libretto like a landscape, a space in which time stands still.

The libretto so conceived could be an accurate representation of the mind. To the doubting, those who would insist that time cannot stand still in a play and does not in *Four Saints*, Stein offers the following parable:

> Magpies are in the landscape that is they are in the sky of a landscape. They are black and white. . . . when they are in the sky they do something that I have never seen any other bird do they hold themselves up and down and look flat against the sky.
>
> A very famous French inventor of things that have to do with stabilisation in aviation told me that what I told him magpies did could not be done by any bird but anyway whether the magpies at Avila do do it or do not at least they look as if they do do it. They look exactly like the birds in the Annunciation pictures the bird which is the Holy Ghost and rests flat against the side sky very high.[20]

Despite the doubts of the expert, the hapless French inventor who serves as her foil, Stein maintains that moving birds stand still against the sky. Impossible? Perhaps, but then Stein insists only that the birds seem stationary. Stein perceives them so because she has seen paintings in which such birds are indeed inanimate and therefore can rest flat against the sky. It is not too fanciful to see Stein's feat in *Four Saints* as comparable to the immobilization of the magpie in the paintings of the Annunciation. Through her "black and white" birds, the words of her text, she conveys an impression of stasis convincing enough to affect our perception of her libretto in performance. When the written words exist as perceptible and energetic language (live birds), they still appear motionless, as do the stage activities they instigate. Through this illusionary landscape shines the geography of Gertrude Stein's mind.

Notes

1. Gertrude Stein did not make a clear distinction between her opera librettos and her plays. She called her second volume of plays *Operas and Plays*, and she designates certain of these texts "operas," specifically: *Four Saints in Three Acts; An Opera to Be Sung* (1927); *A Lyrical Opera Made by Two to Be Sung* (1928); *Madame Recamier*, and *An Opera* (1930). It

is no easier for us to distinguish between these texts and contemporary Stein plays than it is for Stein to do so. In her lecture "Plays," she quotes from *Madame Recamier* as one example of "a great number of plays" (*Lectures in America*, 125), and later, in *Everybody's Autobiography*, she again calls it a play (114). Similarly, she calls *Four Saints* an opera (*Everybody's Autobiography*, 48, 98, 111, and 193), a play (*Everybody's Autobiography*, 194; *Lectures in America*, 125, 129, and 131), and a drama (*Everybody's Autobiography*, 283). Apparently Stein did not see "opera" as a genre distinct from "play." Insofar as *Four Saints* was entirely set to music, we can call it an opera and Stein's text a libretto, keeping in mind that Stein wrote the libretto exactly as if she were writing a play.

2. Eric Bentley, Introduction, *Plays by George Barnard Shaw* (New York: New American Library, 1963), viii.

3. J. L. Styan, *Drama, Stage and Audience* (London: Cambridge University Press, 1975), 4.

4. Susanne Langer, *Feeling and Form: A Theory of Art* (New York: Charles Scribner's Sons, 1953), 310.

5. Andrew K. Kennedy, *Six Dramatists in Search of a Language* (London: Cambridge University Press, 1975), 2.

6. Stein, *The Geographical History of America* (New York: Vintage Books, 1973), 76–77.

7. Ibid., 66.

8. Stein, "Portraits and Repetition," in her *Lectures in America* (1935; rpt. Boston: Beacon Press, 1957), 196–98.

9. Virgil Thomson, *The Musical Scene* (New York: Alfred A. Knopf, 1945), 297–98.

10. Thomson, *Virgil Thomson* (New York: Alfred A. Knopf, 1966), 105.

11. Ibid., 90.

12. Kathleen Hoover and John Cage, *Virgil Thomson: His Life and Music* (New York: Thomas Yoseloff, 1959), 144.

13. Thomson, *Virgil Thomson*, 105.

14. Ibid., 90–91.

15. Thomson quotes Stein as writing on 26 March 1927: "begun Beginning of Studies for an opera to be sung. I think it should be late eighteenth century or early nineteenth century saints. Four saints in three acts. And others. Make it pastoral. In hills and gardens. All four and then additions. We must invent them. But next time you come I will show you a little bit and we will talk some scenes over." The same day in another note to Thomson: "The saints are still enjoying themselves," and four days later, "I think I have got St. Therese onto the stage, it has been an awful struggle and I think I can keep her on and gradually by the second act get St. Ignatius on and then they will be both on together but not at once in the third act. I want you to read it as far as it has gone before you go [to the South of France]" (Thomson, *Virgil Thomson*, 91–92). Despite Stein's avowed wishes, Thomson never read any of the libretto before he left.

16. Richard Bridgman, *Gertrude Stein in Pieces* (New York: Oxford University Press, 1970), 187. By the time she wrote *Four Saints*, Stein had developed the following method of speech notation: "Saint Therese. Who settles a private life." Any portion of the text without such an indication I take to be unassigned, even when a character name is used in it, as in "Saint Therese something like that," or "Saint Therese half indoors and half out of doors." Statements such as these are stage directions, and in any play they are a form of authorial commentary. When character names do not appear, the text is more clearly unassigned. I agree with Richard Bridgman that these unassigned portions belong to Stein, not only because they are unattributed but also because, for the most part, they are about the writer's concerns.

17. Stein, *Four Saints in Three Acts. An Opera to Be Sung*, in her *Operas and Plays*

(hereafter *O&P*) (Paris: Plain Edition, 1932), 11. All further references to this work appear in the text.

18. The five quotes are taken respectively from: 1) Kenneth Burke, "Two Brands of Piety," *Nation*, February 1934, 256; (2) Stark Young, "One Moment Alit," *New Republic*, 7 March 1934, 105; (3) Brooks Atkinson, review of *Four Saints in Three Acts*, *New York Times*, 17 April 1952, 35, col. 1; (4) Miles Kastendieck, "A Unique Experience: A Handsome Show," *New York Journal American*, 17 April 1952, in *New York Theatre Critics' Reviews* (1952); (5) Gilbert Seldes, "Delight in the Theatre," *Modern Music*, March–April 1934, 138.

19. Richard Bridgman, James Mellow, and Linda Simon have each pointed to Stein's use of code names. Stein had early identified Alice with Saint Therese (see Leon Katz, "Weininger and The Making of Americans," *Twentieth Century Literature*, Spring 1978, 14). Given the highly lyrical and climatic ending of this aria, it is difficult to explain the repeated lament, "alas." Although no one has heretofore commented on the phonetic similarity of "alas" and "Alice," a similar connection has been made between the "aider" of "This Is This Dress, Aider" (the last poem in the "Objects" section of *Tender Buttons*) and "Ada," an early code name for Alice. Whether the aria is addressed to Alice or not, about which we can only speculate, it definitely originates from Gertrude Stein and not from Saint Ignatius.

20. Stein, "Plays," in *Lectures in America*, 129.

A Rosy Charm: Gertrude Stein and the Repressed Feminine
Lisa Ruddick*

We have rightly stopped hoping for a single key to Stein's abstract writings that would translate them into ordinary discourse. Yet we keep noticing in her texts bits of what looks like a private code. I believe that there is a code—one that, while hardly making every word or even most of Stein accessible, is more extensive than has been suspected. More importantly, the code is not only a means of referring to Stein's erotic life, although those who have identified disguised lesbian content are accurate.[1] Rather, it is the vehicle for a sophisticated set of insights about gender and culture, insights that we do not ordinarily associate with Stein and that anticipate current psychoanalytic and feminist theory. I offer here a preliminary account of the central themes of *Tender Buttons* and other texts completed about the year 1912. These texts are meditations on the female body and its relation to a symbolic order that suppresses the female.

Stein's early work—particularly *Three Lives* and *The Making of Americans*—is indebted to the psychology of William James.[2] But the ideas of language and attention in slightly later texts, like *Tender Buttons*, both extend and radically deviate from James and from Stein's ideas when she was most influenced by him. Briefly, James divides the mind into a promiscuous and repressive faculty. While a part of us would like to notice

*This essay was written specifically for publication in this volume and is included here by permission of the author.

every sense datum or subconscious fancy that arises, another part keeps practical existence going by making important selections, throwing certain impressions into relief and suppressing others. James calls this faculty "selective attention." Mental life proceeds by an ongoing compromise between selective attention and the indiscriminate tendency that brings new objects into view whether they are likely to be useful to us or not.[3]

The text in which Stein is closest to James is "Melanctha"; the heroine of the story reawakens her lover to the world of sensation by challenging his habits of selection. Melanctha shows Jeff Campbell the minutiae that he has characteristically ignored or dismissed as trivial. What he sees under her guidance is a chaotic field of "new things, little pieces all different."[4] There is a shift, however, in Stein's thinking: with *Tender Buttons* and the texts of 1912, she comes to think of the things that every mind suppresses as images connected with femaleness. Whereas Melanctha did her work by alerting Jeff Campbell to objects like plants and insects, in the later texts the "little pieces" of the world that move into view in moments of perceptual upheaval tend to be pieces of the female body.

The relevant works are *Tender Buttons*, *A Long Gay Book*, *G.M.P.*, and shorter pieces from the same period.[5] First, the female body itself is very much present in these texts, although the references are oblique. Richard Bridgman was the first to notice that *Tender Buttons* is unified by clusters of images, among them "dirt" and "versions of red — pink, scarlet, crimson, rose."[6] Although Bridgman does not analyze these images, they have sexual associations, in *Tender Buttons* and the other texts. Red and roses, for example, are used to suggest menstrual blood, sometimes with a negative association of something shameful or dirty: "A PETTICOAT: A light white, a disgrace, an ink spot, a rosy charm" (*TB*, 471). Or the sexual organs themselves are red roses: "A shallow hole rose on red, a shallow hole in and in this makes ale less [Alice]" (*TB*, 474). Finally, the female body is a white flower stained, marked red, by sexual experience: "A RED STAMP: . . . [L]ilies are lily white . . they dusty will dirt a surface" (*TB*, 465).[7] "The white flower has not been bled."[8]

These images of menstruation and defloration are reinforced by abundant allusions in the texts to "stains," "tiny spots," "bleeding" and "secretions."[9] Stein is doing more than to challenge the reader's delicacy. By focusing on an unconventional or even a suppressed subject, a "disgrace," she is doing just what she began to do with "Melanctha": she brings into view a region of common experience that is conventionally overlooked. James would call this an undoing of selective attention. Stein's task in these texts is not unlike Melanctha's with Jeff Campbell, that of forcing us to concentrate on "little pieces" of the world that are always there but that we normally do not like to think about. And as with the education of Jeff Campbell, part of the difficulty of bringing these little things into view is that of surmounting the reader's automatic resistance or disgust.

For one theme of these texts is that nothing is really disgusting if one looks at it carefully. "[I]t is not dirty. Any little thing is clean" (*TB*, 479–80). This is why the idea of the red spot or the disgrace is often juxtaposed with the theme of seeing: "A BOX: Out of a kindness comes redness . . . out of an eye comes research" (*TB*, 463). "There is no disgrace in looking" (*TB*, 505); on the contrary, the act of looking with care eliminates the illusion of disgrace. The first section of *Tender Buttons* reads, "A kind in glass and a cousin, a spectacle and nothing strange a single hurt color . . ." (461). Among its other meanings, this is an announcement of the author's intent to adjust our focus — give us "glasses" or "spectacles" — so that we will see certain objects (like "hurt colors") in a new way: they are inoffensive, they are "nothing strange."

The title of this entry is "A CARAFE, THAT IS A BLIND GLASS": another of Stein's frequent images for seeing is that of a bottle or glass, with something in it (again, a red thing, a dirty thing, here a "hurt color") that one can inspect with care. "[A] little glass, . . . an elastic tumbler, all this shows that . . . red which is red is a dark color" (*TB*, 505). So the myriad "glasses" in *Tender Buttons* may be either spectacles making us see things newly, or drinking glasses, receptacles containing the objects of inspection. Finally, they may be looking-glasses, mirrors that by reflecting things accurately once again remove the illusion of a stain. "The color is not a stain. It shows what glass is when there is a reflection." A compressed statement of her purposes, in a sketch called "Scenes," suggests that her writing itself is a looking-glass or a tumbler into which she tosses things for scrutiny: "Laugh the basket into a little glass and all the point is painted. So soon is the jewel and so dirty is the splinter" — and yet, she goes on, "it has no splinter." Whatever is in the glass is not "dirty" then, like splinters, but a "jewel."[10]

Perhaps it is putting the case too weakly to say that Stein wants us to see the "little things" she assembles as inoffensive; if they are jewels, they are positively good. The sequence "A PETTICOAT: a white light, a disgrace, an ink spot, a rosy charm" shows a movement not from "disgrace" to mere acceptability but from disgrace to "charm." The stain that seems bad at first is actually appealing. Many of Stein's descriptions of feelings and objects in these texts (including objects not associated with the female body) use the same progression from ugliness or distaste to pleasure. But they may also show a bewildering alternation, as in this description of an unspecified "thing": "to some it is a dreary thing, to some it is a dirty thing, to some it is a solid thing, to some it is a noble thing, . . . to some it is an ugly thing, to some it is a charming thing, . . . to some one it is a frightening thing."[11]

When Stein converts a menstrual spot from a "disgrace" to a "charm," she reverses conventional valuations. Yet in the passage that alternates between "dirty" and "noble," "ugly" and "charming," the effect is not of a reversal but of a collapse of all values. In fact, the two strategies, the inversion and the levelling of conventional categories, are directed toward the same end. Both underscore the fact that our usual hierarchies are not natural. Stein may destabilize illegitimate hierarchies either by neutralizing them, showing that no one thing is finer than another, or by inverting them in individual instances to suggest that discredited objects can be just as "charming" as anything else.

Stein's method of challenging conventional patterns of appraisal is consistent with ideas she first heard formally from William James, whose psychology is dedicated to dignifying perceptual data that we habitually dismiss. But for James the mere disruption of hierarchies does not in itself get us anywhere; the goal of any conceptual upheaval is to generate better hierarchies. He would surely find the mere reversals and alternations of *Tender Buttons* misguided. Stein's program at this stage, which involves the collapse of all stable hierarchies of good and bad, has more in common with contemporary deconstruction than with James's psychology. She unsettles the notion that any one thing is naturally higher or better than another. "It is not more distinguished to be whiter than to be redder, to be taller than to be shorter."[12] Her object is to find a way of judging that cannot be undermined, one that is so free of artificial norms that its meanings are not changed even if one turns one's own perspective (or the object itself) "upside down": "A pale rose is a smell . . . that has upside down the same distinction."[13]

In *Tender Buttons* and the companion texts, many of the objects upon which Stein confers a new distinction are bodily stains, tokens of stigmatized femininity. A number of passages from these texts suggest that by dignifying what is female Stein is engaged in a self-conscious subversion of patriarchal or androcentric values. A comment in *A Long Gay Book*, from a passage about which I will have more to say, refers to a legendary time before women and their bodies were devalued: "Once upon a time there was a reverence for bleeding" (112). Stein restores that reverential attitude, removing the stigma. The collapse of the present dualism that divides the world into good and bad, clean and stained, means the recovery of the feminine that once was valued but now is discredited.

Stein in these years not only writes about the body; she also thinks of herself as writing with the body. During the period of *Tender Buttons*, and even somewhat earlier, Stein conceives of her writings as "secretions" (*LGB*, 110). In "A PETTICOAT," which is short enough to quote again — "a white light, a disgrace, an ink spot, a rosy charm" — the third term standing between the two menstrual images of "a disgrace" and "a rosy charm" is "an ink spot." The association is between the ink spots on Stein's page and the rosy spots on a petticoat. The "white light" that precedes all three terms then refers doubly to the blank page and to the petticoat just before either is marked.[14] Writing-as-secretion for Stein need not always be menstrual or even specifically feminine; it can be a generalized "mark" (*LGB*, 110), or any of a variety of bodily products, as the pun "excreate" in *Tender Buttons* (excrement/create) suggests.[15]

Hélène Cixous is one of a number of feminist critics who have called for a female idiom that will challenge "the phallocentric tradition" by expressing not the superego which censors and categorizes, but the unconscious, which is capacious. Like Stein, she thinks of such writing as writing done with the body, for it involves a suspension of intellectual processes like selective attention. "Write your self. Your body must be heard. Only then will the immense resources of the unconscious spring forth."[16] Although Stein would not share Cixous' idea of the unconscious, her constant imagery of writing as secretion suggests that for her too self-expression involves a subversion of controlled intellectual processes. It happens, half-consciously, like the natural rhythms of the body: "Standing and expressing, opening and holding, turning and meaning, closing and folding, holding and meaning, . . . opening and holding" (*LGB*, 87).[17] This is hardly to suggest that in practice Stein writes by a process of free association or (to raise an old question) of automatic writing. She thinks about what she is doing, but she does not rule out the half-digested thoughts that enter her mind from moment to moment.

Writing about secretions, then, and writing-by-secretion accomplish the same end. Both undermine selective attention and its false hierarchies. For by focusing on bodily blots that are normally overlooked or even thought bad, Stein works against culturally imprinted habits of selective attention. Similarly, by writing *with* spots — with whatever comes out of her — Stein suspends censorship or selective attention in herself. These two different ideas of secretion merge in a passage in *A Long Gay Book*, where Stein also indicates by a pun that "secretion" is a nicely *secret* style that conceals her lesbianism or "difference":

> [L]ife is that which when undertaken is not bashful. Why should it be bashful. Suppose there comes a time that shows there was a difference, is this any disgrace, does this make pride, it does not make pride but it does make secretion, and what is secretion, secretion is that amusement which every little mark shows as merit. A mark is very necessary.   (LGB, 110)

Secretion is both things, a way of writing with one's own "little marks" but also a tolerant kind of writing that dignifies — "shows" the "merit" in — "every little mark."

We have been examining a set of images of secretion in these texts, images that serve to destabilize habitual judgments about what is good or important. A second set of bodily emblems in the text refers to the interior "space" or the womb. This, in Stein's view, is another falsely discredited object. In *Tender Buttons* she paraphrases conventional attitudes about men's and women's bodies:

> . . .[T]hat is one way to breed, breed that. Oh chance to say, oh nice old pole. Next best and nearest a pillar. Chest not valuable. Be papered.
> Cover up . . .   (TB, 476)

The phallus is respected; women (at least those who "breed") are supposed to compliment it: "Oh chance to say, oh nice old pole." They sometimes politely exaggerate: "Next best and nearest a pillar." But the female receptacle, the "chest," is dismissed as "not valuable." Like the "stains" in these texts, moreover, women's bodies are not simply devoid of value but disgraceful, something to be carefully kept out of sight: "Be papered. Cover up."

Stein again reverses the appraisal, and declares women's anatomy good:

> Any space is not quiet it is so likely to be shiny. Darkness very dark. . . . [T]here is that seeding. A little thing in is a little thing. . . . Does it dirty a ceiling. It does not. Is it dainty, it is if prices are sweet. Is it lamentable, it is not. . . .   (*TB*, 482-83)

The "space" is not "dirty" or "lamentable," after all. It is "dainty." For it is the site of fertility or "seeding" — it can have "a little thing in." The passage suggests the possibility of inspecting a seemingly blank space and finding it full of interesting things. It "is *not* quiet"; and if it appears "dark," it turns out to be "shiny" as well. It is not merely an absence.

When Stein speaks of this female "seed-space," she is often referring not to the biological organ that carries babies, but to a mental state that recreates the feeling of the womb, or the primal unity one had with one's own mother. She uses an image of a return to the womb: "MILK: Climb up in sight climb in the whole utter [udder]" (*TB*, 487). This notion of a mental "udder-space" is intelligible in the context of a hidden myth of human development that permeates these texts. The myth is articulated unsystematically, and tends to appear in coded form. But one can make out a central story about loss of the mother, entry into the world of the father, and the imagined recovery of the mother. "Mother" and "father," moreover, mean for Stein something very much like they mean for feminists influenced by Lacan.

The fantasized recovery of the mother repeats the notion of removing the stigma from femininity; once again, Stein resurrects a repressed realm of experience associated with women. The recurring plot in which these ideas are developed contains key images, which include sun, shadow, dirt, cleaning, cooking, seeds, rooms, spaces, spreading, and silence. We recognize these as the ubiquitous symbols of *Tender Buttons*, but they have genuine meanings that make *Tender Buttons* and the companion texts something more than wordplay or stylistic experiment.

The ur-plot begins in an enclosed space — both "pink," because it is made of flesh, and "green" or fertile:

> Tender and not so blue, pink and white, and anything green greener, . . . all the tightness is identified . . . and the space is enthusiastic. This . . . is the beginning of that entry.[18]

The place described is both the uterus and the first stage of life ("the beginning of that entry") before the child is differentiated from the mother: "all the tightness is identified." Nor does the child differentiate objects from one another: the world is a "[l]ump of love, thick potato soup" (p. 250). He or she has not learned to apply mental categories, or to censor impressions by selective attention. The images Stein uses for this stage, in addition to green and "spaces," are wetness (suggesting both fertility and the fluidity of undifferentiated perception), cooking (since the world is like a stew in which things mingle), the house (another "space"), darkness (in which objects are not sharply distinguished), and also colors and taste, since perception in this phase is abundant and unmediated. They combine in passages like the following, from *G.M.P.*, which describes a young boy's[19] early experience at home:

> All the pouring of the rain, all the darkening of the evening, . . . all the little fish-bones cooking, all the principal away and all the comfort of a home, . . . all the open space inclosing, . . . that is one way to expect a person. (249)

This could almost be read as an account of the beginning of life as envisioned by William James. James too thinks of childhood as a period of undifferentiated perception; what he calls selective attention is learned gradually as we acquire practical interests and a stake in the interests of society. Yet Stein's account, unlike James's, situates the child in a gendered world. What she describes is not just infancy but the reign of the mother. "[T]he principal," the father, is "away." He is the absent person referred to in the last clause, the "person" we "expect."

For it is the father who will introduce the symbolic order that breaks up this primal unity. Unlike James, Stein now thinks of the whole problem of language and perception as indissolubly linked to the family triangle. *G.M.P.* contains a short narrative explaining (in Stein's obscure idiom) how the shift from mother to father takes place. Anticipating Lacan, Stein makes the shift hinge on a primal scene and an Oedipal crisis.

Her protagonist of the moment, the same young boy whom we have just observed enjoying the absence of "the principal," walks in one day on a confusing scene: "Toss and spin . . . and roll in the hay in the center of the afternoon. . . . So then the union of the palm tree and the upside down one makes a lying woman escape handling." This witnessed act of intercourse marks a break in his life: "That was the period of that particular punctuation." He now knows that "all the gate is open to a push" — the mother can be entered — "and more [besides himself] can come to stay there." His reaction is the inevitable one: "A season of envy is a storm in the morning" (253–55).

His form of thinking immediately changes. Because he is now in competition with the father, the boy suddenly broods about concepts like "obedience" and "authority" (254, 257). He learns a symbolic system, one that elevates the phallus over the womb: "There is a tail. There is a bewildering distruction [destruction/distrust?] of simple linings" (257). He may even forget the womb: "so thoughtless are the plain painstaking principles. . . . How they do not stay in the deep down. How they do not" (257). It is not fanciful to say that he learns something like phallocentrism.

When, in the maternal orbit, the boy perceived the world as a "thick potato soup," there were no categories of high and low; indeed there were no mental categories at all. But now he is schooled in the name for everything, and its place in a hierarchy: "Name and place and more besides makes the time so gloomy, all the shade is in the sun and lessons have the place of noon" (p. 256). The phrase about the shade and the sun explains what is happening. The sun — Stein uses the symbol repeatedly — stands for the father, who replaces the dark, mingling world of the mother with a field of vision in which everything is differentiated because cast in a bright light. These pages in *G.M.P.* are filled with images of a glaring sun rising in the sky.

But the ascending father also makes shade. While the objects he prizes are brightly lit, his hierarchies simultaneously create a shadow-world, composed of the things he pushes out of view. Thus the world of confused and abundant "colors," the world of the mother, gives way to a simplified world of black and white, good and bad, important and negligible. This is an extreme variety of selective attention. There is no confusion in Stein's saying that "all the shade is in the sun." The father is *both* the sun that exalts certain objects to notice, and the shadow that obscures or suppresses others. Two remarks, then, characterize this phase of life: "Color was disappearing," and, mournfully, "why is it all so changed and so simple, why is there such a long shadow" (260, 264).

One of the things partially suppressed by this new order is the feminine. As the "sun" ascends, the child's first world, the dark world of the mother, is demeaned. The order of the father inconsistently declares it both evil and nonexistent: "[t]he darkness is bad, . . . there is no darkness" (259). This despised darkness is reminiscent of the "chest" or womb in *Tender Buttons* that is both without value and a bad thing, to be covered up. In these passages from *G.M.P.*, there is a double concealment. Not only is the child's own woman-dominated, pre-Oedipal existence pushed under, but the new symbolic order he learns suppresses and devalues the female body. Women are viewed no longer as welcoming womb-spaces but as bearers of particular sorts of clothing; the clothes both stereotype them and literally cover them up. "There is a size corset"; "the authority is mingled with a decent costume" (257, 259). A strange new fiction denies biological facts: "there is no bleeding" (p. 260). This suppression of the female stain, familiar from an earlier context, is accompanied by an obsessional fantasy of getting rid of all sorts of pollution by scrubbing: "So to clean that stinking has that odor." The goal is "[a] state where there is no dirt" (258).

Similarly, while the mother cooked by throwing everything into an earthy "potato soup," the father inaugurates a new bland cuisine whose only object is to sterilize. He boils: "Cooking is establishing a regulation . . . anything that is boiling is not withstanding cooking" (267). The point is to eliminate or lay claim to everything raw, uncivilized, outside the law of "regulation." So "the change is monotonous, . . . it means the baking of any piece of apple and pear and potato" (260–61).

The father, then, tries to transform or destroy rawness and dirt, whether he finds them in the female anatomy or in other alien things. In doing so, he works from a false dichotomy. He labels the female raw or natural, and himself the agent of civilization, yet this is a distortion. The mother herself was a cook, after all, who, with her more impromptu way of putting things together, *mediated* between nature and culture, between raw materials and the dinner table. Perhaps the very dichotomy between nature and culture, male and female, is part of a patriarchal language that artificially divides complex realities into black and white. The point would be reinforced by the fact that the father himself, whether consciously or not, crosses between traditional male and female roles, not only boiling but at times also "baking" (260–61).

One way of coopting or cleaning up women's bodies, in these texts, is by marrying them, thereby entering them into the male economy as objects of exchange. Stein uses two images for such an event: the "sale" of the body or womb, and its "collapse" or impairment. "RED ROSES: A cool red rose and a pink cut pink, a collapse and a sold hole. . . ." (*TB*, 473). The woman's collapse or sale is helped along by aggressive techniques of seduction; it is dangerous to allow one's "purr" to be "rubbed" by a suitor. "Suppose a collapse in rubbed purr, in rubbed purr get. Little sales ladies little sales ladies little saddles of mutton" (*TB*, 475). The "sales ladies" may be either the sold ladies themselves, transformed into "saddles of mutton," or a band of traitorous matchmakers.

The transformation of women into use objects, "saddles of mutton," is symptomatic of an instrumental frame of mind in the world of the father. Even "time," in some obscure way, "was sold" (263). Things are valued insofar as one can own or use them. The same instrumentalism debases language. The mother, in the same long sequence in *G.M.P.*, introduces the boy to language, but to language as play. During the pre-Oedipal phase, "[A] speech is so transferred that alas is not mentioned. . . . The whole time of trial is in the recitation of the vowels and also in the recitation of the figures" (251–52). The child "recites" words and numbers ("figures") for the pleasure of it, as an experiment or "trial." He has fun: there is no "alas." But in the next phase, the free play is lost. Words are not things to be enjoyed but things to be used to get other things. What develops is a "[a] language traded for tobacco, a language traded even for . . . corn." Like everything else in the black-and-white world of the father, language loses its texture, becoming "a language that is so fit to be seen exasperated and reduced and even particular" (274).

This story of the transition from the mother to the father is embedded in all Stein's texts in this period — texts that are not normally thought of as having plots or even discernible subjects. In passages that are superficially unintelligible, Stein repeats the tale:

> Once upon a time there was a reverence for bleeding, at this time there was no search for what came. That which was winsome was unwinding and a clutter a single clutter showed the black white. . . . All this was mightily stirring and littleness any littleness was engaged in spilling. Was there enough there was. Who was the shadow.
>
> The rest was left and all the language of thirty was in the truth. This made it choose just that establishment. . . . A likeness and no vacation. A regularity and obedience. Congratulations. (*LGB*, 113)

The epoch referred to as "once upon a time" is the pre-Oedipal phase, before the female body was suppressed; "there was a reverence for bleeding." (We are able now to be more specific about this passage.) "At this time," there was no selective attention, "no search for what came." Instead the world was perceived whole, like a potato soup or here a great "clutter." It was a "single clutter" because objects were not differentiated. Black and white were not yet defined: the clutter was so profound that it "showed the black white," confusing the contraries. In short, everything was fluid, "mightily stirring" and "spilling." As in the passages from *G.M.P.*, whoever is experiencing this state finds the perceptual chaos thoroughly pleasant: "Was there enough there was."

But this first paragraph ends ominously: "Who was the shadow." The shadow, as before, is the father. As he looms into view, everything changes. He ushers in new sensations of "regularity and obedience," and his medium is "language" (a "language of thirty," perhaps suggesting a marketplace idiom that quantifies things). Nothing goes unclassified: there is "no vacation" from "likeness" or conformity. Stein's bitter comment: "Congratulations."

Yet the word "vacation" here hints at the possibility of a holiday from the Law of the father. This in fact is one way in which the primal plot can end. The important moments of adult life for Stein are those in which a man or a woman slips through a crack in the symbolic order and recovers the maternal world. Many of Stein's old themes, and some important new ones, are compressed in an episode of escape from *G.M.P.*:

> . . . [F]athers are dead. What are fathers, they are different. The casual silence and the joke, the sad supper and the boiling tree. . . . [W]hen the moment and the rejoicing and the elevation and the relief do not make a surface sober, when . . . the season to sow consists in the dark and no titular remembrance, does being weather beaten . . . not

> show a sudden result of not enduring, does it not show a resolution to
> abstain in silence and move South. . . . Perhaps it does nightly, certainly
> it does daily and raw much raw sampling is not succored by the sun.
> (*GMP*, 274–75)

We know already that "fathers" make a "sad supper" by "boiling"
everything into conformity (even, strangely, trees, perhaps in the process
of making paper). But here, suddenly, "fathers are dead." More specifically, some unidentified protagonist moves beyond their reach. For he or
she has enough of the father/sun, and feels "weather beaten." The "sudden
result" is one "of not enduring": the person disclaims the father, resolving
"to abstain in silence," and forgetting patriarchal ties. There is "no titular
remembrance."

He or she escapes, with surprising ease: one need only go under-
ground, or (a synonym Stein likes) "move South." For the father cannot
claim everything; the sun cannot shine everywhere. There is still the
shadow world, the repressed zone "not succored by the sun," which one
can explore at will. Down there, nothing is boiled or regulated; there is
only "raw much raw sampling."

What this means is that the life of immediate or raw perception, the
pre-Oedipal form of life, is submerged by the father but never destroyed.
Throughout adulthood, part of us continues to perceive things as an infant
does. While our practical existence depends on conceptual grids that
"boil" the flavor out of everything, we can relax our categories from time
to time and see that our mind is full of brilliant, pristine data. At such an
instant we take pleasure in the sheer abundance of impressions, useless
from a practical standpoint but vital and invigorating. We stop selecting.
The great burden of instrumental existence is lifted, and we feel "the
moment and the rejoicing and the elevation and the relief." This shift in
perception amounts to a recovery of the domain of the mother, a return to
the early mental state that Stein symbolizes, here as elsewhere, as a dark
seed-space. "The season to sow consists in the dark."

Tender Buttons, the most famous of Stein's "abstract" writings, is not
so abstract as it seems; in fact, it is a prolonged enactment of the return to
the mother. When Stein writes, "MILK: Climb up in sight climb in the
whole utter" (*TB*, 487), part of her point is that one reenters the womb or
udder through "sight" or perception, by seeing things (or hearing, feeling,
or smelling them) in a new way. More accurately it is a primitive way, and
the purpose of her text is to reawaken in us this form of perception. Or—a
slightly different point—we recover the udder by *utterance*, by putting
words together in ways that recall an earlier form of consciousness.

The word "excreate," in which we have already noticed one pun,
contains a second:

> Cocoa and clear soup and oranges and oat-meal. Pain soup, . . .
> suppose it is butter, real is, real is only, only excreate, only excreate a no
> since. A no, a no since, a no since when since. . . . (*TB*, 496)

The images here are reminiscent of the "[l]ump of love, thick potato soup" that Stein used to describe the lively chaos of pre-Oedipal perception in *G.M.P.*. But to reawaken that kind of vision, to turn the world back into rich "cocoa" and "soup" — to get back to what is "real" — one must "excreate innocence," create perceptual innocence by excreating or uncreating the world as one normally knows it.

Stein in *Tender Buttons* has various ways of recreating innocence in the reader. First, she undoes the symbolic order by using words noninstrumentally; even where we can identify discursive content, there is an element of verbal play that distracts us. Like the infant in *G.M.P.*, we experience words as sources of pleasure rather than only as ways of referring to other things. To force us to appreciate the texture of words, Stein uses puns, like "excreate," repetitive or rhythmic sounds, syntactic distortions, and, paradoxically, a sheer overflow of reference that makes the text obscure rather than transparent. "Please could, please could, jam it in not plus more sit in when"; "A little piece of pay of pay owls owls such as pie, bolsters" (*TB*, 474, 494).[20]

Second, Stein restores the perceptual indiscriminacy of the pre-Oedipal phase. She subverts selective attention by piling up objects and actions that demand dispersed attention. When we read "PEELED PENCIL, CHOKE: Rub her coke," or "Black ink best wheel bale brown" (*TB*, 476), we cannot emphasize certain words and slight others without knowing we are missing something. Everything strikes us as important, so we attend to all impressions equally. A third route to innocence is the strategy that was my original subject, Stein's recovery of the repressed feminine by dignifying the female anatomy. If it is true that the thing that makes the symbolic order possible is the elevation of the phallus over the womb, one begins to destabilize the symbolic order by bringing the womb back into view.

To the extent that *Tender Buttons* has a protagonist, he or she too keeps slipping through a chink in the symbolic order. "South, south . . . does silence choke speech or does it not" (p. 503). By going south or under, the speaker escapes the normal hierarchies in which the "speech" of the culture chokes or silences him or her. If the "silent" world, the repressed world that one enters as one goes south, can "choke speech," it is actually greater than the Law of the father.

Or instead of going under, the speaker may enter a fertile space, one that contains "ripe purple":

> Room to comb chickens and feathers and ripe purple, room to curve single plates. . . , room to search a light that is simpler, all room has no shadow.
>
> There is no use there is no use at all in smell, in taste, in teeth, in toast, in anything, there is no use at all and the respect is mutual. (479)

The father is absent: this is the meaning of there being "no shadow." As a result, no one imposes the father's instrumental consciousness. There is "no use" in "anything," and if "the respect is mutual," no one plans to use the speaker either. He or she is back in the pre-Oedipal world of play, the world of the mother where colors, tastes, and all impressions were to be enjoyed rather than used.

Thus the speaker, or Stein herself, is "[c]laiming nothing, not claiming anything" (480). This is true in two senses: she does not try to own or use anything, but she also actively claims *nothing*, stakes out the shadow world that the symbolic order discredited or said was not there. It turns out to be a capacious world after all: "spread into nothing. Spread into nothing" (472). One of the things Stein sees herself doing throughout *Tender Buttons* is to assemble little nothings—trivial objects, fragmentary sensations—and show that they are as noteworthy as anything else.

As it turns out, a good place in which to enjoy a "vacation" from the father is the domestic sphere, the house. For this is one realm, according to Stein, that his hierarchies have trivialized or placed in shadow. Thus, paradoxically, one can do what one wants there; he has not quite occupied or regulated this space. Stein enters an imaginary house in *Tender Buttons* and never leaves it: "The author of all that is in there behind the door." So, she goes on, her job is that of "[e]xplaining darkening," showing the contours of the female world (499). She can do housework here in a lazy, noninstrumental way; we see quite a bit of undirected sweeping and polishing. And there is cooking, too, not of the boiling sort but of a kind that recreates the rich ragout of the mother. This is true metaphorically as well. Where Stein sees a "separation" of things into artificial categories, "so kept well and sectionally," the thing she does is to reintegrate everything. "Put it into the stew, put it to shame" (p. 486).

Stein's imaginative recovery of the mother in *Tender Buttons* is an extraordinary move, for in many of her earlier writings she did not seem to notice or value mothers herself. In works like *Three Lives* and *The Making of Americans*, important fathers were ubiquitous, but for the most part the mothers were contemptible, weak, dying or simply absent. Unlike the fathers, they had no discernible effect on their children. Stein is certainly reversing some profound pattern of repression in her own mind, and discovering that the mother or mother-figures who seemed to be ciphers were important early presences covered up in the course of things.

Thus some of the most touching images in *Tender Buttons* and the companion texts are the incessant images of "filling" and "spreading." These images suggest the womb, but what they often express about it is the presence of a whole universe in what one thought of as only an absence. "So the larger size is not the last of all and the silence is larger. If there is the filling any one is there. . . . This makes all of that precious matter" (*G.M.P.*, 254). Some overlooked, silent space is actually "filling," or already full, and what it contains is "precious matter." These texts are about exploring a space that the culture calls empty—whether it is the female body or the early bond with the mother—and discovering that something is there. The field of vision widens: "there is no empty place."[21] "In every space there is a hint of more" (*TB*, 505).

The maternal and anatomical themes that have been my subject emerged suddenly in Stein's work in 1911–12. Even texts composed over a number of years, like *A Long Gay Book*, are marked by a sharp break after which the new themes dominate. In the same period, Stein's life was changing in ways that, while hardly accounting for the shift in her thinking, point to a consistency between her creative life and issues that were emerging as central in her relationships with other people. The two important events of these years were Stein's alienation from her brother Leo and the beginning of her romantic and domestic life with Alice Toklas. Toklas joined the Stein household in 1909; Leo Stein made his departure from it final in 1913.[22] Stein's self-liberation from a brother who habitually condescended to her and disparaged her work is of a piece with the new refrain in the texts examined in these pages, to the effect that women are not to be contemned but valued.[23] And the relationship with Alice Toklas parallels the maternal theme; although Toklas assumes a variety of roles in Stein's works, ranging from wife to sister, one possibility explored in these texts is that of erotically rediscovering the mother through a female lover, of "climbing in the whole udder."

Whatever their source, the transformations in Stein's thinking affected everything she wrote in this period. My purpose has been to show that Stein's most obscure texts, texts that have received attention only as important stylistic experiments, are in fact filled with ideas, and that the ideas are sophisticated and coherent. We might also fairly call them feminist ideas. Stein is both more intelligible and more centrally interested in issues of gender than has been thought.

One implication of Stein's departure from Jamesian psychology is that the mental paradigm with which she replaced it enabled her to say things about women and their place in the symbolic order. In the short period between *Three Lives* and *Tender Buttons*, Stein moved from a Jamesian notion of selective attention to a psychoanalytic one. By 1912, the transition was complete. The interesting fact of mental life for her was no longer that we suppress or ignore certain facts in the interest of survival — James's point — but that we *repress* aspects of experience in the interest of instituting culture. What we repress is not trivial, as James has it, but important; the very fact that we are so intent on keeping it out of view says as much. And the repressed mental content — pre-Oedipal memories, for example, or discounted impressions — can be excavated at any moment. Her final point is that among the things cast into shadow by the culture are the mother and the female body; in the texts of 1912, she uncivilizes us by bringing these back into view.

Notes

I am indebted to Lauren Berlant, Elizabeth Helsinger, Cass R. Sunstein, and William Veeder for helpful comments on an earlier draft of this paper.

1. See for example Richard Bridgman, *Gertrude Stein in Pieces* (New York: Oxford University Press, 1970), 151–52, and Elizabeth Fifer, "Is Flesh Advisable? The Interior Theater of Gertrude Stein," *Signs* 4 (1979): 472–83.

2. For an extended discussion, see my " 'Melanctha' and the Psychology of William James," *Modern Fiction Studies* 28 (1982–83): 545–56, and "William James and the Modernism of Gertrude Stein," in *Modernism Reconsidered*, ed. Robert Kiely, Harvard English Studies, No. 11 (Cambridge, Mass.: Harvard University Press, 1983), 47–63.

3. William James, *The Principles of Psychology*, 3 vols., in *Works of William James*, ed. Frederick Burkhardt (Cambridge, Mass.: Harvard University Press, 1981), 273, 753.

4. Gertrude Stein, "Melanctha," in *Three Lives* (New York: Random House, 1909), 158.

5. Gertrude Stein, *A Long Gay Book* and *G.M.P.*, in *Matisse Picasso and Gertrude Stein with Two Shorter Stories* (Barton, Vt.: Something Else Press, 1972); *Tender Buttons*, in *Selected Writings of Gertrude Stein*, ed. Carl Van Vechten (New York: Random House, 1962). These texts will be cited parenthetically as *LGB*, *GMP*, and *TB*. In the cases of *A Long Gay Book*, and *G.M.P.*, the issues that concern me emerge toward the end of the texts, preceded by material that resembles that of *The Making of Americans* rather than that of *Tender Buttons*.

6. Bridgman, *Gertrude Stein in Pieces*, 126.

7. I do not believe that my elision here alters the meaning; the quoted passage is part of a dependent clause beginning "If lilies are lily white. . . ."

8. Gertrude Stein, "Portrait of Constance Fletcher," *Geography and Plays* (Boston: Four Seas Press, 1922), 162. Hereafter this text will be cited as *GP*.

9. See for example *TB*, 475, 481; *LGB*, 112; *GMP*, 277.

10. Gertrude Stein, "Scenes. Actions and Disposition of Relations and Positions," *GP*, 97, 115.

11. Gertrude Stein, "Rue de Rennes," *Two: Gertrude Stein and her Brother and Other Early Portraits (1908–1912)* (New Haven: Yale University Press, 1951), 349.

12. "Scenes," 106.

13. Ibid., 115.

14. In " 'The Blank Page' and the Issues of Female Creativity," Susan Gubar discusses certain women writers' fantasies of writing with menstrual and other blood. *Writing and Sexual Difference*, ed. Elizabeth Abel (Chicago: University of Chicago Press, 1982), 73–93.

15. *TB*, 496. Jayne Walker reads the phrase in a similar way; see *The Making of a Modernist: Gertrude Stein from "Three Lives" to "Tender Buttons"* (Amherst: University of Massachusetts Press, 1984), 147.

16. Helene Cixous, "The Laugh of the Medusa," in *The Signs Reader: Women, Gender and Scholarship*, eds. Elizabeth Abel and Emily K. Abel (Chicago: University of Chicago Press, 1983), 284.

17. For a fuller discussion, see Joel Porte, "Gertrude Stein and the Rhythms of Life," *New Boston Review* 1 (June 1975): 16–18.

18. *GMP*, 252. The quotations that follow are from *GMP* except where otherwise noted.

19. We know that he is a boy because of the description of his "Pecker that is red. . . ," 253.

20. For a fuller account of elements of Stein's style that are reminiscent of pre-Oedipal

consciousness, see Marianne DeKoven, *A Different Language: Gertrude Stein's Experimental Writing* (Madison: University of Wisconsin Press, 1983), e.g., 16–17. DeKoven does not argue that Stein thinks of her style in these terms, any more than other experimental writers do. But remarkably, the *content* of these texts indicates that something like the Freudian paradigm of human development is present in Stein's mind.

21. "Scenes," 109.

22. Bridgman, *Gertrude Stein in Pieces*, 361–62.

23. See for example Bridgman, *Gertrude Stein in Pieces*, 108, 114.

The Word-Play of Gertrude Stein   Laura Riding Jackson*

1

A common, and main, propensity in attitudes to language, in this era, has been the downgrading of linguistic discipline as necessarily healthy in its effects. Words are now treated as a legacy from a benighted past, in which they were made too much of. The new educated view of words is: "They have no intrinsic value—let us not be fools over them." In this linguistic anti-traditionalism, the functional properties of words, that is, their meaning-properties, cease to hold interest. Consideration of the rationality of the use of a word has come to be viewed as pedantic piety; the new principle of use is the subservience of the word to the individual user's will—instead of your adapting yourself to it, you make it adapt itself to *you*.

The new verbal modernism—the new linguistic freedom—has two sides, one that is intellectually purposive, and one in which the desertion of discipline is by involuntary default. In the latter state of mind, people find no serious concern in themselves for care in the use of words—and there is no wondering why. The purposive, organized rejection of the values of rational coherence that words have vested in them in their belonging to a language is itself of two kinds. One kind is centered in the terminological fantasy pursued in science-serving philosophy (or, one might say, psychological philosophy). An example of this both extremely ambitious and extremely bizarre, linguistically, is to be seen in Mrs. Susanne Langer's tortuously intricate endeavor to substitute new verbal standards of meaning, derived from scientific systematism, for linguistically normal standards, such as are implicit in the systematic meaning-provisions of language itself. The other form of overthrow of natural linguistic law is centered in stands of literary daring, assumed in the interest of authorial originality and new "creative" literary developments.

*This is a previously unpublished essay and is included here by permission of the author.

Those who adopt this orientation towards words view them, and try to use them, as inert artistic material rather than as the live, organically logical apparatus that they constitute under their identity as language. An impressive example of the second kind of orientation is to be seen in the fanatically persistent efforts of Gertrude Stein to put words together so that, while meaning nothing collectively, they yet appear to amount to something.

The point of Gertrude Stein's verbal experimenting is that, if words used without the rational object of saying something in particular, something definitively "thought," can produce an effect of amounting to something, it will have been established that coherent intellectual intent is not necessary for the successful employment of the resources of language. The writings of Gertrude Stein were seductive in the seeming elemental-ness of their verbal characteristics. Though they were canny contrivances of non-meaning, they invited reception as artifacts that might have been produced in an age of verbal innocence; and they were, indeed, so received, at first by the "advanced" literary public, and, gradually, by more and more of the general public, appreciation in the latter case showing in the form of good-humored tolerance rather than in that of critical satisfaction. There has survived from earlier approving attitudes to what Gertrude Stein did with and to words a settled view that exposure to this results in a healthy disburdening of the mind of the cliché procedures of sophisticated linguistic habit. The actuality is otherwise.

Gertrude Stein's work consists of studied deviations from rational continuity of thought; if allowed to affect the mind, they disrupt its natural rational proclivities. As a *spectacle*, the work looks massively, primitively, simple. But *read*, verbally followed, not just looked at, it could only take the mind on an ever-turning course in which reason is thwarted at every turn. The unhealthy effect of it was not perceived because readers thought of themselves as looking at it, not as reading it. But looked-at words must also be read. Where these words held the eye fascinated, they could make themselves be read, and induce belief that this was, linguistically, something. The procedure appeared to be, in the atmosphere of modernist sympathy with the new in word-ways, a reduc-tion of the sayable to a verbal minimum, a salutary straining of mental simplicity to its extreme. But it went below this minimum, beyond this extreme.

Applying an inverted sort of sagacity, in which the mind prevents the formation of words into statements, so that nothing gets more than partly said, Gertrude Stein constructed sentences that were, in internal make-up, not sentences: they did not make sense. The words were not allowed to carry out their meaning-functions; they were stopped short in these, each word at itself or a little beyond itself. They produced a surface-effect of intended sense because they imitated, queerly, the movement of linguistic rationality, but this was by artistic objective — the author had no interest in sense-depth, sense-accretion. Behind the experimenting of Gertrude Stein there was, besides the drive of personal proclivities, some grounding in early American psychology, which concerned itself with making positives of negatives, and there was also much intimate exposure to the anti-intellectual movements of modern art. She showed, and as if it were a triumph to do this, that the rational impulsion in words was resistible. The exhibition held encouragement for others to try to reduce sense in using words, without expunging all meaning-suggestiveness in them.

Ernest Hemingway was sped on his stylistic course by the inspiration of Gertrude Stein's peculiar version of simplicity. It is difficult, at first or even second or further thought, to see the inspiration of this simplicity in the stylistic rollicking of Joyce, with its play of "arty" refinements of phrase and allusion that tries to outdo in seriousness the seriousness it mocks; but the trail of the new kind of language-savoring worm that speaks language in consuming it can be followed here, and who could say that Gertrude Stein's was not the founding wriggler? Here reference may be pertinently made to the incantatory "a rose is a rose is . . ." of world-wide appeal. The appearance of purest simplicity is false; it is not a simple thing, but astute syntax-flouting and sense-flouting—applause of it is applause of the worm.

Gertrude Stein's writings were not simple manifestations of robust individuality; they did not provide prototypes of constructive revolutionary innovation in linguistic practice. They were early products of a pathological condition, mistakenly associated with liberation from mind-imprisoning verbal conventions, with which modern writing, modern thinking, and modern speaking, have become extensively affected; they illustrate how language can be dehumanized by the ignoring of the standards of rational coherence that are, in intellectual actuality, inseparable from it. Gertrude Stein's planned incoherencies can make a strong initial impression of a liberation from banal sense-constructions. But there is, almost instantly, only a residue of dissociated notions occupying the page-lines in dumb, staring disorder: the basic intention is to let the incoherent have its way. Stein sentences are, indeed, formed of cliché-fragments, pieces of statements, each piece having itself the character of a "stock" phrase, the various pieces being strung together without syntactical scrupling. The following passage is from Gertrude Stein's little book *An Acquaintance With Description*.

> It was easy to be sure that it looked so far away pansy as the let it be as much which is when it is might be so much as much further which which very wide very well and very not and mount. Pansy. Not having counted the pansies it is impossible to say just how many pansies are in it. Very much let it be last which having it to be worn and where can it be if it can be that there is no difference between ridges and between ridges.

It can be seen that this technique of word-use obliterated all categorical difference between making sense and not making sense.

In her personal speaking and correspondence Gertrude Stein strove nostalgically for a normal reasonableness and sagacity of utterance, pursuing with obsessive pertinacity meandering lines of small-talk, and exercising her homely intuition and commonsense shrewdness in aphoristic opinion-pronouncements. While there was the smack of sharp intellect in all this, here, there, everywhere, the sharp and the tart alternating with kindly interest and sentiment, the quality of it all in its totality was a protean vagueness — nothing of it held, nothing definite accumulated. If one joins to this the products of her literary workmanship, one can find a common quality that identifies the whole usefully from the point of view of intellectual history: that is, absolute scepticism.

In its linguistic aspect, Gertrude Stein's scepticism functions through a maximum avoidance, in the use of words, of commitment to meaning. The aversion to linguistic rationality that attended the development of scientific rationality in American nineteenth-century philosophical radicalism found literary outlet in her literally practiced linguistic nonconformism (which, certainly, has connection with her having studied under William James). In her verbal procedure nothing was accepted (seriously) of the intellectual organization that makes language of words — the linguistic value of words was not intellectually recognized. The human aspect of this scepticism is in the pathos and self-contradiction comprised in its sentimental attachment to the idea that the human intelligence is fully respectable without the benefit of words — which are its administrative agents! That is, Gertrude Stein regarded herself and her writing as on the side of the intelligence, and the humane sensibilities generally, although she performed a weird rite of neutralizing the intelligence in her authorial deintellectualizing of language. Given that an energetic mentality can become that passive instrument of an ideology, much of the confusion of Gertrude Stein's intellectual position may be set down to helplessness: though she considered herself to differ from others in not being the product of her education, her position was to a large extent a consequence of a special kind of education. Yet, fitting all her experience to it, she made it emotionally so much her own that she exerted a ponderous influence as a literary popularizer of it. She brought together in her work (as in her person) very many of the paradoxes of modern intellectualism, and found a public to which she could make the queer presentation sound, if not natural, at least proper to the time.

How Gertrude Stein's verbal constructions sounded is how human existence would sound if human beings abandoned their linguistic proficiencies as encumbrances upon the intelligence, yet held on to words as accessories of an intelligent, mentally therapeutic exercise of stupidity. To quote again from *An Acquaintance With Description*:

Pass paper pass please pass pass trees pass trees please pass please pass please pass please as paper as pass as trees. Very likely very nearly likely nearly likely very.

My poetic work has been here and there in the past — and is even occasionally in the present — spoken of as having likenesses to the verbal doings of Gertrude Stein. This is critical purblindness in regard to both. Gertrude Stein and I were at opposite poles in our view of the linguistic functions — and of the spiritual significance of humanness. There was for a time a friendship between us, but I was not insensitive to the destructive implications of what she was doing linguistically; I read into the destructive intent — the seeking of proof, in the word-play, of the possibility of having language-yet-nothingness — an intention and potential of purification. The appeal of pathos in Gertrude Stein's work and personal dispositions was strong: it all seemed so simple, and so innocent. She tried hard to keep it innocent. She wanted to be successfully — naturally, likably, even conventionally — human, and, yet, oh, so much, to be an influentially successful creature of a humanly outré period — modernism. Simple-humanness was not compatible with the inhuman fascination with the disintegrative that came to be ascendant in the world of art and literature of the time; and to wish passionately, as she did, to be a rallying-point at the center of its disorder was to wish herself into continual disappearance and self-resurrection there. Thus is it that the key to what Gertrude Stein was doing in her peculiar mode of word-use is not to be found in it alone. A forceful, dogged will was at work to record exactly how words took their way in her mind, as she let them, so far as was humanly or inhumanly possible, take their way, there. But the will itself had a master, a peculiar modernism with which she had fallen in love.

2

The extent to which Gertrude Stein was at least as much made by as she was the maker of a modernism of a peculiar potency is better understandable now than it could have been in the very time of her involvement in it. For instance, one can see at a distance the weaknesses of that entire literary, artistic, and philosophic movement that, in its young vigor, bristled with empirical impatience, in many forms, towards the rationalists, as unwilling to recognize limits to the understanding. The posture was an invention, it had no intellectual reality except that of being an expression of a general breakdown in intellectual patience, a condition closer to decrepitude of human spiritedness than new animation of human spirit; its vigor was made up of restiveness, fractiousness or querulousness, and what its proponents gave to it of themselves, for what it might give of itself to them. Take away the theatrical backdrop of this modernism: some of its characteristic productions will show a changed appearance. It has been claimed for Gertrude Stein's use of words that it rid words of the exhaustion of their meaning-vitality, suffered in the past, and caused them to stand out in individual freshness. The words of her use, however, are words drained not just of stale accretions of association, but drained of themselves as linguistic entities; they are put to use as aged relics, dissociated not only from their human history but from their very nature as language.

One need not bear down on the fact that Gertrude Stein purused experiments in fatigue-reactions when she was a student of William James, to account for her peculiarities of word-use. Some light might be cast on her word-use and its human significances by the fact of the influence that the thinking of Alfred North Whitehead had with her — she knew him as a friend. He, in his metaphysical speculations, stressed the necessity of a principle of limitations. He called "the ultimate limitation" God.

> . . . and His existence is the ultimate irrationality. For no reason can be given for just that limitation which it stands in His nature to impose. God is not concrete, but He is the ground for concrete actuality. No reason can be given for the nature of God, because that nature is the ground of rationality.

This argument preaches a necessary limit to rationality, as the spiritual principle of existence, and the law of human intelligence. By the argument's terms, a shrunken intellectuality and a shrunken spirituality are the human expression of what is ultimately inexpressible. Gertrude Stein responds to this cramped religious-philosophical-scientific pattern of cosmic explanation with a shrunken linguisticality.

It would take the entire modernism to which Gertrude Stein went to school to account for what she did to words. She learned to believe in, as a ruling abstraction, Reasonless Necessity, with human intelligence incapable of acting as an independent force of accident, under it, to precipitate realities of conscious experiences for itself. She was, in her word-play, the most serious exponent of this modernism in the field of "writing" — the world of literary, and artistic, professionalism. She sacrificed words to its creed, and her own intelligence, apparently without reservations. Among her favorite aphorisms was: "No Jew ever lays down his last cent." If she kept back a last cent, in her dedication to the peculiar nihilistic cultural Renaissance of the time, she has hidden it well. The sacrifice of her intelligence was nearly total — the bits of homely sagacity with which her talk was generally sprinkled were trifles escaped from the major offering. As to words, she made a perfect offering at that altar — or perfect to the extent that words can be denatured into meaning-blank integers (as numbers might be voided of arithmetical sense while continued in their outer identity).

It would be mistaken to think of this word-play as spiritedly imaginative or intuitively directed. It is all done with laborious deliberation; there is no lightness in the play. Gertrude Stein had the genius of total seriousness — the so rare genius. But it was, tragically, squeezed into self-despiting performances in the almost incredibly diminutive confines of her work-design, the meagre reaches of her work's evocation of human reality. One could feel, in the words of her book-writing, and in those of her personal letters identically (as in personal acts towards one), a large initial gesture of good meaning fall fast into a grip of fear of taking *away* from what was pre-committed to a god of time, a god with an insatiable appetite, for whom everything became ever nothing. The verbal and personal atmosphere of her activity was, thus, nervous with a continually aborted generosity. The mood was by genesis grand. What was seen as actually happening was of a striking, impressive, littleness; the dominating quality of the writing was of a tremendously, a passionately, stinted articulatedness.

Others were emboldened by Gertrude Stein's scanting of meaning-content in her use of words to develop various adaptations of the procedure to literary style. The procedure was devoid of considerations of literary style. The underlying concern with her was not with effects of verbal economy, or liberation from conventionalities of literary form. She attacked, as itself a convention, the reality of meaning-content itself, cut down the scope of expression to a supposedly truthful alternative to a supposedly fictitious sense of the humanly important. She made the inconsequential the essential subject of expression, and meaning the mental register or codification of it. The inversion of the importances took in very much more than a mere literary programme could hold, or a programme of art-in-literature, or of literature as a twin or soul-mate of art. It took in *all* meaning: which is to say that it applied itself to the entire field of possible affirmation in a policy of nearly total non-affirmation — one of denial of meaning except for a bare acceptance of language, as word-supply that yielded vehicles, trains, chains of trains, by which to move in tracks of meaning ever away from meaning.

A strong emotional disposition may be imagined to have had part in the forming of Gertrude Stein's general attitudes. The thoroughness of her adoptions of the philosophic implications with which she had had close academic acquaintance — which made the tentative in thought the intellectual objective, as a triumph over the danger of the follies of both intellectual certainty and uncertainty — suggests a personal hopelessness in her inducing the clamping upon herself of the essentially bleak prescription for a modern wisdom that such schooling, taken literally, offered. All the aspects of human love can be imagined to undergo inversion here in importance, along with all aspects of meaning. An inverted romanticism in which the importance of love is minimized in self-protective, self-punitive, emotional discipline might account for the intense, the uninterruptedly sustained severity, of her suppression of meaning-accumulation in her use of words. But it can be assumed as simply perceptible, without speculation, that the meaning-negating, meaning-resisting process pursued in her word-play was backed by an emotional force of the most serious personal temper. The intellectual vigilance of the word-play against sense-structures has for support an emotional vigilance against the happy turns of the happy continuities of utterance. The private story within the public performances of word-play is her own. However, one must not think of her as enacting publicly a private position. She meant the meaning-devastating consequences of the play with all her mind — and if, also, with all her heart, this was by the personal signature to the sincere intention.

Those who took stylistic cues from what Gertrude Stein did with words were literarily self-interested to a degree beyond any personal self-interest attributable to her in her word-procedure. What might be attributable to her of self-interest, in it, is an emotionally earnest throwing of herself personally into the mould of the procedure in all-or-nothing unreservedness of dedicatory fervor. She did not use her chosen procedure personalistically, or with a calculating literary eye — as the adopters of it who adapted it to their writing can be seen to have done, varyingly. Gertrude Stein's work must be viewed as an attempt on a comprehensive scale of purpose to change the intellectual, the literary, the artistic, scene of life in her time, an attempt to rid it of all furniture of definition of any kind, and, with this, of action of commitment to definition of any kind. In advancing this conception of her work-objective, I am not unmindful of the emphasis she put on her being concerned with definition in her various presentations of herself as attaining, now, in this piece of work, now in that, to a finality of understanding of the essential nature of this and that linguistic form: as, what "description" is, what "a sentence," what "a paragraph." Such concern with definition was but the automatic, compulsive, preoccupation of a mind of naturally robust intellectual energeticness curbed in by the adopted intellectual creed of its possessor, the modern philosophical culture she has made the over-mentor of her mind as the mind of one bent on being a force in the general intellectual modernization of the modern world. To probe for basic terms of intellectual principle within the field of the *self-evident* values of linguistic practice, in a modification of that practice from which the very instrument of definition, meaning, was reduced to a minimum just allowing of a token use of words for a token minimum of expressed intellectual action: this was to fortify her intellectual conscience with an illusion of her work's being done at the center of the intellectually crucial value-system of things.

Gertrude Stein pressed out into the scene of twentieth-century intellectual modernism an enormous continual flow of intellectual energy producing what was in its whole a formless quantity of intellectual work. But the diminutive achievements of the purposed mental operations that constituted her work-activity, following one on the other in unbroken succession, had a character of material solidity. Her work, in consequence, juts out into contemporary time — I mean contemporary time in the sense of a single sequence of generations within immediate view — with the massive prominence of a *system* of general mental re-evaluation, more comparable in its rigid purposiveness with such a system of general re-evaluation as the Marxian than with anything in the field of literary, philosophic, or artistic theory. The only question pertinent to it, as being of this nature, is "could it work?" As it was a system set in reverse, for an action of relentless un-doing of all past accretions of definition and value-formations, without any provision in it for a new beyond to its sense and value-nullifying objective, it could only work as something self-reproducing: it is its own product, to be found beginning and ending in itself at whatever period in it attention and examination are applied to it. It is, thus, as an anticipatory funeral monument constructed by a person in substantiation of her living reality as a continuum of individual processes of living consciousness.

Of Gertrude Stein's work, viewed in the terms of the "monument" figure I have suggested, I think it can be said with some realistic pertinence, the figure being applied in a literal sense for simplified accuracy, that the monument was designed not just for self-verification but to stand to moderns as a landmark for innovation in conception of the general human reality, as representable in the form of *words*. For moderns, visitors from successive time-advents of modernity to the monument, it can become only a progressive blank message from its period, and its maker.

I am not a reader of Camus, but I deduce from what I have read about him that he deposited on the landscape of modernity a monument both funerary and exhortatory, intended to be a symbol of attainment to a fullness of nullification in death of a fullness of life, and an inspiration to courage for all extremities to which moderns might feel driven in a quest of capture of the value-secret of nothingness, or the secret of no-value. Against such a literary version of modern tabula rasa making on the human terrain of value, and Marxian political versions of value-nullification, Gertrude Stein's deposition stands out in the impression it makes of personal realness.

Gertrude Stein's words repeat themselves over and over, making, in no matter what cast of expression, no sense — there is no accumulation of sense. Her revolution against sense, and the revolutionary subversions of the other enemies of sense, are resemblant in being efforts to rid the conception of *value* of all association with *values* except as measures that, though lacking a general force of verificality, have a pragmatic serviceability where "things" are endowed with sense within the isolation of particular settings. That is, Gertrude Stein belongs to that modernism for which there is no whole setting of value — which is a philosophic, an artistic, a political, an everything policy for human intelligence after a presumed intellectual deluge that has swept away all the (false, delusory) old orientation signs of a general sense of "things." (The effect of advanced taking-apart of "things" in theoretical investigation to a vanishing-point in ability to put them together again in theoretical summation, with normal processes of understanding pressed towards the brink of the abnormal, is manifest in the key examples of programmatic modernity and in these must be included examples in the field of art, in which the processes of perception have been strained to yield visual conceptions of a universe the reality of which, supposedly, inheres in a capability of rearing itself perpetually into existence from a tabula rasa of fragments of itself.)

The peculiar toughness of Gertrude Stein's exercises in verbal modernity comes of her personal early-formed resolution, adhered to without mercy to herself, her imagination, words themselves, to deal with words as quantities, ponderables, things there, processes impersonal or accidental, a common stock of things not made for use, but found, and put to use. They get no honors of recognition as things of worth, in themselves, in their potencies of expressiveness, their capabilities of being organized into structures of meaning valuable for the ordering of the course of thought — the ordering of human life itself, the relations of human beings with one another. There has been theorizing that, while in her earlier writing she aimed at the rendering of the sea-level verbal functioning of people, flat continuities of ordinariness, successions of words yielding the essence of speaking ordinariness, she later aimed at raising the words to levels of transcendence of their humdrum functionalism, and in the whole accomplished for the word attainment to a reality immune from the impure particularities of meaning — to a consciousness-area where words are restored to a grand primeval generality of reference, taking their user's minds out of themselves into a mystical spiritually basic total generality. But such analysis is a fanciful assimilation of Gertrude Stein's hard modernity to soften versions of verbal, psychological, philosophic, modernity that have served as intellectual substitutes for religion to anti-religious or non-religious aesthetic and literary modernity.

Gertrude Stein's words are not for the uses of any sort of spiritual reorientation. Their reality is that of a realism of disavowal of all but a phenomenological reality in them. They are words stripped to a nudity of psychic inconsequentiality. Users of words in such a condition are themselves in a condition of psychic nudity of mind, in which the mind, utterly neutral to value, plays with words as undifferentiated chequers, in a game ever returning to a restarting. There is no score. The movements on the board do not add up. The play is so seriously conducted, seems so free of stylistic wiles and gambits of literary art, that a sceptical or mocking view of it comes more from those of vulgarian attitude to verbal experiment than to those who take serious interest in it. Behind Gertrude Stein's verbal experimenting is an evidently serious objective, comprehensive in its intended reaches of effects in important fields of mental performance.

How does one talk about, judge seriously of, an unflagging application to making a mental posture of no-meaning a continuously occupiable mental position? If it can be done, and without any other apparent purpose but to show that it is extensively, hugely, possible, and therefore in some way a natural of verbal performance, and of a basic significance as such, must not one try to give it its place in the characterization of outstanding performances, its due of critical description?

3

Very early in my acquaintance with Gertrude Stein's work of work-play, I made an endeavor to place it critically among the conspicuous writing-positions of the time (the early decades of the century) and do proper justice to its substantiality as effort — as work seriously motivated. This I did in an essay entitled, "T. E. Hulme, The New Barbarism, And Gertrude Stein" presented in my book *Contemporaries and Snobs*, of 1928. My purpose, in that essay (which was the base-material of the last portion of *A Survey of Modernist Poetry* [1927]), was to point up the excessive emphasis on literary criticism in the consciousness of those writers of the time who made themselves the vanguard of civilized literary feeling. So dependent was that feeling on literary history, drawing upon it for the formation of *new* positions, offering itself (absurdly) as the harbinger of a new beginning, sophisticated yet of primitive or barbaric vitality, that the anticipated literary productions, as critically depicted, and the actual examples of advance realizations of the new feeling, were feelingless: there was dessication in the motive springs of writing.

I was concerned centrally in the essay to which I have referred with the fate of poetry in a literary atmosphere that, of an "advanced" time-sense, self-consciously late, "new," "different," imposed a barbarically regulatory metaphysic on poetry, a philosophy of criticism for the recreation of poetry according to values "converting poetry into a dogmatic science pledged to the refinement of these values." The values were extracted, supposedly, from the historical actuality of poetry, while the historical actuality itself was left behind: poetry was made, thus, a critical absolute to which the poet automatically conformed in being a poet. What has this to do with Gertrude Stein? I mean to come soon to the connection. I must first touch on the connection of this with myself. To introduce the reference to myself, I shall describe my position as a dedicated poet, believing in poetry and believing also in time, as a reasonable being, but not centering the sense of poetry to the historical sense of *a* time. I was sensitive to the war of historical forces that was claiming the world-population in that period (that, indeed, still claim it) in terms of my identification of both my ground of life and work as poetry. Such was my view of poetry, I seeing it as ground of a universal kind, that my understanding of the poetic potential, and of the entire literary potential as an ultimate bloom of the poetic, had general applicability.

"Freedom," in that time, was a thing of the loosest reference, no more just a thing of "movements" political, philosophical, literary, psychological, something definitionally provided for in their doctrines, but an enormous complex of forces working directly on the individual being, widely, sweepingly, delivering to people's ears and will the message of the time: "*Yours*, the choice, the choices!" And then there were the forces of authority, their old identities erased — obliterated or faded — but they themselves having autochthonous presence in human life, forms of knowledge of internal necessities that the forms of external control have imitated. People felt pressures upon them of a call from the old formal authority-identities, though these were weakened in credit, in their inner sense of necessities internally governing the ultimate realities of being — necessities mainly known by the vague characterization "values." The call spoke thus: "Get you a rule of 'values' — a self-chosen authority." The impression of the time upon very many of the time of a wondering impressionability (what queer important kind of time is this?) was of a peculiar, new twentieth-century mixture of inconsistencies, that made inconsistencies and confusions attending them themselves seem to compose a new truth, to be a revelation of reality as a conjunction of extremes.

Myself, in the midst of this war-play of forces, needed no proddings of "the time" to make free choice of what to do, how to be, nor proddings as to the need of a redefinition of values. My own naturally rising impulsions of freedom-need were intimately accompanied by inward impulsions of a need of values to go by as principles of truth. The matter of "authority" was for me not part of a pattern of forces in which the forces of individual will and those of a power-doctrine existed in varying forms of discrepancy and accommodation. The matter of freedom was for me of one urgency with the matter of truth — the claim of the need of values of truth and that of the need of freedom were one claim. My instincts of recognition of the ills and confusions of understanding where new understandings of the modern human state were put forth were lively. But these instincts in my applications of judgments to specific forms in which the new understandings were expressed were somewhat blunted by my acceptance of poetry as the area of articulate finality, the discovery-ground of values of truth that the tradition of poetry implicitly committed it to being. I comprised within the conception of the poetic function a literal concern with values of truth that, non-literary in the breadth and depth of their reach, were the religious promise in poetry that had kept it spiritually alive, in its vicissitudes in the irregular course of centuries, as mere literature. I therefore felt the philosophical tampering with the nature of poetry that was going on, the prescriptions for new poetic tradition that were no more than critical formulations reducing poetic production to a self-conscious routine of imitation of poetry, as an assault on poetry rather than a direct assault on the speaking human intelligence as informed with a natural truth-principle.

If I had then exercised my sensitivities directly upon the total human disposition of the time to the matter of freedom and authority, and the general human problem of individual choice in relation to that of the need of a commonly recognized truth-principle, and not viewed these problems from the ground of my dedication to poetry, I should have been less worriedly uneasy about the literarily, critically, aesthetically, absolutist prescriptions for the correct modernist mood that were current, and seen the various positions of supposed-to-be intellectually safe spiritual defeatisms that sponsored them as reflections of a great general human sagging of will and spirit. And worried more about that! And I should have comprehended quietly the self-interested, professionalistic motivations of the new philosophics of "creative" action: to save literature, poetry, art, in a world-time in which all the old values that made the world human, or part human, were lost to science and sophisticated weariness, in survival-terms low enough to be compatible with an order of tentative evaluation having suspicion of certainty as its principle of authority.

I was not so much absorbed in contemplating the dismalness of the new critical philosophics, and the "creative" consequences of the following of their prescriptions, as to lose my human good cheer and professional perspective of hope (my human hope lodged in poetry). I wrote in an early book (*Contemporaries and Snobs*: the section from which I quote was subsequently transposed to the collaborative *A Survey of Modernist Poetry*, of which I was the first author): "We might almost say that poetry temporarily turned into philosophy, entangled itself in many introspective absurdities that had nothing to do with poetry. . . ; but that all this was perhaps unfortunately necessary before a position could be reached in which poetry might be normal without being vulgar, and deal naturally with truth without being trite." I looked towards a passing beyond the grim literary dogmatisms of the time to "a greater concentration in both the reader and the poet on poetry as an ever-immediate reality confirmed afresh and independently in each new work rather than as a continuously sustained tradition: confirmed personally rather than professionally."

The sense of my own reality, and of the reality of which my instinct of truth gave me sense, I put in the keeping of a conception of truth as the verbal potential (and proper function) of poetry that had been, indeed, in poetry's long course, the traditional theme of poetic vision. Thus, I kept my head above the literary and general aesthetic and philosophical modern weather of the time, and my heart accessible to some of the downright human actualities encompassed in that weather: and I did not miss the character of Gertrude Stein's position and work in relation to what others were up to, as the joker in the whole pack of cards of the game.

The point I made as to Gertrude Stein in writing in *Contemporaries and Snobs* of the new absolutism which accomplished in Eliot's favorable description of the new intellectual stand, for literature, "the invalidation of the ancient classification," that is, the distinction between *critical* and *"creative,"* was that her use of words planted on the nothingish scene of critically legislated literary modernism an honest-injun Literary Nothing. Eliot said of it ". . . it is not improving, it is not amusing, it is not interesting, it is not good for one's mind. But its rhythms have a peculiar hypnotic power not met with before. It has a kinship with the saxophone. If this is the future, then the future is, as it very likely is, of the barbarians. But this is a future in which we ought not to be interested." But Eliot himself, his unsure guts fortified by the critical philosophy of T. E. Hulme, of which Eliot wrote, "he appears as the forerunner of a new attitude of mind, which should be the twentieth-century mind," was looking to not just a future but a present ruled by a sweeping barbarism, a prescription of an entire beginning literarily anew on severely classical lines. Eliot was also on the side of Nothing, but lacking the sincerity, which Gertrude Stein possessed, of readiness to make good the objective. Whether she believed or not in what she did as Something, she believed in herself. He believed substantially in nothing and believed too little — too little for sincerity — in himself — and was scared to press his issue more than faintly: he did not know how much of an issue he had, could not foresee how far he could go with it. And so he marked time. And so we have the cruel Aprils, the depraved Mays, the wan bravados eked out as with second-hand elegances from rummage-shops of literature and learning.

In other words: occupying a poet-position dissociated from critical politics and philosophies of literary history, and identifying the contemporary critical utmost in sophistication as barbarically destructive (and destructively barbarized), I was able to spot the relative healthiness of Gertrude Stein's acceptance of the seeming challenge of the time to dare to equate modernity with a real barbarism, as compared with the equivocal disposition of the critical definers of a new era of literature and art disembarrassed of the old standard objectives of progress. These raided the past as a mortuary repository for ghostly substance for the supposedly purged present. Gertrude Stein made no deals with the past. She rested — a consistent absolutist of a basic undefinable — at recording just what the succession of pure present evanescent moments admitted of sense-accumulation.

"Everything is the same," Gertrude Stein wrote, "except composition and time, composition and the time of the composition and the time in the composition." That is, there is no real sense-accumulation: there is only the putting down of the words, and nothing can (really) mean anything for long. "No one but Miss Stein," I wrote in that essay, "has been willing to be as ordinary, as simple, as primitive, as stupid, as barbaric, as successful barbarism demands." And, again, I said, commenting on her method of "composition": "It creates duration but makes it absolute by preventing anything from happening in the duration."

4

However mystifying Gertrude Stein's performance may be in its purpose, whatever one may think of it, it does not of itself mystify, there is nothing covert about the performance itself. It is out in the open. There is no behind-the-scenes conspiring, no literary make-up, or costumery employed: this is something enacted on the general floor of the time, not in the theatre of Criticism. She tried to dramatize the time with herself, give it a character, where others tried to use it as "material."

Though the scale of Gertrude Stein's performance was of a worldly bigness, this was a petty worldly bigness, merely. For she equated time with reality, cramming into it, in the name of beauty, human significance, and truths, tidbits of human experience, human expression, human meaning, the content having no wholeness, no reality except that of fragmentary unenduring duration, time as a supreme reality. Time consuming time, the things of time, cannot be spiritualized into transcendence of itself. Nor did she want that! She wanted to voice a grand, overpoweringly simple alternative of general nullity of belief to the long human search for a grand, simple general totality of belief—to disburden her time of more than itself, whether of past or future reference. The trivialities to which this position reduced the intelligent potential of the time in the fields of literature and the arts had a redeeming quality that the performances of the intellectual sophisticates of modernism lacked: her performance was that of one who meant it as a human being for general human purposes, not merely for literary or aesthetic purposes. Her nothing she authenticated with the somethingness of herself: she was there in what she did.

By their geographical and historical circumstances, Americans may be thought of as new people. They cannot avoid doing the different, being the different: this is their human lot, their mission, their good luck. They have being in a concatenation of physical and temporal existence beyond the limits of the world that supplied all the definitions by which human existence familiarized itself with itself. Whatever they do, for worse or better, combines in it a life stress of immediacy and a life stress of finality. It could be the beautiful ultimate of human self-definition. It can be an interminable miscellany of applications of a theory that simplification is the key to all problems. The theory is correct in instinct; but, by resting much self-indulgently at instinct, Americans have tended to simplify problems by omitting as much of them as does not immediately respond to simplification.

I do not mean to, I must not here attempt to, review the manifestations of the response of Americans to the special stimuli of their peculiar position in human circumstance. One could gather illustrations in thick array, from every nationally distinguishable area of activity, of how Americans exercise their sense of there being an American functionality of human decisiveness in edgy conclusion-making that leaves conclusions to be arrived at soon again, and soon again—of how they are given to combining because of the strain under which their human position puts them, boldly conceived extremes of action or performance with extremes of hesitancy. But I shall confine myself to speaking particularistically on this theme, to Gertrude Stein, and then, a little, to myself.

Gertrude Stein attempted to create a norm of extremism in which the contradictions of attitude and performance both finalistic in spirit and temporalistic—having no reality beyond that of an immediate provisional moment—should neutralize each other, and a perfection be achieved thus of nothing left-over from the process, nothing to signify wrong, non-fulfillment of human functionality, incompletion of special destiny. One might call this philosophically instant Hegelianism—something Marx was unable to achieve.

Myself: I have distinguished between the finalistic impulsion and that of immediacy as between a recognized necessity of attaining to a finality of human limit in temporal terms (a coming to a finally determinate sense of human identity, one superseding all past conceptions, and freeing the mind from the rule of these conceptions and a potentiality recognized as implicit in human nature, of transcendence of this finality in a perdurable immediacy of human self-explicitness, and a perfecting, in this, of the human expression of whole reality. In my version of the American version of the principle of human functionality, there have been no contradictions. The stress of a natural finality, even as a stress of annihilation such as that embodied in and typified by death, was subsumed and surpassed in the stress succeeding it with an inevitable rhythm of hope of and confidence in an ultimate integrity of human identity. The element of immediacy, in my envisionments, was the quality of expectation of entrance into a state of a purified fullness of being. There was no vagueness in this expectation. It was neither Nothing nor an indeterminate Something; it was the natural culmination of the sustained fidelity of human nature to the reality of the human reality, and the reality of reality.

I wrote for an announcement of a book of mine, *Though Gently*, published in 1931, the matter of finality in the total question of human self-determination being greatly with me at that time, a description of its contents as "statements in prose and poetry all leading as gently as possible to annihilation and the rest." "Annihilation" was an irony relative to a context in which an effort was made to treat of finalities with a touch both altogether firm and yet quite gentle, in that it was acutely lively with implications of 'the rest.' The rest became, with me, increasingly, the center of my preoccupations, and increasingly the due scene, in my understanding of our humanly best capabilities of presence and attention.

For many, there is a play with ideas of a "rest," to plump out the day of mortal speculation, in sense of dissatisfaction kept, so far as possible, comfortably safe. With Gertrude Stein, there was no "rest"; finality itself was made a denial of itself. The playing was a playing with words, to make them unwrite, unspeak, themselves as fast as they got written, spoken—and, thus, to make human existence at last free of its destiny of making sense of itself, and of Being—of Existence General. It was a terrible misunderstanding of human destiny, fostered by exposure to an unhappy combination of American and other impatiences of modernism co-incident with a giant appetite for functional self-realization—being a Somebody, doing Something.

Addenda
A

I thought, after reading an article on Gertrude Stein in the magazine, *MS*, how it was written out of the environment of her self-picturing—a forceful creation—rather than out of a view of her as occupying the space of a person, the environmental setting not all her personal space.

She was a very hungry woman, and made herself so much her own food. A simplicity of natural feeling coursed along with the literary, the created, simplicity, jostling it and jostled by it. I believe there was a quite strong element of natural simplicity in her feelings towards myself. I have felt that strain of feeling present in her talking to me confidingly of someone—a man. What she told had for me the quality of a natural womanly feeling towards a man; it was not her usual literary-world or art-world off-the-cuff comment, spoken with an assurance that gave it the double edge of a private remark that had also in it stuff of public weight. (I think I ought to introduce here the confidence itself. Perhaps she entrusted it to others. I have never come upon it, or any like it, in the writings of others on her: and suddenly, it seems to me that, in relating it specifically, now, here, I should be performing a service of importance to her, in her enduring presence among us all as a human being. She said to me: "Picasso knows and I know that he is the only man for me and I the only woman for him." The class of comment to which this is, for me, the unique exception to all others to which I was private witness, is illustratable with a characterization of Hemingway as having taken much from her, literarily, and, gone the way of ingratitude, or of Edith Sitwell as perpetually preoccupied with her beauty. But recently my attention was brought to the reproduction, in a magazine issue of past time, of an interview given by Robert Graves: he narrated what I have written above as something told him by Gertrude Stein. We both made visits to her when we were comrades in work. But he had the confidence in confidence from me.)

These two simplicities were the stuff of which she was made. But they did not cohere. The huge genius careerism kept seizing the initiative, the leadership. I have phrased differently the strain to be felt between herself and herself in continuous operation, the unity of her disunity. I said somewhere, to someone, that there was a perverse purpose in her life-zest and labors, which she treated so much as of the nature of a straight-line that she and it evoked response as to virtue—she herself wanting such credit for her work and her life-doings, and to believe it justified.

Sherwood Anderson wrote of her after meeting her: "I admire her because she in her person represents something sweet and healthy in our American life, and because I have an undying faith that what she is up to in her word kitchen in Paris is of more importance to writers of English than the work of many of our more easily understood and more widely accepted word artists."

Americans generally have an appeal for each other, at home and abroad, or it may be called an elementary comfortableness in each other's presence, arising from a special sense of the nature of personal identity that is nurtured within the frame of the American interpretation of the fact of social existence and of the actuality of personal existence. The spirit of this sense is "You or you or you are nothing but yourself, as I am nothing but myself." This "nothing but" principle of identification expressed freedom felt from the obligations of attaching qualifications of special identity to the other one. The social composition of life, per this doctrine, which is a vast simplification of history, is a matter of accident: the general, social, human "we" is a sum of those who *find* themselves together. The individual human being, per this doctrine, is the essential unit of the basic accident of human existence: the actuality of personal existence is both accidental and absolute. "You or you or you are *there*, I am here where I am, I am there along with you, or you or you, you or you or you are here along with me."

To be is, in the American philosophic convenience of reducing human existence to an elementary self-evidentness of the fact of the existence of individual human beings, thus something both of the most matter-of-fact ordinariness and of the most obvious wonderfulness: something both taken for granted and regarded with a surprise that does not wear off. Both attitudes belong to an adoption of an estimate of the natural state of mind of human beings towards the fact of their existence as one of utter ignorance: they begin intellectually at knowing only about themselves, that they are. This is a healthy posture for facing the felt necessity of comprehending just what they are, and an attendant nudging suggestion of a responsibility of living, acting, thinking, being, according to an achieved comprehension of what they are. The catch in it is that it is a healthy preparatory form of self-address to the fulfilling of the role of being a human being. The valuable American "nothing but" or starting-at-the-start mentality loses value little by little as it lets itself become spiritually immobilized in that state as a permanency *within* the limits of which to mature! This amounts to a tendency to contain all the propulsions from the basis of freedom to begin at the beginning within the security of uncompleted maturity—a tendency to cleave to the unfinal as happy ever-revisable fulfillment.

Intellectually busy Americans are given to striving for, each, a point in a trajectory of advance at which advancing movement will find itself stopped in impact upon a presumed natural barrier of sufficiency of individual advance in the direction of maturity. All the *common* feeling characterizing Americans as conscious of human one-another-ness is directed towards the stage of newbornedness, all, into the human opportunity. However at one they may be in their attitude to themselves and one another as adventurers all, in life's potentialities, starting all at the same zero-point of ignorance of the achievable, they part company, all, in a privacy of decision, each, as to how far to try to go individually in advance from the common birth-point in the quest for the possible. And so it is that the charge that falls upon Americans, of all people, as I understand the differences between people in the functions they bring upon themselves by their special different natures, the charge of defining the human being, has not yet had any fulfillment in them but a diminutive truncated version of it.

B

I have written in a comment contained in my notes to Gertrude Stein's letters to me, in reference to a certain remark of hers made in a conversation between herself and myself and another person: "With likeness to Aristotle, Gertrude Stein made use unhesitantly of the obvious. This has two sure advantages: it enables one not to want for words—of either complimentary or sagacious effect, or both kinds in combination—and one is likely to be right, or at least safe from dispute." I should add to this that the uncomplimentary was not absent from her conversational ruminations. But, complimentary or uncomplimentary, all came forth in the quiet and firm flow of an activity of commentary the even-tonedness of which made hearers feel they were listening to words that were of inner and outer speaking, in their utterance. There was no place for agreement or disagreement, provided, in their delivery: they had the authority of words integrated by their speaker in their utterance with her very flesh.

I think I have chanced to make a characterization of Gertrude Stein's performance in words, the written besides the spoken, that illuminates much of her total peculiarity as a worker in the field, the fields, of words. This is, that in her linguistic operations she endeavored to convert the mentality-nature of words into a physicality-nature. What happens where the effort is to physicalize words? While this is an impossibility, that something can be done of this sort, the effort to do it is tenuously describable, with imagination attempted of what Gertrude Stein was trying to do in these inner-outer word-utterance exercises, conversational and literary, that she offered as of mental quality. Effort was exerted by her to isolate the impression-force words have in the operations of the brain from their force as meaning-entities in the life of thought and communication of human beings. In this she proceeded according to the special philosophy she had invented as a principle for verbal functioning without any necessity of coherence other than what bodily sensation itself might automatically supply of coherence to the functioning. The product was, could only be, a pseudo-physical form of articulate mental activity. Whatever the brain stores of sensation-impressions, they cannot do substitute work for thought. The sensorium of the body cannot take the place of the mind.

I see Gertrude Stein, within the frame of this labor of my imagination for constructing a descriptive pattern of her procedure, laying a value of physical force and reality upon a mental activity of hers in which she reduced the mental nature of it to the lowest energy-intensity at which words could have issue in, from, the activity. Delusorily identifying this as a physical operation of mental quality, value, reality, even, in its physical-ity, she applied the technique confidently to both her use of words in her writing-work, and in her personal use of them. In the latter, she indulged herself in an energy-intensity of mental force higher than the bottom level at which she kept it in her formal writing; but it was still of an energy-intensity force greatly, hugely, relaxed from the natural level of intellectual performance. A good deal of mental sense got into her personal use of words, thus, she, however, maintaining uniformly in the personal and formal writer's use of words the posture of one drawing upon her physical sensorium for all her utterance-procedure. What *was* going on was a deliberately low-grade mental activity managed from an intellectual level wilfully maintaining the lower-grade for a purpose of self-release from coherency to which she tried to give a character of virtue.

The perversity of what Gertrude Stein did is difficult to spot as peversity because it is not confined to any particular part or parts of the personal role she played of a dissociated, free intelligence in the society of writers and artists of the early phases of twentieth-century modernism, or of the role she played of a pole of antithesis to all operations and manifestations of intellectual intensity. Dissociation and disavowal of adherence to consecutive movements of intellectual pursuance were perva-sive in her. She made it all into a love-affair with herself. What was herself in this ritual of auto-idolatry? Alas, she made it — the while construing it symbolically as the type of the essential human being — a little of this, a little of that, a little of every element of human identity. Picasso was the male opposite number, doing in paint, in her view, what she did in words. Not to complicate these concluding thoughts on Gertrude Stein with considerations of the basic nature of Picasso's performances, I shall advance a description of her without matching reference to Picasso. She was, by her own created image of herself, as a compendium of human versatility compressing the range of diversity within it to so abbreviated a representation that she was the God of herself.

Through the years, now and then, a question has been insanely raised by someone as to whether I thought I was God. I recall commenting on that proposition very, very, long ago with an ascription to Gertrude Stein of being God rather than myself. This was in very serious play with the possibilities of extreme statement. I meant that I was my careful self, laboring with the difficulties of being exactly what I was as myself among others, and of speaking exactly what my mind thought through to the verge of words. Dismiss those difficulties of being, thinking, speaking, and you absent yourself to an ease of tireless deity-being. To whom? Gertrude Stein has actually won for herself the status of a figure of at least quasi-divinity in literary lore. Timidity of identifying themselves as non-comprehenders of her writing and her intent, or as irreverent disbelievers in the title of what she did to being taken seriously, has become the rule where quasi-worshipfulness is not the rule. Perhaps everyone up to the time of her self-deification was-is to blame, for the great emptiness that had accumulated in human self-knowledge—which Gertrude Stein tried to fill with herself for everyone's edification.

INDEX